Lecture Notes in Computer Science   8968

Commenced Publication in 1973
Founding and Former Series Editors:
Gerhard Goos, Juris Hartmanis, and Jan van Leeuwen

Marc Joye · Amir Moradi (Eds.)

Smart Card Research and Advanced Applications

13th International Conference, CARDIS 2014
Paris, France, November 5–7, 2014
Revised Selected Papers

 Springer

Editors
Marc Joye
Technicolor
Los Altos, CA
USA

Amir Moradi
Ruhr University
Bochum, Nordrhein-Westfalen
Germany

ISSN 0302-9743   ISSN 1611-3349 (electronic)
Lecture Notes in Computer Science
ISBN 978-3-319-16762-6   ISBN 978-3-319-16763-3 (eBook)
DOI 10.1007/978-3-319-16763-3

Library of Congress Control Number: 2015934897

LNCS sublibrary: SL4 – Security and Cryptology

Springer Cham Heidelberg New York Dordrecht London

Printed on acid-free paper

Springer International Publishing AG Switzerland is part of Springer Science+Business Media
(www.springer.com)

Preface

The 13th Smart Card Research and Advanced Application Conference was held in Paris, France, during November 5–7, 2014. The conference was organized by and held at Conservatoire national des arts et métiers (CNAM).

Since 1994, CARDIS is the foremost international conference dedicated to smart card research and applications. Smart cards and secure elements are the basis for many secure systems and play a decisive role in ID management. Established computer science areas like hardware design, operating systems, system modeling, cryptography, verification, and networking got adapted to this fast growing technology and investigate emerging issues resulting from it. Unlike events devoted to commercial and application aspects of smart cards, CARDIS conferences gather researchers and technologists who focus on all aspects of the design, development, deployment, validation, and application of smart cards and secure elements in secure platforms or systems.

CARDIS 2014 received 56 submissions from 21 countries. Each paper was reviewed by at least three independent reviewers. The selection of 15 papers to fill the Technical Program was accomplished based on 170 written reviews. This task was performed by the 26 members of the Program Committee with the help of 52 external sub-reviewers. This year the Program Committee selected a paper to award. To be eligible, the paper had to be co-authored by one full-time student who presented the paper at the conference. This year, the Best Student Paper Award was given to Christine van Vredendaal for the paper titled "Kangaroos in Side-Channel Attacks" written in collaboration with Tanja Lange and Marnix Wakker. The technical program also featured two invited talks and a panel discussion. The first invited speaker, Marc Girault, from Orange Labs, France, presented "A Chip Card Sidelight on Lightweight Crypto." The second invited speaker, Stefan Mangard, from Graz University of Technology, Austria, spoke about "Designing Secure Smart Cards." Further, the panel discussion with the topic of "20 years of CARDIS, 40 years of smart cards: Where do we go from there?" was moderated by David M'Raïhi from Perzo, USA.

We would like to thank the General Chair, Prof. Pierre Paradinas, and the local Organizing Committee for their management as well as the authors of all submitted papers. Moreover, we are grateful to the members of the Program Committee and the external sub-reviewers for their diligent work. We would also like to acknowledge the Steering Committee for giving us the privilege of serving as Program Chairs of CARDIS 2014. We especially thank Prof. Jean-Jacques Quisquater for organizing and publicizing this event and for his help and guidance throughout the process.

November 2014   Marc Joye
Amir Moradi

Organization

CARDIS 2014 was organized by Conservatoire national des arts et métiers (CNAM).

Conference General Chair

Pierre Paradinas Conservatoire national des arts et métiers, France

Conference Program Co-chairs

Marc Joye Technicolor, USA
Amir Moradi Ruhr University Bochum, Germany

Conference Publicity Chair

Jean-Jacques Quisquater Université catholique de Louvain, Belgium

Program Committee

Guillaume Barbu Oberthur Technologies, France
Samia Bouzefrane Conservatoire national des arts et métiers, France
Thomas Eisenbarth Worcester Polytechnic Institute, USA
Viktor Fischer Université de Saint Etienne, France
Aurélien Francillon EURECOM, France
Benedikt Gierlichs Katholieke Universiteit Leuven, Belgium
Christophe Giraud Oberthur Technologies, France
Tim Güneysu Ruhr University Bochum, Germany
Johann Heyszl Fraunhofer-Institut AISEC, Germany
Michael Hutter Graz University of Technology, Austria
Jean-Louis Lanet Université de Limoges, France
Pierre-Yvan Liardet STMicroelectronics, France
Philippe Loubet-Moundi Gemalto, France
Stefan Mangard Graz University of Technology, Austria
Keith Mayes Royal Holloway University of London, UK
David M'Raïhi Perzo, USA
David Oswald Ruhr University Bochum, Germany
Elisabeth Oswald University of Bristol, UK
Eric Peeters Texas Instruments, USA
Emmanuel Prouff ANSSI, France
Thomas Roche ANSSI, France
Pankaj Rohatgi Cryptography Research, USA

Kasuo Sakiyama   University of Electro-Communications, Japan
Akashi Satoh   University of Electro-Communications, Japan
Jörn-Marc Schmidt   secunet Security Networks AG, Germany
François-Xavier Standaert Université catholique de Louvain, Belgium

Additional Reviewers

Philippe Andouard
Costin Andrei
Yoshinori Aono
Josep Balasch
Valentina Banciu
Alberto Battistello
Luk Bettale
Begül Bilgin
Claude Carlet
Guillaume Dabosville
Elke De Mulder
Fabrizio De Santis
Amine Dehbaoui
Ibrahima Diop
Sho Endo
Benoit Feix
Olivier Francis
Daniele Fronte

Hannes Gross
Vincent Grosso
Atsuo Inomata
Eliane Jaulmes
Saqib A. Kakvi
Dina Kamel
Timo Kasper
Thomas Korak
Thinh Le Vinh
Yang Li
Yanis Linge
Victor Lomne
Shugo Mikami
Oliver Mischke
Stephanie Motre
Ryo Nojima
Katsuyuki Okeya
Peter Pessl

Francesco Regazzoni
Franck Rondepierre
Falk Schellenberg
Tobias Schneider
Mostafa Taha
Yannick Teglia
Le Trieu Phong
Michael Tunstall
Lihua Wang
Erich Wenger
Carolyn Whitnall
Johannes Winter
Dai Yamamoto
Xin Ye
Christian T. Zenger
Ralf Zimmermann

Sponsoring Institutions

ANSSI
Serma Technologies
ASR
CEA
Cryptosense
INVIA
Lip6
Oberthur Technologies
Orange
Technicolor

Contents

Public-Key Cryptography

Leakage and Fault Attacks

Java Cards

Memory Forensics of a Java Card Dump

Jean-Louis Lanet[1]($\boxtimes$), Guillaume Bouffard[2,3], Rokia Lamrani[3],
Ranim Chakra[3], Afef Mestiri[3], Mohammed Monsif[3], and Abdellatif Fandi[3]

[1] LHS PEC, INRIA, 263 Avenue Général Leclerc, 35042 Rennes, France
jean-louis.lanet@inria.fr
http://secinfo.msi.unilim.fr/lanet/
[2] Agence Nationale de la Sécurité des Systèmes D'Informations,
51, Boulevard de La Tour-Maubourg, 75700 Paris 07 SP, France
guillaume.bouffard@ssi.gouv.fr
[3] University of Limoges, 123 Avenue Albert Thomas, 87060 Limoges, France

Abstract. Nowadays several papers have shown the ability to dump the EEPROM area of several Java Cards leading to the disclosure of already loaded applet and data structure of the card. Such a reverse engineering process is costly and prone to errors. Currently there are no tools available to help the process. We propose here an approach to find in the raw data obtained after a dump, the area containing the code and the data. Then, once the code area has been identified, we propose to rebuilt the original binary CAP file in order to be able to obtain the source code of the applet stored in the card.

Keywords: Java card · Memory forensics · Reverse engineering · Disassembler · Index of coincidence

1 Introduction

Several attacks have been successful in dumping the memory of the smart card and in particular the EEPROM. Even if the cards are more protected nowadays, it is still possible to get the memory contents. Then, to reverse the content of the dump, one must analyze kilobytes of raw data for obtaining the expected information. At present, there are no tools available for reversing the memory dump for a Java based smart card. The EEPROM memory is made of data for the system and the applications, and their metadata (data descriptors), encrypted data (secure key container), Java CAP file and in particular Java byte code and sometimes native code. For a reverse engineer it is a hard task to find the adequate information and the tools used for reversing a Java Card memory dump are missing. So we have developed a disassembler which is based on natural language recognition and heuristics. Each binary language has a signature that takes into account the probability of occurrence of the language elements. Thus each card embeds at least two languages with two different signatures. Then, for the Java part, a symbolic execution of the recognized program verifies the Java type

M. Joye and A. Moradi (Eds.): CARDIS 2014, LNCS 8968, pp. 3–17, 2015.
DOI: 10.1007/978-3-319-16763-3_1

system for increasing the confidence in the recognition probability. A pattern recognition phase which is card dependent, is then performed to recognize the metadata stored in the card. Having a precise knowledge of the software and in particular the Control Flow Graph (CFG) could be helpful for new attacks or understanding the algorithms.

The rest of the paper is organized as follows: the second section presents the security model of the card and the state of the art concerning the attacks in order to obtain a memory dump. The third section introduces the dump file analyzer and its index of coincidence for recognizing different machine languages. The fourth section explains the Java Card Disassembler and Analyzer (JCDA) implementation followed by experimentation results. Future works and conclusion end this paper.

2   Java Card

The Java platform [12] has been downsized for fitting the smart card constraints. The Java Card technology offers a multi-application environment where sensitive data must be protected against illegal access from another applet. The classical Java technology uses three security elements - type verification, class loader and security managers to protect each applet. Embedding the Java security elements into a smart card is not possible due to the resource constraints. These components have been adapted to the specific requirements of Java Card.

2.1   Security in the Java Card World

To be compliant with the Java security rules, the Java Card security model is split in two parts. One, outside the card (Fig. 1(a)) is in charge of preparing the code to be loaded into the card. It includes a Byte Code Verifier (BCV), a converter and a mechanism to ensure integrity and/or confidentiality of the code to be loaded. The BCV is in charge of verifying the semantics of the Java-program. It ensures that the checked applet file format respects the specification (structural verification) and that all methods are well formed and verify the type system of Java. It is a complex process involving an elaborate program analysis using a very costly algorithm in terms of time consumption and memory usage. Next is the Java Card converter which translates each Java Card package into a Java Card-CAP. A Java Card-CAP is a lightweight Java Card-CLASS based on the tokens. This file format is designed to be optimized for the resource-constraint devices. The organization which provides the applet must sign[1] the application for the on-card loader that will verify the signature. This verification ensures the loader the origin of the code, and thus that the code is compliant with the Java security rules.

---

[1] Due to security reasons, the ability to download code into the card is controlled by a protocol defined by Global Platform [15]. This protocol ensures that the owner of the code has the necessary authorization to perform the action.

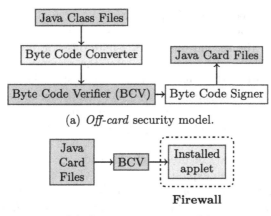

(a) *Off-card* security model.

Firewall

(b) *On-card* security model.

Fig. 1. The Java Card Security Model.

The second part of the security model is embedded into the smart card (Fig. 1(b)). The loader verifies the signature and optionally a BCV might verify the Java security compliance of the Java-Cap file to be installed. Currently, just a few Java Cards embed an on-card BCV component. The applet to be installed is linked after some potential checks. Once an applet is installed, the segregation of different applets is enforced by the firewall which is based on the package structure of Java Card and the notion of context.

2.2 Attacks on Java Card

Recently, the idea to inject physical fault to bypass the BCV's checks has emerged. A legitimate applet which complies with the Java Card security rules is installed into a Java Card. With the help of a fault injection, an attacker can modify some memory content which can lead to exploitable deviant behavior. So the application mutates to execute a malicious byte code which can break the security model. Classically, the fault attacks are used to attack cryptographic algorithm implementations [1,8,14].

Barbu et al. [3] succeed to bypass the embedded smart card BCV. In order to perform it, a correct applet is installed which contains an unauthorized cast between two different objects. Statically, the applet is compliant with the Java Card security rules. If a laser beam hits the bus in such a way that the cast type check instruction is not executed, this applet becomes hostile and can execute any shell code. This type of attack exploits a new method to execute illegal instructions where the physical and logical levels are perturbed. This method succeeds only on some cards and others seem to not be sensitive to this attack.

Bouffard et al. [4], proposed a way to perturb the applet's CFG with a laser beam injection into the smart card's non-volatile memory. The authors described the attack on a loop `for`, but it can be extended with other conditional instructions.

The Java Card specification [12] defines two instructions to branch at the end of a loop, a goto and the goto_w instructions. The first one branches with a 1-byte offset and the second one takes 2-byte offset. Since the smart card's memory manager stores the array data after the memory byte code, a laser fault on the high part of the goto_w parameter can shift the backward jump to a forward one and the authors succeeded to execute the contents of an array. Unlike Barbu et al., Bouffard et al. described a persistent attack to execute their shellcode. Hamadouche et al. [7], proposed a way to obtain Java Card API addresses embedded in the card. With this attack it is possible to use the Java Card internal references to execute a rich shellcode.

Lancia [11] explained an exploitation on Java Card instance allocation based on high precision fault injection. Instead of the Java Virtual machine, each instance created by the Java Card Runtime Environment (JCRE) is allocated in a persistent memory[2]. On the modern Java Card Memory Management Unit (MMU), references are represented by an indirect memory address. This address is an index to a memory address pool which in turn refers to a global instance pool managed by the virtual machine. Like a persistent type confusion, Lancia presented an attack of the global instance pool mechanism in which a laser beam shifts the index referred in the byte code. During the applets execution, the JCRE resolves an index with the associated address in the global instance pool table and have access to another instance of the expected object. This persistent modification may offer information of the card as a part of the smart card memory.

Each attack previously described here gives information about the targeted Java Card. These information can contain a part or the whole Java Card memory (essentially the EEPROM part) as raw data. Generally, this memory fragment contains program's code (virtual and/or native) and data (system and application) needed to well-execute each installed applet. These raw data are called the *dump file*.

Since this work is done without any knowledge of the features implemented in the card, it's of a prime importance to be able to recognize the different elements, to separate code and data. Until now, carving the smart card memory dump is done manually. It s a difficult task, prone to human errors and long. To automate this analysis, we propose a Java Card disassembler to reverse the Java Card memory.

2.3   State of the Art of Memory Carving

Memory analysis is an important part of effective computer forensics. There has been significant research done in improving analysis of memory dump files [17, 18]. Forensic memory analysis starts with collecting the memory from the target machine followed by parsing the memory dump into meaningful artifacts. The

---

[2] The Java Card specification [12] provides some functions to create transient objects. The data of the transient object stored in the RAM memory, but the header of this object is always stored in the persistent memory.

technique consists of several steps: parsing the internal memory structures, retrieving the assembly code and stack from the memory, constructing the control flow graph from the executable code and reversing it and finally identifying the data structures. Unfortunately, these techniques rely on well-known characteristics of the operating system. Furthermore, in most cases, these tools only work on a small number of operating system versions. The absence of a general methodology for forensic log analysis has resulted in ad-hoc analysis techniques such as log analysis [13] and operating system-specific analysis [5].

Schuster [17] proposes an approach to define signatures for executive object structures in the memory and recover the hidden and lost structures by scanning the memory looking for predefined signatures. However, defining a signature that uniquely identifies most of the data structures is not achievable except for a small set of kernel structures.

Walters et al. [18] present an approach for extracting in-memory cryptographic keying material. They have presented an extensible framework which is able to automatically derive object definitions from C source code and extract the underlying objects from memory.

A particular effort has been done for retrieving information from volatile memory that might determine if encryption is being used and extract volatile artifacts and passwords/passphrases [10]. Their approach considers that access to and acquisition of live encrypted data requires that these data must be in the clear in order to be manipulated. Since the contents of an encrypted container or volume are available to the user, then if physical access is gained to the live machine while it is in this state, the contents will also be accessible.

A disassembler recognizes the code section by parsing the whole memory and building the CFG. It recognizes the end of the code by a return instruction and cancels the current analysis if a byte does not represent an instruction.

Most of works on memory carving try to extract data from the dump of general purpose operating system. Of course with such systems, data and code are separated and they proceed by pattern matching for retrieving the data. In our tool, we need first to recognize the virtual and native code and then to recognize the data. Techniques usually used in recognizing code cannot be applied here since some instructions of the code are undocumented.

3   Memory Carving on Java Card

3.1   A Memory Dump

A *dump file* contains a set of binary values which represents a fragment of the smart card memory. The program's code and data can be found in the smart card memory and these information are sensitive.

In the Listing 1.1, a fragment of a Java Card memory dump is presented. The targeted smart card embeds a Java Card 2.2.1 and Global Platform 2.1.1 with 36 kB of EEPROM, 128 kB of ROM and 2 kB of RAM. This dump corresponds to an 88-byte fragment of the EEPROM and starts from the logical address 0x13f8.

Listing 1.1. A fragment of a Java Card memory dump.

```
0x13f0:                         00 0b 81 00 0a 48 65 6c
0x1400: 6c 6f 57 6f 72 6c 64 00 00 02 80 00 00 03 04 02
0x1410: 0c 34 00 00 01 be 81 08 00 0a 00 19 00 25 00 01
0x1420: 2e 00 01 0d 48 65 6c 6c 6f 57 6f 72 6c 65 41 70
0x1430: 70 01 71 00 02 34 04 00 04 06 02 00 00 01 73 01
0x1440: 75 00 05 42 18 8d 08 97 18 01 87 06 18 01 87 07
0x1450: 18 08 91 00 07 87 08 18 01 87 09 1e 29 04 03 29
```

A reversed version of the dump is listed in the Listing 1.2 after intensive work, the first part of the analyzed dump contains metadata (package and class) information. The second part describes the byte code method of a class.

Listing 1.2. The reverse of the value listed in the Listing 1.1

```
0x13f8: 000b 81 00 // Array header: data size: 0x000b,
                //               type: 0x81, owner: 0)
            0a 48 65 6c 6c 6f 57 6f 72 6c 64 // PACKAGE_AID
0x1408: 00 0002 8000 0003 0402 0c34 0000 // Unknown data
0x1414: 01be 81 08 // Array header: data size: 0x01be,
                //               type: 0x81, owner: 08)
        000a 0019 0025 0001 2e00 010d    // Undefined values
        48 65 6c 6c 6f 57 6f 72 6c 64 41 70 70 // APPLET_AID
        01 71 00 02 34 04 00 04 06 02 00 00 01 73 01 75 00
0x1442:    /* method 00: */
           // Method's header
           05 // flags: 0 max_stack: 5
           42 // nargs: 4 max_locals: 2
           // Method's bytecode
           18         // aload_0
           8d 08 97 // invokestatic 0x0897
           18         // aload_0
           01         // aconst_null
           87 06    // putfield_a 06
// To be continued ...
```

In the above sample, the byte codes used are the same as that defined in the Java Card specification [12]. Depending on the card, the program code may be scrambled [2,16] or new and undocumented instructions used. In the previous case, the card *xors* the value of each instruction to mask the code. But even with any masking or encryption, the stored program in the memory always keep the same semantics. In the last case, we have no information about the semantics of the code which can be compressed. For that reason it is impossible to use a simple execution to find the methods. The only way is to use an approximative approach.

3.2 Index of Coincidence

In 1922, Friedman [6] invented the notion of Index of Coincidence (IC) to reverse ciphered message. In cryptography, this technique consists of counting number of times the identical letters appear in the same position in both texts. This count can be calculated either as a ratio of the total or normalized divided by the expected count for a random source model. The IC is computed as defined in the Eq. 1.

$$\text{IC} = \frac{\sum_{i=1}^{c} n_i(n_i - 1)}{N(N-1)/c} \tag{1}$$

where N is the length of the analyzed text and n_i is the frequencies of the c letters of the alphabet ($c = 26$ for a Latin alphabet).

The IC is mainly used both in the analysis of natural-language text and in the analysis of ciphered message (as cryptanalysis). Even when only a ciphered message is available, the coincidences in the ciphered text can be caused by coincidences in the plain message. For example, this cryptanalysis technique is mainly used to attack the Vigenère cipher. The IC for a natural-language like French language is 0.0778, English is 0.0667 and German is 0.0762.

3.3   Finding Java Card Byte Codes

In a Java Card memory *dump file*, it is very difficult to separate the program's data and code. The program's byte code can be assimilated to a language where each instruction has a precise location in the language's grammar.

A Java Card byte code operation is composed by an instruction (between the range 0x00 to 0xB8) and potentially a set of bytes as argument. The Java Card toolchain ensures that the built Java Card byte codes are in compliance with the rules of Java language. The Friedman's approach is mainly based on the analysis of a whole cyphered text. In our case, a *dump file* includes data, byte codes and random values. Random values are a set of bytes which represent old system's values partially overridden or no longer used by the system. To find where a method's byte codes is located, we decided to compute the Friedman's equation upon a sliding window. To determine the IC value for the Java Card byte codes, we tested a set of Java Card byte code built by the Oracle's toolchain. An acceptable IC for Java Card byte codes is located between 0.020 and 0.060.

Computing the IC value upon the sliding window is equivalent to perform the Eq. 1 with each byte inside the interval. With different sizes of the sliding window, IC value is computed. The results are presented in the Fig. 2.

On this figure, the method's area to discover is located between the vertical dashed lines. We show that the optimal size for the sliding windows is between 135 and 150. This range includes false positive closed to the method's area. It is due to the size of the sliding window which includes a part of the method's byte code. False positive are detected by heuristics. We used several heuristics to eradicate the false positives. A code should not embed the value 0x00 which corresponds to the **nop** opcode except for operands. The size of the operands cannot exceed two bytes (except the specific case of the **switch**). The program decides that three consecutive bytes having the value zero cannot represent code.

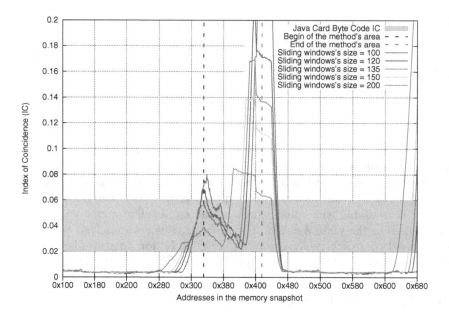

Fig. 2. Searching the optimal sliding window's size.

Another heuristic concerns the undefined byte code, above a given level of such bytes the program cancel the current window.

3.4   Finding Data in a Java Card Memory Dump

Carving raw data requires to characterize the objects manipulated by the system. Any data stored in the smart card belonging to the Java Card world contains a header (or metadata) which describes the data type, data owner and, sometimes, the size of the data. Inside a Java Card, the data can be:

- a package information. The package AID and all the classes in the card should be saved to verify the ownership context during the execution of an applet.
- a class information. A class contains the initialization value of each field, the method's byte code and an AID. A fragment is presented with its package information, in the Listing 1.2.
- the instance of a class which refers to each field sets to the current value (regarding to the life cycle of the instance). The instance of the class is linked with an instance AID which can be different from that of the class AID.
- an array is the last element which contains a header. We discovered empirically that an array header includes the size of the array data, the data type and the owner's context. An example of Java Card array found in a memory dump is shown in the Listing 1.3.

Listing 1.3. A Java Card array found in the memory dump

```
0010    // Data size
81      // type of the data, there it is a byte array
08      // applet's owner context
/* Data */
CA FE CA FE CA FE CA FE CA FE CA FE CA FE CA FE
```

4   JCDA: Java Card Disassembler and Analyzer

To implement the memory carving approach for Java Card, we have developed a tool, named Java Card Disassembler and Analyzer (JCDA) written in Java which aims to reverse a Java Card memory dump. It has been designed to be adapted for the architecture of each Java Card.

To reverse a Java Card memory dump, the JCDA (Fig. 3) requires a card model and a *dump file*. The first one defines the structure of the data contained in the smart card memory dump. This model is a high level abstraction of how the smart card stores objects and associated instances, array, etc. in the memory. This file should be filled by the attacker. This step has not yet been automated, it needs to create in the card objects of different nature (arrays, instances,...) and to compare the state of the memory before and after the creation of the object. The second parameter is a *dump file* of an attacked Java Card.

In our tool, reversing a Java Card memory dump is split in two steps. In the first step, the Java Card Analyzer searches in the Java Card memory *dump file* to locate the Java code or native code. As described previously, to find the Java Card instruction, an automatic process based on the index of coincidence is performed. The card memory model is used to search information about the classes, arrays and other data by using pattern matching.

The second step in the JCDA starts with the disassembling of the Java code recognized in the previous step. Its aim is to reverse each applet installed in the memory dump. The idea is to rebuild a partially stored CAP file in the *dump file*. Once rebuilt, Oracle provides a tool to convert a CAP file to a CLASS file. Then, it becomes obvious to convert the CLASS to Java file, many tools exist for that purpose. In this whole process, the main difficulty consists in regenerating CAP file from an applet installed into the memory. It implies some constraints:

1. Due to software and hardware limitations, information not needed to execute the applet are deleted during the installation file. To restore the complete CAP file, the dependencies between each component are used. For instance, the **Directory** and the **Descriptor** components, often not kept after the installation step, are generated using the information contained in the **Class**, **Method**, and **Static Field** components. Regarding to the smart card's installer implementation, our prototype needs to know how the card stores each CAP file component in memory;

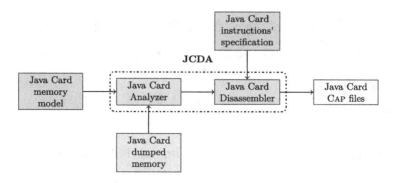

Fig. 3. JCDA Architecture.

2. In a CAP file, the `Import` component refers each class, method, and field imported by the application. Generating this component from a linked and installed applet rises some problems. In fact, each tokens is linked by the smart card internal references during the loading step. To reverse it, a learning step, based on the Hamadouche et al.'s attack [7], which maps the smart card Application Programming Interface (API) is needed. This map links smart card's internal references and the function's name. With the function's name, we are able to rebuild the `Import` component upon the EXPORT files.
3. Finally, the generated CAP file shall be validated by the BCV. This step is mandatory to translate the CAP to CLASS file.

Moreover, the constraints defined by the CAP file dependencies imply to respect a precise order to generate the CAP file components, as illustrated in the Fig. 4. Introduced by this figure, the method component is the keystone of our approach. Indeed, each `Method` contains references to its own class, its class's fields, etc.

For the analyzer, the methods area is a byte stream. To process the CAP file dependencies, the disassembler should find each method present in the dumped

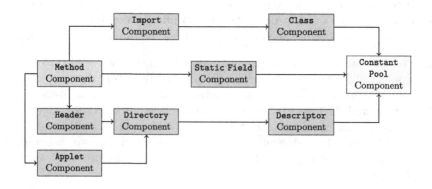

Fig. 4. Order of generation of CAP file components.

area before starting the reverse. This step aims to split the byte stream into a set of method. From the first byte of the method's area, an in-depth analysis is done to detect the end of each method. This analysis is based on the abstract execution of each instruction. In the case of an unknown instruction, the analyzer warns the user for this occurrence. This instruction has be added to the set of specific instructions for this card model. For example, one smart card manufacturer has replaced the `invokestatic` byte code by an undocumented one.

5   Experimental Results

On a smart card snapshot memory, we succeed in detecting the applets byte codes with the IC approach. The analyzer gave information shown in the Listing 1.4 to the disassembler.

Listing 1.4. Linked applet from a memory snapshot.

```
4868  6666  6666  6666  6666  4868  6666  6666  6666  6666  4170  7000
2c00  5480  0102  3400  ff00  0408  0002  0056  ffff  004e  0069  0057
0059  005c  005e  0049  004a  0223  0408  090a  0b04  0062  0019  007e
0009  0062  8019  0085  0000  0083  8007  007d  0000  0092  8002  0075
0000  0110  188d  0897  188b  0101  7a02  308f  ffac  3dcc  ffee  3b7a
0110  0478  0010  7a00  107a  0010  7a01  4004  7801  1010  4278  0110
0478  0010  7a03  2319  8b01  012d  188b  0103  6003  7a10  0681  181a
1007  8118  1c10  0881  181c  1a03  10ca  381a  0410  fe38  1199  998d
08c6  701c  2e11  6789  8d08  c611  9999  8d08  c670  0d28  0411  9999
8d08  c615  0493  7a00  04c1  06ff  ffff  ff00  08c2  06aa  aaaa  aaaa
aaaa  aa00  04c3  0601  0001
```

Regarding to the card model, this snapshotted area is parsed as presented in the Annex A, Listing 1.8. First, we filled, from the dump, some fields inside the **Method**, **Class**, **Header**, **Applet** and the **Static Field** component. Due to the limited size, the initial vector of the static fields is not kept in the card memory. This information is also lost for us. To regenerate the static fields initialization vector, we decided to use the current values another option would be the Java default value. This is one of the limits of the approach.

The next step aims to build the **Constant Pool** component. From the CAP file, this component have purposed to describe the type of each token used by the application. Tokens are used in the **Method**, **Class**, **Static Field** and **Descriptor** components.

In the **Method** component, each instruction with a reference as argument was linked by an internal reference during the CAP file installation. Converting each internal reference creates the set of token used by the application and aims to regenerate the **Import** component. There, the API mapping is used to describe the token to the correct EXPORT file. Once **Import** component is regenerated, we have enough information to create the **Descriptor** and **Constant Pool** components. The Listing 1.5 exhibits a fragment of entries in **Constant Pool** component restored from the dump.

Listing 1.5. Rebuilt Constant Pool component: internal tokens

```
/*0000, 0*/ CONSTANT_ClassRef : 0x0001 // first class
/* offset class constructor 0x0 => method_info[10] (@21) */
/*0004, 1*/ CONSTANT_StaticMethodRef : 0x0021
/*0008, 2*/ CONSTANT_StaticFieldRef  : 0x0006
/*000c, 3*/ CONSTANT_StaticFieldRef  : 0x0008
```

To find the external tokens description, we need to link the references in the *dump file* with the card API to obtain information of each token in the Constant Pool. Then we replace them with an index incremented at each occurrence, Listing 1.6.

Listing 1.6. Rebuilt Constant Pool component: external tokens

```
            // applet's constructor
/*0010, 4*/ CONSTANT_StaticMethodRef : 0x81,0x3,0x1
            // register function's token
/*0014, 5*/ CONSTANT_VirtualMethodRef: 0x81,0x3,0x1
            // APDU.getbuffer function's token
/*0018, 6*/ CONSTANT_VirtualMethodRef: 0x81,0xa,0x1
            // selectingApplet function's token
/*001c, 7*/ CONSTANT_VirtualMethodRef: 0x81,0x3,0x3
            // ISOException.throwIt method's token
/*0020, 8*/ CONSTANT_StaticMethodRef : 0x81,0x7,0x1
            // Exception class' token
/*0024, 9*/ CONSTANT_ClassRef         : 0x80,0x2
```

Finally, when each other components have been regenerated, the Directory component is built.

To validate globally the approach, we checked the regenerated CAP file with the BCV. As shown in the Listing 1.7, our generated file as the correct structure and it contains coherent values regarding the Java Card specification. For this proof of concept we did not regenerate the Java source file but this is not an issue.

Listing 1.7. Analyzing of regenerated CAP file by the Oracle BCV.

```
[INFO:]  Verifier [v3.0.4]
[INFO:]     Copyright (c) 2011, Oracle and/or its affiliates.
            All rights reserved.
[INFO:]  Verifying CAP file dumpedCapFile.cap
[INFO:]  Verification completed with 0 warnings and 0 errors.
```

6   Future Works and Conclusions

We have developed a proof of concept of a tool-chain that allows to recover from raw data application code and objects. In order to find Java code we used the index of coincidence to detect any byte code area. With a pattern matching algorithm, we are able to recover instances in the memory. The JCDA is still an ongoing academic development and currently only few card memory models can be recognized. We only focus for the moment to the byte code language and we need further development for the native language. This will be very useful for the improvement of JCDA development. A second improvement concerns the ability to automate the pattern learning phase for the card model, which is currently a manual process. We only recognize basic objects (array, AID,...) another improvement should be to recognize specific instances like secure containers for key storage. A last improvement for our work is integrating our tool into the IDA Disassembler [9]. IDA is a software which implements all the features required to reverse a computer application. This software is mainly used by security laboratories. One intrinsic limit concerns the initialization vector of the fields for which the information is lost after the applet installation. For example, if the value of a PIN code is stored into a static array its value will never be recoverable which is a good point from the security point of view. As soon as we have a stable version we expect to provide it as open source project for the academic community.

A   Content of a Dumped Area

Listing 1.8. The content of the dump file used for test.

```
48 68 66 66 66 66 66 66 66 66 // PACKAGE AID
/* APPLET Component */
48 68 66 66 66 66 66 66 66 66 41 70 70 // Applet AID
002c //
0054 // @Method Install
// Class Component
// interface_info
80   // -> flag
01   // -> interface_count

// Class_info
0234 // -> super_class_ref
00 // -> declared_instance_size
ff // -> first_reference_index
00 // -> reference_count
04 // -> public_method_table_base
08 // -> public_method_table_count
00 // -> package_method_table_base
02 // -> package_method_table_count
0056 ffff 004e 0069 0057 0059 005c 005e // public_methods

0049 004a // package_methods

// Implemented interface info
0223 // class_ref interface
04 // -> count
[ 08 09 0a 0b ] // index
```

```
/* Method  component  */
0400  6200  1900  7e00  0900  6280  1900  8500
0000  8380  0700  7d00  0000  9280  0200  7500
0001  1018  8d08  9718  8b01  017a  0230  8fff
ac3d  ccff  ee3b  7a01  1004  7800  107a  0010
7a00  107a  0140  0478  0110  1042  7801  1004
7800  107a  0323  198b  0101  2d18  8b01  0360
037a  1006  8118  1a10  0781  181c  1008  8118
1c1a  0310  ca38  1a04  10fe  3811  9999  8d08
c670  1c2e  1167  898d  08c6  1199  998d  08c6
700d  2804  1199  998d  08c6  1504  937a

/* Static  Field  Component  */
0004  c1  06  ff  ff  ff  ff          // byte  array
0008  c2  06  aaaa  aaaa  aaaa  aaaa  // short  array
0004  c3  06  01  00  01  00          // Boolean  array
```

References

1. Aumüller, C., Bier, P., Hofreiter, P., Fischer, W., Seifert, J.P.: Fault attacks on RSA with CRT: concrete results and practical countermeasures. IACR Cryptol. ePrint Arch. **2002**, 73 (2002)
2. Barbu, G.: On the security of Java Card platforms against hardware attacks. Ph.D. thesis, TÉLÉCOM ParisTech (2012)
3. Barbu, G., Thiebeauld, H., Guerin, V.: Attacks on java card 3.0 combining fault and logical attacks. In: Gollmann, D., Lanet, J.-L., Iguchi-Cartigny, J. (eds.) CARDIS 2010. LNCS, vol. 6035, pp. 148–163. Springer, Heidelberg (2010)
4. Bouffard, G., Iguchi-Cartigny, J., Lanet, J.-L.: Combined software and hardware attacks on the java card control flow. In: Prouff, E. (ed.) CARDIS 2011. LNCS, vol. 7079, pp. 283–296. Springer, Heidelberg (2011)
5. Dolan-Gavitt, B.: Forensic analysis of the windows registry in memory. Digit. Invest. **5**, 26–32 (2008)
6. Friedman, W.F.: The Index of Coincidence and Its Applications in Cryptography. Aegean Park Press, Laguna Hills (1922)
7. Hamadouche, S., Bouffard, G., Lanet, J.L., Dorsemaine, B., Nouhant, B., Magloire, A., Reygnaud, A.: Subverting byte code linker service to characterize java card API. In: Seventh Conference on Network and Information Systems Security (SAR-SSI), pp. 75–81, 22–25 May 2012. https://sarssi2012.greyc.fr/
8. Hemme, L.: A differential fault attack against early rounds of (Triple-)DES. In: Joye, M., Quisquater, J.-J. (eds.) CHES 2004. LNCS, vol. 3156, pp. 254–267. Springer, Heidelberg (2004)
9. Hex Rays: IDA Pro Disassembler and Debugger
10. Klein, T.: All your private keys are belong to us. Technical report, trapkit (Feb 2006)
11. Lancia, J.: Java card combined attacks with localization-agnostic fault injection. In: Mangard, S. (ed.) CARDIS 2012. LNCS, vol. 7771, pp. 31–45. Springer, Heidelberg (2013)

12. Oracle: Java Card 3 Platform, Virtual Machine Specification, Classic Edition 3.0.0. Oracle (September 2011)
13. Peikari, C., Chuvakin, A.: Security Warrior - Know Your Enemy. O'Reilly, Sebastopol (2004)
14. Piret, G., Quisquater, J.-J.: A differential fault attack technique against spn structures, with application to the AES and KHAZAD. In: Walter, C.D., Koç, Ç.K., Paar, C. (eds.) CHES 2003. LNCS, vol. 2779, pp. 77–88. Springer, Heidelberg (2003)
15. Platform: Card Specification v2.2. (March 2006)
16. Razafindralambo, T., Bouffard, G., Thampi, B.N., Lanet, J.-L.: A dynamic syntax interpretation for java based smart card to mitigate logical attacks. In: Thampi, S.M., Zomaya, A.Y., Strufe, T., Alcaraz Calero, J.M., Thomas, T. (eds.) SNDS 2012. CCIS, vol. 335, pp. 185–194. Springer, Heidelberg (2012)
17. Schuster, A.: Searching for processes and threads in microsoft windows memory dumps. Digit. Invest. 3(Supplement–1), 10–16 (2006)
18. Walters, A., Petroni, N.: Integrating volatile memory forensics into the digital investigation process. In: Blackhat Hat DC (2007)

Heap ... Hop!
Heap Is Also Vulnerable

Guillaume Bouffard[1,2]([✉]), Michael Lackner[3], Jean-Louis Lanet[4],
and Johannes Loinig[5]

[1] University of Limoges, 123 Avenue Albert Thomas, 87060 Limoges, France
guillaume.bouffard@ssi.gouv.fr
[2] Agence Nationale de la Sécurité des Systèmes D'Informations,
51, Boulevard de La Tour-Maubourg, 75700 Paris 07 SP, France
[3] Institute for Technical Informatics,
Graz University of Technology, Graz, Austria
michael.lackner@tugraz.at
[4] INRIA LHS-PEC, 263 Avenue Général Leclerc, 35042 Rennes, France
jean-louis.lanet@inria.fr
[5] NXP Semiconductors Austria GmbH, Gratkorn, Austria
johannes.loinig@nxp.com

Abstract. Several logical attacks against Java based smart card have
been published recently. Most of them are based on the hypothesis that
the type verification was not performed, thus allowing to obtain dynamically a type confusion. To mitigate such attacks, typed stack have been
introduced on recent smart card. We propose here a new attack path for
performing a type confusion even in presence of a typed stack. Then we
propose using a Fault Tree Analysis a way to design efficiently counter
measure in a top down approach. These counter measures are then evaluated on a Java Card virtual machine

Keywords: Java Card · Logical attack · Transient persistent heap ·
Counter measures

1 Introduction

Today most of the smart cards are based on a Java Card Virtual Machine(JCVM).
Java Card is a type of smart card that implements the standard Java Card 3.0
[18] in one of the two editions "Classic Edition" or "Connected Edition". Such
a smart card embeds a virtual machine, which interprets application byte codes
already romized with the operating system or downloaded after issuance. Due
to security reasons, the ability to download code into the card is controlled by
a protocol defined by Global Platform [9]. This protocol ensures that, the code
owner has the required credentials to perform the particular action.

A smart card can be viewed as a smart and secure container which stores
sensitive assets. Such tokens are often the target of attacks at different levels:
pure software attacks, hardware based, *i.e.* side channel of fault attacks but

© Springer International Publishing Switzerland 2015
M. Joye and A. Moradi (Eds.): CARDIS 2014, LNCS 8968, pp. 18–31, 2015.
DOI: 10.1007/978-3-319-16763-3_2

also mixed attacks. Security issues and risks of these attacks are ever increasing and continuous efforts to develop countermeasures against these attacks are sought. This requires a clear understanding and analysis of possible attack paths and methods to mitigate them through adequate software/hardware countermeasures. The current smart cards are now well protected against pure logical attacks with program counter bound checks, typed stack and so on. For such smart cards, we propose in this paper, two new attacks that target the heap of the JCVM. The first one is on the transient heap while the second allows a type confusion on the permanent heap.

Often countermeasures are designed in a bottom-up approach, in such a way that they cut efficiently the attack path but a new avatar of an attack path can be found easily. We propose here to use a top down approach to mitigate the attack by protecting the assets instead of blocking the attack path.

The remaining of the paper is organized as follows: the second section introduces the related works on logical attacks. The third section presents our contributions on the heap: the transient array and the type confusion. Then, in the fourth section, we propose some counter measures designed with a top down approach and we evaluate them in term of performance. Finally, in the last section, we conclude.

2   State of the Art of the Logical Attacks

Logical attacks are based on the fact that the runtime relies on the Byte Code Verifier (BCV) to avoid costly tests. Then, once someone find an absence of a test during runtime, there is a possibility that it leads to an attack path. An attack aims to confuse the applet's control flow upon a corruption of the Java Card Program Counter or perturbation of the data.

2.1   Fooling the Control Flow Graph

Misleading the application's control flow purposes to execute a shellcode stored somewhere in the memory. The aim of EMAN1 attack [12], explained by Iguchi-Cartigny et al., is to abuse the Firewall mechanism with the unchecked static instructions (as `getstatic`, `putstatic` and `invokestatic`) to call malicious byte codes, this behavior is allowed by the Java Card specification. In a malicious CAP file, the parameter of an `invokestatic` instruction may redirect the Control Flow Graph (CFG) of another installed applet in the targeted smart card. The EMAN2 [6] attack was related to the return address stored in the Java Card stack. They used the unchecked local variables to modify the return address, while Faugeron in [8] uses an underflow on the stack to get access to the return address.

When a BCV is embedded, installed an ill-formed applet is impossible. To bypass an embedded BCV, new attacks exploit the idea to combine software and physical attacks. Barbu et al. presented and performed several combined attacks such as the attack [3] based on the Java Card 3.0 specification leading to the circumvention of the Firewall application. Another attack [2] consisting of tampering the Application Protocol Data Unit (APDU) that leads to access the APDU buffer array at any time. They also discussed in [1] about a way to disturb the operand stack with a combined attack. It also gives the ability to alter any method regardless of its java context or to execute any byte code sequence, even if it is ill-formed. This attack bypasses the on-card BCV [4]. In [6], Bouffard et al. described how to change the execution flow of an application after loading it into a Java Card. Recently, Razafindralambo et al. [20] introduced a combined attack based on fault enabled viruses. Such a virus is activated by hitting with a laser beam, at a precise location in the memory, where the instruction of a program (virus) is stored. Then, the targeted instruction mutates one instruction with one operand to an instruction with no operand. Then, the operand is executed by the JCVM as an instruction. They demonstrated the ability to design a code in a such way that a given instruction can change the semantics of the program. And then a well-typed application is loaded into the card but an ill-typed one is executed. Hamdouche et al. [11] introduced a mutation analysis tool to check the ability of an application to come a malicious one.

Hamadouche et al. [10] described various techniques used for designing efficient viruses for smart cards. The first one is to exploit the linking process by forcing it to link a token with an unauthorized instruction. The second step is to characterize the whole Java card API by designing a set of CAP files which are used to extract the addresses of the API regardless of the platform. The authors were able to develop CAP files that embed a shellcode (virus). As they know all the addresses of each method of the Application Programming Interface (API), they could replace instructions of any method. In [20], they abuse the on board linker in such a way that the application is only made of tokens to be resolved by the linker. Knowing the mapping between addresses to tokens thanks to the previous attack, they have been able to use the linker to generate itself the shellcode to be executed.

We have presented attacks which perturb the application's control flow. Cheating the CFG leads to execute malicious bytecode or prevent any instruction to correctly finish. Another approach is exploiting the Java Card heap to access to unauthorized fields.

2.2   Exploiting the Java Card Heap

Lancia [13] exploited the Java Card instance allocator of Java Card Runtime Environment (JCRE) based on high precision fault injection. Each instance created by the JCRE is allocated in a persistent memory. The Java Card specification [18] provides some functions to create transient objects. The data of the transient object are stored in the RAM memory, but the header of this object is always stored in the persistent memory. On the modern Java Card using Memory Management Unit (MMU), references are represented by an indirect memory address. This address is an index to a memory address pool which in turn refers to a global instance pool managed by the virtual machine.

In this section, we have introduced logical attacks on Java Card from the literature. In this paper, we focus on the heap security. In the next section, I will present new ways to break the Java Card heap integrity.

3   Logical Attacks Against the Java Card Heap

From the state of the art, reading the memory needs to write at least 2 bytes to read few bytes. This method stresses the memory and will need more than 65,000 writing to the same cell. So 10 or 20 executions of a shellcode will kill the card reaching the stress threshold of the EEPROM. We need to have a smarter shellcode. To improve this approach we purpose to use transient array.

A transient array is an array where the data are stored in RAM and its descriptor is stored in EEPROM, precisely in the owner's heap area. Thus a transient array lost its content during power off but not the reference, there is no *natural* garbage collection. Unlike the EEPROM, one can write indefinitely in RAM area. So, using a transient array is better to dump RAM and EEPROM parts to avoid memory stress. To understand how a transient array is stored in the smart card, we created a simple applet which gets the transient array address and reads data at this address.

3.1   Transient Arrays on Java Card

So, using a transient array is better to dump RAM and EEPROM parts to avoid memory stress. To understand how a transient array is stored in the smart card, we created a simple applet which gets the transient array address and reads data at this address.

An implementation of the transient array's header is the following at the EEPROM area address:

```
0x8E85: 0x00 0x04 0x5B 0x30 0x6C 0x88 0x00 0x0A 0x05 0xB9
```

Where 0x0004 is the size of the structure without the metadata corresponding to the header. In the header part the byte 0x5B corresponds to the transient byte array type. The three next bytes are probably the security context 0x30 0x6C 0x88. It remains the four last bytes as pseudo data. After several experimentation, we understood that 0x000A represents the size of the data in RAM and 0x05B9 its address as shown in the Fig. 1.

We have disclosed how a transient array is design in a card implementation, focus on how to modify one. Confusing one purposes us to read and write anywhere in the memory.

3.2   Type Confusion Upon the Java Card Heap

The Java Card heap contains the runtime data for all class instances and allocated arrays. The instance data can be a reference to an object, an instance of

Permanent Array

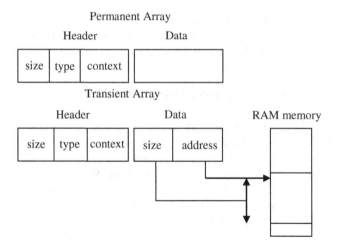

Fig. 1. Structure of transient and permanent arrays.

a class or a numerical value. In the Java Card architecture, the heap is a persistent element stores in the EEPROM area. Due to the limited resources, the instance data are often not typed. To have access to the instance fields, the Java Card specification [18] defines getfield_<t>_this and putfield_<t>_this as typed instructions on a t typed element. The type t can be a reference (<t> is replaced by a), a short value (type is s), etc. The getfield_<t>_this instruction pushes the field value onto the stack. On the opposite, the putfield_<t>_this instruction stores the latest pushed value. From the stack point of view, the last element must be a t type.

Latest smart cards based on Java Card technology increasingly implement typed stack. To succeed a type confusion on this kind of platform, I propose to exploit the untyped instance fields. Let us assume the code shown in the Listing 1.1. On a card which no embeds any BCV, this method aims at converting a given reference given in parameter to a short value returned.

Listing 1.1. Receive reference of an object by type confusion over instance fields.

```
short getObjectAddress (object object) {
  02 // flags: 0 max_stack : 2
  12 // nargs: 1 max_locals: 2
  /*005f*/ L0: aload_1 // object reference given in
     parameter
  /*0060*/     putfield_a_this 0
  /*0062*/     getfield_s_this 0
  /*0064*/     sreturn
}
```

In the Listing 1.1, the field 0 is accessed as a reference (at 0x60) and as a short value (at 0x62). In the case of the use of a typed stack, only two types are supported, the short and reference types. The `putfield_a_this` instruction (at 0x60) saved the value given in parameter into the field 0. The `getfield_s_this` (from 0x62) pushes the value of the field 0 to stack as a short. A type confusion can then be performed on the instance fields. There, the reference given as parameter is then returned as a short value. From the Java Card stack side, the type of each manipulated element is correct. Nonetheless, a type confusion has been performed during the field manipulation.

In this section, we have explained a new typed confusion attack on Java Card smart cards which embed typed stack. As the stack mechanism cannot be confused, we focused on the instance fields which are often untyped. Thus, the type confusion attack moves on the Java Card stack to the instance fields.

3.3   Setting up Transient Array Metadata to Snapshot the Memory

Based on the function shown in the Listing 1.1, we are able to update this reference to point out a fake transient array. Stored in a Java array, we succeed in retrieve its reference upon on the type confusion explained in the previous section. On the targeted platform, each transient array has the same metadata's pattern. The transient array's header can be so update with our properties.

Some cards prevent accessing to transient array out of a specific heap area. On the targeted card, a typed stack is embedded but no BCV. So, using static instruction abuse of the firewall [12] to read and write anywhere in memory, as shown in the Listing 1.2. This code can be executed through the EMAN2 [6] attack. Assume that the transient array size and the data address are located from 0x8E9D.

Listing 1.2. Executing the basic shellcode

```
18 FF      sspush 0x00FF
80 8E 9B putstatic_s 0x8E9B //size: 0x00FF
18 00      sspush 0x00FE
80 8E 9D putstatic_b 0x8E9D //address: start from 0x00FE
7A         return
```

There, we are able to set the size and the address of our transient data to cover from 0 for `0xFFFF` bytes, i.e., the whole memory. This behavior is accepted by the targeted card and this corrupted transient array can be used to read the complete memory. Fooling transient array is more efficient than the attacks presented in the state of the art: we need to write only few bytes in memory to obtain an array which can be read normally.

Once this shellcode is executed, we have to copy the array in the APDU buffer slicing it into slots of 255 bytes to fit the size of the APDU buffer. Unfortunately, the ROM is always unread by this approach. The values returned at the ROM area are filled with 0. With attack as EMAN2 [6], the dumping shellcode needs to write around 65,000 times into a particular cell. There, we have improved the dump with only one write into each cell for 255 read bytes. We reduced greatly the execution time[1] and minimized the memory stress.

---

[1] Writing in EEPROM needs to erase which is time consuming.

4   Countermeasures

The security of the Java Card sandbox model is threaten by two main types of attacks. The first are, as used by the proposed attack of this paper, logical attacks by uploading malicious applets. The second class are fault attacks (laser beam) which threaten the integrity of the memory.

4.1   Counteract Fault Attack on the Java Heap

The common fault attack model, which is also used in this work, is that an adversary can set[2] bytes inside the card memory to 0x00 or 0xFF. This model is called *precise byte error* and is presented in Table 1. The difficulty for an attacker to set bits inside the card to either 0x0 or 0x1 is called *precise bit error* and is currently no realistic fault model.

Table 1. Current fault models to evaluate possible countermeasures and security threats on Java Cards [7, with modifications].

Fault Model	Precision	Location	Timing	Fault Type	Difficulty
precise bit error	bit	precise control	precise control	BSR[a], random	++
precise byte error	byte	loose control	precise control	BSR, random	+
unknown byte error	byte	loose control	loose control	BSR, random	-
random error	variable	no control	loose control	random	–

[a] bit set or reset.

The transient array objects in the heap contain the size (2 bytes) and start address (2 bytes) of the array fields. Due to the *precise byte error* fault model an adversary is able to set the size field to 0xFFFF. This enables again a full memory dump of the RAM even if no malicious applet is installed. Therefore, it is a substantial need to protect the array object headers against fault attacks.

Fault attacks can either inject transient faults or permanent faults into the memory. An industrial often used countermeasure against these transient faults are multiple readings from the same address and the comparison if all read-out values are equal. The change for a successful attack by circumventing the multiple readings by additional fault attacks is a negative exponential distribution.

Unfortunately, a multiple read is no protection against an attacker which uses a strong enough laser to permanently change the values of a memory cell. A multiple read on a permanently changed memory cell always results in the same read-out value. Therefore, to counteract such a permanent fault, a statically calculated checksum is needed. This checksum is re-calculated during run-time and compared to the statically calculated one. Generally the checksum countermeasure, compared to multiple reads, consumes more run-time performance and requires additional non-volatile memory.

---

[2] Memory encryption results in a logical read-out value which is random.

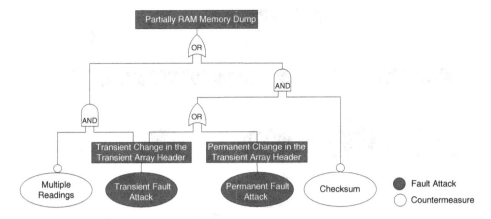

Fig. 2. Fault tree overview of the different possible attack paths to fulfill a partial memory dump of the RAM by a fault attack. Furthermore, effective countermeasures against the two general types of fault attacks are listed.

In summary to counteract transient fault attacks we propose to perform multiple readings on the accessed object header elements. To counteract permanent and transient faults on the object header we propose as countermeasure a checksum. An overview of the attack paths and countermeasures against these fault attacks is shown in Fig. 2. Multiple readings on the object header counteract transient fault attacks. Checksums counteract transient faults and permanent faults on the object header.

4.2   Logical Attack on the Java Heap

Unfortunately, the proposed checksums and multiple reads over the object headers in the Java heap, to counteract fault attacks, is not an effective countermeasure against logical attacks. By a logical attack it is quite easily possible to study the algorithm of the checksum creation and create valid checksums for manipulated object headers. Therefore, other countermeasures must be found to counteract logical attacks.

To find an appropriate countermeasure an attack tree for the proposed attack of this work is shown in Fig. 3. Starting from the lower left it is shown that the causes of the execution of illegal bytecodes can be either a logical attack with the absence of an on-card BCV or a fault attack. The presence of illegal bytecodes is a cause to successfully perform a type confusion attack between *integral data* or *reference*. The type confusion can be either performed on the operand stack or, as proposed in this work, on instance fields of objects. This type confusion is the first main requirement for the full RAM memory dump attack of this work. The second requirement is the manipulation of the integrity of the transient array object header. This integrity violation can be reached by various kind of the proposed attacks EMAN1 [12], EMAN2 [6], and EMAN4 [6].

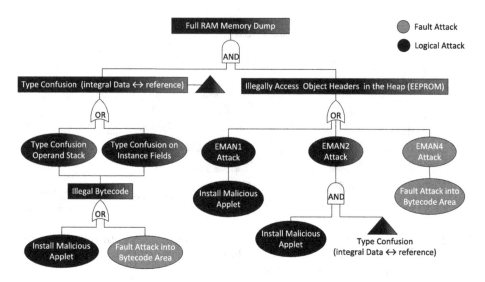

Fig. 3. Fault tree overview of the different possible attack paths and needed attack preconditions to fulfill the memory dump attack of this work.

EMAN1 relies on the fact that illegal static variables are not checked during run-time by the Java Card firewall. EMAN2 relies on the fact that it is possible to overwrite the Java frame return address by a bytecode with an illegally index of bytecode accessing the local variables. The return address is overwritten with the address of a Java array which is previously received by a type confusion attack. EMAN4 relies on a fault attack during run-time which illegally changes the operands of a `goto_w` bytecode. This attack results in a jump and execution of a Java array filled with malicious bytecodes.

To install applets on Java cards a secret key must be known which is only available for authorized authorities. Nohl [16] presented in 2013 an attack to crack this key (DES encryption) which enables the installation of malicious applets. Based on Nohls presented information the industry created guidelines to counteract this attack. Therefore, we assume that the installation of malicious applets on currently available credit cards or bank cards is again a very unlikely security threat.

Therefore, half of the starting points of the attacks of this work, previously presented in Fig. 3, are not available on industrially used Java Cards. Furthermore, Java Cards are becoming more and more powerful which will most probably result in an available on-card verification process which only accepts applets which only contain harmless operations. Resource optimized on-card verification algorithms are presented in different works [5, 14].

Nevertheless, the attack preconditions of this work (type confusion and access to the object header) can be also reached by uploading a valid applet and turning them into a malicious one. This transformation is done by performing fault attacks into the bytecode area. Therefore, additional security mechanisms must be integrated when operands or opcodes are fetched from the bytecode area. Various countermeasures [15,21–23] are proposed to protect the integrity of the bytecode area.

Protect Integrity of the Bytecode Area: The replacement of the typically not used bytecode NOP (0x00) is proposed in [23] to counteract the threat of skipping bytecodes. The authors of [15] create a fingerprint of an applet which is based on the position of critical bytecodes/values (0x00, 0xFF, branch, jump, subroutine call, return) inside a method. This fingerprint is than checked during run-time. Another countermeasure against the illegal execution of arbitrary bytecodes is the encryption of the bytecode based on a secret key and the memory address where the bytecode is stored [21]. The authors in [22] propose to divide the bytecodes of a method into basic blocks. During an off-card preprocessing step checksums are calculated over these basic blocks and stored into the applet as an additional component. During run-time the checksums are re-calculated and compared to the off-card calculated checksums.

Based on the required level of security all of these countermeasures are a possible solution to counteract integrity attacks into the bytecode area. These attacks are needed as a starting point of an attacker to reach the goal of turning valid applets into malicious one. These malicious applets are the starting point to create the proposed memory dump attack of this work on industrially used Java Cards.

5   Experimental Results

The measurements of this work are based on a Java Card prototype implementation which is based on the Java Card specification [17,18]. We integrated our countermeasures into this prototype to counteract fault attacks which manipulate the array headers in the Java heap.

The JCVM is compiled with μVision3 which is a development tool especially for low cost processors based on the 8-bit 8051 platform. The performance results are based on the supplied memory-accurate 8051 instruction set simulator of the μVision IDE. The tested Java Card applets HelloWorld and Wallet are obtained from the official Java Card software development kit (SDK). The Calculator applet is self programmed. Note that the performance overhead measurements are normalized to a JCVM implementation which do not perform the additionally proposed countermeasures during run-time.

5.1   Fault Attack Countermeasures on the Object Header

Checksum: A checksum is statically calculated over the size and pointer element of each Java array header in the heap. The checksum is based on a XOR operation and has a length of one byte. Each array object header of our prototype, even the permanent arrays, contain a size and address field shown in

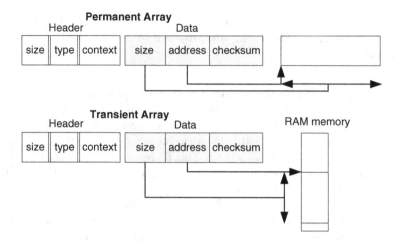

Fig. 4. Structure of transient and permanent arrays in the prototype implementation.

Fig. 4. For permanent arrays the address field points into the non-volatile memory (EEPROM). Therefore, the object header must be secured for permanent and transient arrays.

The checksum calculation and writing is performed during the execution of the `<t>newarray` bytecodes and the creation of a transient array by calling the Java Card API method `JCSystem.makeTransientByteArray()`. During runtime this checksum is re-calculated at each security-critical access to the array object header (e.g., `aaload`, `sstore`, `arraylength`).

Double Read: The double read is done when the size or pointer elements of the array object header are accessed by security-critical bytecodes. During the creation of the array header the write operation of the size and pointer element is checked by an immediate reading and comparison of the written values.

Execution Time Overhead: The run-time overhead of the checksum and double reads is shown in Fig. 5. The execution time of the `newarray` bytecode is quite long even if no additional security checks are performed which results in a low percentage overhead increase. Compared to this the `saload` bytecode, which loads a short value from an array, has an additional overhead of +9 % for double reads and +22 % for the checksum re-calculation.

The creation of a new Java array is in generally performed one time during the installation process of an applet. The overall applet execution time for different applets and bytecodes are presented in Table 2. The overall applet time measurements does include the sending of APDU commands for the selection of the applet, sending of commands to communicate with the applet, and the reception of results. Overall the additional checks do not significantly increase the overall execution time of the measured applets. The highest overall measured

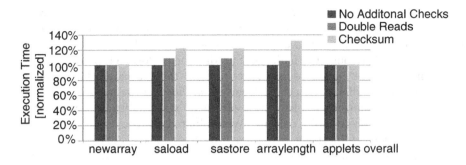

Fig. 5. Graphical representation of the performance impact of the additional double read and checksum calculations for selected bytecodes and the overall time of the measured applets.

time increase is only around +1 % for the self written Calculator applet and the checksum countermeasure. The double reads increase the Calculator applet by only around +0.5 %. Therefore, the higher security of the checksums, with regard to permanent memory faults, is paid with the price of one additional byte per array header and a doubling of the execution time overhead.

Table 2. Performance overhead overview of the double read and checksum counter-measures.

Java Bytecodes	Java Card Applet	Double Read	Checksum
`<t>newarray`		+1 %	+2 %
`<t>aload`		+9 %	+22 %
`<t>astore`		+9 %	+22 %
`arraylength`		+6 %	+22 %
	HelloWorld	+0.2 %	+0.5 %
	Wallet	+0.3 %	+0.9 %
	Calculator	+0.5 %	+1 %

6 Conclusion

Smart card designers now take into account the possibility to execute ill typed application even if the loaded applet is well typed. The combined attacks allow to use laser based attack to execute hostile applets. For this reason, designers protect dynamically the execution. Unfortunately, the attack paths can be subtle and the counter measures must protect the assets and not the attack paths. We presented two new attack paths that target the heap. The attack on the transient array can be obtained via a laser on the size field. The exploitation allows to parse completely the memory without stressing the EEPROM. The second one exploits a type confusion even in presence of a typed stack.

We proposed, through the fault tree paradigm to perform a top down analysis to design the counter measures in order to improve their coverage. This approach avoid to mitigate different attack with several *ad-hoc* counter measures. We proposed different solutions implemented currently at the software level, but we plan to integrate them into hardware. We evaluated the cost in term of performances, the memory footprint being less important. The evaluation brought to the fore that such counter measures are affordable for the smart card domain.

References

1. Barbu, G., Duc, G., Hoogvorst, P.: Java card operand stack: fault attacks, combined attacks and countermeasures. In: Prouff [19], pp. 297–313
2. Barbu, G., Giraud, C., Guerin, V.: Embedded eavesdropping on java card. In: Gritzalis, D., Furnell, S., Theoharidou, M. (eds.) SEC 2012. IFIP AICT, vol. 376, pp. 37–48. Springer, Heidelberg (2012)
3. Barbu, G., Hoogvorst, P., Duc, G.: Application-replay attack on java cards: when the garbage collector gets confused. In: Barthe, G., Livshits, B., Scandariato, R. (eds.) ESSoS 2012. LNCS, vol. 7159, pp. 1–13. Springer, Heidelberg (2012)
4. Barbu, G., Thiebeauld, H., Guerin, V.: Attacks on java card 3.0 combining fault and logical attacks. In: Gollmann, D., Lanet, J.-L., Iguchi-Cartigny, J. (eds.) CARDIS 2010. LNCS, vol. 6035, pp. 148–163. Springer, Heidelberg (2010)
5. Berlach, R., Lackner, M., Steger, C., Loinig, J., Haselsteiner, E.: Memory-efficient On-card Byte Code Verification for Java Cards. In: Proceedings of the First Workshop on Cryptography and Security in Computing Systems. CS2 2014, pp. 37–40. ACM, New York (2014)
6. Bouffard, G., Iguchi-Cartigny, J., Lanet, J.L.: Combined software and hardware attacks on the java card control flow. In: Prouff [19], pp. 283–296
7. Dubreuil, J., Bouffard, G., Thampi, B.N., Lanet, J.L.: Mitigating Type Confusion on Java Card. IJSSE **4**(2), 19–39 (2013)
8. Faugeron, E.: Manipulating the frame information with an underflow attack. In: Francillon, A., Rohatgi, P. (eds.) CARDIS 2013. LNCS, vol. 8419, pp. 140–151. Springer, Heidelberg (2014)
9. GlobalPlatform: Card Specification. GlobalPlatform Inc., 2.2.1 edn., January 2011
10. Hamadouche, S., Bouffard, G., Lanet, J.L., Dorsemaine, B., Nouhant, B., Magloire, A., Reygnaud, A.: Subverting byte code linker service to characterize java card api. In: Seventh Conference on Network and Information Systems Security (SAR-SSI), pp. 75–81 (22–25 May 2012)
11. Hamadouche, S., Lanet, J.L.: Virus in a smart card: Myth or reality? J. Inf. Secur. Appl. **18**(2–3), 130–137 (2013)
12. Iguchi-Cartigny, J., Lanet, J.L.: Developing a Trojan applets in a smart card. J. Comput. Virol. **6**(4), 343–351 (2010)
13. Lancia, J.: Java card combined attacks with localization-agnostic fault injection. In: Mangard, S. (ed.) CARDIS 2012. LNCS, vol. 7771, pp. 31–45. Springer, Heidelberg (2013)
14. Leroy, X.: Bytecode verification on Java smart cards. Softw. Pract. Exper. **32**(4), 319–340 (2002)

15. Morana, G., Tramontana, E., Zito, D.: Detecting Attacks on Java Cards by Fingerprinting Applets. In: Reddy, S., Jmaiel, M. (eds.) WETICE, pp. 359–364. IEEE (2013)
16. Nohl, K.: Rooting SIM Cards. Speak at the Black Hat USA 2013 (2013)
17. Oracle: Java Card 3 Platform, Runtime Environment Specification, Classic Edition. No. Version 3.0.4, Oracle. Oracle America Inc., Redwood City, September 2011
18. Oracle: Java Card 3 Platform, Virtual Machine Specification, Classic Edition. No. Version 3.0.4, Oracle. Oracle America Inc., Redwood City (2011)
19. Prouff, E. (ed.): CARDIS 2011, vol. 7079. Springer, Heidelberg (2011)
20. Razafindralambo, T., Bouffard, G., Lanet, J.-L.: A friendly framework for hiding *fault enabled virus* for java based smartcard. In: Cuppens-Boulahia, N., Cuppens, F., Garcia-Alfaro, J. (eds.) DBSec 2012. LNCS, vol. 7371, pp. 122–128. Springer, Heidelberg (2012)
21. Razafindralambo, T., Bouffard, G., Thampi, B.N., Lanet, J.-L.: A dynamic syntax interpretation for java based smart card to mitigate logical attacks. In: Thampi, S.M., Zomaya, A.Y., Strufe, T., Alcaraz Calero, J.M., Thomas, T. (eds.) SNDS 2012. CCIS, vol. 335, pp. 185–194. Springer, Heidelberg (2012)
22. Sere, A., Iguchi-Cartigny, J., Lanet, J.L.: Evaluation of Countermeasures Against Fault Attacks on Smart Cards. Int. J. Secur. Appl. 5(2), 49–61 (2011)
23. Séré, A.A.K., Iguchi-Cartigny, J., Lanet, J.L.: Automatic detection of fault attack and countermeasures. In: Serpanos, D.N., Wolf, W. (eds.) WESS. ACM (2009)

Software Countermeasures

Study of a Novel Software Constant Weight Implementation

Victor Servant[1]([✉]), Nicolas Debande[2], Houssem Maghrebi[1],
and Julien Bringer[1]

[1] SAFRAN Morpho, 18, Chaussée Jules César, 95520 Osny, France
{victor.servant,houssem.maghrebi,julien.bringer}@morpho.com
[2] SERMA Technologies (ITSEF), 3, Avenue Gustave Eiffel, 33608 Pessac, France
n.debande@serma.com

Abstract. While in the early 2000's lots of research was focused on Differential Power Analysis of first and second-order, it seems the recent trend is of even higher-order. As this order grows, countermeasures such as masking need to be designed in a more generic way. In this paper, we introduce a new constant weight implementation of the AES extending the idea of the software dual-rail countermeasure proposed by Hoogvorst et al. at COSADE 2011. Notably, we illustrate its practicality on 16-bit microcontroller in terms of speed and complexity. This countermeasure applies to all devices that leak a function of the Hamming weight of the internal variables. Under this assumption, our constant weight implementation is theoretically inherently resistant to side-channel attacks of any order. A security evaluation is conducted to analyze its resistance when the leakage slightly deviates from the Hamming weight assumption. It reveals that the countermeasure remains as good as several well-known masking countermeasures. Moreover, the proposed countermeasure offers the possibility to detect some classes of faults.

Keywords: Constant weight · Information theoretic analysis · Side-channel analysis · AES · Software implementation

1 Introduction

Since the introduction of Differential Power Analysis (DPA) by Kocher [12], Side-Channel Analyses (SCA) have become important issues for the security of cryptographic devices. During the two last decades, a lot of efforts have been dedicated towards the research about SCA and the development of corresponding countermeasures.

A very common countermeasure to protect implementations of block ciphers against SCA is to randomize the sensitive variables by *masking* techniques. The core principle of masking is to ensure that every sensitive variable is randomly

---

Nicolas Debande — Work done when the author was at SAFRAN Morpho.

split into at least two shares so that the knowledge of a strict sub-part of the shares does not give information on the shared variable itself. Masking can be characterized by the number of random masks used per sensitive variable. So, it is possible to give a general definition for a dth-order masking scheme: every sensitive variable Z is randomly split into $d + 1$ shares $M_0, \cdots, M_d$ in such a way that the relation $M_0 \perp \cdots \perp M_d = Z$ is satisfied for a group operation $\perp$ (e.g. the XOR operation in Boolean masking) and no tuple of strictly less than $d + 1$ shares depends on Z. Obviously, a dth-order masking can be theoretically defeated by a $(d+1)^{\text{th}}$-order SCA attack that jointly involves all the $d+1$ shares.

In the literature, several provably secure higher-order masking schemes have been proposed, see for instance [3,23] and [5]. But, due to their large penalty factors (complexity and speed), these countermeasures are unpractical for an everyday use of a smartcard.

In this paper, we perform an in-depth analysis of an alternative to masking countermeasure which consists in coding the data with a fixed *Hamming weight* value, and perform all operations following this fashion. It is often assumed that a device leaks information based on the Hamming weight of the data being operated on, or the Hamming distance between the processed data and its initial state. This assumption is quite realistic and many security analyses in the literature have been conducted following this model [2,17]. This paper introduces a new variety of *constant weight* codes which can be used to secure software implementations of block ciphers. Typically, we show that assuming a Hamming weight leakage function (or even some small variations of it), it is possible to prevent side-channel attacks.

The rest of the paper is structured as follows. We first recall the two published constant weight (dual-rail) implementations of a block-cipher in software and look into their advantages and drawbacks in Sect. 2. Then, we describe a new solution for a constant weight implementation in Sect. 3, and apply it to the AES in Sect. 4. Finally, we conduct an information theoretic analysis in Sect. 5, and a security analysis in Sect. 6 to evaluate our proposed scheme. The conclusion and some perspectives are in Sect. 7.

2   Previous Works

Hoogvorst *et al.* [10] presented a *dual-rail* implementation of PRESENT [1] in 2011. The paper aimed at proving that one could rather easily protect a block cipher in software using constant weight coding style rather than using masking. The idea was straightforwardly taken from existing dual-rail hardware, and consists in encoding one bit *s.t.* $0 \rightarrow 01$ and $1 \rightarrow 10$ (or the inverse).

The adaptation of this solution to software implementation required computing tables performing all basic operations such as XOR, AND, *etc.* In the end, the execution is 9 times slower than their original unsecured implementation. The memory cost is minimal: only very little non-volatile memory is required to store the tables (256 for the Sbox and 16 bytes for the XOR operation) and an unchanged RAM cost. Given the theoretical protection offered by such an implementation, it seems a very attractive choice cost-wise. Note that the complexity to achieve such a protection was minimal thanks to the very lightweight structure of PRESENT (only two types of operations used) and to the assumption that the expanded keys were already in dual-rail representation. No side-channel analysis was conducted and it is argued that this coding style seems limited to lightweight ciphers, or AES in a different field representation.

The authors in [8] introduce an improvement on the previous idea which drastically simplifies the XOR operation. Moreover, a side-channel and performance analysis of PRESENT and Lightweight Block cipher under this form are presented. No vulnerability appears when targeting the S-box output. The overhead in execution time is almost negligible.

However, the trick used to accelerate a XOR operation induces a leakage. The authors noticed that for any pair of variables (A, B), we have $C(A) \oplus C(B) \oplus 01 = C(A \oplus B)$, where C denotes the chosen dual-rail code. Performing a constant weight XOR does not require an access to a precomputed table this way. They argue that performed in some precise order, these operations do not leak a potential secret value. This works if one assumes there is only a single secret value XORed with a non-secret. Unfortunately, this assumption cannot be made for the second round of PRESENT and for the AES, as the XORs performed during the first MixColumns operation contain information on the secret key in both operands, making a side-channel attack possible.

In [22], Rausy *et al.* present a balancing strategy based on the execution of binary operators only. This balancing protection uses *dual-rail* with two bits in the registers, selected to be as similar as possible in terms of leakage, and S-Boxes are computed using a bit-slice representation.

All the aforementioned works tried to enforce the dual-rail representation. In this paper, we turn our attention to other classes of constant weight strategy.

3   A Constant Weight AES

3.1   The AES Algorithm

The AES [15], formerly known as Rijndael has been the international standard for symmetric ciphers and much research has focused on securing it against side-channel attacks since its adoption in 2000. It can be described as having four layers: a Substitution (*SubBytes*), a permutation (*ShiftRows*), a mixing phase (*MixColumns*) and a Key Addition (*AddRoundKey*).

The *SubBytes* phase is a nonlinear transformation in $GF(2^8)$ and is often implemented as a table lookup in software. *ShiftRows* is simply a sequence of byte swaps. *MixColumns* is a matrix multiplication of all 16 bytes of the AES state with a constant matrix, it can be implemented as several bitwise XORs and field multiplications. Those multiplications are based on an operation called *Xtimes*, which is the multiplication of a polynomial (represented as a byte) by X over $GF(2^8)$. This procedure is a simple bit test and a shift, plus a conditional XOR with a constant. It could also be implemented as a table look-up to avoid timing attacks. The last operation, *AddRoundKey*, is a simple XOR between the state values and a round key.

3.2   Constant Weight Codes

Constant weight codes have a simple definition: it is any code that has all its words of a given weight, say ω. In the following, we denote (x,y)-code the set of values of weight x over y bits, which contains $\binom{y}{x}$ elements. The dual-rail representation is a specific case of these codes, but it is not the only option one should consider in a software setting. It is adapted to the hardware environment as one has to deal with pair-wise balancing of wires. In software, one could simply use the code with the smallest cardinal available to encode the input set of data. A 4-bit data set contains 16 elements. The $(3,6)$-code presented in Table 1 (the set of 6-bit words of Hamming Weight 3) contains 20 elements, and is therefore large enough to encode the previous 4-bit set. Encoding (non-linearly) in this way could simply be a random assignment. For the rest of this paper, we will refer to the $(3,6)$-code simply by $\mathcal{C}$.

Table 1. $(3,6)$-code

0 → 000111	4 → 010011	8 → 011010	12 → 100110
1 → 001011	5 → 010101	9 → 011100	13 → 101001
2 → 001101	6 → 010110	10 → 100011	14 → 101010
3 → 001110	7 → 011001	11 → 100101	15 → 101100

3.3   Encoded Operations

Let us denote by $\mathcal{C}(A)$ (respectively $\mathcal{C}(B)$) the encoded form of the variable A (respectively B) in a constant weight representation. Then, the operation $A \perp B$ (where $\perp$ is any operation like XOR, AND $etc.$) can be performed in a non-leaking manner using a precomputed table T such that: $T[(\mathcal{C}(A) \ll n) \parallel \mathcal{C}(B)] = \mathcal{C}(A \perp B)$, where n is either the size of the codewords ($e.g.$ $n = 6$ for the $(3,6)$-code) or the size of a processor word ($i.e.$ $n = 8$) That is, if we prepare an index in this table by appending one encoded value to the other and then fetch the result from T, we get the encoded result of $A \perp B$.

For AES, we have to encode 8-bit values. Straightforwardly done, it would take up to 16 bits per state byte in dual-rail. The table for the S-box precomputed to fit this code would span 128 Kbytes of data, which is not a reasonable option for a conventional smartcard. Instead, in [10] authors propose to use the $GF(2^4)$ representation of AES. The S-box is then performed as a sequence of inverses and multiplications in that same field. This variant is expected to perform slowly due to these operations, see [16] for example. We aim to provide an alternative that performs fast and occupies an acceptable memory space.

For AES block cipher, the smallest code that can encode all of the 256 possible elements of the state is the $(5,11)$-code (462 elements). The table for performing the S-box would be indexed by 11 bits, thereby spanning 2048 elements of 11 bits each, which would amount to 4 KBytes in a realistic implementation. This is acceptable, but the problem arises from the XOR operation. In dual-rail, it could be done 2 bits by 2 bits, but with the $(5, 11)$-code it is not possible anymore, as this encoding is non-linear. To perform a XOR, a 22 bits index is needed under this form. Of course, this exceeds by far the capacity of any smartcard, so this code is a bad choice. Instead of coding a whole 8-bit variable W into a constant weight word, we split it into two 4 bits words (a high word HB and a low word LB) and encode each of them separately, but using the same $\mathcal{C}$:

$$W = \underbrace{0011}_{HB}\ \underbrace{1011}_{LB},\ \ \mathcal{C}(W) = \underbrace{001110}_{c(HB)}\ \underbrace{100101}_{c(LB)}$$

This way, linear operations can be performed on the two halves separately at a much lower memory cost. The table for the S-box is now indexed by $6+6 = 12$ bits, which is 4096 elements, and it is the same cost for the XOR. The operations cannot be made at once in this case though. As the Arithmetic Logic Unit (ALU) can only retrieve a byte from memory, we need two accesses to obtain both the HB and the LB of the S-box result. We end up with three tables of 4 KBytes each: one for the S-box's high bytes, one for the low bytes, and one for the XOR. The instruction sequence performing a XOR between two $(3, 6)$-codewords A and B, equal respectively to $(aaaaaa)$ and $(bbbbbb)$ in binary, is shown in Listing 1.1. Displayed on the right is the state of the 16-bit registers used. We stress the fact that line 5 is here to prevent any leakage in the Hamming distance model.

```
1   mov     ax, #0          // ax = 00000000 00000000
2   mov     Rh, A           // ax = 00aaaaaa 00000000
3   mov     Rl, B           // ax = 00aaaaaa 00bbbbbb
4   xor     ax, &table      // ax = ddaaaaaa ddbbbbbb
5   mov     bx, #0          // bx = 00000000 00000000
6   mov     bx, [ ax ]      // bx = 00000000 00cccccc = C(A xor B)
```

Listing 1.1. Table accesses in constant weight (x86 assembly style)

All performed operations meet the constant Hamming weight specifications. The constraints on the address format (2 bits set in the middle (dd)) is easily treated by modern compilers, which usually allow declaring tables at a specific address (*e.g.* the IAR compiler with the @ keyword).

4   Encoding the AES

In this section, we show how the various operations of the AES could be implemented in a constant weight fashion. There are mainly three different types of operations:

(i) Non-linear transformations of one word, *i.e.* SubBytes;
(ii) Two-operand operations, *i.e.* XOR;
(iii) Linear transformations of one word, *i.e.* Xtimes.

In the sequel, we denote by A_h (respectively A_l) the most significant (respectively the least significant) 4 bits of a byte A ($A = A_h \parallel A_l$).

Computation of type (i). The SubBytes operation will be performed in two accesses: one for the MSB of the result which will be put in register R_h, and another for the LSB which will be stored in register R_l such that:

$$R_h \leftarrow high\_subbytes[\ (\mathcal{C}(A_h) \ll 8)\ ||\ \mathcal{C}(A_l)\ ] = \mathcal{C}(SubBytes(A_h)),$$
$$R_l \leftarrow low\_subbytes[\ (\mathcal{C}(A_h) \ll 8)\ ||\ \mathcal{C}(A_l)\ ] = \mathcal{C}(SubBytes(A_l)).$$

Computation of type (ii). It is a similar case for the XOR operation, but it needs two operands A and B:

$$R_h \leftarrow xor\_table[\ (\mathcal{C}(A_h) \ll 8)\ ||\ \mathcal{C}(B_h)\ ] = \mathcal{C}(A_h \oplus B_h),$$
$$R_l \leftarrow xor\_table[\ (\mathcal{C}(A_l) \ll 8)\ ||\ \mathcal{C}(B_l)\ ] = \mathcal{C}(A_l \oplus B_l).$$

Computation of type (iii). At first, one could implement Xtimes just like the S-box as a one-operand full-length table access. This would add 8 more KBytes to the implementation and disregard the linearity of the operation. Instead, one can write the matrix M of Xtimes as:

$$M = \begin{pmatrix} 0\,0\,0\,0\,0\,0\,1\,0 \\ 0\,0\,0\,0\,0\,1\,0\,0 \\ 0\,0\,0\,0\,1\,0\,0\,0 \\ 0\,0\,0\,1\,0\,0\,0\,1 \\ 0\,0\,1\,0\,0\,0\,0\,1 \\ 0\,1\,0\,0\,0\,0\,0\,0 \\ 1\,0\,0\,0\,0\,0\,0\,1 \\ 0\,0\,0\,0\,0\,0\,0\,1 \end{pmatrix}$$
$$\underbrace{}_{M_h}\ \underbrace{}_{M_l}$$

where M_h and M_l are two (8×4) matrices such that $M = [M_h||M_l]$. Then, this linear operation consists in a XOR of two products of an (8×4) matrix by a 4-bit vector:

$$M \cdot A = (M_h \cdot A_h^T) \oplus (M_l \cdot A_l^T).$$

The necessary tables for M_h and M_l only use 256 bytes of non-volatile memory in total, which is almost negligible compared to the S-box.

4.1   Implementation Performance and Comparison

The whole implementation had to be done in assembly and using several macros. The code could be smaller as loops had to be fully unrolled - our macros could not easily allow use of variable indexes. The execution time is also reduced for the same reason. The Key Expansion phase was on-the-fly and in constant weight coding as well.

Encoded bytes were always written on registers previously set to 0, thereby preventing any Hamming distance leakage of the form $\mathcal{C}(A) \oplus \mathcal{C}(B)$, which is not constant weight. We compared our $(3, 6)$-code version to a C version of the AES on the same platform. For a fair comparison, it was checked that the compiler did optimize the unprotected version as much as possible. The results are enclosed in Table 2.

Table 2. Implementation results

Version	Speed (Cycles)	Code size (Ko)
AES unprotected	3.490	2,8
AES using $(3, 6)$-code	14.625	24,0

From Table 2, one can conclude that the protected version of the AES using $(3, 6)$-code is about $4, 2$ times slower, and $8, 5$ times bigger in code size.

In the following, we compare this implementation to existing higher-order masking schemes applied to block ciphers. As the targeted platforms are different we can only evaluate the performance in terms of loss compared to an unprotected version on the same platform, hence the scores in Table 3 are given as factors (*e.g.* $\times 2$ means the secured implementation is twice as slow as the unprotected one on the same microcontroller).

From Table 3, one can see that the Rivain-Prouff masking scheme of order 3 applied to AES takes 271.000 cycles according to [19], whereas the unprotected AES takes only 2.000 cycles. The performance loss would be $\times 135$ in this case.

4.2 Fault Detection Capability and Memory Consumption

Only 256 bytes of each 4 KBytes table will be used by the cipher during normal operation. This seems like a waste of space but actually yields a very interesting feature of this countermeasure which is fault detection.

We filled all unused values of our tables with 0's, a value which is not in the $(3, 6)$-code. If a random byte fault occurs on the state of the AES, then the 0 value will be returned with probability $(4096 - 256)/4096 = 93, 75\%$. This makes a variant of an infective computation method [6], as the 0 will propagate to all future operations within the cipher and the ciphertext will have 0 values in place of key-dependent values for the affected bytes. Testing whether a fault was injected or not incurs no overhead (simple zero-test of ciphertext bytes). Also,

Table 3. Theoretical resistance of higher-order masking and constant weight schemes against attacks in the Hamming Weight or Distance model.

Method and cipher	Resistance Order	Speed loss	Fault Detection
Higher-order masking schemes			
Masking (AES) [9]	1	$\times 1,7$	
Rivain-Prouff (AES) [19]	1	$\times 64,0$	
Kim-Hong-Lim (AES) [11]	3	$\times 41,0$	
Genelle-Prouff (AES) [5]	3	$\times 90,0$	
Rivain-Prouff (PICARO) [19]	2	$\times 6,1$	
Constant weight Schemes			
Dual-rail (PRESENT) [10]	Any	$\times 9,0$	93,75 %
(3,6)-code (AES)	**Any**	**$\times 4,2$**	**93,75 %**

any one-bit fault can be detected. This fault detection rate provides a strong advantage over all classical masking schemes, which do not inherently provide this detection capability.

Another advantage worth mentioning is that the RAM cost of this constant weight implementation is limited to 64 bytes (instead of 32 for the unprotected variant). Although RAM costs increases with the order of the masking schemes, in our case it is constant for any order.

5   Information Theoretic Analysis

As argued on the evaluation framework introduced in [24], the robustness of a countermeasure encompasses two dimensions: its amount of leakage irrespective of any attack strategy and its resistance to specific attacks. So, the evaluation of protected implementations should hold in two steps. First, an information theoretic analysis determines the actual information leakage. Second, a security analysis determines the efficiency of various attacks in exploiting this leakage.

Following this evaluation framework, we start with an information theoretic analysis. Under the Hamming weight assumption, it is obvious that the constant weight countermeasure is leakage-free. In fact, the mutual information is null since all manipulated variable have a constant Hamming weight. Therefore we investigate the consequences of a leakage function deviating from the Hamming Weight assumption on our proposed countermeasure. For instance, we assume that the leakage function is a polynomial of higher degree. Actually, the assumption that all the bits leak identically and without interfering does not hold in real hardware [25]. Also, it has been shown that with specific side channel capturing systems the attacker can distort the measurement. For instance, in [18], the authors show that with a home-made magnetic coil probing the circuit at a crucial location, the rising edges can be forced to dissipate 17 % more than the falling edges.

Thus, we study how the the constant weight countermeasure is resilient to imperfections of the leakage model. To do so, we consider the leakage function used in [7], *i.e.* which is a polynomial one of the form:

$$L(Z) = \sum_i a_i \cdot z_i + \sum_{i,j} b_{i,j} \cdot (z_i \cdot z_j) + \sum_{i,j,k} c_{i,j,k} \cdot (z_i \cdot z_j \cdot z_k), \qquad (1)$$

where z_i denotes the ith bit of the sensitive value Z and a_i, $b_{i,j}$ and $c_{i,j,k}$ are some weighting coefficients.

To evaluate the information revealed by the constant weight countermeasure, we compute the *Mutual Information Metric* (MIM) between the sensitive variable and the leakage function under two conditions:

1. **First case:** All bits of a sensitive variable leak identically, but interfere with each other (*i.e.* in Eq. (1) $\forall i\ a_i = a \in \{0,1\}$, $\forall i,j\ b_{i,j} = b \in \{0,1\}$, $\forall i,j,k\ c_{i,j,k} = c \in \{0,1\}$).
2. **Second case:** The bits of a sensitive variable leak randomly and interfere with each other (*i.e.* in Eq. (1) $\forall i\ a_i \in \{0,1\}$, $\forall i,j\ b_{i,j} \in \{0,1\}$, $\forall i,j,k\ c_{i,j,k} \in \{0,1\}$).

Table 4. MIM for polynomial leakage functions with perfect bits transition.

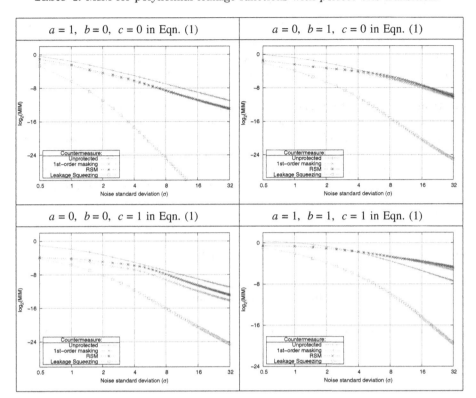

For the sake of comparison, we proceed similarly for several well-known countermeasures. We list hereafter the considered implementations with their corresponding leakage functions:

- Unprotected implementation: $O = L(Z) + N$, where N is a normally distributed noise variable of standard deviation σ (*i.e.* $N \sim \mathcal{N}(0, \sigma^2)$).
- Rotating S-box Masking (RSM) [14]: $O = L(Z \oplus M') + N$, where M' is a low entropy mask chosen within a code.
- Classical first-order Boolean masking[1]: $O = L(Z \oplus M) * L(M) + N$, where M is a full entropy mask.
- Leakage Squeezing[2] [13]: $O = L(Z \oplus M) + L(B(M)) + N$, where B is a bijection chosen within a binary code as well.
- Dual-rail [10]: $O = L(D(Z)) + N$, where D is the dual-rail encoding.
- (3,6)-code: $O = L(\mathcal{C}(Z)) + N$.

---

[1] For this implementation, the leakage corresponds to a bivariate attack, when the product combination is used by the adversary.

[2] This leakage function corresponds to a hardware implementation. To the best of our knowledge, the leakage squeezing countermeasure has never been adapted into a software implementation, therefore we only consider an univariate leakage in our simulation.

5.1   First Case: Perfect Bits Transition

The results are shown in Table 4. It is noteworthy that the mutual information for our constant weight countermeasure, as well as for the dual-rail countermeasure, is null whatever σ is. In fact, if all bits leak identically, the leakage function is always constant independently of the values of (a,b,c) and its degree has no influence on the quantity of information leaked. However, the results of our investigation show that for all other countermeasures, the higher the degree of the leakage function, the higher the leaked information. For instance, if the leakage function is a cubic one (*i.e.* $c = 1$), the RSM and the first-order masking lead to a first-order security against bivariate side-channel attacks since the slope of their corresponding MIM curves is equal to 2. Furthermore, these curves are parallel to the one of the unprotected implementation. Concerning the leakage squeezing countermeasure, it ensures a second-order security against univariate side-channel attacks (*i.e.* the slope is equal to 3).

5.2   Second Case: Random Bits Transition

In this case, we consider that the bits leak differently. From the results plotted in Table 5, the following observations can be emphasized:

Table 5. MIM for polynomial leakage functions with random bits transition.

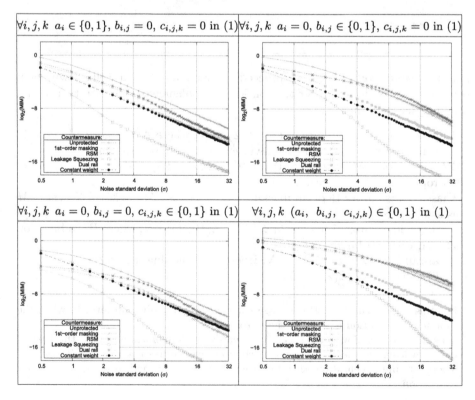

- Our proposed countermeasure offers a first-order resistance against univariate side-channel attacks and remains all the same as good as the first-order Boolean masking and the RSM countermeasure. In fact, their corresponding MIM curves have a slope equal to 2.
- When considering high noise values, the quantity of mutual information leaked by the constant weight countermeasure is lower than a first-order masking, for instance. Hence, a first-order attack will succeed, but the adversary will need more traces when dealing with the constant weight countermeasure.

6   Security Analysis

As a complement to the information theoretic analysis carried out in Sect. 5, we conduct in this section a security analysis to evaluate the resistance of our proposed countermeasure.

6.1   Higher-Order Side-Channel Resistance in the Hamming Weight Model

To prove the resistance of our countermeasure against higher-order SCA attacks in the perfect Hamming model, we have computed the *optimal correlation coefficient* defined in [21] by $f_{opt}(z) = E[\ (O(Z) - E[O(Z)])^d \mid Z = z\ ]$, where $O(Z)$ denotes the leakage function on the sensitive variable Z and satisfies $O(Z) = HW(\mathcal{C}(Z)) + N$. The noise is denoted by $N \sim \mathcal{N}(0, \sigma^2)$. Then, the optimal correlation coefficient rewrites:

$$\begin{aligned} f_{opt}(z) &= E[\ (HW(\mathcal{C}(Z)) + N - E[HW(\mathcal{C}(Z)) + N])^d \mid Z = z\ ] \\ &= E[\ (HW(\mathcal{C}(Z)) + N - HW(\mathcal{C}(Z)) - E[N])^d \mid Z = z\ ] \\ &= E[\ N^d\ ]. \end{aligned}$$

The last equality is only dependent on the noise, not on the sensitive variable $Z = f(X, K)$, where f denotes any operation using the input variable X and the key K. In that case this means the attack does not work, independently of the order d. Note that switching from Hamming weight leakage protection to Hamming distance protection only requires setting destination registers to 0 before storing the result of a sensitive operation into them. Therefore, this security analysis applies for both leakage models, given a proper implementation.

6.2   Side-Channel Resistance in the Imperfect Model

In this section, we evaluate the soundness of the proposed constant weight implementation when the leakage slightly deviates from the rules involved to design this countermeasure. First, we analyse if our implementation shows some vulnerabilities against first-order CPA attack, and then we examine how robust it is against a stochastic online attack [4]. The purpose of this stochastic approach is to deduce the global activity associated to arbitrary chosen events occurring during the encryption (typically a bit-flipping). Although the Hamming weight of each manipulated word remains constant at any time, we expect that the stochastic online approach can exploit differences from a bit register to another, especially if the leakage function deviates from the Hamming weight model as highlighted in the previous information theoretic analysis.

For comparison purpose, we computed the success rate of CPA and stochastic online attack on an unsecured software implementation of AES over 1.000 independent experiments. Concerning the constant weight AES implementation, we performed these *distinguishers* over 20.000 independent experiments. In our practical attack scenario, we considered the following simulated leakage model:

$$O = \sum_{i=1}^{8} a_i \cdot z_i + N, \tag{2}$$

where a_i are some weighting coefficients following a Gaussian law $\mathcal{N}(1, \sigma_e)$, z_i is the ith bit of the sensitive value Z (equals S-box$[X \oplus K]$ for the unprotected AES, and equals $\mathcal{C}(\text{S-box}[X \oplus K])$ for the $(3, 6)$-code constant weight implementation) and N is an environmental noise $s.t.$ $N \sim \mathcal{N}(0, \sigma)$. This model allows us to simulate the leakages by taking into account a slight deviation from the Hamming weight leakage model. The results of these attacks are shown on Fig. 1 for $\sigma_e = 0.1$ and $\sigma = 2$.

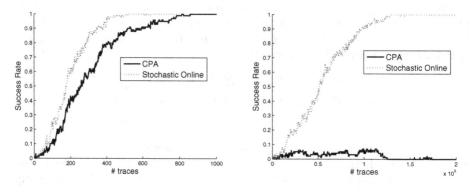

Fig. 1. CPA and stochastic online attacks on unsecured AES implementation (left) and constant weight implementation (right)

From Fig. 1 the following observations can be emphasized:

– As expected, the CPA attack is no longer efficient on the secured implementation even if the leakage model deviates from the Hamming weight assumption.
– Considering the stochastic online attack results, one can see that the unprotected implementation is easily broken. In fact, about 400 traces suffices to achieve a success rate of 100 %. As expected and revealed by the information theoretic analysis, the $(3, 6)$-code implementation performs worse when the bit-flipping is random. Indeed, the success rate of the stochastic online attack reaches 100 % with 140 K traces, although this represents a gain of robustness of about a factor 350.

7   Conclusion

An investigation on whether the AES could be implemented in a constant weight fashion on a 16-bit smartcard was conducted. Instead of using a dual-rail code, we chose an "m out of n" code that enables fast operations at an acceptable memory cost. We have argued that our proposal is a leak-free countermeasure under some realistic assumptions about the leakage model. The solution has been evaluated within an information-theoretic study, proving its security against SCA under the Hamming weight assumption. When the leakage function deviates slightly from this assumption, our solution still achieves good results. On the performance side, it was shown our $(3, 6)$-code AES is faster at execution than most generic higher-order masking schemes, and also comes with some fault detection capability at no cost; a feature which masking schemes lack.

Acknowledgments. This work has been partially funded by the ANR projects E-MATA HARI and SPACES.

References

1. Bogdanov, A.A., Knudsen, L.R., Leander, G., Paar, C., Poschmann, A., Robshaw, M., Seurin, Y., Vikkelsoe, C.: PRESENT: an ultra-lightweight block cipher. In: Paillier, P., Verbauwhede, I. (eds.) CHES 2007. LNCS, vol. 4727, pp. 450–466. Springer, Heidelberg (2007)
2. Brier, E., Clavier, C., Olivier, F.: Correlation power analysis with a leakage model. In: Joye, M., Quisquater, J.-J. (eds.) CHES 2004. LNCS, vol. 3156, pp. 16–29. Springer, Heidelberg (2004)
3. Coron, J.-S.: Higher order masking of look-up tables. In: Nguyen, P.Q., Oswald, E. (eds.) EUROCRYPT 2014. LNCS, vol. 8441, pp. 441–458. Springer, Heidelberg (2014)
4. Doget, J., Prouff, E., Rivain, M., Standaert, F.-X.: Univariate side channel attacks and leakage modeling. J. Crypt. Eng. **1**(2), 123–144 (2011)
5. Genelle, L., Prouff, E., Quisquater, M.: Thwarting higher-order side channel analysis with additive and multiplicative maskings. In: Preneel, B., Takagi, T. (eds.) CHES 2011. LNCS, vol. 6917, pp. 240–255. Springer, Heidelberg (2011)
6. Gierlichs, B., Schmidt, J.-M., Tunstall, M.: Infective computation and dummy rounds: fault protection for block ciphers without check-before-output. Cryptology ePrint Archive, Report 2012678 (2012). http://eprint.iacr.org
7. Grosso, V., Standaert, F.-X., Prouff, E.: Low entropy masking schemes, revisited. In: Francillon, A., Rohatgi, P. (eds.) CARDIS 2013. LNCS, vol. 8419, pp. 33–43. Springer, Heidelberg (2014)
8. Han, Y., Zhou, Y., Liu, J.: Securing lightweight block cipher against power analysis attacks. In: Zhang, Y. (ed.) Future Wireless Networks and Information Systems. LNEE, vol. 143, pp. 379–390. Springer, Heidelberg (2012)
9. Herbst, C., Oswald, E., Mangard, S.: An AES smart card implementation resistant to power analysis attacks. In: Zhou, J., Yung, M., Bao, F. (eds.) ACNS 2006. LNCS, vol. 3989, pp. 239–252. Springer, Heidelberg (2006)
10. Hoogvorst, P., Duc, G., Danger, J.-L.: Software implementation of dual-rail representation. In: COSADE (2011)

11. Kim, H., Hong, S., Lim, J.: A fast and provably secure higher-order masking of AES S-box. In: Preneel, B., Takagi, T. (eds.) CHES 2011. LNCS, vol. 6917, pp. 95–107. Springer, Heidelberg (2011)
12. Kocher, P.C., Jaffe, J., Jun, B.: Differential power analysis. In: Wiener, M. (ed.) CRYPTO 1999. LNCS, vol. 1666, pp. 388–397. Springer, Heidelberg (1999)
13. Maghrebi, H., Carlet, C., Guilley, S., Danger, J.-L.: Optimal first-order masking with linear and non-linear bijections. In: Mitrokotsa, A., Vaudenay, S. (eds.) AFRICACRYPT 2012. LNCS, vol. 7374, pp. 360–377. Springer, Heidelberg (2012)
14. Nassar, M., Souissi, Y., Guilley, S., Danger, J.-L.: RSM: a small and fast countermeasure for AES, secure against first- and second-order zero-offset SCAs. In: DATE (TRACK A: "Application Design", TOPIC A5: "Secure Systems"), pp. 1173–1178. IEEE Computer Society, Dresden, Germany, 12–16 March 2012
15. NIST/ITL/CSD. Advanced Encryption Standard (AES). FIPS PUB 197, November 2001. http://csrc.nist.gov/publications/fips/fips197/fips-197.pdf
16. Oswald, E., Schramm, K.: An efficient masking scheme for AES software implementations. In: Song, J.-S., Kwon, T., Yung, M. (eds.) WISA 2005. LNCS, vol. 3786, pp. 292–305. Springer, Heidelberg (2006)
17. Peeters, E., Standaert, F.-X., Donckers, N., Quisquater, J.-J.: Improved higher-order side-channel attacks with FPGA experiments. In: Rao, J.R., Sunar, B. (eds.) CHES 2005. LNCS, vol. 3659, pp. 309–323. Springer, Heidelberg (2005)
18. Peeters, É., Standaert, F.-X., Quisquater, J.-J.: Power and electromagnetic analysis: Improved model, consequences and comparisons. Integ. VLSI J. **40**, 52–60 (2007). doi:10.1016/j.vlsi.2005.12.013. Embedded Cryptographic Hardware
19. Piret, G., Roche, T., Carlet, C.: PICARO – a block cipher allowing efficient higher-order side-channel resistance. In: Bao, F., Samarati, P., Zhou, J. (eds.) ACNS 2012. LNCS, vol. 7341, pp. 311–328. Springer, Heidelberg (2012)
20. Preneel, B., Takagi, T. (eds.): CHES 2011. LNCS, vol. 6917. Springer, Heidelberg (2011)
21. Prouff, E., Rivain, M., Bévan, R.: Statistical analysis of second order differential power analysis. Cryptology ePrint Archive, Report 2010/646 (2010). http://eprint.iacr.org/
22. Rauzy, P., Guilley, S., Najm, Z.: Formally proved security of assembly code against leakage. IACR Cryptol. ePrint Arch. **2013**, 554 (2013)
23. Rivain, M., Prouff, E.: Provably secure higher-order masking of AES. In: Mangard, S., Standaert, F.-X. (eds.) CHES 2010. LNCS, vol. 6225, pp. 413–427. Springer, Heidelberg (2010)
24. Standaert, F.-X., Malkin, T.G., Yung, M.: A unified framework for the analysis of side-channel key recovery attacks. In: Joux, A. (ed.) EUROCRYPT 2009. LNCS, vol. 5479, pp. 443–461. Springer, Heidelberg (2009)
25. Veyrat-Charvillon, N., Standaert, F.-X.: Mutual information analysis: how, when and why? In: Clavier, C., Gaj, K. (eds.) CHES 2009. LNCS, vol. 5747, pp. 429–443. Springer, Heidelberg (2009)

Balanced Encoding to Mitigate Power Analysis: A Case Study

Cong Chen[✉], Thomas Eisenbarth, Aria Shahverdi, and Xin Ye

Worcester Polytechnic Institute, Worcester, MA, USA
{cchen3,teisenbarth,ashahverdi,xye}@wpi.edu

Abstract. Most side channel countermeasures for software implementations of cryptography either rely on masking or randomize the execution order of the cryptographic implementation. This work proposes a countermeasure that has constant leakage in common linear leakage models. Constant leakage is achieved not only for internal state values, but also for their transitions. The proposed countermeasure provides perfect protection in the theoretical leakage model. To study the practical relevance of the proposed countermeasure, it is applied to a software implementation of the block cipher Prince. This case study allows us to give realistic values for resulting implementation overheads as well as for the resulting side channel protection levels that can be achieved in realistic implementation scenarios.

1 Introduction

Embedded implementations of cryptography are a popular target for side channel attacks. With the advent of the Internet of Things, an ever-increasing number of embedded devices enters our lives and homes. These devices handle and exchange possibly sensitive information, raising the need for data security and privacy. High-end security solutions such as the processors found in passports and security smart cards come with an abundance of hardware protection to mitigate all kinds of physical and side channel attacks. However, most embedded devices are consumer-grade products that usually have to rely on unprotected off-the-shelf microprocessors. Only a limited number of methods are available to protect cryptographic software against side channel attacks on such a platform. A popular countermeasure is masking, such as random precharge for registers or full masking schemes [10]. One of the biggest problems for getting a high level of protection of microprocessors is that masking is only effective if the processor has a low signal-to-noise ratio [3,13]. On modern embedded processors, this is usually not the case, requiring the combination of masking with other countermeasures that decrease the signal-to-noise ratio. Due to the fixed architecture of processors, real hiding countermeasures that achieve leakage reduction are hard to achieve. Proposed countermeasures for embedded software cryptosystems are mostly randomization countermeasures, i.e. leakage is not reduced, but rather randomized in time. Examples include shuffling [17,19] or random delays [6].

This work explores a true hiding countermeasure in software. The idea is to ensure a constant leakage for all intermediate states. There is some limited

© Springer International Publishing Switzerland 2015
M. Joye and A. Moradi (Eds.): CARDIS 2014, LNCS 8968, pp. 49–63, 2015.
DOI: 10.1007/978-3-319-16763-3_4

prior work proposing constant Hamming weight (HW) encodings of intermediate states. In [9], a secure assembly coding style based on the concept of Dual-Rail Precharge Logic (DPL) was proposed. The authors claim that a constant activity can be achieved using their specific data representation and programming rules. Their work is purely theoretic, no experimental results to support their idea were presented. Furthermore, the computation protocol did not completely prevent Hamming distance (HD) leakage. In [14], the authors present the methods and tools to generate DPL style code automatically. In [8], a similar data representation called Bitwise Balanced enCoding scheme was proposed. This scheme appears to be flawed: the XOR operation will leak information of one of the two inputs, as we explain later. They also just present simulation results that assume an idealized leakage. Hence, that work also lacks any analysis of real-world applicability.

In this work, we present new constant-leakage encodings. As prior works, we require intermediate states to be represented by constant Hamming weight encodings. We go beyond prior studies by showing that requiring constant Hamming distance transitions between states is also feasible. Unlike prior work, we actually implement the counteremeasure, allowing us to realistically judge resulting implementation overheads. More importantly, we evaluate the achieved leakage reduction on a modern 8-bit microcontroller. We show how the constant leakage can be implemented not only for state representations, but also for state transitions, This allows us to apply the encodings to create a protected implementation of the Prince block cipher.

As most countermeasures, this countermeasure cannot provide perfect protection by itself. The leakage of real-world microprocessors deviates from linear and balanced models like the Hamming weight or Hamming distance model. However, forcing the side channel adversary to exploit the non-linear and imbalanced components of the leakage requires more sophisticated attacks and an increasing number of leakage observations. In other words, the countermeasure can effectively decrease the signal-to-noise ratio. The proposed countermeasure is orthogonal to masking or randomization countermeasures. Hence it can easily be combined with those to achieve an even higher overall resistance.

The remainder of the contribution is structured as follows: Related work is discussed in Sect. 2. The new encoding scheme is introduced in Sect. 3 and applied to Prince in Sect. 4. Section 5 explains our leakage evaluation and Sect. 6 presents implementation results and the outcome of the leakage evaluation.

2   Background

This section introduces the related work on balanced encodings to counteract SCA in both hardware and software implementations, as well as a short introduction to the Prince block cipher to which the countermeasure will be applied.

2.1   Balanced Logic for Hardware Implementation

Dual-Rail Precharge Logic (DPL) aims to achieve constant activity at the gate level. In a DPL style circuit, any gate that generates logic bit A is accompanied with a complementary gate that generates logic bit $\bar{A}$. That is, the logic bit pair $(A, \bar{A})$ is used to represent A. Note that the Hamming weight of the pair is always constant as 1. Besides, in order to obtain constant Hamming distance, the bit pair is precharged to $(0, 0)$ before evaluation. Hence, the gate transitions from $(0, 0)$ to either $(0, 1)$ or $(1, 0)$ leaks data independent power consumption or EM emissions. Based on this idea, many DPL style have been proposed such as WDDL [18], MDPL [12] and DRSL [5]. All these DPL variants aim to protect the hardware crypto systems against SCA.

2.2   Balanced Logic for Software Implementation

Solutions to reproduce DPL in software have been proposed in the past few years. The basic idea of these solutions is the same in that the data in the register or RAM is represented using balanced encoding. Each bit of an intermediate state is converted to two complementary bits. For example, logical bit 1 is encoded as 01 and logical bit 0 is encoded as 10. 11 and 00 are taken as invalid values.

In [9], Hoogvorst et al. showed a generic assembly coding methodology using DPL style. They redefined the instructions of the standard microprocessor using DPL macros which combines a series of normal instructions to achieve precharge (by moving 0s to the data register) and evaluation (by concatenating operands and indexing in a lookup table). The activity of precharge phase is constant since overwriting the balanced data register with all $'0'$ causes constant bit flips. During the evaluation phase, the activity of each normal instruction is either constant or irrelevant with the sensitive data. Given the new instructions, the normal assembly code can be transformed to the DPL style code. In [4], Chen et al. also proposed a software programming style to generate a Virtual Secure Circuit (VSC). The basic idea of VSC is to use complementary instructions in a balanced processor to emulate the DPL circuits' behavior.

Han et al. proposed in [8] a balanced encoding scheme for block ciphers. Instead of proposing protection for individual instructions, they propose specific protections for the operations of the cipher, such as KeyAddition and S-box lookups. For example in their KeyAddition layer one balanced encoded key bit (01 or 10) is XORed with one plaintext bit. The plaintext bit is encoded by repetition code (00 for 0 or 11 for 1) so that the result is 01 or 10, i.e. an internal state bit correctly encoded with a balanced encoding. Obviously, the operation may leak information of the plaintext input, even in the Hamming weight leakage model, but this information is not useful for differential side channel attacks. However, this method can only be applied to the initial KeyAddition where the plaintext is known. For the following rounds, the intermediate data may still leak useful information. Since no alternative XOR is introduced, we do not think this scheme can be applied in an appropriate way to protect cryptographic implementations. Furthermore, the S-box operation also cannot prevent Hamming distance leakage.

2.3   The Prince Block Cipher

The Prince block cipher is a lightweight cipher, featuring a 64-bit block size and a 128-bit key size [1]. Prince has been optimized for low latency and a small hardware footprint. Its round function has several similarities to the AES: it features KeyAddition, S-box, ShiftRows and MixColumns operations. However, these operations are performed on a 4-by-4 array of 4-bit nibbles. This 4-bit oriented design makes Prince—unlike AES—a suitable candidate for a constant Hamming weight encoding on 8-bit microcontrollers. Prince has 12 rounds, and the last six apply the inverse operations of the first six. The 64-bit round key remains constant in all rounds, but is augmented with a 64-bit round constant to ensure variation between rounds. The remaining 64 key bits are used for pre- and post-whitening of the state. A feature of Prince is that encryption and decryption only differ in the round key. A detailed description of an unprotected microcontroller implementation of the Prince can be found in [15].

3   General Balanced Encoding Countermeasure

The non-balanced encoding of the algorithmic inputs and internal states usually causes side channel leakage during the execution of crypto primitives. The leakage can be exploited from classical side channel attacks such as DPA, CPA or MIA. The proposed countermeasure aims at encoding the internal states with longer bit length but resulting in constant Hamming weight of state and constant Hamming distance between two consecutive states. This trade-off sacrifices some memory and efficiency but achieves a balanced representation internal data and therefore mitigates the impact of side channel threats.

Formally, the balanced encoding requires the uniform distribution of Hamming weight for all codewords. Namely, every codeword should have the same Hamming weight, like the idea of constant-weight code or (m of n code). Clearly, the natural binary encoding is not such a candidate (e.g. $HW(0) \neq HW(1)$) since the resulting distribution of Hamming weight is binomial rather than uniform. The idea of balancing encoding can be realized only if using more than necessary bit length. A balanced encoding uses an embedding mapping τ from the natural binary encoded space $\mathcal{C} = \mathbb{F}_2^m$ for all $c \in \mathcal{C}$ into an extension $\mathbf{ext}(\mathcal{C}) = \mathbb{F}_2^n$ with $n > m$. In order to satisfy the constant Hamming weight of the new codeword, a necessary condition is that $C_n^{n/2} \geq 2^m$, where the image $\tau(\mathcal{C})$ sits entirely in the subset $S_{n/2} = \{u \in \mathbb{F}_2^n \mid HW(u) = n/2\}$.

Secondly, the newer encoding should preserve the basic bivariate operations $f(\cdot, \cdot)$ like xor and more complicated univariate operation $g(\cdot)$ such as the nonlinear S-box mapping. More precisely, for any $v_1, v_2 \in \mathcal{C}$, it should hold that $\tau(f(v_1, v_2)) = \tilde{f}(\tau(v_1), \tau(v_2))$, where $\tilde{f}$ is the n-bit adjustment of the m-bit operation f. Similarly, for any $v \in \mathcal{C}$, it should hold that $\tau(g(v)) = \tilde{g}(\tau(v))$. Preserving such operations ensures the validity of the algorithmic evolution.

Thirdly, we also want such balanced encoding that achieves constant Hamming distance between any two consecutive states. This may not be easily realized with the choice of the codeword by requiring $HW(\tau(v) \oplus \tilde{g}(\tau(v)))$ being constant for any $v \in \mathcal{C}$. But it can be easily achieved with implementation tricks such as flushing registers before overwriting them with new values. That is, in order to mitigate the leakage generated from overwriting values, say for example, the state representation $\tau(v)$ which is stored in register $R1$ needs to be replaced by the univariate functional output $\tilde{g}(\tau(v))$, the procedure is first to store the output $\tilde{g}(\tau(v))$ at a different pre-cleared register $R2$, then clear register $R1$ and finally copy the register value from $R2$ back to $R1$ and free the temporary register $R2$. This approach sacrifices the efficiency of the code, but prevents Hamming distance leakage from overwriting the state. Another solution is to apply different balanced encodings to the two consecutive states to achieve not only constant Hamming weight but constant Hamming distance as well. More details of this solution will be given in the following section.

4   A Case Study Based on the Prince Cipher

In this section, we use Prince as an example to present the balanced encoding scheme. Prince is a nibble-based block cipher, as detailed in Sect. 2.3. Since our target platform is an 8-bit processor, a simple balanced encoding can be achieved by simply adding complementary bits, as done for dual-rail logic styles. That way, each state nibble is encoded as a 8-bit balanced encoding by inserting the complementary bits. For any nibble $b_3 b_2 b_1 b_0$ where b_i is one bit data, the complementary nibble is $\bar{b}_3 \bar{b}_2 \bar{b}_1 \bar{b}_0$, where $\bar{b}_i$ is the inverse of b_i. Concatenating these two nibbles forms a balanced encoding $\bar{b}_3 \bar{b}_2 \bar{b}_1 \bar{b}_0 b_3 b_2 b_1 b_0$. An alternative is the encoding $\bar{b}_3 b_3 \bar{b}_2 b_2 \bar{b}_1 b_1 \bar{b}_0 b_0$. Theoretically, under the Hamming weight leakage assumption, any sequence of those bits can be used as a balanced encoding because the Hamming weight is always 4. In the following we will use two different such encodings, i.e. $enc_I = \bar{b}_3 b_3 \bar{b}_2 b_2 \bar{b}_1 b_1 \bar{b}_0 b_0$, which we refer to as *encoding I*, and $enc_{II} = b_0 \bar{b}_2 b_1 b_3 \bar{b}_1 b_2 \bar{b}_0 \bar{b}_3$, which we refer to as *encoding II*. Both of the encodings ensure the constant Hamming weight of states. The *encoding II* is used to guarantee the constant Hamming distance between state transitions and the way this specific encoding is determined will be explained in the following section.

KeyAddition with Constant HW/HD. In the unprotected Prince implementation, the KeyAddition operation is denoted as $r_3 r_2 r_1 r_0 = b_3 b_2 b_1 b_0 \oplus k_3 k_2 k_1 k_0$ where k is the subkey, b is a state nibble before the KeyAddition and r is the result of KeyAddition. For the protected Prince, we want an XOR-addition where secret inputs and outputs have a balanced encoding. However, for the initial key whitening at the input of the cipher, the plaintext input can be assumed not critical. Hence, only the output r and the key k are mapped to encoding I, i.e. $\bar{r}_3 r_3 \bar{r}_2 r_2 \bar{r}_1 r_1 \bar{r}_0 r_0$ and $\bar{k}_3 k_3 \bar{k}_2 k_2 \bar{k}_1 k_1 \bar{k}_0 k_0$. As in [8], we can simply XOR-add k in encoding I to b encoded as $b_3 b_3 b_2 b_2 b_1 b_1 b_0 b_0$ to realize the partially-protected XOR. This way, the Hamming weight of r is constant as well as the Hamming distance between r and b. The encoding for b does not satisfy the balanced encoding requirement, but has instead double Hamming weight leakage. Therefore, this only works for the initial KeyAddition where the plaintext is known.

After the first KeyAddition, the state becomes sensitive and need the balanced encoding. Hence, for the KeyAddition inside each round, b uses encoding I. Instead, we map k to the encoding $k_3 k_3 k_2 k_2 k_1 k_1 k_0 k_0$, resulting in a remaining *constant* leakage for the round keys. Since the leakage is constant, it is not exploitable by CPA or DPA. Note that this leakage can also be avoided by using the XOR addition described in the following MixColumns section. It is more costly than the above described XOR variant, but all inputs and outputs have a balanced encoding and all transitions a constant Hamming distance.

Table Lookup with Constant HW/HD. The S-box operation can be described as $s_3 s_2 s_1 s_0 = S(r_3 r_2 r_1 r_0)$ where $S(\cdot)$ denotes the S-box, r denotes an input nibble, and s denotes the output. To protect it, a new lookup table based on the balanced encoding is designed in order to minimize the leakage. The S-box operation is denoted as $\bar{s}_3 s_3 \bar{s}_2 s_2 \bar{s}_1 s_1 \bar{s}_0 s_0 = S'(\bar{r}_3 r_3 \bar{r}_2 r_2 \bar{r}_1 r_1 \bar{r}_0 r_0)$ where the $S'(\cdot)$ represents the new S-box. Therefore the Hamming weight of S-box output bits is constant. Note that, unlike the regular S-box of size of 1×16, the new S-box is a 16×16 table where the only 16 positions contain the output value and all other positions are unused. The new S-box prevents the Hamming weight leakage but cannot prevent the Hamming distance leakage. One solution is to precharge the target register with zero before writing s into it. An alternative is applying encoding II to s, which is found by exhaustive search in all the possible encodings. For the Prince cipher, the S-box output in encoding II can be denoted as $s_0 \bar{s}_2 s_1 s_3 \bar{s}_1 s_2 \bar{s}_0 \bar{s}_3$. In this way, the Hamming weight of S-box output is still constant as 4 and the Hamming distance between input in encoding I and output in encoding II becomes constant as $HD(enc_I(r), enc_{II}(s)) = 4$.

The cost of using two different encodings is an additional reordering layer which coverts encoding II back to encoding I. This is because the following operations such as MixColumns and ShiftRows are based on encoding I. A straightforward idea for reordering is the bit rotation which can be implemented using AND, LSL, LSR and OR instructions. AND instruction is used to pick out each single bit in encoding II by zeroing the other bits. Then we shift it to its position in encoding I. Finally, we combine all bits together to form encoding I. The disadvantage is that it is time consuming and it still causes side channel leakage. Instead, we can implement the reordering layer as a 16x16 lookup table R. The reordering table take the encoding II as input and output encoding $\bar{s}_3 s_3 \bar{s}_2 s_2 \bar{s}_1 s_1 s_0 \bar{s}_0 = R(enc_{II}(s))$. Note that, the output of R is a variant of encoding I by swapping the two LSBs. This is because $HD(enc_I(s), enc_{II}(s))$ is either 2 or 4 but $HD(\bar{s}_3 s_3 \bar{s}_2 s_2 \bar{s}_1 s_1 s_0 \bar{s}_0, enc_{II}(s))$ is constant as 4. Then, the output of R is XORed with 0x03 which swaps the two LSBs back to encoding I.

MixColumns with Constant HW/HD. The MixColumns operation can be implemented as XOR operations between the intermediate data. Unlike the XOR operation in KeyAddition, all the data involved in the MixColumns operation are sensitive and must hence be encoded in balanced encoding scheme to avoid the information leakage. Thus we need to design a new **constant XOR operation** instead of reusing the XOR from the KeyAddition. After the S-box substitution, the data in MixColumns operation are represented in encoding I. Denote the two operands of the constant XOR are as follows: $x : \bar{x}_3 x_3 \bar{x}_2 x_2 \bar{x}_1 x_1 \bar{x}_0 x_0$ and $y : \bar{y}_3 y_3 \bar{y}_2 y_2 \bar{y}_1 y_1 \bar{y}_0 y_0$. The XOR result is $z : \bar{z}_3 z_3 \bar{z}_2 z_2 \bar{z}_1 z_1 \bar{z}_0 z_0$. The constant XOR can be implemented using the following steps: .

Step 1: Divide the operand x into two parts and construct two new bytes as $x_L : \bar{x}_3 x_3 \bar{x}_2 x_2 \bar{x}_3 x_3 \bar{x}_2 x_2$ and $x_R : \bar{x}_1 x_1 \bar{x}_0 x_0 \bar{x}_1 x_1 \bar{x}_0 x_0$. In AVR microcontroller, this step can be easily done by AND, SWAP and OR instructions. For operand y, we construct y_L and y_R in the same way. The following code to the generate x_L can also be applied to the generation of x_R, y_L and y_R.

Input: r1 = x
Output: x_L

```
1   ldi r16, 0xF0
2   ldi r17, 0xF0
3   and r16, r1     ; Cut off the right nibble of x
4   and r17, r1     ; Cut off the right nibble of x
5   swap r17        ; Swap the left nibble to the right
6   or r16, r17     ; Generate x_L
```

Step 2: Do the regular XOR operation between x_L and 0xA5 to generate x'_L : $x_3 x_3 x_2 x_2 \bar{x}_3 \bar{x}_3 \bar{x}_2 \bar{x}_2 = x_L \oplus (10100101)_b$. Then $z_L = x'_L \oplus y_L = \bar{z}_3 z_3 \bar{z}_2 z_2 z_3 \bar{z}_3 z_2 \bar{z}_2$. We also can generate z_R with the similar operations.

Input: r16 = x_L, r18 = y_L
Output: z_L

```
1   ldi r17, 0xA5
2   eor r16, r17    ; Convert x_L to x_L'
3   eor r16, r18    ; Generate z_L
```

Step 3: Combine the most significant nibble of z_L and the least significant nibble of z_R to construct $z : \bar{z}_3 z_3 \bar{z}_2 z_2 \bar{z}_1 z_1 \bar{z}_0 z_0$.

Input: r1 = z_L, r2 = z_R
Output: z

```
1   ldi r16, 0xF0
2   ldi r17, 0x0F
3   and r16, r1     ; Cut off the least significant nibble of z_L
4   and r17, r2     ; Cut off the most significant nibble of z_R
5   or r16, r17     ; Generate z
```

Note that all above instructions operate on constant Hamming weight representations. Furthermore, there are no transitions that feature a non-constant Hamming distance in any operands. Hence, while costly, this XOR operation is free of Hamming weight or Hamming distance leakages in the operands.

5   Evaluation Methodology

The analyzed countermeasure is secure if each bit of the secret state s leaks in the same way, i.e. linearly and with the same weight. However, practical devices never have such a perfect leakage. To evaluate the leakage properties on the constant weight encoding on a real device, we analyze the leakage behavior of different evaluation approaches. Besides correlation-based DPA, we also perform a mutual information-based evaluation.

5.1   Correlation-Based DPA

Correlation-based DPA was originally proposed by Brier *et al.* [2]. The typical leakage model is the Hamming weight of the S-box output. The studied countermeasure is designed to not feature such a leakage at all. However, since real devices will never feature a perfect Hamming-weight leakage, it is still interesting to analyze whether the remaining leakage of a protected implementation is still exploitable by a CPA. The predicted secret state for our CPA is the Hamming weight of a single S-box output. Another popular analysis is single-bit DPA. As before we apply correlation, but this time using a single bit of the S-box output as leakage model. As the Hamming-weight based CPA, this attack does not work in an idealized environment where each bit leaks in the same way: One of the two bits used to represent the value of a certain bit will always be one, the other zero. However, in practice no two lines leak alike. Hence, bit leakages should be recoverable, but be impeded by the countermeasure.

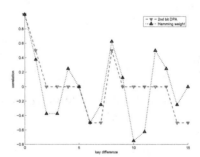

Fig. 1. CPA results on output bit 2 of the unprotected Prince S-box and on the Hamming weight of the unprotected Prince S-box for the correct key (or correctly predicted S-box input, index 0) and incorrect keys (or incorrectly predicted inputs, all other indices). The vertical axis shows the resulting correlation while the horizontal axis indicates the offset from the correct key (or S-box input value). Basically all indices besides 0 that exhibit a significant correlation are considered *Ghost peaks*, showing that Hamming weight based CPA might not be the wisest choice to attack Prince.

Note that both CPA and bit-wise DPA do not behave very well for the Prince block cipher: even in a perfect (Hamming weight) leakage environment, an unprotected implementation features strong *"ghost peaks"*, as depicted in Fig. 1. These ghost peaks make the distinction of the correct key more difficult. However, since the behavior is predictable, they can also be used to improve the attack, as discussed e.g. in [11].

5.2 Mutual Information Based Evaluation

A popular method for evaluating the side channel resistance of an implementation is mutual information. It was proposed as a side channel leakage metric for evaluation in [16] and refined for practical experiments in [7]. The goal is to evaluate the leakage L of a critical intermediate state s. The evaluated intermediate state for the Prince cipher is one nibble. The initial state is a nibble of the plaintext p, which is known. KeyAddition and round constant addition are mere permutations of the state, as are S-box and ShiftRows operations. Since mutual information is computed over all states, the changing labeling does not change the mutual information, i.e. it can be precisely computed through the aforementioned operations even without knowing the key. The MixColumns operation, however, mixes information from different state nibbles, i.e. output nibbles no longer depend on a single input nibble. This means that, during and after the MixColumns operation the meaning of the mutual information that is computed on one nibble finally drops off. However, since the typical target—the S-box output—is fully covered, the leakage typically exploited by any univariate attacks targeting only the first round will be identified by mutual information computed on individual state nibbles. The mutual information $I(S; L)$ between the leakage L and the states S is computed as $I(S; L) = H(S) - H(S|L)$ where $H(S|L)$ is the conditional entropy of S, knowing the leakage L. It is given as

$$H(S|L) = -\sum_{l \in \mathcal{L}} \left(Pr(l) \sum_{s \in \mathcal{S}} Pr(s|l) \log Pr(s|l) \right), \tag{1}$$

where l and s are specific observations of the leakage and state, respectively. Given univariate templates $\mathcal{N}(\mu_s, \sigma_s)$ for each state value s and each point of the leakage, we have the probability density for observing a leakage l at that point given as $p(l|s) = \mathcal{N}(\mu_s, \sigma_s)$. Following Bayes' Theorem, we get $p(s|l) = \frac{p(l|s)Pr(s)}{Pr(l)}$ and, since all observations and states are equiprobable, we can derive

$$Pr(s|l) = \frac{p(l|s)}{\sum_{s^* \in \mathcal{S}} p(l|s^*)},$$

as typically done for templates. Plugging this back into Eq. (1), we can solve Eq. (1) by computing and summing over all $Pr(s|l^*)$ for each $l^* \in \mathcal{L}_T$, where $\mathcal{L}_T$ is the test (or evaluation) set.

6   Evaluation Results

To verify the balanced encoding scheme, we performed side channel evaluation on three implementations and compared the results between them.

2Prince. The first implementation is the unprotected nibble-parallel Prince implementation from [15], in which the 16-nibble states are stored in 8 registers. All round operations process two nibbles in parallel in order to achieve better performance. This implementation feature should result in slightly increased noise if the adversary only predicts a single nibble.

Balanced Prince. The second implementation is the protected Prince using encoding I only. In this case, the precharge phase is added to the S-box lookup to achieve not only constant HW but constant HD as well.

Double-Balanced Prince. The third one is also the protected Prince but using both encoding I and encoding II. This implementation differs from the second one in that the constant HD is obtained by using encoding II at the S-box output followed by a reordering layer.

We used an 8-bit AVR microcontroller to run the implementations. The performance and memory usage of the implementations are presented below. An automatic power measurement platform was established using a PC, a differential probe and an Tektronix DPO5000 series oscilloscope. A total of 100,000 power traces with random plaintext inputs were obtained for each implementation. Each implementation was analyzed using Hamming weight based CPA as a reference attack. Next, Mutual Information is used as a metric to quantify the leakage and compare the implementations. To make our numbers more reliable, we use 10-fold cross-validation on the computation of the mutual information.

6.1   Implementation Results

First we compare the performance of the three analyzed implementations. Table 1 compares the computation time per encrypted block and resource consumption in terms of code size and RAM usage. The code size increases significantly for the protected implementations, i.e. by a factor of 3. At the same time the performance decreases by a factor of 7. This is because each round operation costs more resources in order to obtain constant activity.

Table 2 shows the contribution of specific operations to the overall resource consumption. In particular, the code size and performance are broken down into the KeyAddition (KA), byte substitution (SB), and the mixing (M) operations of the Prince cipher. For example, the S-box of the protected implementations and the unprotected one are of the same size (256 byte, not included in the table code size calculation), but the unprotected one performs two S-box lookups in parallel. Similarly, either a precharge phase (for the Balanced implementation) or a reordering layer (for the Double-Balanced implementation) had to be added in order to gain constant Hamming distance transitions, also resulting in a significant increase in memory and clock cycles. Additionally, the conversion between normal data and balanced encoded data for the plaintext and ciphertext also adds overhead. The worst overhead is due to the M-Layer, or more precisely the constant leakage XOR, which uses 58 more clock cycles than regular XOR instruction.

Table 1. Performance comparison of the three analyzed implementations.

Implementation	Encryption Time in clock cycles	Code Size in Bytes	RAM Usage in Bytes
2Prince [15]	3253	1574	24
Balanced	28214	3700	472
Double-Balanced	29498	4100	472

Table 2. Performance and cost comparison for the KeyAddition (KA), byte substitution (SB), and the mixing (M) layers for the three analyzed implementations.

Implementation	Operation	Performance in clock cycles	Code Size in Bytes
2Prince [15]	KA	72	80
	SB	41	36
	M	162	286
Balanced	K	57	68
	SB	90	62
	M	2156	1193
Double-Balanced	KA	57	68
	SB &RO	180	129
	M	2156	1193

6.2 CPA Results

We first performed CPA on all of the three implementations. Each CPA predicts the Hamming weight of the output of a single S-box. To compare the leakage of the implementations—rather than distinguishing the correct key—we use the Hamming weight of the all 16 S-box outputs under a known key as the power model. The results are presented in Fig. 2. The correlation between the measurements and power model is greatly reduced in the protected scenarios. For the unprotected implementation, the correlation coefficients range from 0.6 to 0.8 which is only about 0.1 to 0.3 in the protected implementations. Note that a few of the 16 nibbles feature a much stronger leakage than the others in the protected cases (cf. Fig. 2(b) and (c)). This might be an implementation artifact and not due to the countermeasure itself. Similarly, the double-balanced implementation features its strongest leakage in the reordering layer. The results show that the balanced encoding scheme is effective in reducing the Hamming weight leakage. However, due to differences in the leakage of individual bits, the leakage does not completely disappear.

Figure 3 compares the trend of the correlation coefficients of the implementations (vertical axis) over the number of power traces (horizontal axis). We can observe that the correct subkey hypothesis can be easily distinguished from the wrong key guesses with as little as one hundred traces for the unprotected Prince in Fig. 3(a). However, for both Balanced Prince and Double-Balanced

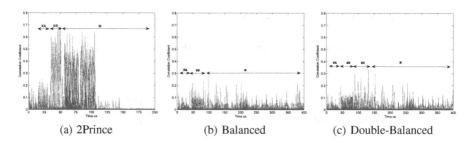

(a) 2Prince   (b) Balanced   (c) Double-Balanced

Fig. 2. Result of CPA of three Prince implementations on the S-box output. The unprotected implementation (a) leaks significantly stronger than the two protected implementations (b) and (c). (KA: KeyAddition; SB: S-box Lookup; RO: reordering M: Mixing Layer)

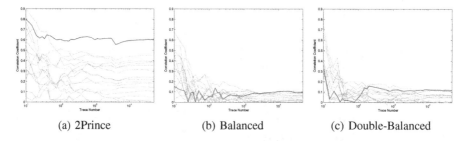

(a) 2Prince   (b) Balanced   (c) Double-Balanced

Fig. 3. CPA results for the Hamming weight of the S-box output for the unprotected implementation (a) and the two protected implementations (b) and (c). The vertical axis indicates the absolute value of the correlation coefficient; The horizontal axis indicates the number of traces used. The comparison of the three plots shows the significant improvement resulting from the balanced encodings, if applied correctly. Plot (a) clearly shows the effect of the ghost peaks mentioned in Sect. 5.

Prince in Fig. 3(b) and (c), the correlation coefficient is significantly smaller and it is hard to distinguish the correct key hypothesis, even for as many as 50,000 observations. Note that this problem is not obvious in Fig. 2, since that figure only contains correlations for the correct subkey hypotheses.

6.3   Mutual Information Based Leakage Analysis

To compare the implementations in a leakage-model independent setting, we apply the mutual information based methodology introduced in Sect. 5.2 during the first round of the Prince implementation. We apply it in two different ways: First, by using classical univariate templates with an individual mean and variance for each possible nibble state; Next, by using reduced univariate templates with an individual mean for each nibble state, but a common variance for all templates. The latter approach allows to only evaluate first-order leakages.

Figure 4 shows the mutual information for all 16 state nibbles for the first round, as derived from full univariate templates. Figure 5 shows the mutual

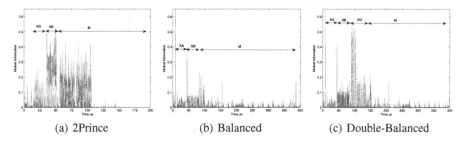

(a) 2Prince   (b) Balanced   (c) Double-Balanced

Fig. 4. Mutual information between the state and the leakage for the unprotected (a), Balanced (b), and Double-Balanced (c) implementations during the first round.

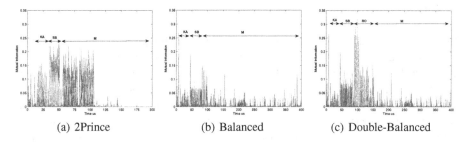

(a) 2Prince   (b) Balanced   (c) Double-Balanced

Fig. 5. First order mutual information between the state and the leakage for the unprotected (a), Balanced (b), and Double-Balanced (c) implementations during the first round.

information for all 16 state nibbles only for the first order leakage, as derived from the reduced univariate templates. Both plot families behave very similar, with the first-order MI being slightly lower in all cases. This indicated that the implementations on the AVR feature significant non-linear components in the leakage function. The first-order MI is more appropriate to predict the resistance against first-order attacks such as DPA and CPA. More interestingly, the leakage drops significantly for the protected implementations. In fact, the mutual information goes down by as much as 50 %. Especially the leakage of the S-box operation drops even more strongly, from .5 for the unprotected implementation to as low as .1 for the protected ones. That is, there is a single nibble that exhibits a huge leakage for the protected implementations. This is always the first nibble. To remove the leakage, we reordered the nibbles for the computation of the S-box. Surprisingly, whichever nibble is computed first, it exhibits this strong leakage. We claim this to be an implementation artifact. Similarly, there is a leakage right before the KeyAddition starts. Again, we do not have a good explanation for this leakage. However, unlike the S-box leakage, this one is not problematic, as information before the KeyAddition is plaintext, i.e. known to the attacker. As hinted at by the CPA results, both Figs. 4(c) and 5(c) show that the Reordering layer still leaks a significant amount of information.

As a result, the Balanced implementation has a weaker leakage than the one of the Double-Balanced implementation. The stronger leakage for the second implementation occurs in the reordering layer. This was not expected, since it is implemented to have a constant Hamming weight and Hamming distance.

In summary, the balanced implementation is a better choice for devices that have a strong Hamming weight leakage and is a valuable new addition to the family of countermeasures in software. The Double-Balanced implementation is slightly less efficient, but suffers from the strong leakage of the reordering layer. A more careful implementation of the reordering layer could reduce the maximum leakage of the Double-Balanced implementation. One should be able to avoid the reordering layer completely by customizing operations in the Mix-Columns layer, but we did not further explore this route.

7   Conclusion

This work performs the first practical evaluation of the balanced encoding countermeasure in software. While promising in theory, its standalone effectiveness on the modern microcontroller platform used for this study is significant, especially for CPA, but far from perfect. The countermeasure is of high relevance, as it is orthogonal to other software countermeasures such as shuffling and masking, i.e. it can be applied in addition to those. This is of high relevance for platforms that feature high signal-to-noise ratios, such as modern microcontrollers. It is also noteworthy that implementation costs are higher than conjectured, e.g. in [9]. Overall, we believe that this countermeasure technique is useful for lightweight ciphers in cases where additional hiding countermeasure are desirable.

Acknowledgments. This material is based upon work supported by the National Science Foundation under Grant No. #1261399 and Grant No. #1314770. We would like to thank the anonymous reviewers for their helpful comments.

References

1. Borghoff, J., Canteaut, A., Güneysu, T., Kavun, E.B., Knezevic, M., Knudsen, L.R., Leander, G., Nikov, V., Paar, C., Rechberger, C., Rombouts, P., Thomsen, S.S., Yalçın, T.: PRINCE – a low-latency block cipher for pervasive computing applications. In: Wang, X., Sako, K. (eds.) ASIACRYPT 2012. LNCS, vol. 7658, pp. 208–225. Springer, Heidelberg (2012)
2. Brier, E., Clavier, C., Olivier, F.: Correlation power analysis with a leakage model. In: Joye, M., Quisquater, J.-J. (eds.) CHES 2004. LNCS, vol. 3156, pp. 16–29. Springer, Heidelberg (2004)
3. Chari, S., Jutla, C.S., Rao, J.R., Rohatgi, P.: Towards sound approaches to counteract power-analysis attacks. In: Wiener, M. (ed.) CRYPTO 1999. LNCS, vol. 1666, p. 398. Springer, Heidelberg (1999)
4. Chen, Z., Sinha, A., Schaumont, P.: Implementing virtual secure circuit using a custom-instruction approach. In: Proceedings of the 2010 International Conference on Compilers, Architectures and Synthesis for Embedded Systems, pp. 57–66 (2010)

5. Chen, Z., Zhou, Y.: Dual-rail random switching logic: a countermeasure to reduce side channel leakage. In: Goubin, L., Matsui, M. (eds.) CHES 2006. LNCS, vol. 4249, pp. 242–254. Springer, Heidelberg (2006)
6. Coron, J.-S., Kizhvatov, I.: Analysis and improvement of the random delay countermeasure of CHES 2009. In: Mangard, S., Standaert, F.-X. (eds.) CHES 2010. LNCS, vol. 6225, pp. 95–109. Springer, Heidelberg (2010)
7. Durvaux, F., Standaert, F.-X., Veyrat-Charvillon, N.: How to certify the leakage of a chip? In: Nguyen, P.Q., Oswald, E. (eds.) EUROCRYPT 2014. LNCS, vol. 8441, pp. 459–476. Springer, Heidelberg (2014)
8. Han, Y., Zhou, Y., Liu, J.: Securing lightweight block cipher against power analysis attacks. In: Zhang, Y. (ed.) Future Computing, Communication, Control and Management. LNEE, vol. 143, pp. 379–390. Springer, Heidelberg (2012)
9. Hoogvorst, P., Duc, G., Danger, J.-L.: Software implementation of dual-rail representation. In: 2nd International Workshop on Constructive Side-Channel Analysis and e Secure Design – COSADE 2011, 24–25 February 2014
10. Mangard, S., Oswald, E., Popp, T.: Power Analysis Attacks: Revealing the Secrets of Smartcards. Springer, Heidelberg (2007)
11. Pan, J., van Woudenberg, J.G.J., den Hartog, J.I., Witteman, M.F.: Improving DPA by peak distribution analysis. In: Biryukov, A., Gong, G., Stinson, D.R. (eds.) SAC 2010. LNCS, vol. 6544, pp. 241–261. Springer, Heidelberg (2011)
12. Popp, T., Mangard, S.: Masked dual-rail pre-charge logic: DPA-resistance without routing constraints. In: Rao, J.R., Sunar, B. (eds.) CHES 2005. LNCS, vol. 3659, pp. 172–186. Springer, Heidelberg (2005)
13. Prouff, E., Rivain, M.: Masking against side-channel attacks: a formal security proof. In: Johansson, T., Nguyen, P.Q. (eds.) EUROCRYPT 2013. LNCS, vol. 7881, pp. 142–159. Springer, Heidelberg (2013)
14. Rauzy, P., Guilley, S., Najm, Z.: Formally proved security of assembly code against power analysis: a case study on balanced logic (2013). https://eprint.iacr.org/2013/554.pdf
15. Shahverdi, A., Chen, C., Eisenbarth, T.: AVRprince - An Efficient Implementation of PRINCE for 8-bit Microprocessors. Technical report, Worcester Polytechnic Institute (2014). http://users.wpi.edu/~teisenbarth/pdf/avrPRINCEv01.pdf
16. Standaert, F.-X., Malkin, T.G., Yung, M.: A unified framework for the analysis of side-channel key recovery attacks. In: Joux, A. (ed.) EUROCRYPT 2009. LNCS, vol. 5479, pp. 443–461. Springer, Heidelberg (2009)
17. Tillich, S., Herbst, C.: Attacking state-of-the-art software countermeasures—a case study for AES. In: Oswald, E., Rohatgi, P. (eds.) CHES 2008. LNCS, vol. 5154, pp. 228–243. Springer, Heidelberg (2008)
18. Tiri, K., Verbauwhede, I.: A logic level design methodology for a secure DPA resistant ASIC or FPGA implementation. In: Proceedings of the conference on Design, automation and test in Europe, pp. 10246. IEEE Computer Society (2004)
19. Veyrat-Charvillon, N., Medwed, M., Kerckhof, S., Standaert, F.-X.: Shuffling against side-channel attacks: a comprehensive study with cautionary note. In: Wang, X., Sako, K. (eds.) ASIACRYPT 2012. LNCS, vol. 7658, pp. 740–757. Springer, Heidelberg (2012)

On the Cost of Lazy Engineering
for Masked Software Implementations

Josep Balasch[1], Benedikt Gierlichs[1], Vincent Grosso[2],
Oscar Reparaz[1(✉)], and François-Xavier Standaert[2]

[1] Department of Electrical Engineering-ESAT/COSIC and iMinds, KU Leuven,
Kasteelpark Arenberg 10, 3001 Leuven-Heverlee, Belgium
oscar.reparaz@esat.kuleuven.be
[2] ICTEAM/ELEN/Crypto Group, Université catholique de Louvain,
Louvain-la-Neuve, Belgium

Abstract. Masking is one of the most popular countermeasures to mitigate side-channel analysis. Yet, its deployment in actual cryptographic devices is well known to be challenging, since designers have to ensure that the leakage corresponding to different shares is independent. Several works have shown that such an independent leakage assumption may be contradicted in practice, because of physical effects such as "glitches" or "transition-based" leakages. As a result, implementing masking securely can be a time-consuming engineering problem. This is in strong contrast with recent and promising approaches for the automatic insertion of countermeasures exploiting compilers, that aim to limit the development time of side-channel resistant software. Motivated by this contrast, we question what can be hoped for these approaches – or more generally for masked software implementations based on careless assembly generation. For this purpose, our first contribution is a simple reduction from security proofs obtained in a (usual but not always realistic) model where leakages depend on the intermediate variables manipulated by the target device, to security proofs in a (more realistic) model where the transitions between these intermediate variables are leaked. We show that the cost of moving from one context to the other implies a division of the security order by two for masking schemes. Next, our second and main contribution is to provide a comprehensive empirical validation of this reduction, based on two microcontrollers, several (handwritten and compiler-based) ways of generating assembly codes, with and without "recycling" the randomness used for sharing. These experiments confirm the relevance of our analysis, and therefore quantify the cost of lazy engineering for masking.

1 Introduction

Masking is a widely deployed countermeasure to protect block cipher implementations against side-channel attacks. It works by splitting all the sensitive variables occurring during the computations into $d + 1$ shares. Its security proofs (such as given, e.g. for the CHES 2010 scheme of Rivain and Prouff [24])

© Springer International Publishing Switzerland 2015
M. Joye and A. Moradi (Eds.): CARDIS 2014, LNCS 8968, pp. 64–81, 2015.
DOI: 10.1007/978-3-319-16763-3_5

ensure the so-called dth-order property, which requires that *every tuple of at most d intermediate variables in the implementation is independent of any sensitive variable.* Ensuring this property (ideally) guarantees that the smallest key-dependent statistical moment in the leakage distribution is $d + 1$. It has been shown (in different, more or less specialized settings [6,10,21,27]) that the data complexity of side-channel attacks against such implementations increases exponentially with the number of shares. More precisely, in the usual context of (close to) Gaussian noise, this data complexity is proportional to $(\sigma_n^2)^d$, with σ_n^2 the noise variance. In practice though, security proofs for masking heavily rely on an independence assumption. Namely, the (ideal) hope is that the leakage function manipulates the shared intermediate variables independently. Whenever this assumption is not fulfilled, all bets are off regarding the security of the implementation. For example, a leakage function that would re-combine the different shares would directly lead to an implementation that is as easy to attack as an unprotected one. As a result, the main question for the proofs in [6,10,21] to provide concrete security improvements is whether this assumption is respected in practice.

Unfortunately, experiments have shown that the independent leakage assumption does not always hold in actual hardware and software. Many physical effects can be the cause of this issue. For hardware implementations, glitches are a well-identified candidate [15]. For software implementations, the problem more frequently comes from memory transitions (e.g. captured by a Hamming distance model) [8]. From this empirical observation, different strategies could be followed. One can naturally try to enforce independent leakages at the hardware or software level, but current research rather concludes negatively in both cases [8,17]. A more promising approach is to deal with the problem at the algorithmic level. For example, threshold implementations and solutions based on multi-party computations can provide "glitch-resistance" [20,25]. But the first solution is rather specialized to hardware devices (see, e.g. [5,18] for applications to the AES), while the second one implies strong performance overheads [12]. In the following, we pursue a third direction for the software case, and investigate the security guarantees that can be obtained if we simply ignore the problem.

For this purpose, we start by formalizing the types of leakage functions that can be encountered in practice (namely value-based vs. transition based, generic vs. specific). As any formalization effort, we do not claim that it perfectly corresponds to actual measurements. Yet, we will show that it captures some important physical effects to a sufficient extent for our conclusions to be supported by practical experiments. Next, our first contribution is to provide a couple of reductions from security claims obtained for one type of leakage functions to security claims for another type. Our most interesting result shows that a dth-order security proof obtained against value-based leakages leads to a $\lfloor \frac{d}{2} \rfloor$th-order security proof against transition-based ones. As the main question for such reductions to be relevant is whether they can be confirmed by actual implementations, our second and main contribution is to provide a comprehensive analysis of two case-studies of masked software (namely, in an Atmel AVR and an 8051 microcontroller). More precisely, we show empirical evidence that implementations masked with one mask (two shares) and proved first-order secure against value-based leakages are insecure in our devices with transition-based leakages, while two-mask (three-share) ones are indeed first-order secure in the same context. Furthermore, we show that our conclusions hold both for handwritten assembly codes and for C code compiled with various flags. We also study the impact of recycled randomness in these case studies. We finally combine these security analyses with an evaluation of the performance overheads due to the increased number of shares needed to reach a given masking order, and sub-optimally compiled codes.

Besides their theoretical interest, we believe these conclusions are important for security engineers, since they answer a long standing open question regarding the automated insertion of countermeasures against side-channel attacks. Our proofs and experiments suggest that a single C code of a masked block cipher can indeed provide concrete security on two different devices, at the cost of an artificially increased number of shares. The overheads caused by this increased order correspond to the "cost of lazy engineering" suggested by our title, which is to balance with the significant gains in terms of development time that automation allows. As a result and maybe most importantly, these results validate an important line of research trying to exploit compilers to replace the manual insertion of countermeasures by expert developers [4,19,23]. Our findings suggest that such an approach can be feasible for masking.

2 Definitions

Following previous works on masking, we denote any key-dependent intermediate variable appearing in an unprotected implementation as a *sensitive variable*. Taking the example of the secure multiplication of two shared secrets in Algorithm 1 in [24], a and b are sensitive variables.

We further denote as *intermediate variables* the set of all the variables appearing in a masked implementation, bar loop counters. These intermediate variables should not be sensitive if masking is well implemented, since each share should be independent of the key in this case. For example, the set of intermediate variables in Algorithm 1 in [24] is given by:

$$\mathcal{V} = \{a_i\} \cup \{b_i\} \cup \{r_{i,j}\} \cup \{a_i \times b_j\} \cup \{r_{i,j} \oplus a_i \times b_j\}$$
$$\cup \{a_j \times b_i\} \cup \{(r_{i,j} \oplus a_i \times b_j) \oplus a_j \times b_i\} \cup \{a_i \times b_i\}$$
$$\cup \{a_i \times b_i \oplus_{j=0}^{i-1} [(r_{i,j} \oplus a_i \times b_j) \oplus a_j \times b_i] \oplus_{j=i+1}^{d} r_{i,j}\}. \tag{1}$$

The security proof of the masking scheme in [24] (and following works) was typically obtained for value-based leakage functions that we define as follows:

Definition 1 (Value-Based Leakage Functions). *Let $\mathcal{V}$ be a set of intermediate variables and $\mathsf{L}(.) = \mathsf{L_d}(.) + N$ be a leakage function made of a deterministic part $\mathsf{L_d}(.)$ and an (additive) random noise N. This leakage function is value-based if its deterministic part can only take values $v \in \mathcal{V}$ as argument.*

By contrast, the flaws in [8] come from the fact that the software implementation considered by the authors was leaking according to a Hamming-distance model. The following transition-based leakage functions aim at formalizing this issue:

Definition 2 (Transition-Based Leakage Functions). *Let $\mathcal{V}$ be a set of intermediate variables and $\mathcal{T} := \{v \oplus v' \mid v, v' \in \mathcal{V}\} \cup \mathcal{V}$ be the set of all the transitions between these intermediate variables. A leakage function $\mathsf{L}(.)$ is transition-based if its deterministic part $\mathsf{L_d}(.)$ can only take values $t \in \mathcal{T}$ as argument.*

Note that this type of transitions, based on the bitwise XOR between the values v and v', is motivated by practical considerations (since it generalizes the Hamming distance model). Yet, even more general types of transitions, e.g. the concatenation $v \| v'$, would not change our following conclusions – it would only make the bound of Theorem 1 more tight in certain cases (see next).
We further define generic vs. specific leakage functions as follows:

Definition 3 (Generic Leakage Functions). *A value-based (resp. transition-based) leakage function associated with an intermediate variable $v \in \mathcal{V}$ (resp. transition $t \in \mathcal{T}$) is generic if its deterministic part is a nominal mapping from this variable to a leakage variable $l_d \in \mathcal{L_d}$, such that the set of deterministic leakages $\mathcal{L_d}$ has the same cardinality as the set of values $\mathcal{V}$ (resp. transitions $\mathcal{T}$).*

The identity mapping is a typical example of generic leakage function[1].

Definition 4 (Specific Leakage Functions). *A value-based (resp. transition-based) leakage function associated with an intermediate variable $v \in \mathcal{V}$ (resp. transition $t \in \mathcal{T}$) is specific if its deterministic part is a mapping from this variable to a leakage variable $l_d \in \mathcal{L_d}$, such that the set of deterministic leakages $\mathcal{L_d}$ has smaller cardinality than the set of values $\mathcal{V}$ (resp. transitions $\mathcal{T}$).*

The frequently considered Hamming weight and distance functions are typical examples of specific (value-based and transition-based) leakage functions.

3 Reductions

From these definitions, a natural question is whether a proof of security obtained within one model translates into a proof in another model. As we now detail, three out of the four possible propositions are trivial (we recall them for completeness). The last one is more intriguing and practically relevant.

Lemma 1. *A proof of dth-order side-channel security obtained within a generic model implies a proof of dth-order security in a specific model.*

Proof. This directly derives from Definitions 3 and 4. By moving from one to the other, we only reduce the amount of information provided to the adversary (since we reduce the cardinality of the set of possible deterministic leakages).

---

[1] This definition differs from the one of "generic power model" in [3] since it relates to the leakage function, while the latter one relates to the adversary's model.

Lemma 2. *A proof of dth-order security obtained within a specific model does not imply a proof of dth-order security in a generic model.*

Proof. A counterexample can be found in [13] for low-entropy masking schemes.

Lemma 3. *A proof of dth-order side-channel security obtained within a transition-based model implies a proof of dth-order security in a value-based model.*

Proof. Similarly to Lemma 1, this directly derives from Definitions 1 and 2. By moving from one to the other, we only reduce the amount of information provided to the adversary (since we reduce the input range of the leakage function).

We will need the following lemma to prove our last result.

Lemma 4. *The information obtained from any subset of at most $\lfloor \frac{d}{2} \rfloor$ elements in a set $\mathcal{T}$ can be obtained from a subset of d elements in a set $\mathcal{V}$.*

Proof. Let $\mathcal{S}_\mathcal{T} \subset \mathcal{T}$ such that $\#(\mathcal{S}_\mathcal{T}) < \lfloor \frac{d}{2} \rfloor$. We show that $\exists \, \mathcal{S}_\mathcal{V} \subset \mathcal{V}$ such that $\#(\mathcal{S}_\mathcal{V}) < d$, and $\mathcal{S}_\mathcal{T}$ can be built from $\mathcal{S}_\mathcal{V}$ as follows (with $\#(.)$ the cardinality of a set). $\forall t \in \mathcal{S}_\mathcal{T}$, if $t \in \mathcal{V}$, then $\mathcal{S}_\mathcal{V} = \mathcal{S}_\mathcal{V} \cup \{t\}$, else $\exists \, v, v' \in \mathcal{V}$ such that $t = v \oplus v'$ and $\mathcal{S}_\mathcal{V} = \mathcal{S}_\mathcal{V} \cup \{v, v'\}$. Since $\#(\mathcal{S}_\mathcal{T}) < \lfloor \frac{d}{2} \rfloor$, and we add at most 2 elements in $\mathcal{S}_\mathcal{V}$ per element in $\mathcal{S}_\mathcal{T}$, we directly have that $\#(\mathcal{S}_\mathcal{V}) < d$.

It directly leads to the following theorem:

Theorem 1. *A proof of dth-order side-channel security obtained within a value-based model implies a proof of $\lfloor \frac{d}{2} \rfloor$th-order security in a transition-based model.*

Proof. If there existed a subset of transitions $\mathcal{S}_\mathcal{T}$ with less than $\lfloor \frac{d}{2} \rfloor$ elements which can be used to mount a successful side-channel attack, then there would exist a subset $\mathcal{S}_\mathcal{V}$ with less than d elements that can be used to mount a successful side-channel attack as well. As this second attack is impossible by hypothesis, such a set $\mathcal{S}_\mathcal{T}$ cannot exist and the implementation is at least $\lfloor \frac{d}{2} \rfloor$th-order secure.

This bound is tight for Boolean masking. If $x = v_0 \oplus v_1 \oplus \ldots v_{d-1} \oplus v_d$, we can see that $x = t_0 \oplus \cdots \oplus t_{\lfloor \frac{d}{2} \rfloor}$, with $t_i = v_{2i} \oplus v_{2i+1}$ for $0 \leq i < \lfloor \frac{d}{2} \rfloor$ and $t_{\lfloor \frac{d}{2} \rfloor} = v_d$ if d even, and $t_{\lfloor \frac{d}{2} \rfloor} = v_{d-1} \oplus v_d$ if d is odd. By contrast, it is not tight for other types of masking schemes such as inner product or polynomial [1,22]. However, it would be tight even for those masking schemes in the context of concatenation-based transitions (i.e. if using $v \| v'$ rather than $v \oplus v'$ in Definition 2).

4 Experiments

In view of the simplicity of Theorem 1, one can naturally wonder whether it captures real-world situations. That is, is it sufficient for a careless designer to double the security order to obtain some guarantees for his masked implementations? In the rest of the paper, we investigate this question in various practically-relevant scenarios. For this purpose, we will focus on secure S-box

---

Algorithm 1. Masked key addition and inversion.

Require: Shares $(p_i^0)_i, (p_i^1)_i, (k_i^0)_i, (k_i^1)_i$ satisfying $\oplus_i p_i^0 = p^0, \oplus_i p_i^1 = p^1, \oplus_i k_i^0 = k^0, \oplus_i k_i^1 = k^1$; with k^0 fixed and $k^1 \neq k^0$ fixed

Ensure: Shares $(c_i^0), (c_i^1)$ satisfying $\oplus_i c_i^0 = (p^0 \oplus k^0)^{-1}, \oplus_i c_i^1 = (p^1 \oplus k^1)^{-1}$

1: **for** i from 0 to 1 **do**
2:     **for** j from 0 to d **do**
3:         $x_j \leftarrow p_j^i \oplus k_j^i$
4:     **end for**
5:     $(c_0^i, \ldots, c_d^i) \leftarrow \text{SecInv}(x_0, \ldots, x_d)$
6: **end for**

---

computations. As explained in [24], this is usually the most challenging part of a masked block cipher. In the case of AES that we will consider next, the method exploits a representation of the S-box with power functions in $GF(2^8) \equiv GF(2)[x]/x^8 + x^4 + x^3 + x + 1$ (see Algorithm 3 in [24]). We will implement it for two key additions followed by two inversions (see Algorithm 1). Note that we are aware that the masked inversion scheme proposed by Rivain and Prouff exhibits a small bias as presented by Coron et al. in [9], however, this does not affect our results and conclusions, as explained in the full version of this paper [2].

Concretely, we made several implementations of Algorithm 1, which is complex enough to exercise registers, ALU, RAM and ROM. Note that we provide input plaintext and key bytes to the implementations in $d + 1$ shares each. This ensures that the device does not process unmasked variables, unless the shares are explicitly combined by the implementation, which is highly relevant for our testing procedure. We investigate the impact of the following parameters:

- Programming language: we contrast handwritten assembly (ASM) and compiled C code. For both ASM and C we implemented straightforwardly with little attention to secure the implementations.
- Device architecture: we provide results for an Atmel AVR and for an 8051 compatible microcontroller.
- Compiler flags: we assess the impact of compiler flags. We compiled the C code with default options and with several combinations of flags that influence the degree of optimization as well as the order in which registers are assigned.
- Masking order: we implemented everything for $d = 1$ (2 shares) and for $d = 2$ (3 shares).
- Mask re-use: since randomness is expensive on low cost microcontrollers an implementer might decide to re-use random masks. We contrast implementations that use *fresh* randomness for the processing of each input byte (initial masking, SecMult, RefreshMasks) and implementations that *recycle* the randomness from the processing of the first byte for the processing of the second byte. Since our microcontrollers do not have an internal source of randomness, we provide uniformly distributed random numbers from the measurement PC.

4.1   Implementation Details

Our main target platform is an AVR ATmega163 microcontroller in a smart card body. It internally provides 16 kBytes of flash memory and 1 kByte of data memory. Implementations are processed by `avr-gcc` (ver. 4.3.3) from the WinAVR tools (ver. 20100110).

The implementation of the secure inversion requires support for arithmetic in the finite field $GF(2^8)$. Multiplication over $GF(2^8)$ is implemented using `log` and `alog` tables [28]. This method requires two read-only tables of 256 bytes each and allows to compute the product of two *non-zero* field elements in 3 table lookups. Since a straightforward implementation of this technique may exhibit SPA leakage when handling 0 inputs, we implemented an SPA-resistant version of Kim et al. as in [14]. This version, illustrated in Algorithm 2, avoids `if/else` statements and expresses the logical conditions in the form of elementary arithmetic operations.

Algorithm 2. SPA-resistant multiplication over $GF(2^8)$ [14].

Require: Field elements a, $b \in GF(2^8)$, `log` and `alog` tables
Ensure: Field element $a \times b \in GF(2^8)$
  1: $(c, s) = \log[a] + \log[b]$ /* c holds carry bit, s the lower 8 bits */
  2: $r = \text{alog}[c + s]$
  3: **return** $(a\&\&b) \cdot r$ /* && indicates logical AND condition */

Assembly. Our assembly implementations are tailored to the target AVR architecture and optimized for speed. We have developed codes for each of the tested masking orders, i.e. one for $d = 1$ and one for $d = 2$. Our routine for field multiplication takes 22 cycles. More than a third of this time is devoted to achieve a constant flow of operations to securely implement line 3 in Algorithm 2. Both `log` and `alog` tables are stored in program memory. All raisings to the power of two are implemented as lookup tables in program memory. While this requires the storage of $3 \times 256 = 768$ bytes, it results in a significant performance increase. Further speed-ups are achieved by aligning all tables on a 256 byte boundary (0×100). This ensures all addresses of the cells differ only in the lower byte and allows for more efficient handling of pointers.

C language. One of the goals of our experiments is to devise and evaluate platform-independent C code. Declaring and accessing program memory arrays in AVR requires the use of special attributes in `avr-gcc`[2]. Consequently, we cannot take advantage of storing lookup tables in program memory and the implementation becomes more restricted in terms of storage than its ASM counterpart. Our C routine for multiplication over $GF(2^8)$ follows the code given in Algorithm 2. The two `log` and `alog` tables take half of the available space in RAM. Because of this we opt to perform field squarings as field multiplications,

---

[2] See http://www.nongnu.org/avr-libc/user-manual/pgmspace.html.

i.e. without using lookup tables. This saves 768 bytes of memory arrays with respect to the assembly implementations, but results in larger execution times and more randomness requirements.

4.2 Testing Procedure

The security evaluation of cryptographic implementations with respect to side-channel attacks is a topic of ongoing discussions and an open problem. Since long, implementations are evaluated (in academia) by testing their resistance to state-of-the-art attacks. However, it is well known that this is a time-consuming task with potentially high data and computational complexity. In addition, an implementation that resists known attacks may still have vulnerabilities that can be exploited by new attacks. Hence, this style of evaluation can lead to a false sense of security, but it also stimulates improvements of the state-of-the-art. In 2009, Standaert et al. [26] proposed a framework for the evaluation of cryptographic implementations w.r.t. side-channel attacks. For univariate analysis (i.e. analysis of each time sample separately), their information-theoretic metric shows how much information is available to an attacker in a worst-case scenario. It directly corresponds to the success rate of a (univariate) template attack adversary and captures information present in *any* statistical moment of the leakage distributions. For multivariate analysis (i.e. joint analysis of time samples) the technique relies on heuristics regarding the selection of time samples, just as well as all state-of-the-art attacks. The technique has strong requirements w.r.t. data and computational complexity. For our evaluations, computing the metric is beyond feasible, but it would also be inappropriate as we are interested in testing specific statistical moments of the measured distributions for evidence of leakage (while a worst-case evaluation typically exploits all the statistical moments jointly). We therefore adopt the relatively novel approach to evaluation called *leakage detection*. Contrary to the classical approach of testing whether a given attack is successful, this approach decouples the detection of leakage from its exploitation. And contrary to the IT metric, this approach can be tuned in order to evaluate specific statistical moments of the measured distributions.

For our purpose we use the *non-specific* t-test based fixed versus random leakage detection methodology of [7,11]. It has two main ingredients: first, chosen inputs allow to generate two sets of measurements for which intermediate values in the implementation have a certain difference. Without making an assumption about how the implementation leaks, a safe choice is to keep the intermediate values fixed for one set of measurements, while they take random values for the second set. The test is *specific*, if particular intermediate values or transitions in the implementation are targeted (e.g. S-box input, S-box output, Hamming distance in a round register, etc.). This type of testing requires knowledge of the device key and carefully chosen inputs. On the other hand, the test is *non-specific* if *all* intermediate values and transitions are targeted at the same time. This type of testing only requires to keep all inputs to the implementation fixed for one set of measurements, and to choose them randomly for the second set. Obviously, the *non-specific* test is extremely powerful. The second ingredient is a simple, robust and efficiently computable statistical test to determine if the two sets of measurements are significantly different (to be made precise below).

In our experiments, all implementations receive as input $4(d+1)$ shares $(p_i^0)_i, (p_i^1)_i, (k_i^0)_i, (k_i^1)_i$ of the plaintext and key bytes. The (unshared) key bytes (k_0, k_1) are fixed with $k_0 \neq k_1$. We obtain two sets of measurements from each implementation. For the first set, we fix the values $p^0 = k^0$ and $p^1 = k^1$ such that, without masking, the input of the inversion function would be zero, which is likely to be a "special" case. Indeed, all the intermediate results through the exponentation to the power of 254 would be zero. We denote this set $\mathcal{S}_{fixed}$. For the second set, the values of p_0 and p_1 are drawn at random from uniform. We denote this set $\mathcal{S}_{random}$. Note that we obtain the measurements for both sets interleaved (one fixed, one random, one fixed, one random, etc.) to avoid time-dependent external and internal influences on the test result. A power trace covers the execution of steps 1 to 6 in Algorithm 1.

We then compute Welch's (two-tailed) t-test:

$$t = \frac{\mu(\mathcal{S}_{fixed}) - \mu(\mathcal{S}_{random})}{\sqrt{\frac{\sigma^2(\mathcal{S}_{fixed})}{\#\mathcal{S}_{fixed}} + \frac{\sigma^2(\mathcal{S}_{random})}{\#\mathcal{S}_{random}}}}, \tag{2}$$

(where μ is the sample mean, σ^2 is the sample variance and $\#$ denotes the sample size) to determine if the samples in both sets were drawn from the same population (or from populations with the same mean). The *null hypothesis* is that the samples in both sets were drawn from populations with the same mean. In our context, this means that the masking is effective. The alternative hypothesis is that the samples in both sets were drawn from populations with different means. In our context, this means that the masking is not effective.

At each point in time, the test statistic t together with the degrees of freedom ν, computed with the Welch-Satterthwaite equation allow to compute a p value to determine if there is sufficient evidence to reject the null hypothesis at a particular significance level $(1 - \alpha)$. The p value expresses the probability of observing the measured difference (or a greater difference) by chance if the null hypothesis was true. In other words, small p values give evidence to reject the null hypothesis.

As in any evaluation, one is left with choosing a threshold to decide if an observed difference is significant or not. Typical significance levels in statistics are 0.05 and 0.00001 [16]. However, here we aim at choosing the threshold in a less arbitrary, data-driven way. To this end, we run a test "random-vs-random". In this test, measurements in both groups come from the same population (population of traces with random plaintext) so we know that the null hypothesis is true. We compute the test statistic t based on a random partition into two groups, keep its largest absolute value and repeat the experiment 200 times, each iteration with a fresh random partition into two sets. The highest absolute t-value we observed was 5.6088. For orientation, note that for large sample sizes the probability to observe a single t-value with absolute value ≥ 4.5 *by chance* is approximately 0.001 % [11]. The fact that we observe several t-values with absolute value ≥ 5 by chance can be attributed to the length of the traces we used for this test (5 million time samples). In light of this result, we select a conservative threshold of ±5 for the statistic t in all experiments to determine if an observed difference in means of the two sets is significant or not.

Further, also this type of evaluation is limited by the number of measurements at hand. In case the test does not show sufficient evidence of leakage, repeating the same evaluation with more measurements might do.

4.3 Security Results

We measure the power consumption of the AVR platform as the voltage drop over a 50 Ohm shunt resistor placed in the GND path. For all code evaluations we set the device's clock at 3.57 MHz and the oscilloscope's sampling rate at 250 MS/s. Results are presented in form of plots of t-values on the y-axis and time on the x-axis. Recall that the t-test is applied to each time sample individually. Superposed, we plot a threshold of ±5 for the statistic t. For clarity, we include an auxiliary trigger signal in the upper part of the figure to indicate the beginning and the end of each byte's processing, i.e. masked key addition followed by masked field inversion.

Assembly. We begin by evaluating the AVR assembly implementation corresponding to the masking order $d = 1$ (two shares). The results are shown in Fig. 1. The first input byte is processed until time sample $\approx 3 \times 10^4$, while processing of the second byte starts at time sample $\approx 4 \times 10^4$. The left plot corresponds to the implementation with fresh randomness. The right plot is the result for recycled randomness. Both experiments are performed using a set of 1 000 measurements: 500 corresponding to $\mathcal{S}_{fixed}$ and 500 corresponding to $\mathcal{S}_{random}$.

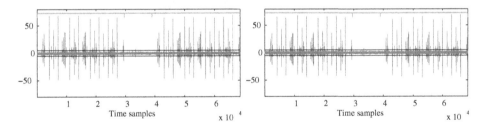

Fig. 1. T-test evaluation. Assembly, $d = 1$. Left: fresh randomness, 1 k traces. Right: recycled randomness, 1 k traces. Clear evidence of first-order leakage.

Figure 1 shows clear excursions of the t-test statistic beyond the defined thresholds, rejecting the null hypothesis. This indicates the existence of obvious univariate first-order leakage, in the form of identical patterns in each byte processing. There is no appreciable difference between using fresh versus recycled randomness. The outcome of this first experiment is however not surprising: as our platform is known to leak transitions, a (straightforward) implementation with masking order $d = 1$ is likely to be vulnerable to univariate attacks (see, e.g. [8] for similar findings). Perhaps more important, the results of the evaluation serve to validate the soundness of our testing methodology.

The situation changes when we evaluate the case $d = 2$ (three shares), as illustrated in Fig. 2. Even by increasing the number of measurements to 10 000, the t-test does not reject the null hypothesis for both scenarios. This indicates that any attack exploiting univariate first-order information (i.e., mean traces for each unshared value) is expected to fail, since there is no information about intermediate values in the first statistical moment. Interestingly, this result shows a first constructive application of Theorem 1. Starting with an implementation with second-order security in a value-based leakage model, we are able to achieve first-order security on a device with a transition-based leakage behavior. Finally, note that all our claims regarding the evaluation for $d = 2$ are restricted to first-order scenarios. In fact, attacks exploiting second or higher statistical moments are expected to succeed in breaking the implementation. We addressed this point in more detail in page 16 (together with the previously mentioned flaw exhibited at FSE 2013). Besides, and as already mentioned, all evaluations are inherently limited to the number of measurements at hand. In this respect, one may imagine that more measurements would allow detecting a first-order leakage. Yet, we note that in all our following experiments, whenever we claim no evidence of first-order leakages, second-order leakages were identified with confidence. This suggests that even if first-order leakages could be detected, their informativeness would be limited compared to second-order ones.

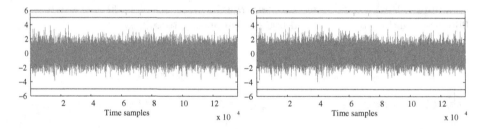

Fig. 2. T-test evaluation. Assembly, $d = 2$. Left: fresh randomness, 10 k traces. Right: recycled randomness, 10 k traces. No evidence of first-order leakage.

C language. A natural follow-up question is whether the results obtained so far hold for the case of C implementations. In the following we evaluate the results of our platform-independent C code. For the first set of tests we initially switch off the `avr-gcc` compiler flags for optimization, i.e. we use the option -O0.

Figure 3 shows the results obtained for the case $d = 1$ (two shares). As expected, the evaluation of the $d = 1$ implementation on our AVR platform indicates univariate first-order leakage. This result is consistent with its assembly counterpart. The main difference is that the absolute value of the statistic t at time samples beyond the ± 5 threshold is smaller, probably due to the leakage being more scattered. After all, code resulting from compiling C is expected to be more sparse code than concise, hand-crafted assembly. Illustrative of this effect is also the considerable increase in length of our measurements, from 70 000 samples to 1 200 000 samples.

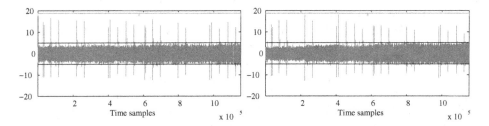

Fig. 3. T-test evaluation. C, no flags, $d = 1$. Left: fresh randomness, 1 k traces. Right: recycled randomness, 1 k traces. Clear evidence of first-order leakage.

The results obtained for $d = 2$ (three shares) are given in Fig. 4. Here we observe a substantial difference between the fresh randomness and recycled randomness scenarios. While the left plot does not exhibit excursions beyond the threshold, the right plot does unexpectedly suggest clear univariate leakage. In fact, the statistic t shows a particular pattern not bound to a few time samples. Rather differently, it gradually increases over time and it only appears during the second half of the trace, i.e. during the processing of the second input byte with recycled randomness.

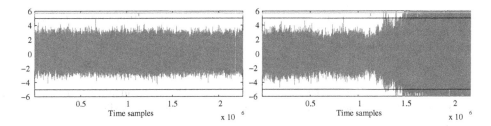

Fig. 4. T-test evaluation. C, no flags, $d = 2$. Left: fresh randomness, 10 k traces. Right: recycled randomness, 10 k traces. Evidence of first order leakage.

We have verified that these results are caused by a non-constant time behavior of our compiled code. Although our C routines are written following seemingly constant-time and SPA-resistant algorithms [14], the avr-gcc compiler generates code with conditional execution paths. More specifically, the compiler transforms the Boolean evaluation $a\&\&b$ into a series of TST (test for zero and minus) and BREQ (branch if equal) commands in assembly, regardless of the choice of compiler flags. This results in variable execution time (and flow) depending on the value(s) of the input(s). From this, we conclude that the pseudo-code given in Algorithm 2 is equivalent to the original use of `if` / `else` statements, and therefore fails in providing resistance against SPA.

Note that it is unclear whether this leakage due to time variations can be exploited by univariate first-order attacks. While any practically exploitable first-order leakage will show up in the statistic t, the contrary is not true, i.e. not all leakage identified by the t-test may be practically exploitable. In order to confirm the identified origin of the leakage, we implement a new C routine for multiplication in $GF(2^8)$ that does not directly evaluate the Boolean condition $a\&\&b$. Instead, our code follows a series of time-constant operations which are equivalent to the Boolean statement. The results obtained from evaluating this code are depicted in Fig. 5. No obvious leakage is observed in either of the two scenarios, verifying that the shapes in Fig. 4 are indeed caused by misalignments due to timing differences. As a downside, note that the performance of our platform-independent SPA-resistant code degrades significantly. The number of samples per measurement increases from 2 500 000 to 8 500 000, which in turn makes our analyses more difficult to carry out.

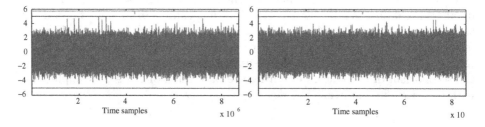

Fig. 5. T-test evaluation. C, no flags, $d = 2$, secure routine for multiplication in $GF(2^8)$. Left: fresh randomness, 10 k traces. Right: recycled randomness, 10 k traces. No evidence of first-order leakage.

These results are interesting since they moderate the applicability of Theorem 1 for compiled codes. That is, while this theorem nicely predicts the impact of transition-based leakages on the security order of our implementations, it does not prevent the existence of other flaws due to a careless implementation leading to data-dependent execution times. That is, whenever taking advantage of compilers, designers should still pay attention to avoid such SPA flaws, e.g. by ensuring constant-time implementations. Note that this remains an arguably easier task than ensuring DPA security, which therefore maintains the interest of our theorem even in this case.

Compiler options. A relevant scenario for the security evaluation of C code is to determine the impact of compiler flags. To this end, we provide the security evaluation for different compilation processes with `avr-gcc`. In particular, we analyze the effects for different degrees of optimization (flag `-O`) and for different

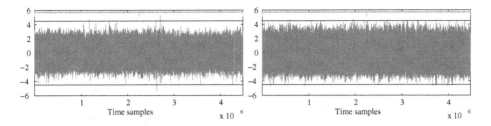

Fig. 6. T-test evaluation. C, -O1, $d = 2$. Left: fresh, right: recycled randomness.

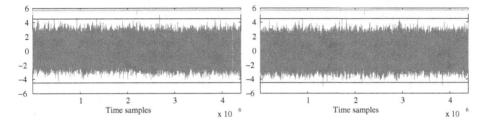

Fig. 7. T-test evaluation. C, -O2, $d = 2$. Left: fresh, right: recycled randomness.

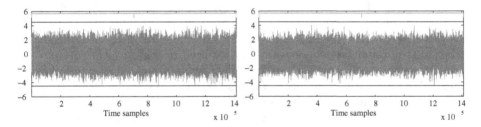

Fig. 8. T-test evaluation. C, -O3, $d = 2$. Left: fresh, right: recycled randomness.

assignment of registers (flag -morder). As can be seen in Figs. 6, 7 and 8, these changes do not significantly affect our security conclusions.

They do have however quite strong impact on the performance, in terms of both code size and cycle count. A detailed summary of the performance figures for each of the 30 combinations of compiler flags and masking orders is provided in Table 1. As one may expect, the implementations leading to a better speed vs. memory trade-off are programmed in assembly. The fastest C implementations (with flag -O3) are ten times slower than their assembly counterpart. Recall that due to data memory constraints, C implementations perform field squaring as field multiplication. In addition, achieving a time and flow constant implementation of Algorithm 1 in [24] in C is more complex than in assembly. In fact, while a multiplication over $GF(2^8)$ in assembly takes 22 cycles, the fastest one achieved in C (again with flag -O3) requires 150 cycles. This explains the great difference in performance numbers.

Table 1. Implementation results for masking order $d = 1$ (left) and $d = 2$ (right).

Language	Flags	ROM (bytes)	Speed (cycles)	Language	Flags	ROM (bytes)	Speed (cycles)
ASM	n/a	2 820	627	ASM	n/a	3 588	1 168
C	-O0	2 806	38 005	C	-O0	2 886	72 880
C	-O1	1 776	18 611	C	-O1	1 956	35 752
C	-O2	1 626	17 677	C	-O2	2 018	35 083
C	-O3	3 866	5 017	C	-O3	4 310	11 211
C	-Os	1 606	17 722	C	-Os	2 002	35 443
C	-morder1 -O0	2 926	38 116	C	-morder1 -O0	3 006	73 018
C	-morder1 -O1	1 770	18 341	C	-morder1 -O1	1 952	35 247
C	-morder1 -O2	1 630	17 669	C	-morder1 -O2	2 024	35 071
C	-morder1 -O3	3 874	5 017	C	-morder1 -O3	4 318	11 051
C	-morder1 -Os	1 610	17 714	C	-morder1 -Os	2 010	35 443
C	-morder2 -O0	2 818	38 487	C	-morder2 -O0	2 898	73 056
C	-morder2 -O1	1 780	18 645	C	-morder2 -O1	1 958	35 809
C	-morder2 -O2	1 634	17 939	C	-morder2 -O2	2 030	35 600
C	-morder2 -O3	3 868	5 029	C	-morder2 -O3	4 312	11 139
C	-morder2 -Os	1 614	17 984	C	-morder2 -Os	2 014	35 960

Other platforms. A final question of interest is whether the previous results hold for devices other than AVR. To this end, we perform a second set of experiments with the C implementations on an 8051 processor. Our results confirm that this is indeed the case, albeit with certain differences regarding the shape of the statistic t and the number of traces required to achieve clear results.

In this setup, both program and data memory are provided as external components. We process our C implementations using the Keil C51 toolchain (v9.02) and setting the compiler flags to speed optimization. The ASIC core is clocked at 7 MHz and the sampling rate of the oscilloscope is set at 250 MS/s. Power measurements are obtained by capturing the voltage drop over a 50 Ohm resistor in the V_{dd} path.

The evaluation results are illustrated in Fig. 9 for the case of fresh randomness. The left plot depicts the outcome of the t-test for $d = 1$ (2 shares). The existence of univariate first-order leakage is confirmed by clear peaks appearing symmetrically along the processing of each byte. The shape of the excursions beyond the ±5 threshold is different than the one obtained for the AVR. Also, we need to evaluate the t-test with a larger number of measurements in order to clearly detect first-order leakage. As usual in the context of empirical evaluations, such a situation is hard to explain formally. Nevertheless, we believe two main reasons are the cause for this. First, the more noisy nature of the measurement setup. And second, the less leaky behavior of the targeted 8051 core. For the sake of completeness, we present the results for $d = 2$ (3 shares) in the right plot of Fig. 9. Similar to AVR, there is no evidence of univariate first-order leakage after processing 10 000 traces. Although we expect bivariate second-order leakage to be present in these measurements, we have not attempted to detect it. The reason for this is the expensive computation and storage required to jointly process all possible sample pairs within such long traces (of millions of time samples).

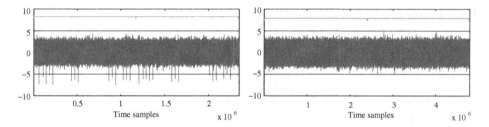

Fig. 9. T-test evaluation. C, no flags, 8051 platform, fresh randomness. Left: $d = 1$, 10 k traces. Right: $d = 2$, 10 k traces. First-order leakage visible only in the left plot.

Bivariate leakage. The bivariate second-order analysis can be found in the extended version of this paper [2] which can be found online here: http://eprint.iacr.org/2014/413. We successfully identified bivariate second-order leakage using a t-test based methodology. This is an expected result, and it serves to confirm that we indeed used enough traces for the previous univariate first-order analysis. For details, we refer the reader to the extended version of this paper.

5 Concluding Remarks

Confirmed by numerous experiments, the results in this paper first suggest a simple and natural way to convert security proofs obtained against value-based leakage models into security guarantees of lower order against transition-based ones. As a result, they bring a theoretical foundation to recent approaches to side-channel security, trying to automatically insert countermeasures such as masking in software codes. From a pragmatic point of view though, this positive conclusion should be moderated. On the one hand, just looking at the security order, we see that compiled codes can bring similar guarantees as handwritten assembly. On the other hand, reaching such a positive result still requires paying attention to SPA leakages (e.g. data-dependent execution times). Furthermore, compiled codes generally imply significant performance overheads. Yet, we hope that our results can stimulate more research in the direction of design automation for side-channel resistance, combining low development time and limited implementation overheads.

Acknowledgements. F.-X. Standaert is a research associate of the Belgian Fund for Scientific Research (FNRS-F.R.S.). Oscar Reparaz is funded by a PhD fellowship of the Fund for Scientific Research - Flanders (FWO). Benedikt Gierlichs is a Postdoctoral Fellow of the Fund for Scientific Research - Flanders (FWO). This work has been funded in parts by the European Commission through the ERC project 280141 (CRASH), by the Hercules foundation (AKUL/11/19) and by the Research Council KU Leuven: GOA TENSE (GOA/11/007).

References

1. Balasch, J., Faust, S., Gierlichs, B., Verbauwhede, I.: Theory and practice of a leakage resilient masking scheme. In: Wang, X., Sako, K. (eds.) ASIACRYPT 2012. LNCS, vol. 7658, pp. 758–775. Springer, Heidelberg (2012)
2. Balasch, J., Gierlichs, B., Grosso, V., Reparaz, O., Standaert, F.-X.: On the cost of lazy engineering for masked software implementations. Cryptology ePrint Archive, Report 2014/413 (2014). http://eprint.iacr.org/
3. Batina, L., Gierlichs, B., Prouff, E., Rivain, M., Standaert, F.-X., Veyrat-Charvillon, N.: Mutual information analysis: a comprehensive study. J. Cryptology **24**(2), 269–291 (2011)
4. Bayrak, A.G., Regazzoni, F., Bruna, D.N., Brisk, P., Standaert, F.-X., Lenne, P.: Automatic application of power analysis countermeasures. IEEE Trans. Comput. **99**(PrePrints), 1 (2013)
5. Bilgin, B., Gierlichs, B., Nikova, S., Nikov, V., Rijmen, V.: A more efficient AES threshold implementation. In: Pointcheval, D., Vergnaud, D. (eds.) AFRICACRYPT. LNCS, vol. 8469, pp. 267–284. Springer, Heidelberg (2014)
6. Chari, S., Jutla, C.S., Rao, J.R., Rohatgi, P.: Towards sound approaches to counteract power-analysis attacks. In: Wiener, M. (ed.) CRYPTO 1999. LNCS, vol. 1666, pp. 398–412. Springer, Heidelberg (1999)
7. Cooper, J., DeMulder, E., Goodwill, G., Jaffe, J., Kenworthy, G., Rohatgi, P.: Test Vector Leakage Assessment (TVLA) methodology in practice. In: International Cryptographic Module Conference (2013). http://icmc-2013.org/wp/wp-content/uploads/2013/09/goodwillkenworthtestvector.pdf
8. Coron, J.-S., Giraud, C., Prouff, E., Renner, S., Rivain, M., Vadnala, P.K.: Conversion of security proofs from one leakage model to another: a new issue. In: Schindler, W., Huss, S.A. (eds.) COSADE 2012. LNCS, vol. 7275, pp. 69–81. Springer, Heidelberg (2012)
9. Coron, J.-S., Prouff, E., Rivain, M., Roche, T.: Higher-order side channel security and mask refreshing. In: Moriai, S. (ed.) FSE 2013. LNCS, vol. 8424, pp. 410–424. Springer, Heidelberg (2014)
10. Duc, A., Dziembowski, S., Faust, S.: Unifying leakage models: from probing attacks to noisy leakage. In: Nguyen, P.Q., Oswald, E. (eds.) EUROCRYPT 2014. LNCS, vol. 8441, pp. 423–440. Springer, Heidelberg (2014)
11. Goodwill, G., Jun, B., Jaffe, J., Rohatgi, P.: A testing methodology for side channel resistance validation. NIST non-invasive attack testing workshop (2011). http://csrc.nist.gov/news_events/non-invasive-attack-testing-workshop/papers/08_Goodwill.pdf
12. Grosso, V., Standaert, F.-X., Faust, S.: Masking vs. multiparty computation: how large is the gap for AES? In: Bertoni, G., Coron, J.-S. (eds.) CHES 2013. LNCS, vol. 8086, pp. 400–416. Springer, Heidelberg (2013)
13. Grosso, V., Standaert, F.-X., Prouff, E.: Low entropy masking schemes, revisited. In: Francillon, A., Rohatgi, P. (eds.) CARDIS 2013. LNCS, vol. 8419, pp. 33–43. Springer, Heidelberg (2014)
14. Kim, H., Hong, S., Lim, J.: A fast and provably secure higher-order masking of AES S-Box. In: Preneel, B., Takagi, T. (eds.) CHES 2011. LNCS, vol. 6917, pp. 95–107. Springer, Heidelberg (2011)
15. Mangard, S., Popp, T., Gammel, B.M.: Side-channel leakage of masked CMOS gates. In: Menezes, A. (ed.) CT-RSA 2005. LNCS, vol. 3376, pp. 351–365. Springer, Heidelberg (2005)

16. Mather, L., Oswald, E., Bandenburg, J., Wójcik, M.: Does my device leak information? an *a priori* statistical power analysis of leakage detection tests. In: Sako, K., Sarkar, P. (eds.) ASIACRYPT 2013, Part I. LNCS, vol. 8269, pp. 486–505. Springer, Heidelberg (2013)
17. Moradi, A., Mischke, O.: Glitch-free implementation of masking in modern FPGAs. In: HOST, pp. 89–95. IEEE (2012)
18. Moradi, A., Poschmann, A., Ling, S., Paar, C., Wang, H.: Pushing the limits: a very compact and a threshold implementation of AES. In: Paterson, K.G. (ed.) EUROCRYPT 2011. LNCS, vol. 6632, pp. 69–88. Springer, Heidelberg (2011)
19. Moss, A., Oswald, E., Page, D., Tunstall, M.: Compiler assisted masking. In: Prouff, E., Schaumont, P. (eds.) CHES 2012. LNCS, vol. 7428, pp. 58–75. Springer, Heidelberg (2012)
20. Nikova, S., Rijmen, V., Schläffer, M.: Secure hardware implementation of nonlinear functions in the presence of glitches. J. Cryptology **24**(2), 292–321 (2011)
21. Prouff, E., Rivain, M.: Masking against side-channel attacks: a formal security proof. In: Johansson, T., Nguyen, P.Q. (eds.) EUROCRYPT 2013. LNCS, vol. 7881, pp. 142–159. Springer, Heidelberg (2013)
22. Prouff, E., Roche, T.: Higher-order glitches free implementation of the AES using secure multi-party computation protocols. In: Preneel, B., Takagi, T. (eds.) CHES 2011. LNCS, vol. 6917, pp. 63–78. Springer, Heidelberg (2011)
23. Regazzoni, F., Cevrero, A., Standaert, F.-X., Badel, S., Kluter, T., Brisk, P., Leblebici, Y., Ienne, P.: A design flow and evaluation framework for DPA-resistant instruction set extensions. In: Clavier, C., Gaj, K. (eds.) CHES 2009. LNCS, vol. 5747, pp. 205–219. Springer, Heidelberg (2009)
24. Rivain, M., Prouff, E.: Provably secure higher-order masking of AES. In: Mangard, S., Standaert, F.-X. (eds.) CHES 2010. LNCS, vol. 6225, pp. 413–427. Springer, Heidelberg (2010)
25. Roche, T., Prouff, E.: Higher-order glitch free implementation of the AES using secure multi-party computation protocols - extended version. J. Cryptographic Eng. **2**(2), 111–127 (2012)
26. Standaert, F.-X., Malkin, T.G., Yung, M.: A unified framework for the analysis of side-channel key recovery attacks. In: Joux, A. (ed.) EUROCRYPT 2009. LNCS, vol. 5479, pp. 443–461. Springer, Heidelberg (2009)
27. Standaert, F.-X., Veyrat-Charvillon, N., Oswald, E., Gierlichs, B., Medwed, M., Kasper, M., Mangard, S.: The world is not enough: another look on second-order DPA. In: Abe, M. (ed.) ASIACRYPT 2010. LNCS, vol. 6477, pp. 112–129. Springer, Heidelberg (2010)
28. De Win, E., Bosselaers, A., Vandenberghe, S., De Gersem, P., Vandewalle, J.: A fast software implementation for arithmetic operations in $GF(2^n)$. In: Kim, K.-C., Matsumoto, T. (eds.) ASIACRYPT 1996. LNCS, vol. 1163. Springer, Heidelberg (1996)

Side-Channel Analysis

Efficient Stochastic Methods: Profiled Attacks Beyond 8 Bits

Marios O. Choudary and Markus G. Kuhn[(✉)]

Computer Laboratory, University of Cambridge, Cambridge, UK
{osc22,mgk25}@cl.cam.ac.uk

Abstract. Template attacks and stochastic models are among the most powerful side-channel attacks. However, they can be computationally expensive when processing a large number of samples. Various compression techniques have been used very successfully to reduce the data dimensionality prior to applying template attacks, most notably Principal Component Analysis (PCA) and Fisher's Linear Discriminant Analysis (LDA). These make the attacks more efficient computationally and help the profiling phase to converge faster. We show how these ideas can also be applied to implement stochastic models more efficiently, and we also show that they can be applied and evaluated even for more than eight unknown data bits at once.

Keywords: Side-channel attacks · Template attack · Stochastic model · PCA · LDA

1 Introduction

The most powerful side-channel attacks for inferring secret data (passwords, cryptographic keys, etc.) processed inside tamper-resistant hardware use profiling. An attacker first characterizes the signals leaking out of a device while it processes known data values, thereby measuring their probabilistic relationship with the resulting unintended power-supply or electromagnetic emissions (*profiling phase*). The attacker can then use this leakage model to determine the maximum-likelihood data values from the signals leaking out of an identical device that processes unknown data (*attack phase*).

Two such profiling techniques have been described in the literature: the "template attack" [1] and the "stochastic model" [2]. Template attacks are very general in that they use all available information from the side-channel traces to form a probabilistic model for each possible data value (Sect. 2.1). In contrast, the stochastic method models the leakage through a small number of functions of a data word (e.g. the value of each bit), resulting in fewer parameters to estimate, thereby trading generality of the model for efficiency of profiling (Sect. 2.2).

One of the main difficulties with implementing these attacks is dealing with a large number of leakage variables, such as oscilloscope traces with thousands of samples. Several compression techniques have been proposed to reduce the

© Springer International Publishing Switzerland 2015
M. Joye and A. Moradi (Eds.): CARDIS 2014, LNCS 8968, pp. 85–103, 2015.
DOI: 10.1007/978-3-319-16763-3_6

dimensionality of leakage traces, while preserving most of the side-channel information (Sect. 3). Particularly successful were the application of Principal Component Analysis (PCA) [3] and Fisher's Linear Discriminant Analysis (LDA) [7] to this end. Last year [12], we presented very efficient ways of implementing template attacks with both, and demonstrated in a detailed comparison that those are the most efficient techniques proposed so far.

The question arises, whether similar benefits can be achieved with the stochastic methods [7]. In this paper, we show how to do so, in particular how to adapt the PCA and LDA methods to stochastic models (Sect. 4). We propose four efficient ways for estimating the PCA and LDA parameters, to preserve the overall efficiency of the stochastic method.

We then use the *Grizzly* dataset [12], which provides real data from an unprotected 8-bit microcontroller, to evaluate all our methods for implementing stochastic models, and we also compare them with template attacks (Sect. 5). The results show that our methods provide indeed very efficient implementations of stochastic models, while preserving their profiling efficiency.

Finally, we demonstrate how to profile and evaluate stochastic models simultaneously for more than eight bits (Sect. 6), and we show that our applications of LDA and PCA are particularly helpful in this context.

2   Profiled Attacks

In a profiled attack (template or stochastic model), we need physical access to a pair of identical devices, which we refer to as the *profiling* and the *attacked* device. We wish to infer some secret value $k\star \in \mathcal{S}$, processed by the attacked device at some point. For an 8-bit microcontroller, $\mathcal{S} = \{0, \ldots, 255\}$ might be the set of possible byte values manipulated by a particular machine instruction.

We assume that we determined the approximate moments of time when the secret value $k\star$ is manipulated and we are able to record signal traces (e.g. supply current or electro-magnetic waveforms) around these moments. We refer to these traces as "raw" *leakage vectors*, which we write as $\mathbf{x}^{r\prime} = [x_1, \ldots, x_{m^r}]$, where $x_j \in \mathbb{R}$ ($1 \le j \le m^r$) is a sample at time index j.[1]

2.1   Template Attacks

During the *profiling* phase we record n_p leakage vectors $\mathbf{x}^r_{ki} \in \mathbb{R}^{m^r}$ ($1 \le i \le n_p$) from the profiling device for each possible value $k \in \mathcal{S}$, and combine these as row vectors $\mathbf{x}^r_{ki}{}'$ in the leakage matrix $\mathbf{X}^r_k \in \mathbb{R}^{n_p \times m^r}$.

Typically, the raw leakage vectors $\mathbf{x}^r_{ki}$ provided by the data acquisition device contain a large number m^r of samples (random variables), due to high sampling rates used. Therefore, we might *compress* them before further processing, as explained in Sect. 3. We refer to such compressed leakage vectors as $\mathbf{x}_{ki} \in \mathbb{R}^m$ and combine all of these as rows into the compressed leakage matrix $\mathbf{X}_k \in \mathbb{R}^{n_p \times m}$. (Without a compression step, we would have $\mathbf{X}_k = \mathbf{X}^r_k$ and $m = m^r$.)

---

[1] Throughout this paper $\mathbf{x}'$ is the transpose of $\mathbf{x}$.

Using $\mathbf{X}_k$ we can compute the template parameters $\bar{\mathbf{x}}_k \in \mathbb{R}^m$ and $\mathbf{S}_k \in \mathbb{R}^{m \times m}$ for each possible value $k \in \mathcal{S}$ as

$$\bar{\mathbf{x}}_k = \frac{1}{n_{\mathrm{p}}} \sum_{i=1}^{n_{\mathrm{p}}} \mathbf{x}_{ki}, \qquad \mathbf{S}_k = \frac{1}{n_{\mathrm{p}} - 1} \sum_{i=1}^{n_{\mathrm{p}}} (\mathbf{x}_{ki} - \bar{\mathbf{x}}_k)(\mathbf{x}_{ki} - \bar{\mathbf{x}}_k)' = \frac{1}{n_{\mathrm{p}} - 1} \widetilde{\mathbf{X}}_k{}' \widetilde{\mathbf{X}}_k, \tag{1}$$

$\bar{\mathbf{x}}_k$ is the sample mean, $\mathbf{S}_k$ is the sample covariance matrix and $\widetilde{\mathbf{X}}_k$ is the leakage matrix $\mathbf{X}_k$ with $\bar{\mathbf{x}}_k$ subtracted from each row.

In the *attack* phase, we try to infer the secret value $k\star \in \mathcal{S}$ processed by the attacked device. We obtain n_{a} leakage vectors $\mathbf{x}_i \in \mathbb{R}^m$ from the attacked device, using the same recording technique and compression method as in the profiling phase, resulting in the leakage matrix $\mathbf{X}_{k\star} \in \mathbb{R}^{n_{\mathrm{a}} \times m}$. Then, for each $k \in \mathcal{S}$, we compute a *discriminant score* $\mathrm{d}(k \mid \mathbf{X}_{k\star})$, and try all $k \in \mathcal{S}$ on the attacked device, in order of decreasing score (optimised brute-force search, e.g. for a password or cryptographic key), until we find the correct $k\star$. If the leakage vectors $\mathbf{x}_i$ can be modeled well by a multivariate normal distribution, which is generally the case and what we also observed in our experiments, then the classic approach is to use a discriminant based on the probability density function (pdf) of this distribution:

$$\mathrm{d}_{\mathrm{PDF}}^{\mathrm{joint}}(k \mid \mathbf{X}_{k\star}) = \prod_{\mathbf{x}_i \in \mathbf{X}_{k\star}} \frac{1}{\sqrt{(2\pi)^m |\mathbf{S}_k|}} \exp\left(-\frac{1}{2}(\mathbf{x}_i - \bar{\mathbf{x}}_k)' \mathbf{S}_k^{-1} (\mathbf{x}_i - \bar{\mathbf{x}}_k)\right). \tag{2}$$

However, if the actual covariance $\boldsymbol{\Sigma}$ is independent of k, we can use a *pooled* sample covariance matrix [10, 12]

$$\mathbf{S}_{\mathrm{pooled}} = \frac{1}{|\mathcal{S}|(n_{\mathrm{p}} - 1)} \sum_{k \in \mathcal{S}} \sum_{i=1}^{n_{\mathrm{p}}} (\mathbf{x}_{ki} - \bar{\mathbf{x}}_k)(\mathbf{x}_{ki} - \bar{\mathbf{x}}_k)', \tag{3}$$

to better estimate $\boldsymbol{\Sigma}$, and then use the discriminant score [6, 12]

$$\mathrm{d}_{\mathrm{LINEAR}}^{\mathrm{joint}}(k \mid \mathbf{X}_{k\star}) = \bar{\mathbf{x}}_k' \mathbf{S}_{\mathrm{pooled}}^{-1} \left(\sum_{\mathbf{x}_i \in \mathbf{X}_{k\star}} \mathbf{x}_i \right) - \frac{n_{\mathrm{a}}}{2} \bar{\mathbf{x}}_k' \mathbf{S}_{\mathrm{pooled}}^{-1} \bar{\mathbf{x}}_k, \tag{4}$$

which avoids numerical pitfalls and is very efficient, being linear in $\mathbf{x}_i$. Throughout our experiments, described in the following sections, we observed that the covariances $\mathbf{S}_k$ are indeed similar. Particular implementations that cause the covariances $\mathbf{S}_k$ to be significantly different are outside the scope of this paper.

2.2 Stochastic Models

Stochastic models were introduced by Schindler et al. [2] as another kind of profiled attack, where the profiling phase can be more efficient than for template attacks. Here, we assume that each sample x_j $(1 \leq j \leq m)$ of a leakage trace $\mathbf{x}_i$

is modeled as a combination of a deterministic part $\delta_j(k)$, which takes as input a value k, and a random part ρ_j, which models the noise:[2]

$$x_j = \delta_j(k) + \rho_j. \tag{5}$$

This model can be used to attack any target k, similarly to the template attacks in the previous section.

The deterministic function $\delta_j(k)$ is modeled as a linear combination of base functions $g_{jb} : \mathcal{S} \to \mathbb{R}$, with

$$\delta_j(k) = \sum_{b=0}^{u-1} \beta_{jb} \cdot g_{jb}(k), \tag{6}$$

where $\beta_{jb} \in \mathbb{R}$. The essential idea behind stochastic models is to find a good set of base functions that matches well the leakage of the values k. A common and generally good option for 8-bit architectures is to use the set of $u = 9$ base functions known as $\mathcal{F}_9$, for which $g_{j0}(k) = 1$ and $g_{jb}(k) = \mathrm{bit}_b(k)$. We used $\mathcal{F}_9$ successfully in our 8-bit experiments (Sect. 5), but in some cases, including XORs between bits [2,4], can improve results (Sect. 6).

During profiling, instead of acquiring n_p leakage traces $\mathbf{x}_{ki}^r$ for each candidate k and then use (1, 3) to compute the mean vectors $\bar{\mathbf{x}}_k$ and covariance $\mathbf{S}_{\mathrm{pooled}}$ needed for template attacks, we only use a *total* of N leakage traces $\mathbf{x}_i^r \in \mathbb{R}^{m^r}$ from a uniform distribution of the values $k \in \mathcal{S}$. As with template attacks, we generally compress these leakage traces to obtain the compressed traces $\mathbf{x}_i \in \mathbb{R}^m$ ($m \ll m^r$, see Sect. 4). Then, we combine all these leakage traces into the leakage matrix $\mathbf{X} \in \mathbb{R}^{N \times m}$ and let k^i represent the value of k corresponding to the trace $\mathbf{x}_i$. Next, for each sample index $j \in \{1, \dots, m\}$ we build the matrix

$$\mathbf{F}_j = \begin{bmatrix} g_{j0}(k^1) & g_{j1}(k^1) & \cdots & g_{ju-1}(k^1) \\ g_{j0}(k^2) & g_{j1}(k^2) & \cdots & g_{ju-1}(k^2) \\ \vdots & \vdots & \ddots & \vdots \\ g_{j0}(k^N) & g_{j1}(k^N) & \cdots & g_{ju-1}(k^N) \end{bmatrix} \tag{7}$$

and use the stochastic model

$$\mathrm{col}_j(\mathbf{X}) = \mathbf{d}_j + \mathbf{r}_j = \mathbf{F}_j \mathbf{v}_j + \mathbf{r}_j, \tag{8}$$

---

[2] The original description [2] used a deterministic function $\delta_j(d_i, k)$ with two parameters, to capture any combination of a plaintext value d_i and key value k in an encryption algorithm, and then used a mapping function that reduced this combination into a value to be modeled by the set of base functions g_{jb}. However, the most common mapping is the XOR between d_i and k [2,8] or the XOR between these and a mask value [5]. Therefore, in most cases, a single value (e.g. the XOR result) is modeled by the base functions. If we want to target several values (e.g. for masking [2,5] one might use base functions that depend on both a mask y and the XOR between this mask, a plaintext and a key), we simply concatenate the bits of these values (e.g. $k = [\mathrm{bits\ mask} | \mathrm{bits\ XOR}]$).

where $\mathrm{col}_j(\mathbf{X})$ contains the leakage samples x_j of all traces $\mathbf{x}_i \in \mathbf{X}$, $\mathbf{v}_j' = [\beta_{j0}, \ldots, \beta_{ju-1}]$, $\mathbf{r}_j' = [\rho_j^1, \ldots, \rho_j^N]$, and $\mathbf{d}_j' = [\delta_j(k^1), \ldots, \delta_j(k^N)]$. To find the vector of coefficients $\mathbf{v}_j$, we try to minimize the distance $\|\mathrm{col}_j(\mathbf{X}) - \mathbf{F}_j\mathbf{v}_j\|^2$, leading to the solution

$$\mathbf{v}_j = (\mathbf{F}_j'\mathbf{F}_j)^{-1}\mathbf{F}_j'\mathrm{col}_j(\mathbf{X}). \tag{9}$$

Note that the matrix inversion in (9) requires $\mathrm{rank}(\mathbf{F}_j) = u$ [12], that is $\mathbf{F}_j$ must have u independent rows and columns.

In practice, we may use the same set of base functions (e.g. $\mathcal{F}_9$) for all samples j (or at least for a subset of all samples). In this case, we can drop the subscript j from (7) and use the same $\mathbf{F}$ for all samples j, turning (8) into $\mathbf{X} = \mathbf{F}\mathbf{V} + \mathbf{R}$, allowing us to compute all the coefficients at once as

$$\mathbf{V} = [\mathbf{v}_1, \ldots, \mathbf{v}_m] = (\mathbf{F}'\mathbf{F})^{-1}\mathbf{F}'\mathbf{X}, \tag{10}$$

which is computationally more efficient. The coefficient vectors $\mathbf{v}_j$, computed with either (9) or (10), can be used with (6) to compute the deterministic part $\delta_j(k)$ of a sample x_j for any value k. Note that this deterministic part is assumed to be noise-free, since the noise is captured by the term ρ_j. Therefore, as mentioned also by Gierlichs et al. [4], we can use the values $\delta_j(k)$ to compute the stochastic mean vectors $\hat{\mathbf{x}}_k \in \mathbb{R}^m$ as

$$\hat{\mathbf{x}}_k' = [\delta_1(k), \ldots, \delta_m(k)]. \tag{11}$$

While these correspond to the template mean vectors $\bar{\mathbf{x}}_k$ from (1), they depend very much on the choice of base functions.

In order to also use the noise information, we need to compute a covariance matrix $\hat{\mathbf{S}} \in \mathbb{R}^{m \times m}$, similar to the pooled covariance $\mathbf{S}_{\mathrm{pooled}}$ from (3). The available N traces that were used to estimate the coefficients $\mathbf{v}_j$ are good for this purpose[3], since in (5) the deterministic part $\delta_j(k)$ approximates the noise-free part, *common* to all the N traces. Therefore, the noise vector $\mathbf{z} \in \mathbb{R}^m$ *specific* to each trace $\mathbf{x}_i$ can be computed as

$$\mathbf{z}_i' = [\rho_1^i, \ldots, \rho_m^i], \quad \rho_j^i = x_j^i - \delta_j(k^i). \tag{12}$$

These vectors can then be used to compute the noise matrix

$$\mathbf{Z} = \begin{bmatrix} \mathbf{z}_1' \\ \vdots \\ \mathbf{z}_N' \end{bmatrix} = \begin{bmatrix} \rho_1^1 & \cdots & \rho_m^1 \\ \vdots & \ddots & \vdots \\ \rho_1^N & \cdots & \rho_m^N \end{bmatrix}, \tag{13}$$

and finally, we can estimate the covariance matrix as

---

[3] Schindler et al. [2], as well as following publications [5,8], suggest to use an *additional* disjoint training set of N_2 traces to compute the covariance matrix $\hat{\mathbf{S}}$. However, this requirement was never clearly motivated. In the appendix of an extended version of this paper [14] we show results that sustain our claim.

$$\hat{\mathbf{S}} = \frac{1}{N-1} \sum_{i=1}^{N} \mathbf{z}_i \mathbf{z}_i{}' = \frac{1}{N-1} \mathbf{Z}'\mathbf{Z}. \tag{14}$$

In the attack step, we proceed as in template attacks, using the linear discriminant from (4), but replacing the template mean vectors $\bar{\mathbf{x}}_k$ with the vectors $\hat{\mathbf{x}}_k$ from (11), and the pooled covariance $\mathbf{S}_{\text{pooled}}$ with the covariance $\hat{\mathbf{S}}$ from (14).

3   Compression Methods for Template Attacks

As mentioned earlier, during a profiled attack we should first compress the leakage traces $\mathbf{x}_i^{\text{r}} \in \mathbb{R}^{m^{\text{r}}}$ into $\mathbf{x}_i \in \mathbb{R}^m$ ($m \ll m^{\text{r}}$), in order to reduce the number of variables involved while at the same time keeping as much information as possible. It turns out that the choice of compression method is an essential step for the success of profiled attacks. The first proposed methods [1] relied on selecting some samples that maximise the data-dependent signal, but this can be error-prone. Later, Principal Component Analysis (PCA) [3] and Fisher's Linear Discriminant Analysis (LDA) [7] helped to maximise the information used in the attack step with a very small number m of samples. Last year [12], we provided a detailed analysis of these compression methods in the context of template attacks, and showed that LDA can provide a significantly better attack than the sample selection methods. Below we briefly describe these methods in the context of template attacks, and in Sect. 4 we show how to adapt them efficiently for use with stochastic models.

3.1   Sample Selection

For the sample selection method we first compute a signal strength estimate s_j for each sample j ($1 \leq j \leq m^{\text{r}}$), and then select some of the samples having the largest s_j. We used either one sample per clock (*1ppc*) or 20 samples per clock (*20ppc*) among the 5 % samples having the highest s_j. Common estimates s_j are the difference of means (DOM) [1] (which can also be computed using the absolute difference [12], as we do in this paper), the Signal to Noise Ratio (SNR) [9] and the sum of squared pairwise t-differences (SOST) [4].

3.2   PCA

For PCA, we define the sample *between groups* matrix

$$\mathbf{B} = \sum_{k \in \mathcal{S}} (\bar{\mathbf{x}}_k^{\text{r}} - \bar{\mathbf{x}}^{\text{r}})(\bar{\mathbf{x}}_k^{\text{r}} - \bar{\mathbf{x}}^{\text{r}})' \in \mathbb{R}^{m^{\text{r}} \times m^{\text{r}}}, \tag{15}$$

where $\bar{\mathbf{x}}_k^{\text{r}} = \frac{1}{n_{\text{p}}} \sum_{i=1}^{n_{\text{p}}} \mathbf{x}_{ki}^{\text{r}}$ are the mean vectors over the *raw* traces $\mathbf{x}_{ki}^{\text{r}}$ and $\bar{\mathbf{x}}^{\text{r}} = \frac{1}{|\mathcal{S}|} \sum_{k \in \mathcal{S}} \bar{\mathbf{x}}_k^{\text{r}}$. Then, we obtain the first m eigenvectors $[\mathbf{u}_1, \ldots, \mathbf{u}_m] = \mathbf{U}^m \in \mathbb{R}^{m^{\text{r}} \times m}$ of $\mathbf{B}$, which contain most of the information about the means, i.e. that can be used to separate well the mean vectors $\bar{\mathbf{x}}_k^{\text{r}}$. For this purpose, we can use the Singular Value Decomposition (SVD) $\mathbf{B} = \mathbf{U}\mathbf{D}\mathbf{U}'$, where $\mathbf{D}$ is a diagonal matrix having the eigenvalues (corresponding to $\mathbf{U}$) on its diagonal, and retain only the first m columns of $\mathbf{U}$.[4] We can use visual inspection of the eigenvalues [3], the cumulative percentage of variance [12], or we can also consider the DC contribution of each of the eigenvectors $\mathbf{u}_j$ [13], to select the best value m. Finally, we can compute the projected leakage matrix

$$\mathbf{X}_k = \mathbf{X}_k^{\mathrm{r}}\mathbf{U}^m \tag{16}$$

and obtain the PCA-based template parameters $(\bar{\mathbf{x}}_k, \mathbf{S}_{\mathrm{pooled}})$ using (1, 3).

3.3 LDA

For LDA, we use the between groups matrix $\mathbf{B}$ and the pooled covariance $\mathbf{S}_{\mathrm{pooled}}$ from (3), computed from the *raw* traces $\mathbf{x}_i^{\mathrm{r}}$, and combine the eigenvectors $\mathbf{a}_j \in \mathbb{R}^{m^{\mathrm{r}}}$ of $\mathbf{S}_{\mathrm{pooled}}^{-1}\mathbf{B}$ into the matrix $\mathbf{A} = [\mathbf{a}_1, \dots, \mathbf{a}_m]$. Then, we use the diagonal matrix $\mathbf{Q} \in \mathbb{R}^{m \times m}$, with $Q_{jj} = (\frac{1}{\mathbf{a}_j'\mathbf{S}_{\mathrm{pooled}}\mathbf{a}_j})^{\frac{1}{2}}$, to scale the matrix of eigenvectors $\mathbf{A}$ and obtain $\mathbf{U}^m = \mathbf{A}\mathbf{Q}$. Finally, we use $\mathbf{U}^m$ to project the raw leakage matrices as $\mathbf{X}_k = \mathbf{X}_k^{\mathrm{r}}\mathbf{U}^m$. Using this approach, the resulting covariance matrix of the projected traces becomes the identity matrix, so we only need to use the template mean vectors $\bar{\mathbf{x}}_k$ obtained from (1).

4 Compression Methods for Stochastic Models

4.1 Sample Selection

All the sample selection methods from Sect. 3 can be adapted for stochastic models by using (11) and (14) to compute the stochastic mean vectors $\hat{\mathbf{x}}_k$ and covariance matrix $\hat{\mathbf{S}}$, and then using these to obtain the desired signal-strength estimate s_j. In addition, Schindler et al. [2] proposed to use $s_j = \sum_{b=1}^{u-1}\beta_{jb}^2$, i.e. the norm of the data-dependent coefficients, which we refer to as *bnorm* in this paper. We used this sample selection method with stochastic models.

4.2 PCA and LDA

Using PCA, and in particular LDA, significantly improved the application of template attacks, and Standaert et al. [7] mentioned that *"Combining data dimensionality reduction techniques with stochastic models is a scope for further research."* However, until now, the sole published attempt to apply PCA to stochastic models, by Heuser et al. [11], is inefficient. As we have shown earlier, for template attacks, the goal of PCA is to find the eigenvectors $\mathbf{u}_j$ such that the projection in (16) maximises the distance between the compressed

---

[4] Archambeau et al. [3] show an alternative method for obtaining the matrix $\mathbf{U}$, that can be more efficient when $m^{\mathrm{r}} > |\mathcal{S}|$. This is generally the case, when attacking an 8-bit target, but may not hold when k is a 16-bit target, as in Sect. 6.

traces corresponding to different values k. Instead of using the eigenvectors of $\mathbf{B}$ ("supervised approach"), Heuser et al. [11] used those of the *raw* covariance matrix $\hat{\mathbf{S}}^{\mathrm{r}}$, computed as in (14), to project the leakage traces. While this removes the correlation between leakage samples, it does not maximise the discrimination between means, since the matrix $\hat{\mathbf{S}}^{\mathrm{r}}$ contains no information about the different *raw* mean vectors $\hat{\mathbf{x}}_k^{\mathrm{r}}$, obtained from (11), thereby forming an "unsupervised approach". We suspect that the lack of 'mean' information in $\hat{\mathbf{S}}^{\mathrm{r}}$ is also the reason why only the first eigenvalue was significant in the results of Heuser et al., which lead them to use a univariate attack. We verified that, for the *Grizzly* dataset [12], this *unsupervised PCA* method provides no useful attack (i.e. the guessing entropy did not decrease).

We now provide four efficient methods for implementing PCA and LDA with stochastic models. All these methods work in three main steps. In the first step, for which we offer two methods (labelled "S" and "T" below), we compute the matrix $\hat{\mathbf{B}}$, as an approximation of the *between groups* matrix $\mathbf{B}$ from (15), and the *raw* covariance matrix $\hat{\mathbf{S}}^{\mathrm{r}}$ (only needed for LDA). Next, we use either PCA or LDA to obtain the matrix of eigenvectors $\mathbf{U}^m$, and use that to compress the *raw* leakage matrix $\mathbf{X}^{\mathrm{r}} \in \mathbb{R}^{N \times m^{\mathrm{r}}}$ into $\mathbf{X} \in \mathbb{R}^{N \times m}$. Finally, for the third step, we use the stochastic model, on the compressed (projected) traces, to model each sample x_j of a *compressed* trace $\mathbf{x}_i = [x_1, \ldots, x_m] \in \mathbf{X}$.

Note that the "S" methods apply the stochastic method *twice*, once on raw traces and once on compressed traces, placing the PCA or LDA compression algorithm into a *stochastic model sandwich*. The general method is shown in Fig. 1, Algorithm A.

S-PCA. Our first PCA method for stochastic models (named *S-PCA*) relies on the stochastic model from Sect. 2.2, to build the mean vectors $\hat{\mathbf{x}}_k^{\mathrm{r}}$ of the *raw* traces. In the first step, we use these vectors to compute $\hat{\mathbf{B}}$ (see Algorithm B), and in the second step, we obtain $\mathbf{U}^m$ as the eigenvectors of $\hat{\mathbf{B}}$ (see Sect. 3.2).

T-PCA. Our second PCA method for stochastic models (*T-PCA*) is based on the observation that the matrix $\mathbf{B}$ in (15) may be approximated from a subset $\mathcal{S}_s \subset \mathcal{S}$ of values k. Therefore, in the first step, we obtain *raw* traces for the subset $\mathcal{S}_s$, and we use the resulting leakage matrices $\mathbf{X}_k^{\mathrm{r}}$ to compute the matrix $\hat{\mathbf{B}}$ (see Algorithm C). In the second step, we obtain $\mathbf{U}^m$ as the eigenvectors of $\hat{\mathbf{B}}$. Note that for this method (as well as for *T-LDA*, described next), we need two sets of *raw* traces: (a) the N traces in $\mathbf{X}^{\mathrm{r}}$ (used in step 2 and then, compressed, in step 3), and (b) the $|\mathcal{S}_s| \cdot n_{\mathrm{p}}$ traces for the matrices $\mathbf{X}_k^{\mathrm{r}}$ ($k \in \mathcal{S}_s$).

S-LDA and T-LDA. We also propose two methods for using LDA with stochastic models: *S-LDA* and *T-LDA*. These are very similar to their PCA counterparts, with S-LDA using Algorithm B, and T-LDA using Algorithm C, to compute $\hat{\mathbf{B}}$. The main difference is that, besides the matrix $\hat{\mathbf{B}}$, we also need to compute the covariance matrix $\hat{\mathbf{S}}^{\mathrm{r}} \in \mathbb{R}^{m^{\mathrm{r}} \times m^{\mathrm{r}}}$ of the *raw* traces. Then,

Algorithm A: generic for all PCA/LDA methods

Require: $\mathbf{X}^r \in \mathbb{R}^{N \times m^r}$
Step 1:
1: Obtain the matrix $\hat{\mathbf{B}}$ (Algorithm B or C),
   and the matrix $\hat{\mathbf{S}}^r$ (Algorithm D or E, LDA only)
Step 2:
2: Obtain the matrix $\mathbf{U}^m$ from $\hat{\mathbf{B}}$ (PCA)
   or $\hat{\mathbf{S}}^{r-1}\mathbf{B}$ (LDA)
3: $\mathbf{X} \leftarrow \mathbf{X}^r\mathbf{U}^m$, $\mathbf{X} \in \mathbb{R}^{N \times m}$
Step 3:
4: Compute $\mathbf{F}$ (same for all samples)   ▷ See (7)
5: $\mathbf{V} = [\mathbf{v}_1, \ldots, \mathbf{v}_m] \leftarrow (\mathbf{F}'\mathbf{F})^{-1}\mathbf{F}'\mathbf{X}$
   where $\mathbf{v}_j' = [\beta_{j0}, \ldots, \beta_{ju-1}]$
6: **for all** $k \in S$ **do**
7:    $\hat{\mathbf{x}}_k' = [\delta_1(k), \ldots, \delta_m(k)], \; \delta_j(k) \leftarrow \sum_{b=0}^{u-1} \beta_{jb} \cdot g_{jb}(k)$
8: **end for**
9: **for** $i \leftarrow 1, \ldots, N$ **do**
10:    $\mathbf{z}_i' = [\rho_1^i, \ldots, \rho_m^i], \; \rho_j^i \leftarrow x_j^i - \delta_j(k^i)$
11: **end for**
12: $\mathbf{Z}' = [\mathbf{z}_1, \ldots, \mathbf{z}_N]$
13: $\hat{\mathbf{S}} \leftarrow \frac{1}{N-1}\mathbf{Z}'\mathbf{Z}$
14: Use $(\hat{\mathbf{x}}_k, \hat{\mathbf{S}})$ in the attack step

Algorithm C: compute $\hat{\mathbf{B}}$ for T-PCA/T-LDA

Require: $\mathbf{X}_k^r \in \mathbb{R}^{n_p \times m^r}, \forall k \in S_s$
1: **for all** $k \in S_s$ **do**
2:    $\bar{\mathbf{x}}_k^r \leftarrow \frac{1}{n_p}\sum_{i=1}^{n_p} \mathbf{x}_{ki}^r$
3: **end for**
4: $\bar{\mathbf{x}}^r \leftarrow \frac{1}{|S_s|}\sum_{k \in S_s} \bar{\mathbf{x}}_k^r$
5: $\hat{\mathbf{B}} \leftarrow \sum_{k \in S_s}(\bar{\mathbf{x}}_k^r - \bar{\mathbf{x}}^r)(\bar{\mathbf{x}}_k^r - \bar{\mathbf{x}}^r)'$

Algorithm B: compute $\hat{\mathbf{B}}$ for S-PCA/S-LDA

Require: $\mathbf{X}^r \in \mathbb{R}^{N \times m^r}$
1: Compute $\mathbf{F}$ (same for all samples)   ▷ See (7)
2: $\mathbf{V}^r = [\mathbf{v}_1, \ldots, \mathbf{v}_{m^r}] \leftarrow (\mathbf{F}'\mathbf{F})^{-1}\mathbf{F}'\mathbf{X}^r$
   where $\mathbf{v}_j' = [\beta_{j0}, \ldots, \beta_{ju-1}]$
3: **for all** $k \in S$ **do**
4:    $\hat{\mathbf{x}}_k^{r'} = [\delta_1(k), \ldots, \delta_{m^r}(k)], \; \delta_j(k) \leftarrow \sum_{b=0}^{u-1} \beta_{jb} \cdot g_{jb}(k)$
5: **end for**
6: $\hat{\mathbf{x}}^r \leftarrow \frac{1}{|S|}\sum_{k \in S} \hat{\mathbf{x}}_k^r$
7: $\hat{\mathbf{B}} \leftarrow \sum_{k \in S}(\hat{\mathbf{x}}_k^r - \hat{\mathbf{x}}^r)(\hat{\mathbf{x}}_k^r - \hat{\mathbf{x}}^r)'$

Algorithm D: compute $\hat{\mathbf{S}}^r$ for S-LDA

Require: $\mathbf{X}^r \in \mathbb{R}^{N \times m^r}$
1: Compute $\mathbf{F}$ (same for all samples)   ▷ See (7)
2: $\mathbf{V}^r = [\mathbf{v}_1, \ldots, \mathbf{v}_{m^r}] \leftarrow (\mathbf{F}'\mathbf{F})^{-1}\mathbf{F}'\mathbf{X}^r$
   where $\mathbf{v}_j' = [\beta_{j0}, \ldots, \beta_{ju-1}]$
3: **for** $i \leftarrow 1, \ldots, N$ **do**
4:    $\mathbf{z}_i' = [\rho_1^i, \ldots, \rho_{m^r}^i], \; \rho_j^i \leftarrow x_j^i - \delta_j(k^i),$
      $\delta_j(k^i) \leftarrow \sum_{b=0}^{u-1} \beta_{jb} \cdot g_{jb}(k^i)$
5: **end for**
6: $\mathbf{Z}' = [\mathbf{z}_1, \ldots, \mathbf{z}_N]$
7: $\hat{\mathbf{S}}^r \leftarrow \frac{1}{N-1}\mathbf{Z}'\mathbf{Z}$

Algorithm E: compute $\hat{\mathbf{S}}^r$ for T-LDA

Require: $\mathbf{X}_k^r \in \mathbb{R}^{n_p \times m^r}, \forall k \in S_s$
1: **for all** $k \in S_s$ **do**
2:    $\bar{\mathbf{x}}_k^r \leftarrow \frac{1}{n_p}\sum_{i=1}^{n_p} \mathbf{x}_{ki}^r$
3: **end for**
4: $\hat{\mathbf{S}}^r \leftarrow \frac{1}{(n_p-1)|S_s|}\sum_{k \in S_s}\sum_{i=1}^{n_p}(\mathbf{x}_{ki}^r - \bar{\mathbf{x}}_k^r)(\mathbf{x}_{ki}^r - \bar{\mathbf{x}}_k^r)'$

Fig. 1. Algorithms needed to implement PCA and LDA with stochastic models.

we can obtain $\mathbf{U}^m$ from the eigenvectors of $\hat{\mathbf{S}}^{r-1}\hat{\mathbf{B}}$, as explained in Sect. 3.3. Algorithms D and E show how to obtain $\hat{\mathbf{S}}^r$ for S-LDA and T-LDA, respectively. In Fig. 2, we show the first four PCA eigenvectors of the *Grizzly* dataset for template PCA, S-PCA, T-PCA with different random subsets S_s, and the unsupervised PCA, along with the coefficients β_{jb}. For the unsupervised PCA, it is clear that the eigenvectors fail to provide useful information. For the other methods, the first two eigenvectors are very similar. This suggests that S-PCA and T-PCA can produce eigenvectors similar to those from template attacks. Note that for S-PCA and S-LDA we can only obtain a maximum of u eigenvectors corresponding to non-zero eigenvalues, because that is the maximum number of independent vectors used in the computation of $\hat{\mathbf{B}}$ (see Algorithm B).

5   Evaluation on 8-Bit Data

We use the *Grizzly* dataset [12] to compare the template attacks (TA) with stochastic models (SM). The *Grizzly* dataset contains $n_p = 3072$ *raw* traces $\mathbf{x}_{ki}^r$ for each $0 \le k \le 255$ (786432 traces in total), which we randomly divide into a training set and an attack set. Each *raw* trace $\mathbf{x}_{ki}^r$ has $m^r = 2500$ samples, corresponding to the current consumption of several consecutive LOAD instructions executed by the unprotected 8-bit Atmel XMEGA 256 A3U microcontroller.

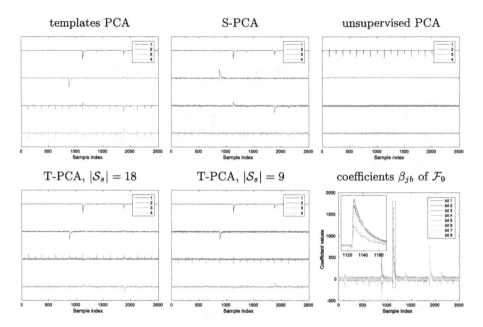

Fig. 2. Normalized eigenvectors for different PCA methods, along with coefficients β_{jb} of $\mathcal{F}_9$ computed via (10).

A single instruction loads the value k, while the other instructions load the constant value 0. Note that the value k affects the traces over several clock cycles.

5.1   Guessing Entropy

To evaluate the overall *practical* success of a profiled attack we use the *guessing entropy*, following our definition in [12], which estimates the (logarithmic) average cost of an optimised brute-force search. The guessing entropy approximates the expected number of bits of uncertainty remaining about the target value $k\star$, by averaging the results of the attack over all $k\star \in \mathcal{S}$. The lower the guessing entropy, the more successful the attack has been and the less effort remains to search for the correct $k\star$. For all the results shown in this paper, we compute the guessing entropy (g) on 10 random selections of traces $\mathbf{X}_{k\star}$ and plot the average guessing entropy over these 10 iterations.

5.2   Results on 8-Bit Data

In Fig. 3, we show the results of SM using our PCA/LDA methods, along with TA using PCA/LDA for $m = 4$. For TA, we used $n_{\mathrm{p}} = 1000$ traces per value k during profiling, while for SM we used different N and subsets $\mathcal{S}_s$. We also show the results for SM and TA using *1ppc* ($m = 10$) and *20ppc* ($m = 80$), computed using the absolute difference of means [12].

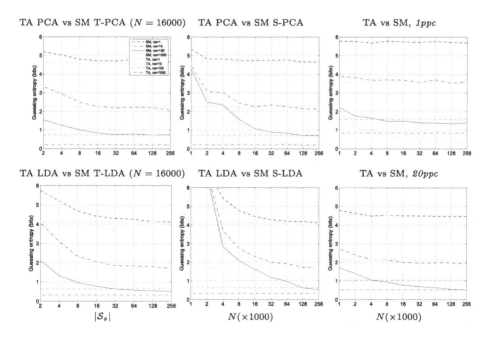

Fig. 3. Comparing TA with SM using PCA, LDA, *1ppc* and *20ppc* with different N and n_a. For TA we used $n_p = 1000$.

From these figures, we can observe several things. Firstly, it is clear that all the SM methods provide a guessing entropy equal to or better than their TA equivalent, even when supplied with a much smaller amount of training data. Therefore, our results confirm the observations of Standaert et al. [8], that SM can be at least one order of magnitude more efficient than TA. Theoretically, given enough training data, SM cannot perform better than TA. However, with a limited number of profiling traces, SM may outperform TA when the leakage is modeled well by the chosen base functions. With 256×1000 profiling traces from the *Grizzly* dataset, SM reaches nearly 0-bit guessing entropy with 1000 attack traces, whereas TA does not (Fig. 3, bottom right). Furthermore, if we want to use profiled attacks against data having more than 8 bits, as we show in the next section, the SM may be the only practical choice.

Secondly, we can observe that both S-PCA and T-PCA reach the TA boundary quicker than S-LDA and T-LDA. We believe this to be the case because the PCA methods only depend on $\hat{\mathbf{B}}$ (the approximation of $\mathbf{B}$), while the LDA methods depend on both $\hat{\mathbf{B}}$ and $\hat{\mathbf{S}}^r$.

Thirdly, we observe that, for large n_a, the *T-PCA*, *T-LDA*, *S-PCA*, *S-LDA*, and *20ppc* methods provide similar results, but for small n_a, the best results are obtained by LDA. In particular, note that, using *T-LDA* and *S-LDA*, we can reach 4.1 bits of entropy when $n_a = 1$, while this limit is unreachable for *1ppc* (5.7 bits), *20ppc* (4.5 bits) or PCA (4.7 bits).

From the TA, we knew that PCA and LDA are the most efficient compression methods. Now, we have seen that our PCA/LDA implementations for SM can achieve the same performance. On the other hand, the SM provide more efficient profiling than TA and, moreover, the SM may be the only viable solution to implement profiled attacks against more than 8-bit targets. Therefore, our proposed methods (*S-PCA*, *S-LDA*, *T-PCA* and *T-LDA*) combine the best compression methods (PCA, LDA) with the most efficient profiled attack (SM).

6   Profiled Attacks on 16-Bit Data and More

So far, most publications on profiled attacks have focused on 8-bit attacks. The possibility of attacking 16 bits was mentioned in passing [11], but we are not aware of any public description of the challenges involved in attacking 16-bit data. Therefore, we now consider and demonstrate a profiled 16-bit attack.

6.1   Considerations for the Attacker

It is not feasible to mount a template attack on much more than 8 bits, as we need to obtain leakage traces for *each* value k to compute and store the mean vectors $\bar{x}_k$. However, for the stochastic model, all we need is a selection of traces from a random subset of values k, to estimate the coefficient vectors v_j, from which we can derive any desired stochastic mean vector $\hat{x}_k$. The remaining limitation is that, in the attack phase, we still need to compute the discriminant d_{LINEAR} from (4) over all possible values k. While doing so for $|\mathcal{S}| = 2^{32}$ candidate values is no problem with normal PCs, attempting to do this for 2^{64} candidates would certainly require special hardware.

6.2   Considerations for Evaluation Laboratories

Even if stochastic methods are practical given a *single* attack trace x_i, a problem that remains, in particular for evaluation labs, is computing the guessing entropy [12], which requires to store n_a traces for *each* value $k\star \in \mathcal{S}$ and run the attack on each of these. This is not practical for values having 16 bits or more. However, one practical solution is to run the attack merely over a subset $\mathcal{S}_s$ of the target values $k\star$ and estimate the expected value of the guessing entropy over these. We refer to this measure as the *sampled guessing entropy* (SGE).

6.3   Efficient Attacks and Evaluations on More Than 8-Bit

The complexity of d_{LINEAR} is $O(m^2 + n_a \cdot m)$. However, that implies the use of a covariance in (4). But with LDA, we no longer use a covariance matrix (see Sect. 3), so the complexity of d_{LINEAR} reduces to $O(m + n_a \cdot m) = O(n_a \cdot m)$. Then, an attacker who simply wants to find the most likely k, requires a computation of complexity $O(|\mathcal{S}| \cdot n_a \cdot m)$ when using LDA (since we need to compute d_{LINEAR} for each $k \in \mathcal{S}$), and $O(|\mathcal{S}|(m^2 + n_a \cdot m))$ when using PCA or sample selection. If

n_a is of a lower order than m, then the use of LDA will provide a computational advantage to an attacker. Also, both PCA and LDA will typically work with an m much smaller than that required for sample selection. In our experiments, on the *Grizzly* dataset, we used $m = 4$ for PCA and LDA, while for *20ppc* we use $m = 80$ (sample selection benefits from using many samples per clock [12]). In the extreme case $n_a = 1$, an attack using LDA will be about 1600 times faster than using *20ppc*, and PCA will be about 400 times faster than *20ppc*. For larger traces, covering many clock cycles (e.g. for a cryptographic algorithm), we expect this difference to increase. Therefore, our PCA and LDA implementations for SM can offer great computational advantage.[5]

An evaluator who wants to compute the SGE will run the attack for each $k\star \in \mathcal{S}_s$. Therefore, the complexity of the evaluation is $O(|\mathcal{S}_s| \cdot |\mathcal{S}| \cdot n_a \cdot m)$ for LDA and $O(|\mathcal{S}_s| \cdot |\mathcal{S}| \cdot (m^2 + n_a \cdot m))$ for PCA or sample selection. However, we can optimise the computation of the SGE by precomputing $\mathbf{y}_k = \hat{\mathbf{x}}_k' \hat{\mathbf{S}}^{-1}$, and $z_k = \mathbf{y}_k' \hat{\mathbf{x}}_k$, which require a computation of $O(|\mathcal{S}|m^2)$. With these values, the discriminant $\mathrm{d}_{\mathrm{LINEAR}}$ can be computed as

$$\mathrm{d}_{\mathrm{LINEAR}}^{\mathrm{fast}}(k \mid \mathbf{X}_{k\star}) = \mathbf{y}_k' \left(\sum_{\mathbf{x}_i \in \mathbf{X}_{k\star}} \mathbf{x}_i \right) - \frac{n_a}{2} z_k, \tag{17}$$

which has complexity $O(n_a \cdot m)$. Therefore, the evaluation of the partial guessing entropy can be done with complexity $O(|\mathcal{S}|m^2 + |\mathcal{S}_s| \cdot |\mathcal{S}| \cdot n_a \cdot m)$. For PCA, the value m may be comparable to or smaller than $|\mathcal{S}_s|$ and therefore an evaluation using $\mathrm{d}_{\mathrm{LINEAR}}^{\mathrm{fast}}$ will run as fast as an evaluation using LDA. However, if we need to use a sample selection method with very large m, then the evaluation will be considerably slower. Remember also that, while *1ppc* with low m may be as fast as LDA in this case, we confirmed in Fig. 3 that both PCA and LDA provide better results than *1ppc*.

These considerations show that the choice of compression method depends also on who will need to use it: an attacker who only wants the correct $k\star$, or an evaluator who wants to know the average attack cost. In both cases, our LDA and PCA methods will help.

6.4 Results on 16-Bit Data

In order to verify that an attack on 16-bit data is feasible, and to obtain an estimate on the actual run time, we used the same device as in the *Grizzly* dataset: an Atmel XMEGA 256 A3U, with similar data acquisition setup for current traces. In order to obtain 16-bit data, we varied the 8-bit values processed by two consecutive LOAD instructions, thus obtaining leakage traces that depend on 16-bit values. Using this scenario, we cannot evaluate the limit of SM on a 16-bit parallel bus, but we can evaluate the feasibility of profiled attacks on more

---

[5] We also note that, for SM with sample selection, we should use *bnorm* (see Sect. 4.1), as that is more computationally efficient than the other methods for estimating the signal-strength estimate s_j.

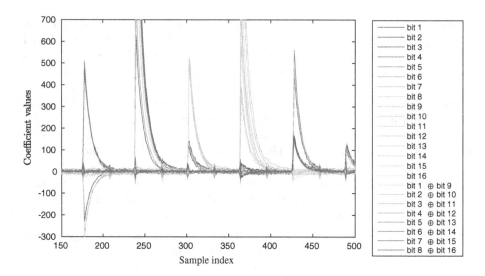

Fig. 4. Contribution of coefficients β_{jb} in $\mathcal{F}_{17}$ (bits 1 to 16) and $\mathcal{F}_{17x}$ ($\mathcal{F}_{17}$ enhanced with XOR between bits of 8-bit halves) for the *Panda* dataset. Pipelining causes leakage of the two 8-bit halves to overlap (e.g. around sample 300). Their consecutive processing also leaks their XOR value (e.g. around sample 430). While the β_{jb} for bits 1–16 are not exactly identical for $\mathcal{F}_{17}$ and $\mathcal{F}_{17x}$, the difference is visually indistinguishable.

than 8 bits of data. For this dataset, which we call *Panda*, we acquired $n_p = 200$ traces for each of the $2^{16} = 65536$ values $k \in \mathcal{S}$ ($N = 13\,107\,200$ traces in total). Each trace has $m^r = 500$ samples, recorded with $125\,\mathrm{MS/s}$ using the HIRES mode of our Tektronix TDS 7054 oscilloscope (which provides ≈ 10.5 bits per sample by averaging 40 consecutive 8-bit samples acquired internally at $5\,\mathrm{GS/s}$), and contained data over 5 LOAD instructions, of which two contained our target data and the other three processed the constant value 0. We split this data into two sets, for profiling and attack. In addition we also acquired $n_p = 1000$ traces for a selection of $|\mathcal{S}_s| = 512$ random values k (512000 traces in total), which we used for the estimation of $\hat{\mathbf{B}}$ and $\hat{\mathbf{S}}^r$ with T-PCA and T-LDA. For the implementation of the SM we simply extended the set of base functions to include the individual contributions of all the 16 bits of the values k, resulting in the set $\mathcal{F}_{17}$. The contribution of each base function is shown in Fig. 4.

In Fig. 5, we show our results for the full 16-bit attack. For our SM versions of PCA and LDA we used $m = 10$. With most methods, the guessing entropy converges after only about $N = 1000 \times 2^4 = 16000$ traces, which confirms the efficiency of stochastic models. S-LDA reduces the guessing entropy below 4 bits when using $n_a = 100$ traces, which means that, in this case, we can find the correct $k\star$ in a brute-force search attack with at most 16 trials, on average. S-PCA, S-LDA and T-PCA are better than *20ppc*, but T-LDA is not. Both S-PCA and S-LDA are better than T-PCA and T-LDA, which suggests that the subset of $|\mathcal{S}_s| = 512$ values we used for the estimation of the T-PCA/T-LDA

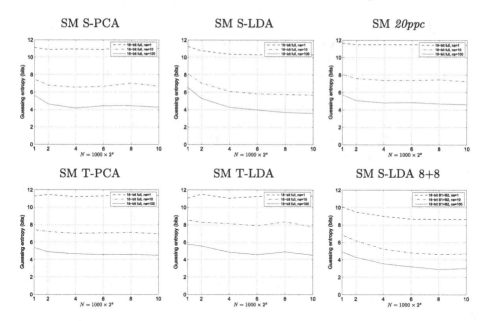

Fig. 5. Results of full 16-bit $\mathcal{F}_{17}$ attack for pipelined data, with *S-PCA*, *S-LDA*, *20ppc*, *T-PCA*, *T-LDA*, and results from *S-LDA* on 8 bits at a time, using different N and n_a. We tried $N = 1000 \cdot 2^x$, where x is the value shown on the logarithmic x-axis. For *T-PCA* and *T-LDA*, we used $|\mathcal{S}_s| = 512$.

parameters $\hat{\mathbf{B}}$ and $\hat{\mathbf{S}}^r$ was not enough to reach the full potential of PCA and LDA. Therefore, for attacks on more than 8 bits the methods S-PCA and S-LDA may be the best option, as they can use all the available N traces with the stochastic model for both the modeling of the compressed mean vectors $\hat{\mathbf{x}}_k$ (step 3 in Algorithm A), as well as for the modeling of *all* the raw vectors $\hat{\mathbf{x}}_k^r$ (lines 3–5 in Algorithm B). This in turn can result in a better estimation of the matrix $\hat{\mathbf{B}}$ (step 1 in Algorithm A), than what can be achieved with a small subset of real vectors $\bar{\mathbf{x}}_k^r$ for the T-PCA and T-LDA methods.

In the bottom-right of Fig. 5, we also show the results when performing the SM attack separately, for each of the two bytes of our target value (i.e. during profiling we only consider one byte known, while the varying value of the other represents noise). We computed the results by adding the guessing entropy from each 8-bit attack. This figure shows that, in our particular scenario, performing two 8-bit attacks (each with $\mathcal{F}_9$) provided better results than any of the 16-bit attacks with $\mathcal{F}_{17}$. This could potentially be due to several factors. Firstly, by attacking only 8 bits, there are fewer parameters to be estimated during the attack (e.g. the SM coefficients). Secondly, the signal-to-noise ratio in the acquisition setup might have been too low to provide sufficient separation between the $|\mathcal{S}| = 2^{16}$ classes to be distinguished by our classifier. Finally, the base function set $\mathcal{F}_{17}$ may simply not have adequately modeled the leakage. The latter turned out to be the main factor, which was easily fixed. Our 16-bit target value

$k = [k_1|k_2]$ is composed of two 8-bit halves (k_1 and k_2), which are processed consecutively in the XMEGA CPU. If these two values pass through the same parts of the circuit, their XOR difference is likely to affect part of the leakage traces. Therefore, we also evaluated an attack where the stochastic model included the XOR between the bits of k_1 and k_2, resulting in the set $\mathcal{F}_{17x}$ (see Fig. 4).

Figure 6 shows the results of our SM attacks using S-PCA (left) and S-LDA (right) with $\mathcal{F}_{17x}$. We see that, using $\mathcal{F}_{17x}$, both S-PCA and S-LDA perform better than with $\mathcal{F}_{17}$. Also, in this case S-LDA reduces the guessing entropy to about one bit, which is far better than any of the other results, including the attack on k_1 and k_2 separately. Therefore, a 16-bit attack can perform better than two 8-bit attacks, if a model is used that also takes into consideration differences between the bits, as we did in $\mathcal{F}_{17x}$.

In Table 1, we show the execution times for the main steps of an evaluation using S-PCA. This table shows that SM attacks are feasible, at least computationally, on 16-bit data. All the steps can be extended for 32-bit data and more. The only steps that depend on the number of bits are the computation of the raw vectors $\hat{\mathbf{x}}_k^r$ and the computation of the compressed vectors $\hat{\mathbf{x}}_k$ for all $k \in \mathcal{S}$, and the computation of the SGE. These steps depend *linearly* on k, so a straight-forward extension to 32-bit may require 65536 times more time. That

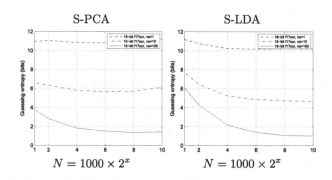

Fig. 6. Results of SM attack using $\mathcal{F}_{17x}$ with S-PCA (left) and S-LDA (right).

Table 1. Approximate time required for the main steps of an evaluation using S-PCA on 16 bits with $\mathcal{F}_{17}$ and $N = 64000$

Step	Time
Obtaining $\mathbf{V}$ on raw data (Algorithm B, step 2)	40 s
Approximating raw mean vectors $\hat{\mathbf{x}}_k^r$ (Algorithm B, steps 3–5)	32 s
Computing PCA parameters (Algorithm A, step 2)	2 s
Obtaining $\mathbf{V}$ on compressed data (Algorithm A, step 5)	38 s
Obtaining $\hat{\mathbf{x}}_k$ for all k (Algorithm A, steps 6–8)	28 s
Obtaining $\hat{\mathbf{S}}$ (Algorithm A, steps 9–13)	33 s
Compute SGE using $|\mathcal{S}_s| = 256$ with m of the same order as n_a	210 s

means that, for an attacker who only wants to find what the most likely target $k\star$ is, the attacks would take 24 days for the computation of the raw vectors $\hat{\mathbf{x}}_k^r$, 21 days for the computation of the compressed vectors $\hat{\mathbf{x}}_k$ and 15 hours for the attack step. However, it seems that for an evaluator it would be impractical to compute the SGE on 32-bit data for large $|\mathcal{S}_s|$.

7 Conclusions

In this paper, we have shown how to implement the PCA and LDA compression methods, which have so successfully boosted the performance of template attacks in the past, also for stochastic models. As both techniques implement coordinate transforms based on singular-value decomposition of covariance matrices, there were two opportunities to apply a stochastic model: first before the compression step, on raw traces, to aid estimating the matrices required by the compression method, and secondly, on the compressed traces that they output, to better estimate the mean vectors for each data value. In addition, we investigated a variant in which the matrices for the compression step are instead estimated directly, as in the template attacks, but using only a subset of all possible data values, which also boosts the performance of the profiling phase.

We have shown that, for 8-bit attacks, our PCA and LDA methods for stochastic models can obtain the same or even better results than their respective implementations on template attacks. Combining the compression efficiency of PCA and LDA with the profiling efficiency of stochastic models allows us to extract the most out of profiled attacks. Moreover, we have shown that, from a computational perspective, LDA can provide a significant advantage to an attacker, which for our experiments may result in an attack step that is 1600 times faster than using sample selection. For an evaluator, both LDA and PCA will be very helpful in obtaining efficient evaluations of profiled attacks.

We also performed an evaluation on 16-bit data, which allowed us to confirm that: (a) our PCA and LDA implementations provide good results, and (b) stochastic attacks are feasible, at least computationally, on 16-bit data. Extrapolating the run-time of our evaluation, even an attack on 32 bits appears computationally feasible (requiring in the order of 45 days for the profiling step and 15 hours for the attack step on our PC).

Our results also showed that two separate 8-bit attacks performed better than a 16-bit attack, which could be attributed to several factors, such as fewer parameters to be estimated, or a limitation in the acquisition setup and attack method to distinguish a 16-bit value. However, when adding the contribution of the XOR between the two 8-bit halves of our target value to the 16-bit model, we obtained better results. This showed that simply expanding the attack to 16 bits is not guaranteed to improve the results, because the larger number of parameters that need to be estimated reduced the accuracy achievable with a given set of traces, and in such situations, an attack targeting two 8-bit halves separately can actually perform better. A 16-bit attack, however, can perform better if a more informative model is used, such as taking into consideration differences between the bits, as we did in $\mathcal{F}_{17x}$, in which case the attack could outperform the individual 8-bit attacks.

Data and Code Availability: In the interest of reproducible research we make available our data and related MATLAB scripts at:

http://www.cl.cam.ac.uk/research/security/datasets/grizzly/

Acknowledgement. The first author is a recipient of the Google Europe Fellowship in Mobile Security, and this research was supported in part by this fellowship. The opinions expressed in this paper do not represent the views of Google unless otherwise explicitly stated.

References

1. Chari, S., Rao, J.R., Rohatgi, P.: Template attacks. In: Kaliski, B.S., Koç, Ç.K., Paar, C. (eds.) CHES 2002. LNCS, vol. 2523, pp. 13–28. Springer, Heidelberg (2003)
2. Schindler, W., Lemke, K., Paar, C.: A stochastic model for differential side channel cryptanalysis. In: Rao, J.R., Sunar, B. (eds.) CHES 2005. LNCS, vol. 3659, pp. 30–46. Springer, Heidelberg (2005)
3. Archambeau, C., Peeters, E., Standaert, F.-X., Quisquater, J.-J.: Template attacks in principal subspaces. In: Goubin, L., Matsui, M. (eds.) CHES 2006. LNCS, vol. 4249, pp. 1–14. Springer, Heidelberg (2006)
4. Gierlichs, B., Lemke-Rust, K., Paar, C.: Templates vs. stochastic methods. In: Goubin, L., Matsui, M. (eds.) CHES 2006. LNCS, vol. 4249, pp. 15–29. Springer, Heidelberg (2006)
5. Lemke-Rust, K., Paar, C.: Analyzing side channel leakage of masked implementations with stochastic methods. In: Biskup, J., López, J. (eds.) ESORICS 2007. LNCS, vol. 4734, pp. 454–468. Springer, Heidelberg (2007)
6. Karsmakers, P., et al.: Side channel attacks on cryptographic devices as a classification problem, KU Leuven, COSIC, internal report, 2007. https://www.cosic.esat.kuleuven.be/publications/article-2450.pdf
7. Standaert, F.-X., Archambeau, C.: Using subspace-based template attacks to compare and combine power and electromagnetic information leakages. In: Oswald, E., Rohatgi, P. (eds.) CHES 2008. LNCS, vol. 5154, pp. 411–425. Springer, Heidelberg (2008)
8. Standaert, F.-X., Koeune, F., Schindler, W.: How to compare profiled side-channel attacks? In: Abdalla, M., Pointcheval, D., Fouque, P.-A., Vergnaud, D. (eds.) ACNS 2009. LNCS, vol. 5536, pp. 485–498. Springer, Heidelberg (2009)
9. Mangard, S., Oswald, E., Popp, T.: Power Analysis Attacks: Revealing the Secrets of Smart Cards, 1st edn. Springer, Heidelberg (2010)
10. Oswald, D., Paar, C.: Breaking Mifare DESFire MF3ICD40: power analysis and templates in the real world. In: Preneel, B., Takagi, T. (eds.) CHES 2011. LNCS, vol. 6917, pp. 207–222. Springer, Heidelberg (2011)
11. Heuser, A., Kasper, M., Schindler, W., Stöttinger, M.: A new difference method for side-channel analysis with high-dimensional leakage models. In: Dunkelman, O. (ed.) CT-RSA 2012. LNCS, vol. 7178, pp. 365–382. Springer, Heidelberg (2012)

12. Choudary, O., Kuhn, M.G.: Efficient template attacks. In: Francillon, A., Rohatgi, P. (eds.) CARDIS 2013. LNCS, vol. 8419, pp. 253–270. Springer, Heidelberg (2014)
13. Choudary, O., Kuhn, M.G.: Template attacks on different devices. In: Prouff, E. (ed.) COSADE 2014. LNCS, vol. 8622, pp. 179–198. Springer, Heidelberg (2014)
14. Choudary, M.O., Kuhn, M.G.: Efficient stochastic methods: profiled attacks beyond 8 bits, extended version, Cryptology ePrint Archive, Report 2014/885 (2014). https://eprint.iacr.org/2014/885.pdf

Kangaroos in Side-Channel Attacks

Tanja Lange[1], Christine van Vredendaal[1,2]([✉]), and Marnix Wakker[2]

[1] Department of Mathematics and Computer Science,
Eindhoven University of Technology, P.O. Box 513,
5600 MB Eindhoven, The Netherlands
tanja@hyperelliptic.org, c.v.vredendaal@tue.nl
[2] Brightsight B.V., Delftechpark 1, 2628 XJ Delft, The Netherlands
wakker@brightsight.com

Abstract. Side-channel attacks are a powerful tool to discover the cryptographic secrets of a chip or other device but only too often do they require too many traces or leave too many possible keys to explore. In this paper we show that for side channel attacks on discrete-logarithm-based systems significantly more unknown bits can be handled by using Pollard's kangaroo method: if b bits are unknown then the attack runs in $2^{b/2}$ instead of 2^b. If an attacker has many targets in the same group and thus has reasons to invest in precomputation, the costs can even be brought down to $2^{b/3}$.

Usually the separation between known and unknown keybits is not this clear cut – they are known with probabilities ranging between 100 % and 0 %. Enumeration and rank estimation of cryptographic keys based on partial information derived from cryptanalysis have become important tools for security evaluations. They make the line between a broken and secure device more clear and thus help security evaluators determine how high the security of a device is. For symmetric-key cryptography there has been some recent work on key enumeration and rank estimation, but for discrete-logarithm-based systems these algorithms fail because the subkeys are not independent and the algorithms cannot take advantage of the above-mentioned faster attacks. We present ϵ-enumeration as a new method to compute the rank of a key by using the probabilities together with (variations of) Pollard's kangaroo algorithm and give experimental evidence.

Keywords: Side-channel attacks · Template attacks · Key enumeration · Rank estimation · Discrete logarithms · Pollard-kangaroo method · Precomputation

1 Introduction

In security evaluations it is important to investigate how well cryptographic implementations fare against side-channel attacks (SCA's). Numerous of these

This work was supported by the Netherlands Organisation for Scientific Research (NWO) under grant 639.073.005. Permanent ID of this document: c1c4c98f98c7ca3cb1b1f4208b95e8b8. Date: February 15, 2015.

© Springer International Publishing Switzerland 2015
M. Joye and A. Moradi (Eds.): CARDIS 2014, LNCS 8968, pp. 104–121, 2015.
DOI: 10.1007/978-3-319-16763-3_7

attacks are known: In this paper we will be most interested in the Template Attacks introduced by Chari, Rao and Rohatgi [3]. These attacks are among the strongest possible attacks in the sense that they extract all possible information of the samples S measured from a secret-key operation. They assume access to an identical device as used by the target and use it to produce precise multivariate characterizations of the noise of encryptions with different keys. By a process of iterative classification they then attempt to derive the key used when measuring S. At each iteration a few bits are added to the templates. Each set of a few bits is called a subkey.

In [3] iterative classification was performed until only a few candidates for the key were left. We however accept being left with a larger number of possibilities of which we are 100 % sure that they are the likeliest keys according to our attack results and then continue to enumerate the remaining keys. This might be faster than continuing to attack and hoping to get more significant results. The motivation for this approach is the guy in the security evaluation lab. He starts his template attack and if he were to spend a long enough time he might find the key. However if he is able to enumerate 2^b keys, then the lab guy might as well stop the measurements after reducing the space of the remaining keys to an interval of size 2^b. By pruning the space further he will only risk throwing out the actual key even though he could have enumerated it. Another motivation for our approach is that there are some implementations where it does not matter how long the guy stays in the lab, the power traces will not give away more information. In this case we will still have a (larger) space of possibilities we need to enumerate based on all the information we were able to get.

When we have the results of such a SCA we can take two approaches. The first is the black-box approach of key enumeration. A key enumeration algorithm takes the SCA results as input and return keys k in order of likelihood. The position of a k in such an ordering is called its rank r. For symmetric-key cryptography some research has been done on this subject. Pan, van Woudenberg, den Hartog and Witteman [10] described a sub-optimal enumeration method with low storage requirements and an optimal method that required more storage. Veyrat-Charvillon, Gérard, Renauld, and Standaert [17] improved the optimal algorithm to require less storage and be able to enumerate more keys faster.

The second way of looking at a SCA result is the white-box approach of rank estimation. This method is particularly relevant for security evaluation labs. Using modern technology it is feasible to enumerate 2^{50} to 2^{60} keys, but when a key is ranked higher, we can only say that its rank is higher than $\sim 2^{60}$ (the rank at which the memory is exceeded). For security evaluations of the encryption algorithm however more accuracy is required. A rank estimation algorithm is able to extract information about the rank r of k without enumerating all the keys. For symmetric cryptography like AES such an algorithm was put forth by Veyrat-Charvillion, Gérard and Standaert in [18].

Our contribution in this paper is to extend these works to public-key cryptography, specifically Elliptic-Curve Cryptology (ECC [9]). Using the (partial) information from a template attack on the subkeys of a key k used in Diffie-Hellman

Key Exchange, k might be recovered by enumerating the most likely candidates. Contrary to the assumptions in the previously mentioned algorithms, the information on the subkeys is not independent for ECC and therefore we cannot use the existing algorithms. On the bright side, in ECC we are working with cyclic groups and we can use this structure to speed up enumeration. This way, enumeration can be interpreted as finding the solution to the Discrete Logarithm Problem (DLP) by using partial information on the subkeys. We present our own algorithm which utilizes Pollard's kangaroo methods (see [5,11,12,14,16]) to enumerate with an error margin ϵ. In trade for this error margin we are able to enumerate a space of ℓ keys in $O(\sqrt{\ell})$ group operations.

If we make use of a precomputation table like was proposed in [1] we can reduce the expense per key to $O(\sqrt[3]{\ell})$ operations. This improvement of Pollard's methods lends itself particularly well to use in side-channel attacks. The creation of the precomputation table costs $O(\sqrt[3]{\ell^2})$ group operations and a specific table can only be used to speed up solving of DLPs in one particular group and interval length. So creating the table is only useful if we want to perform an attack a lot of times on the same length interval of a certain subgroup, but this is a fairly common scenario since many smart card vendors implement the NIST P-256 curve for which the curve equation and the base point are standardized. This means that security evaluation labs can create the most commonly needed tables beforehand and re-use them every time an attack is performed on an implementation for this curve.

We end this introduction with noting that even though the results in this paper are posed in the setting of elliptic curves, the techniques are applicable to solving a DLP in any cyclic group.

2   Background

This section gives a short description of methods to solve the Discrete Logarithm Problem (DLP) in a group of prime order n. The "square-root methods" solve this problem on average in $O(\sqrt{n})$ group operations. We will use additive notation since the main application is to is to solve the DLP on an elliptic curve E over a finite field $\mathbb{F}_p$ but the methods work in any group. Let $P, Q \in E(\mathbb{F}_p)$ be in a cyclic group; the goal is to find an integer k such that $Q = kP$.

2.1   A Short History of Discrete Logarithm Algorithms

A well known method is Shanks' Baby-Step-Giant-Step (BSGS) method [13]. It uses a table to find collisions between baby steps $0P, P, \ldots, (m - 1)P$ and giant steps $Q - 0P, Q - mP, Q - 2mP, Q - 3mP, \ldots$, where $m \approx \sqrt{n}$. This finds $k = k_0 + k_1 m$ as the collision of $k_0 P$ and $Q - k_1 mP$ in $O(m)$ steps. A drawback of this method it that it has a storage requirement of m elements, which is a more serious limitation than $O(m)$ computation. If the discrete logarithm k is known to lie in an interval $[a, b]$ of length ℓ then choosing $m \approx \sqrt{\ell}$ gives a runtime of $O(\sqrt{\ell})$.

The Pollard-ρ method [11] gives a solution to the storage problem. It uses a deterministic random walk on the group elements with the goal of ending up in a cycle (which can be detected by Floyd's cycle finding algorithm). The walk is defined in such a way that the next step in the walk depends solely on the representation of the current point and that a collision on the walk reveals the discrete logarithm k. Van Oorschot and Wiener [16] introduced a parallel version of the Pollard-ρ method which gives a linear speed-up in the number of processors used. They use distinguished points: a point is a distinguished point if its representation exhibits a certain bit pattern, e.g., has the top 20 bits equal to zero. Whenever one of the parallel random walks reaches such a point it is stored on a central processor. A collision between two of these distinguished points almost surely reveals the value of the key. This method is an improvement over BSGS in that the storage requirements are minimal, but the algorithm is probabilistic and it cannot be adapted to search an interval efficiently.

Pollard's kangaroo method solves the latter problem. It reduces the storage to a constant and is devised to search for the solution of a DLP in an interval of length ℓ. The mathematical ingredients, the algorithm and improvements are the topic of the remainder of this section.

2.2 Mathematical Aspects of Kangaroos

To adequately explain Pollard's kangaroo method we first have to dive into the notion of a mathematical kangaroo. We define a kangaroo by the sequence of its positions $X_i \in \langle P \rangle$. Its starting point is $X_0 = s_0 P$ for a certain starting value s_0 and the elements that follow are a pseudo-random walk. The steps (or rather jumps) of a kangaroo are additions with points from a finite set of group elements $S = \{s_1 P, \ldots, s_L P\}$.

The step sizes s_i are taken such that their average is $s = \beta\sqrt{\ell}$ for some scalar β. To select the next step we use a hash function $H : \langle P \rangle \to \{1, 2, \ldots, L\}$ and we compute the distance by defining $d_0 = 0$ and then updating it for every step as follows

$$d_{i+1} = d_i + s_{H(X_i)}, \quad i = 0, 1, 2, \ldots,$$
$$X_{i+1} = X_i + s_{H(X_i)}P, \quad i = 0, 1, 2, \ldots.$$

This results in a kangaroo which after i jumps has travelled a distance of d_i and has value $(s_0 + d_i)P$.

2.3 Pollard's Kangaroo Method

The original algorithm that Pollard presented in [11] works as follows: Suppose we know that the value k in $Q = kP$ is in the interval $[a, b]$ of length $\ell = b - a + 1$. We introduce two kangaroos. The first one is the tame kangaroo T and we set it down at the point bP. We tell him to take $N = O(\sqrt{\ell})$ jumps and then stop. The point at which he stops and how far the kangaroo travelled to get there are recorded. This information can be seen as a trap meant to catch the second kangaroo. The trap consists of the endpoint $X_N = (b + d_N)P$ and the travelled distance d_N. Then a second, wild, kangaroo W is let loose at the unknown starting point $X'_0 = Q = kP$ following the same instructions determining jumps. The crucial fact upon which this algorithm is based is that if at any point the path of the wild kangaroo crosses with that of the tame one, meaning that they land on the same point, their remaining paths are the same. So if the wild kangaroo starts jumping and crosses the tame one's path, then there is a jump M at which $X'_M = X_N$. From this we have $(k + d'_M)P = (b + d_N)P$ and $k = b + d_N - d'_M$ and we will detect this collision since $X'_{M+j} = X_{N+j}$, so the wild kangaroo will eventually meet the tame one.

Van Oorschot and Wiener [16] also presented a parallel version of this algorithm which even for just two kangaroos gives an improvement. Here instead of one trap, multiple traps are set: a fraction $1/w$ of the group elements which satisfy a certain distinguishing property $\mathcal{D}$ are defined as the distinguished set. Here w is taken to be $\alpha\sqrt{\ell}$, where α is some small constant (usually smaller than 1). A central server then records the distance and location of any kangaroo reaching a point in $\mathcal{D}$. We again have a wild and a tame kangaroo. Instead of starting at the end of the interval however, the tame kangaroo now starts in the middle at some point cP. Instead of finishing their entire paths, the kangaroos now jump alternately. Whenever one of them jumps to a distinguished point, their relevant information (position, distance, offset of starting point, kangaroo type) $= (X_i, d_i, c_i, Y)$ is recorded in a hash table which hashes on the X_i. When two kangaroos of different types have been recorded in the same entry of the hash table, we can derive the answer to the DLP.

Let us analyze this algorithm. The distance between the two kangaroos at the starting position is at most $(a - b + 1)/2 = \ell/2$ and on average $\ell/4$. If we take $s = \beta\sqrt{\ell}$, then the average number of jumps needed for the trailing kangaroo to catch up to the starting point of the front kangaroo is $\ell/4s$. Now we use that the probability of missing the front kangaroo's trail after passing its starting point for i steps is $(1 - 1/s)^i \approx e^{-i/s}$ (we can use this approximation as s is large) and get that it takes s steps on average to hit the trail. Lastly, both kangaroos have to hop far enough to hit a distinguished point. If $1/w$ is the fraction of group elements that are distinguished, then w steps are needed on average before hitting a distinguished point. The total average number of steps is the $2(\ell/4s + s + w) = 2(\alpha + \beta + 1/4\beta)\sqrt{\ell}$, in which α and β can be optimized experimentally.

This algorithm can be improved even further by using 3 or 4 kangaroos (see [5]), but in this paper we consider the 2-kangaroo version.

2.4   Pollard's Kangaroo Method with Precomputation

Pollard's kangaroo method can be sped up using precomputation. Bernstein and Lange [1] suggest to first produce a table of T distinguished points. Selecting the distinguished-point property and creating the table is then similar to setting a trap at every distinguished point in a desert, then sending a bunch of kangaroos into said desert and recording in a table which traps are most popular.

Then when we are ready to send in the wild kangaroo we really want to trap we already know where he is most likely to fall in.

The algorithm works as follows. In the precomputation phase we start a lot of walks from random values yP and continue these walks until they reach a distinguished point at $(y+d)P$. We record $(y+d, (y+d)P)$ in the precomputation table $\mathcal{T}$. We keep starting new walks until T different distinguished points are found (or sample for longer and keep the most popular ones). As [1] notes, these walks should be independent from Q.

In the main computation phase we start random walks that are dependent on Q. We let a kangaroo on $X_0' = Q$ hop until it reaches a distinguished point. If this point is in the table we have solved our DLP. If not we start a new walk at $Q + xP$ for some small random x. For each new walk we use a new randomization of Q and continue this way until a collision is found.

If enough DLPs in this group need to be solved so that precomputation is not an issue — or if a real-time break of the DLP is required — they propose to use $T \approx \sqrt[3]{\ell}$ precomputed distinguished points, walk length $w \approx \alpha\sqrt{\ell/T}$, i.e., $w \approx \alpha\sqrt[3]{\ell}$, with α an algorithm parameter to be optimized, and a random step set $\mathcal{S}$ with mean $s \approx \ell/4w$. This means that the precomputed table $\mathcal{T}$ takes $O(\sqrt[3]{\ell^2})$ group operations to create but can be stored in $\approx \sqrt[3]{\ell}$. This reduces the number of group operation required to solve a DLP to $O(\sqrt[3]{\ell})$ group operations, essentially a small number of walks.

3 ϵ-Enumeration

Now that we have the mathematical background covered, we continue to enumeration in side-channel attacks. Our goal is to enumerate through SCA results and give a rank estimation for a key similar to what was done in [17,18] for SCAs on implementations of symmetric cryptography. To do this we first have to model the result of SCA on ECC.

3.1   The Attack Model

We will assume a template attack like Chari, Rao and Rohatgi performed in [3]. In this attack we use our own device to make a multivariate model for each of the possibilities for the first bits of the key. When we then get a power sample of the actual key, we compute the probability of getting this shape of power sample given the template for each possible subkey. These probabilities will be our SCA results.

We can iterate this process by taking a few bits more and creating new templates, but making these requires a lot of storage and work. At the same time, they will either confirm earlier guesses or show that the wrong choice was made. At each iteration we only include the most likely subset of the subkeys from the previous iteration. Discarding the other possibilities creates a margin of error that we want to keep as small as possible.

In Chari [3] the aim was to recover *all* the bits of the key with a high success rate. Our goal is to minimize the overall attack time — the time for the measurements plus the time for testing (and generating) key candidates. We do not require to only be left with a couple of options at the end of the attack of which one is correct with a high probability. We accept ending the experiments being left with a larger number of possibilities of which we are close to 100 % sure that they are the likeliest keys according to our attack results. After this we wish to enumerate them in the order of their posterior probabilities. We show how this can be faster than continuing to measure and hoping to get more significant results.

The results of the measurement and evaluation can be visualized as depicted in Fig. 1.

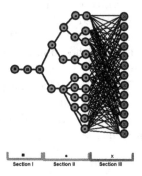

Fig. 1. The graphical representation the SCA result

We will call this visualization the enumeration tree. It consists of three sections. The first section consists of the subkey bits that we consider recovered. After the iterations of the template attack all options but one were discarded. Section II consists of the subkeys that we have partial information on, but not enough to reduce the number of likely subkeys to one. The last section consists of the subkeys that we have very little to no information on. It contains all possible subkeys per layer.

The idea is that each node $n_{i,j}$ in the representation is located in the i'th level (starting with 1 at the root) and corresponds to the j'th choice for subkeys $k_{i,1}, k_{i,2} \ldots ,$. For each node $n_{i,j}$ there is an associated subkey $k_{i,j}$ and a posterior probability $q_{i,j}$. This is the probability that subkey i is equal to $k_{i,j}$ given that the path up to its parent node is correct. So if the nodes on the path to $n_{i,j}$ are $n_{1,x_1}, n_{2,x_2}, \ldots, n_{i-1,x_{i-1}}, n_{i,j}$, then the probability $q_{i,j}$ associated with this node is

$$q_{i,j} = \Pr[k_i = k_{i,j} | k_1 = k_{1,x_1}, k_2 = k_{2,x_2}, \ldots, k_{i-1} = k_{i-1,x_{i-1}}]. \qquad (1)$$

Then we can also associate with each node a probability $p_{i,j}$ that represents the posterior probability of the key consisting of the subkeys represented by the nodes leading up to it (including itself). This probability is then

$$p_{i,j} = q_{i,j} \cdot \prod_{h=1}^{i-1} q_{1,x_h}. \tag{2}$$

In sections I and II the subkeys that were discarded during the attack and are not in the model might have a combined small probability p_ϵ. We assume that these probabilities are negligible (otherwise more nodes should be included in section II or the transition between section I and II should have moved closer to the root) and thus assume that the sum of the probabilities $p_{i,j}$ of each level of the tree is 1.

3.2   Enumeration in an Interval

The brute-force approach an attacker could take to enumerate the keys is to sort the nodes of the rightmost layer of section II by posterior probability p_{ij} and then for each choice brute-force all the options in section III. However using the algorithms from Sects. 2.3 and 2.4 we can do better. Enumerating section III of a node is equivalent to computing the keys in an interval. Therefore we can use the Pollard-kangaroo algorithms to speed up the enumeration. The downside of this approach is that without searching the whole interval we can never say with 100 % certainty that the key is not in the interval. However, in return we are able to speed up enumeration in an interval of size ℓ to $O(\sqrt{\ell})$ group operations or even to $O(\sqrt[3]{\ell})$ if we have the luxury of a precomputation table. We do have to note that even though we will call this process of searching the interval enumeration, it is a different kind than the enumeration in [17]. In that algorithm each key enumerated had to be checked for correctness against the encryption in an exhaustive-search manner. Using the kangaroo algorithms means that we search for a collision between group elements and only after this happens we can compute and double-check correctness against the public key of the cryptosystem attacked. This is much more sophisticated and much faster than the brute-force approach of having to check every key. The rank r of k now reflects the number of group operations required to find k after the end of the experimental session. It also means that we have only $O(\sqrt{\ell})$ ranks and they are dependent on the parameters used in the algorithm. To accurately reflect the uncertainty in this kind of enumeration, we introduce the following definition.

Definition 1. *Let the key $\hat{k}$ that we wish to find have rank $\hat{r}$. In an ϵ-enumeration we check keys in such a way that when we have enumerated up to rank r, then there is a $(1 - \epsilon)$ probability that $\hat{r} > r$.*

If we want to perform such an ϵ-enumeration we have to have a stopping criterion. This criterion dictates how many group operations we have to do in order to get the probability of having missed our actual key below the ϵ bound. We have the following theorem.

Theorem 1. *Assume that the private key $\hat{k}$ lies in the interval of size ℓ. Let the average step size of the kangaroos be $s = \beta\sqrt{\ell}$. Let the probability of hitting a* *distinguished point be* $\theta = c/\sqrt{\ell}$ *and assume the distinguished points are spread uniformly over the whole group. Lastly we assume that the hash function H and the step set in the improved Pollard-kangaroo algorithm of Sect. 2.3 is sufficiently random. Then for $x > \ell/(4s)$ the average probability of not finding $\hat{k}$ in $2x$ steps, i.e. x hops per kangaroo, of that algorithm is*

$$\epsilon(x) = e^{-\frac{x}{s}+\frac{\ell}{4s^2}} + \left(e^{\theta\left(\frac{\ell}{4s}+2-x\right)} - e^{2\theta-\frac{1}{s}\left(x-\frac{\ell}{4s}\right)}\right)/\left(s - se^{\left(\theta-\frac{1}{s}\right)}\right). \qquad (3)$$

Proof. Recall that in this algorithm we had 2 kangaroos placed in the interval and they alternate their jumps. In this proof we analyze the x steps of the back kangaroo and compute the average probability that it does not collide with the front kangaroo even though they were both placed in the same interval. First the back kangaroo needs to catch up to the front one. The number of steps to do this is on average $\ell/4s$. Given that the back kangaroo takes x steps we now have $y = x - \ell/(4s)$ steps left on average. To avoid a recorded collision in these remaining y steps we either have to avoid the trail of the front kangaroo, or hit it after i steps and avoid distinguished points for the next $y - i$ steps. We assumed the hash function H to be sufficiently random, so the average probability of avoiding the trail is $(1 - 1/s)$ for each step taken and the chance of missing a distinguished point is $(1 - \theta)$ in each step. Thus we have the average approximate probability of avoiding detected collisions as follows

$$\left(1 - \frac{1}{s}\right)^{x-\frac{\ell}{4s}} + \sum_{i=0}^{x-\frac{\ell}{4s}-1}\left(1 - \frac{1}{s}\right)^{i}\frac{1}{s}(1 - \theta)^{x-\frac{\ell}{4s}-i-2}.$$

We can approximate the second part of this equation as follows

$$\sum_{i=0}^{x-\frac{\ell}{4s}-1}\left(1 - \frac{1}{s}\right)^{i}\frac{1}{s}(1 - \theta)^{x-\frac{\ell}{4s}-i-2} \approx \frac{1}{s}\sum_{i=0}^{x-\frac{\ell}{4s}-1}e^{\frac{-i}{s}}e^{-\theta\left(x-\frac{\ell}{4s}-i-2\right)}$$

$$= \frac{e^{\theta\left(\frac{\ell}{4s}+2-x\right)}}{s}\sum_{i=0}^{x-\frac{\ell}{4s}-1}e^{\frac{-i}{s}}e^{\theta i}.$$

This in turn then evaluates to

$$\frac{e^{\theta\left(\frac{\ell}{4s}+2-x\right)}}{s}\sum_{i=0}^{x-\frac{\ell}{4s}-1}\left(e^{\theta-\frac{1}{s}}\right)^{i} = \frac{e^{\theta\left(\frac{\ell}{4s}+2-x\right)}}{s}\cdot\frac{1 - e^{\left(\theta-\frac{1}{s}\right)\left(x-\frac{\ell}{4s}\right)}}{1 - e^{\left(\theta-\frac{1}{s}\right)}}$$

$$= \frac{e^{\theta\left(\frac{\ell}{4s}+2-x\right)} - e^{2\theta-\frac{1}{s}\left(x-\frac{\ell}{4s}\right)}}{s - se^{\left(\theta-\frac{1}{s}\right)}}.$$

So indeed we have our average probability of

$$\epsilon(x) = \left(1 - \frac{1}{s}\right)^{x-\frac{\ell}{4s}} + \frac{e^{\theta\left(\frac{\ell}{4s}+2-x\right)} - e^{2\theta-\frac{1}{s}\left(x-\frac{\ell}{4s}\right)}}{s - se^{\left(\theta-\frac{1}{s}\right)}}$$

$$\approx e^{-\frac{x}{s}+\frac{\ell}{4s^2}} + \frac{e^{\theta\left(\frac{\ell}{4s}+2-x\right)} - e^{2\theta-\frac{1}{s}\left(x-\frac{\ell}{4s}\right)}}{s - se^{\left(\theta-\frac{1}{s}\right)}}. \qquad \square$$

Note that this equation is only valid for values of $x > \frac{\ell}{4s}$, otherwise $\epsilon(x) = 1$.

We now analyze the situation of using Pollard's kangaroo algorithm with a precomputation table. For this we make a hypothesis on the distribution of distinguished points and the number of points covered by each walk: Let the precomputation table $\mathcal{T}$ consist of the first found T different distinguished points $D_i = t_i P$. Let the average walk length be $w = \alpha\sqrt{\ell/T}$ and the average step size of the kangaroos be $s \approx \ell/(4w)$ such that the average distance of a walk is $\approx \ell/4$. Since the points in $\mathcal{T}$ are different their paths are disjoint. They cover on average Tw points. Assume that these points are uniformly distributed over $\{P, 2P, \ldots, \gamma \ell P\}$ for some value of γ. In Sect. 4 we will present experiments showing that $\gamma = \max\limits_{1 \leq i \leq T} t_i/\ell - \min\limits_{1 \leq i \leq T} t_i/\ell$ is a good fit.

Theorem 2. *Let $\hat{k}$ lie in an interval of size ℓ. Let the average walk length be $w = \alpha\sqrt{\ell/T}$ and the average step size of the kangaroos be $s \approx \ell/(4w)$. Under the hypothesis made above, $\mathcal{T}$ represents tW points distributed uniformly over $\{P, 2P, \ldots, \gamma \ell P\}$ for some value of γ. The average probability that the Pollard-kangaroo algorithm with precomputation (Sect. 2.4) does not find $\hat{k}$ in y independent walks of the algorithm is*

$$\epsilon(x) = e^{\frac{-\alpha^2 y}{\gamma}}. \tag{4}$$

Proof. Under the hypothesis the probability of the wild kangaroo hitting the trail of one of the table points' kangaroos is on average $(Tw)/(\gamma\ell) = \alpha^2/(\gamma w)$ at each step. Since the walk takes on average w steps the probability of avoiding a collision is

$$\left(1 - \alpha^2/(\gamma w)\right)^w \approx e^{\frac{-\alpha^2}{\gamma}}.$$

We assume independent walks, so we have that the probability that after y walks we have not found a collision is

$$\prod_{i=1}^{y} e^{\frac{-\alpha^2}{\gamma}} = e^{\frac{-\alpha^2 y}{\gamma}}.$$

which is the result we desired.   □

3.3   Further Considerations and Optimizations

Combining Intervals. If we have adjacent intervals in the enumeration tree we might combine these intervals to speed up the search. If they are of the same length then searching the intervals separately simply means searching twice as long. Combining two intervals in the kangaroo method reduces the search time by a factor $\sqrt{2}$. When we do this we do have to take the posterior probabilities of the intervals into account. If we simply combine all adjacent intervals in the enumeration tree and search them in the order of the subinterval with the highest posterior probability then it might happen that an interval ranked high separately is not searched because it is not part of some large combined interval. We therefore only combine intervals if they also have subsequent posterior probabilities. For the precomputation case of the algorithm we also have to take the availability of tables into account. We only combine intervals if we have a table and step set corresponding to that newly created interval length.

Restarts. We described the general kangaroo algorithm to have the kangaroos continue along their paths after finding a distinguished point. For the standard rho method [2] show the benefits of restarting walks after a distinguished point is found. If we do not use a precomputation table then doing restarts means redoing the initial phase of the two kangaroos catching up to each other and the error function will decrease at a slower rate. This is only advantageous if the kangaroos ended up in a loop they cannot get out. If we detect such a loop, the kangaroo(s) can be restarted. If $\ell \ll n$ the probability of ending in a loop is very small. On the other hand, we do not have the problem of the initial catching up phase. Therefore we restarted walks if they exceeded $20w$ steps. An advantage of using the improved Pollard-kangaroo algorithm without precomputation tables is that there is a probability of finding the solution of a DLP in an adjacent interval because the kangaroos naturally venture out in the direction of larger discrete logarithms. This is also an argument against doing restarts. Even though the current interval was chosen for the good reason of having the highest posterior probability among those not considered, yet, it is an added benefit that one might accidentally find a solution in another interval. If the tame kangaroo is started in interval I_1 of size ℓ, but the key was actually in adjacent interval I_2, then after a longer initial catch-up phase there is a probability of collisions. We could estimate this probability with an error function like we did for I_1 to reduce search time, but the longer the kangaroos jump the bigger the variance gets and the less accurate the error function is going to be. Therefore we do not advise to include this extra probability into the considerations.

Parallelization. There are two levels at which the ϵ-enumeration method can be parallelized: One level is the underlying kangaroo algorithm using distinguished points; the second level is dividing the intervals over the processors used, i.e., we could simply place one interval search on each processor, or we could have all processors search one of the intervals, or use a combination of the two. Using multiple processors for a single interval only makes sense if the interval is sufficiently large and many walks are needed (so rarely with precomputation) and if the posterior probability is significantly higher. If a lot of intervals have a similar probability it might be better to search them in parallel.

ϵ-Rank Estimation. Now that we have a definition of ϵ-enumeration we can easily extend it to estimating ranks of keys that we cannot ϵ-enumerate in feasible time. To do this we have to adapt the attack on the device using the key $\hat{k}$. When discarding keys of a too low probability from future templates we do store the subkey in the enumeration tree with their probabilities. They are however not included in new templates, so the corresponding branch of the enumeration tree will not grow any more. After finishing the measurement we can determine with the error function for each interval with a higher posterior probability than the one that contains $\hat{k}$ how many steps we would (on average) take in this interval. The sum of these quantities is then an estimated lower bound for the rank of $\hat{k}$. We can use a similar method to determine an estimated upper bound.

4   Experimental Results

This section presents representative examples of our implementations. We ran our experiments on a Dell Optiplex 980 using one core of an Intel Core i5 Processor 650 / 3.20 GHz. We re-used parts of the Bernstein/Lange kangaroo C++ code used for [1]. Our adaptations will be posted at http://www.scarecryptow.org/publications/sckangaroos. For ease of implementation we used the group $\mathbb{F}_p^*$ as was used in [1], which uses a "strong" 256-bit prime (strong meaning that $\frac{p-1}{2}$ is also prime) and a generator g, which is a large square modulo p. Although in the previous sections we focussed on elliptic curves, both those and $\mathbb{F}_p^*$ are cyclic groups and thus these results hold for both. We set the interval size to $\ell = 2^{48}$ and at each run took a random h in the interval for a new DLP.

For the experiments without precomputation we made use of distinguished points to find the collision, which were recorded in a vector table that was searched each time a new distinguished point was found. We chose the probability of landing in a distinguished point to be $2^{-19} = \frac{2^5}{\sqrt{\ell}}$ by defining a point as distinguished if the least-significant 19 bits in its representation were zero, i.e., if the value modulo $w = 2^{19}$ was zero. The step function selected the next step based on the value modulo 128, the 128 step sizes were taken randomly around $\sqrt{\ell}$.

Step Sets. The goal of this paper is not to find the optimal parameters for the kangaroo algorithm. The choice of step set is however relevant for usability of the error function of Eq. 3. As can be seen Eq. 3 only uses the mean of the step set and not its actual values, so it is possible to create one that will not adhere to the error function at all. Even if we choose the step set randomly it can contain dependencies and this makes the error function less accurate. We can see this in the top graph of Fig. 2.

We did 8192 experiments and saw that the error function in blue is a rather good approximation for the fraction of unsolved DLPs in red for the first 10 million steps of step set $\mathcal{S}_1$ of the wild kangaroo and from 25 million onward. In between these values we see some unexpected behavior. It might be that our step set contains some dependencies, e.g., it might be that the step set contains too many steps in a certain equivalence class; meaning that the probability of missing the trail is larger than $(1 - 1/s)$ per step. We were not able to visually identify what the problem was. By trying a different seed for the random step set we found $\mathcal{S}_2$ which behaved nicely according to our expectations as can be observed in the bottom graph of Fig. 2. For concrete attacks it is advisable to run a few tests to check the quality of the step function.

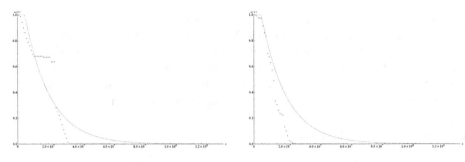

Fig. 2. The theoretic function $\epsilon(x)$ for the kangaroo method without precomputations and the experimental results using two random step sets $\mathcal{S}_1$ and $\mathcal{S}_2$ with $\beta \approx 1$. Top: $\beta = 0.978$. Bottom: $\beta = 0.971$

Combining Intervals. We were able to find similar results for intervals where we combined two adjacent intervals of length 2^{48} to one of size 2^{49}. We observed the same problem of good and bad step sets. With trying three step sets, we got a step set that had the error function as an upper bound for the experiments. These graphs are similar to the graphs before and therefore ommitted. They did confirm that by combining the intervals we can search twice the keyspace in approximately $\sqrt{2}$ times the steps.

Using Precomputation. We again searched for DLPs in an interval of length 2^{48}. Our 128 step sizes however were now uniformly chosen between 0 and $\ell/4w$ instead of around $\beta\sqrt{\ell}$ for some β. Each DLP $h = g^y$ was chosen randomly and each walk starting from it was randomized in the interval between $y - 2^{40}$ and $y + 2^{40}$. For the precomputation we used a table of size $N = T = \sqrt[3]{\ell} = 2^{16}$. We used the first T distinguished points found as table points and computed $\gamma = 1.923$ as $\max_{1 \leq i \leq T} t_i/\ell - \min_{1 \leq i \leq T} t_i/\ell$, for the T table elements of the form g^{t_i}. We used an average walklength of $w = 2^{15}$ such that $\alpha = 0.5$. Using 2097152 experiments we got the results on the top of Fig. 3. We see that the error function is a good upper bound for the experimental results. We continued with the same experiment for an interval of length $\ell = 2^{50}$. We used a table of $T = 104032 \approx \sqrt[3]{\ell}$ table points and found $\gamma = 1.853$. We used an average step set of $w = 2^{16}$ such that $\alpha \approx 0.630$. Using 2097152 experiments we got the results on the bottom of Fig. 3. We again see that the error function is a good approximation for the experiments.

Other parameters than α and γ can influence the performance of the algorithm. The error function does not reflect information on the step set other than its mean, nor on how often distinguished points were found but it relies on the hypothesis that the table covers about wT points and these are uniformly distributed over $\{P, 2P, \ldots, \gamma P\}$.

Considerations about the step set are even more relevant when preparing the precomputation table by making $N > T$ walks and selecting for T the T

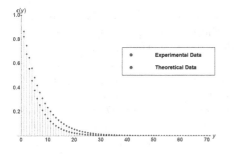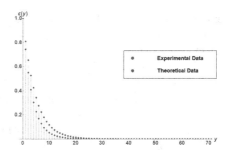

Fig. 3. The theoretic function $\epsilon(y)$ for the kangaroo method with precomputation and the experimental results using a step set with $s \approx \frac{\ell}{4w}$. Top: $\ell = 2^{48}$. Bottom: $\ell = 2^{50}$.

points with the largest number of ancestors (longest walks leading up to them, distinguished points found with multiplicity).

For the ϵ-enumeration we suggest to include a parameter σ in the exponent of the error function $\epsilon(y) = e^{\sigma \alpha^2 y / \gamma}$ that is determined experimentally. After determining the step set and table we can run the algorithm on different randomly chosen DLPs, much like we did in our experiments, and determine a value for σ. After this the error function is ready to be used in a security evaluation.

ϵ-Enumeration. The result is that according to our best found results we can ϵ-enumerate in an interval of length ℓ in the steps displayed in Table 1.

Table 1. Required group operations for ϵ-enumeration

ϵ	$1.0 \cdot 10^{-1}$	$1.0 \cdot 10^{-3}$	$1.0 \cdot 10^{-5}$	$1.0 \cdot 10^{-7}$	$1.0 \cdot 10^{-9}$
$N = T = 0, \sigma = 1$	$4.2 \cdot \sqrt{\ell}$	$10.8 \cdot \sqrt{\ell}$	$17.6 \cdot \sqrt{\ell}$	$24.3 \cdot \sqrt{\ell}$	$31.0 \cdot \sqrt{\ell}$
$N = T = \sqrt[3]{\ell}, \sigma = 1$	$18 \cdot \sqrt[3]{\ell}$	$54 \cdot \sqrt[3]{\ell}$	$89 \cdot \sqrt[3]{\ell}$	$124 \cdot \sqrt[3]{\ell}$	$160 \cdot \sqrt[3]{\ell}$
$N = T = \sqrt[3]{\ell}, \sigma = 1.12$	$16 \cdot \sqrt[3]{\ell}$	$48 \cdot \sqrt[3]{\ell}$	$79 \cdot \sqrt[3]{\ell}$	$111 \cdot \sqrt[3]{\ell}$	$142 \cdot \sqrt[3]{\ell}$
$N = 2T = 2 \cdot \sqrt[3]{\ell}, \sigma = 1$	$5 \cdot \sqrt[3]{\ell}$	$14 \cdot \sqrt[3]{\ell}$	$23 \cdot \sqrt[3]{\ell}$	$32 \cdot \sqrt[3]{\ell}$	$41 \cdot \sqrt[3]{\ell}$
$N = 2T = 2 \cdot \sqrt[3]{\ell}, \sigma = 1.28$	$4 \cdot \sqrt[3]{\ell}$	$11 \cdot \sqrt[3]{\ell}$	$18 \cdot \sqrt[3]{\ell}$	$25 \cdot \sqrt[3]{\ell}$	$32 \cdot \sqrt[3]{\ell}$
$N = 8T = 8 \cdot \sqrt[3]{\ell}, \sigma = 1$	$5 \cdot \sqrt[3]{\ell}$	$14 \cdot \sqrt[3]{\ell}$	$23 \cdot \sqrt[3]{\ell}$	$31 \cdot \sqrt[3]{\ell}$	$40 \cdot \sqrt[3]{\ell}$
$N = 8T = 8 \cdot \sqrt[3]{\ell}, \sigma = 1.40$	$4 \cdot \sqrt[3]{\ell}$	$10 \cdot \sqrt[3]{\ell}$	$16 \cdot \sqrt[3]{\ell}$	$23 \cdot \sqrt[3]{\ell}$	$29 \cdot \sqrt[3]{\ell}$

There are a couple of remarks to be made. We took only semi-optimized parameters. What we mean by this is that we did some experiments to find a reasonable step set, but as the purpose of our research was not to find the best parameters for Pollard-kangaroo algorithms, we did not fully optimize the step set. The results might thus be improved with optimal parameters. We observe that the higher N is relative to T, the fewer group operations are necessary to drop below the margin of error. Increasing the value of N improves the functionality of the algorithm more than the variables α and γ reflect. This is seen in the experimental values of σ. It increases as N increases. We also see that increasing N from T to $2T$ makes a big difference in the required group operations. The effect of increasing N even further to $8T$ does not have the same magnitude.

Although even small speed-ups are always nice, we also have to take the time it takes to create the tables into account. For $N = T$ it took us just over 9 billion group operations and under 19 min to create the table. This is equal to $1.4\sqrt[3]{\ell^2}$ multiplications. When we increased N to $2T$ it took about 50 minutes and $3.8\sqrt[3]{\ell^2}$ group operations. Finally, when we took N up to $8T$ it took approximately 9 hours and 2.5 million walks of in total $161544244922 \approx 37.6\sqrt[3]{\ell^2}$ group operations. This is doable for evaluation companies, even if they have to make a lot of tables, but doing many more might not have enough yield for the time it takes.

We see that we can determine how many group operations we have to do on average for different degrees of confidence. If we increase the confidence by a factor 100 the constant c in $c\sqrt{\ell}$ or $c\sqrt[3]{\ell}$ increases linearly. This means that if we use the $N = 8T$ precomputation table and we do $170\sqrt[3]{\ell}$ steps in an interval of length 2^{48} we can 2^{-128}-enumerate it in less than $2^{23.5}$ group operations. This is a massive improvement over brute-force enumerating all 2^{48} keys in an interval. The new ranking method that is induced by such an enumeration is also a much more accurate measure of the security of a device. Security evaluation labs could more confidently estimate how secure an implementation is.

5   Comparison and Conclusion

This is the first paper studying key enumeration and rank estimates for public key cryptosystems. Gopalakrishnan, Thériault, and Yao [8] studied key recovery for ECC if a side-channel attack only provided some bits of the key. In contrast to our model they assume that the known bits are absolutely correct and do not discuss the possibility that we might have partial information on a subkey. If we were to make an enumeration tree of such a result it would solely consist of sections I and III. Although their assumption makes enumeration a lot easier it is not very realistic. Often there are too few bits fully recovered to make searching the remaining key space feasible. Using not only fully recovered bits but also the partial information we can search an interval smartly and possibly recover the solution to the DLP where [8] could not. Finally, they do not consider enumeration and rank computation.

5.1   Comparison

One important assumption of the model covered in this paper so far is that we have not only information about specific subkeys, but also that these keys are adjacent and start from the most significant bits. This is true for the very common case of implementations using windowing methods (including signed and sliding) starting from the most significant bits. However, we can adjust our method to the scenarios considered in [8] as we will now discuss.

The first scenario in their paper is that contiguous bits of the key are revealed. These bits can be the most significant bits, the least significant bits or be somewhere in the middle. So far we considered the first case but our model can be easily adapted to the others:

- If the least significant bits are revealed, then our tree would get inverted. Searching section III would then require a slight adaptation of the algorithms used on it. Searching it with for instance Pollard kangaroo would require searching in equivalence classes instead of an interval. This adaptation means the probability of finding our solution 'accidentally' in a neighboring interval becomes zero. Creating tables in the Bernstein/Lange precomputation is still possible; we would shift each instance of the DLP to the same equivalence class.
- If bits somewhere in the middle are revealed the model would become more complicated. We would get a bow-shaped model with 2 sections II and III. There are 5 sections; the third contains known bits, on the second and fourth we have partial information and we have no information on the remaining sections. Enumerating through the sections III would become more complicated, though not impossible.

The second scenario [8] poses is that the information is not on any specific bits, but on the square-and-multiply chain. In this case the enumeration tree of Fig. 1 would become a binary tree. Searching the sections is the same as before.

We now present an application that is not mentioned in [8] but is realistic for an ECC scenario. A common speed up for scalar multiplication using the base point P is to include $P' = 2^m P$ in the system parameters, where the group order n is of length $2m$, and compute kP as $(k_0 + 2^m k_1)P = k_0 P + k_1 P'$. This halves the number of doublings required to compute kP (see Straus [15]) and reduces the overhead of dummy instructions introduced to perform one addition per doubling. When such an implementation is attacked, we will know the MSBs of k_0 and k_1 with much higher probability than their lower bits. This results in an enumeration tree of six sections: sections I and IV contain known bits, for sections II and V we have partial information, and we have little to no information on sections III and VI. Enumeration in such a structure is not straightforward with the methods we presented so far. If section III is small enough, we can brute-force it and use ϵ-enumeration in section VI, but realistically sections III and VI have equal size. To compute the key we have to adapt the kangaroo algorithms to simultaneously hop intervals and equivalence classes. This is achieved by algorithms for multidimensional DLPs which have been studied by Gaudry and Schost in [7]. The running time is $O(\sqrt{\ell_1 \ell_2})$ if the section III and VI are intervals of length ℓ_1 and ℓ_2. An improved version of this algorithm was presented by Galbraith and Ruprai in [6]. We have not devised an error function for these algorithms, but expect results similar to Theorems 1 and 2.

Lastly, it was pointed out to us by a kind anonymous reviewer that there are attacks on ECC where in fact the subkeys are independent (see e.g. [4,19,20]). In this case the rank estimation algorithm of [18] is applicable. The methods in this paper can then still be used as a comparison method; it is more realistic to compare dependent subkey attacks to independent ones with a ϵ-rank than the brute-force rank.

5.2 Conclusion

In summary, we showed that kangaroos can be very useful in making SCA on ECC more efficient:

- Once section III is below 80 bits and section II not too wide there is no point in letting the lab guy do further measurements since a standard PC can casually do the 2^{40} group operations to break the DLP.
- In cases where measurements cannot be pushed further by physical limitations (restricted number of measurements, limits on what templates can be measured) our improvements allow retrieving the key in some situations in which previous methods could not.
- Theoretical kangaroos can be used to estimate the rank of the key in white-box scenarios to determine whether a sufficiently motivated attacker could mount the attack to break the system and we present error functions to use in ϵ-enumeration.

References

1. Bernstein, D.J., Lange, T.: Computing small discrete logarithms faster. In: Galbraith, S., Nandi, M. (eds.) INDOCRYPT 2012. LNCS, vol. 7668, pp. 317–338. Springer, Heidelberg (2012)
2. Bernstein, D.J., Lange, T., Schwabe, P.: On the correct use of the negation map in the Pollard rho method. In: Catalano, D., Fazio, N., Gennaro, R., Nicolosi, A. (eds.) PKC 2011. LNCS, vol. 6571, pp. 128–146. Springer, Heidelberg (2011)
3. Chari, S., Rao, J.R., Rohatgi, P.: Template attacks. In: Kaliski, B.S., Koç, Ç.K., Paar, C. (eds.) CHES 2002. LNCS, vol. 2523, pp. 13–28. Springer, Heidelberg (2003)
4. Clavier, C., Feix, B., Gagnerot, G., Roussellet, M., Verneuil, V.: Horizontal correlation analysis on exponentiation. In: Soriano, M., Qing, S., López, J. (eds.) ICICS 2010. LNCS, vol. 6476, pp. 46–61. Springer, Heidelberg (2010)
5. Galbraith, S.D., Pollard, J.M., Ruprai, R.S.: Computing discrete logarithms in an interval. Math. Comput. **82**(282), 1181–1195 (2013)
6. Galbraith, S., Ruprai, R.S.: An improvement to the Gaudry-Schost algorithm for multidimensional discrete logarithm problems. In: Parker, M.G. (ed.) Cryptography and Coding 2009. LNCS, vol. 5921, pp. 368–382. Springer, Heidelberg (2009)
7. Gaudry, P., Schost, É.: A low-memory parallel version of Matsuo, Chao, and Tsujii's algorithm. In: Buell, D.A. (ed.) ANTS 2004. LNCS, vol. 3076, pp. 208–222. Springer, Heidelberg (2004)
8. Gopalakrishnan, K., Thériault, N., Yao, C.Z.: Solving discrete logarithms from partial knowledge of the key. In: Srinathan, K., Rangan, C.P., Yung, M. (eds.) Indocrypt 2007. LNCS, vol. 4859, pp. 224–237. Springer, Heidelberg (2007)
9. Hankerson, D., Menezes, A.J., Vanstone, S.: Guide to Elliptic Curve Cryptography. Springer-Verlag New York Inc., Secaucus (2003)

10. Pan, J., van Woudenberg, J.G.J., den Hartog, J.I., Witteman, M.F.: Improving DPA by peak distribution analysis. In: Biryukov, A., Gong, G., Stinson, D.R. (eds.) SAC 2010. LNCS, vol. 6544, pp. 241–261. Springer, Heidelberg (2011)
11. Pollard, J.M.: Monte Carlo methods for index computation (mod p). Math. Comput. **32**, 918–924 (1978)
12. Pollard, J.M.: Kangaroos, monopoly and discrete logarithms. J. Cryptol. **13**(4), 437–447 (2000)
13. Shanks, D.: Class number, a theory of factorization, and genera. In: Lewis, D.J. (ed.) 1969 Number Theory Institute. Proceedings of Symposia in Pure Mathematics, Providence, Rhode Island, vol. 20, pp. 415–440. American Mathematical Society (1971)
14. Stein, A., Teske, E.: The parallelized Pollard kangaroo method in real quadratic function fields. Math. Comput. **71**(238), 793–814 (2002)
15. Straus, E.G.: Addition chains of vectors (problem 5125). Am. Math. Mon. **70**, 806–808 (1964). http://cr.yp.to/bib/entries.html#1964/straus
16. van Oorschot, P.C., Wiener, M.J.: Parallel collision search with cryptanalytic applications. J. Cryptol. **12**(1), 1–28 (1999)
17. Veyrat-Charvillon, N., Gérard, B., Renauld, M., Standaert, F.-X.: An optimal key enumeration algorithm and its application to side-channel attacks. In: Knudsen, L.R., Wu, H. (eds.) SAC 2012. LNCS, vol. 7707, pp. 390–406. Springer, Heidelberg (2013)
18. Veyrat-Charvillon, N., Gérard, B., Standaert, F.-X.: Security evaluations beyond computing power. In: Johansson, T., Nguyen, P.Q. (eds.) EUROCRYPT 2013. LNCS, vol. 7881, pp. 126–141. Springer, Heidelberg (2013)
19. Walter, C.D.: Sliding windows succumbs to big mac attack. In: Koç, Ç.K., Naccache, D., Paar, C. (eds.) CHES 2001. LNCS, vol. 2162, pp. 286–299. Springer, Heidelberg (2001)
20. Witteman, M.F., van Woudenberg, J.G.J., Menarini, F.: Defeating RSA multiply-always and message blinding countermeasures. In: Kiayias, A. (ed.) CT-RSA 2011. LNCS, vol. 6558, pp. 77–88. Springer, Heidelberg (2011)

Combining Leakage-Resilient PRFs and Shuffling
Towards Bounded Security for Small Embedded Devices

Vincent Grosso[(✉)], Romain Poussier, François-Xavier Standaert, and Lubos Gaspar

ICTEAM/ELEN/Crypto Group, Université catholique de Louvain,
Louvain-la-Neuve, Belgium
vincent.grosso@uclouvain.be

Abstract. Combining countermeasures is usually assumed to be the best way to protect embedded devices against side-channel attacks. These combinations are at least expected to increase the number of measurements of successful attacks to some reasonable extent, and at best to guarantee a bounded time complexity independent of the number of measurements. This latter guarantee, only possible in the context of leakage-resilient constructions, was only reached either for stateful (pseudo-random generator) constructions, or large parallel implementations so far. In this paper, we describe a first proposal of stateless (pseudo-random function) construction, for which we have strong hints that security bounded implementations are reachable under the constraints of small embedded devices. Our proposal essentially combines the well-known shuffling countermeasure with a tweaked pseudo-random function introduced at CHES 2012. We first detail is performances. Then we analyze it against standard differential power analysis and discuss the different parameters influencing its security bounds. Finally, we put forward that its implementation in 8-bit microcontrollers can provide a better security vs. performance tradeoff than state-of-the art (combinations of) countermeasures.

1 Introduction

Securing block cipher implementations in small embedded devices is a challenging problem. Popular countermeasures include masking, shuffling or the insertion of random delays, for which state-of-the-art solutions can be found in [3,16,20]. In practice, such countermeasures are usually combined in order to reach high security levels – which raises the question of which combinations bring the best security vs. efficiency tradeoffs. For example, mixing masking with shuffling has been shown to be an effective solution [9,17], while mixing masking with random delays may be easier to cryptanalyze [5]. These type of combinations essentially aim at reducing the amount of information leakage per block cipher execution.

More recently, an orthogonal approach has attracted the attention of cryptographers, of which the goal is to limit the adversary's power by bounding its data complexity (i.e. number of plaintexts for which the leakage can be observed) or number of measurements. This approach is usually referred to as *re-keying* [11] or

© Springer International Publishing Switzerland 2015
M. Joye and A. Moradi (Eds.): CARDIS 2014, LNCS 8968, pp. 122–136, 2015.
DOI: 10.1007/978-3-319-16763-3_8

leakage-resilient cryptography [6] in the literature. From an application point-of-view, the most interesting primitives are stateless ones – Pseudo-Random Functions (PRFs), typically – since they provide essentially the same functionalities as block ciphers (so are useful, e.g. for encryption, authentication, hashing). In this context, the standard construction is the tree-based one from Goldreich, Goldwasser and Micali (GGM) [8]. Its leakage-resilience has first been analyzed under a random-oracle based assumption in [18]. A modified construction exploiting an "alternating structure" has then been proven secure in the standard model by Dodis and Pietrzak [4]. Faust et al. next succeeded to get rid of this alternating structure and to prove the GGM construction in the standard model, at the cost of some additional randomness requirements. Eventually, Yu Yu and Standaert showed how to relax these randomness requirements in minicrypt [21], and Abdalla et al. studied how to improve the efficiency of these constructions by exploiting a skip-list data structure [1]. All these previous results were obtained for non-adaptive leakage functions (i.e. pre-determined by the hardware).

In practice, the hope of leakage-resilient constructions is to obtain security-bounded implementations, in the sense that the time complexity of the best side-channel attack is lower-bounded, independent of the number of measurements performed by the adversary. Unfortunately, a recent report from Belaïd puts forward that this hope is not reached with the previously listed leakage-resilient PRFs[1]. This work further shows that the combination of leakage-resilient PRFs with masking does not lead to any significant security improvements. In this context, the only positive (heuristic) result of security bounded implementation was obtained for the tweaked PRF construction proposed by Medwed et al. at CHES 2012 [15], that takes advantage of hardware parallelism and carefully chosen plaintexts. The main idea of this tweak is to exploit plaintexts of the shape $p = (b, b, \ldots, b)$, i.e. where all the bytes entering the key additions are the same. Intuitively, if these bytes are manipulated in parallel, they create a "key-dependent algorithmic noise" that is hard to exploit by side-channel adversaries and may (under certain conditions) lead to security-bounded implementations. However, this positive result only applied to hardware implementations so far.

In this paper, we investigates whether more positive results can be obtained for software implementations, by combining the CHES 2012 tweaked PRF with the shuffling countermeasure. We next denote this proposal as the Shuffled PRF (SPRF) construction. The main motivation behind such a proposal is that key-dependent algorithmic noise can be produced by the parallel manipulation of carefully chosen plaintexts $p = (b, b, \ldots, b)$. Hence, since the impact of a shuffling is (under certain conditions) to emulate the noise of large parallel implementations within the constraints of small embedded devices, this combination could be effective. For this purpose, we first describe a framework allowing us to analyze the security of SPRF implementations against standard DPA attacks [13], and put forward that it depends on two main parameters: first, the amount of

---

[1] In short, because these (stateless) PRF constructions can only bound the adversary's data complexity, by contrast with (stateful) leakage-resilient Pseudo-Random number Generators (PRGs) that bound the adversary's number of measurements.

direct leakage on the S-box computations and permutation used for shuffling; second, the amount of *indirect leakage*, essentially due to the fact that the power consumed to compute different S-boxes may depend on the resource used and execution time. We then show that one type of indirect leakages (namely, different resources leaking differently at the same time sample) is beneficial to the adversary, while the other type (namely, the same resource leaking differently at different time samples) is detrimental. This suggests simple guidelines for cryptographic hardware designers willing to improve the security of SPRFs. We finally apply our results to the challenging case-study of an 8-bit microcontroller, and show that security-bounded implementations can be obtained under actual (direct and indirect) leakages. To the best of our knowledge, it is the first time that such a positive result is obtained for a small embedded device. Furthermore, and compared to the hardware construction in [15], our software scheme has the additional advantage that all operations (i.e. the key additions and S-boxes, but also MixColumns and the key scheduling) are shuffled with a 16-permutation. This mitigates possible weaknesses due to adversaries targeting one out of four MixColumns, hence reducing the key-dependent algorithmic noise.

2 Background

2.1 Leakage-Resilient PRFs

We first describe the GGM construction evaluated on an input $x \in \{0,1\}^n$ under a key $k \in \{0,1\}^n$, next denoted $\mathsf{F}_k(x)$. It requires n stages and $2n$ random plaintexts p_b^i, with $b \in \{0,1\}$ and $1 \le i \le n$. Each stage consists in a block cipher execution, where an intermediate key k^i is computed from the previous intermediate key k^{i-1} and the plaintext $p_{x(i)}^i$ (i.e. $k^i = \mathsf{E}_{k^{i-1}}\big(p_{x(i)}^i\big)$, with $x(i)$ the ith bit of x, k^0 initialized to k and the output $\mathsf{F}_k(x)$ set to k^n. Taking AES as an example, this implies computing $n = 128$ block cipher executions to produce a single output. The tweak proposed in [15] is to use more (namely, 256) plaintexts of a specific shape per stage, leading to a total of 16 stages (plus one output whitening). For this purpose, the input is first split in 16 bytes denoted as $x = (x_1, x_2, \ldots, x_{16})$. Next and as illustrated in Fig. 1, each stage updates the intermediate key as $k^{i+1} = \mathsf{E}_{k^i}(p_{x_{i+1}})$, with $1 < i \le 16$ and plaintexts of a specific shape $p_{x_i} = (x_i, x_i, \ldots, x_i)$. Eventually, the output is defined as $\mathsf{F}_k(x) = \mathsf{E}_{k^{16}}(p)$ (with p an additional plaintext). Intuitively, the combination of a parallel implementation with the carefully selected plaintexts creates key-dependent algorithmic noise, and the output whitening prevents attacks exploiting the ciphertext (given that the block cipher is secure against SPA).

2.2 Shuffled AES Implementation

Shuffling is a countermeasure against side-channel attacks that aims to randomize the execution of an algorithm over time. It has been applied to the AES in [9,20]. The main parameter influencing its security is the number of permutations randomizing each operation. Taking the simple example of the AES

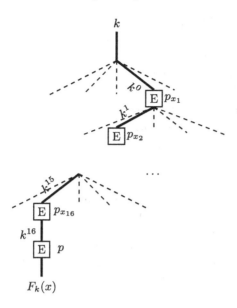

Fig. 1. Efficient leakage-resilient PRF.

S-boxes, one can choose between executing them according to a random index (among 16 possible ones) that is just incremented, or according to a random permutation (among 16! possible ones). It has been shown in [20] that the first solution (although cheaper) may lead to very efficient attacks. In particular, an implementation protected with such a Random Start Index (RDI) may be as weak as an unprotected one for low noise levels. As a result, our following investigations will only consider shuffling based on a random permutation.

Besides the generation of a permutation vector (that is common to all solutions), different alternatives exist to implement a shuffled AES. The straightforward method requires an indirect indexing of the operands. That is, a counter is used to index a permutation vector, and the result is used to index the operand vector. Thus, instead of operating on registers directly, two RAM accesses are required for each (read or write) access to operands. This naturally leads to quite large cycle counts. A more efficient solution proposed at ASIACRYPT 2012 is to randomize the execution path. For this implementation, the assembly code of every transform is split into 16 independent blocks of instructions. Each of these 16 blocks is augmented with a label. This allows identifying its address in ROM. Furthermore, every transform is associated with an array of 17 16-bit words, where the first 16 words hold the addresses of the 16 blocks, and the 17th holds the address of the return instruction. During the execution of the cipher, the addresses are first re-ordered according to a previously generated permutation. Then, whenever entering a transform, a pointer is set to the beginning of the array in order to execute its 16 blocks of instructions in random order.

Note that the implementations with double indexing and randomized execution path from [20] that we re-use in the following paid attention to shuffle *all* the

Table 1. SPRF performances compared to masking [16].

Implementation	Cycles count $\times 10^3$
First-order masking	129
Second-order masking	271
Third-order masking	470
SPRF (double indexing)	788
SPRF (rand. exec. path)	252

AES operations with a 16-permutation. For this purpose, MixColumns is implemented in sets of 16 independent instructions based on xtime operations and three dummy key schedulings are interleaved with the real one (since the AES key scheduling only has four independent operations). Based on these choices, the cycle count of a SPRF implementation in an Atmel AVR micro-controller is given in Table 1, and compared with (1st-, 2nd- and 3rd-order) masking.

3   Evaluation Framework

In order to analyze the security of SPRF implementations, we will use the standard DPA attacks defined in [13]. Furthermore, as our goal is to approach worst-case evaluations, we will consider the profiled setting of template attacks [2], and quantify their complexity with the security graphs described in [19].

Since the SPRF construction essentially relies on a shuffled AES design, the main challenge for our following investigations is to efficiently exploit the leakages of such implementations. In particular, and as previously discussed in [20] this requires to combine information obtained from the permuted operations in a meaningful way. As usual in side-channel attacks, we will target the first-round S-boxes and consider different (more or less ideal) models for this purpose.

Starting with the simplest situation, we can assume that all the S-boxes leak in the same manner (as in [15]), e.g. according to a Hamming weight function. This provides the adversary with 16-element vectors defined as:

$$\mathbf{L_u} = [\mathsf{HW}(\mathsf{S}(x_0 \oplus k_0)) + N_0, \ldots, \mathsf{HW}(\mathsf{S}(x_{15} \oplus k_{15})) + N_{15}],$$

in the unprotected case, with N_i a Gaussian-distributed random noise with variance σ_n^2. Moving to a shuffled implementation, the vector becomes:

$$\mathbf{L_s} = [\mathsf{HW}(\mathsf{S}(x_{\mathsf{p}(0)} \oplus k_{\mathsf{p}(0)})) + N_0, \ldots, \mathsf{HW}(\mathsf{S}(x_{\mathsf{p}(15)} \oplus k_{\mathsf{p}(15)})) + N_{15}],$$

with p the permutation used in the shuffling. Eventually, the SPRF construction will additionally force the same single value for all bytes, that is:

$$\mathbf{L_{\mathrm{sprf}}} = [\mathsf{HW}(\mathsf{S}(x \oplus k_{\mathsf{p}(0)})) + N_0, \ldots, \mathsf{HW}(\mathsf{S}(x \oplus k_{\mathsf{p}(15)})) + N_{15}].$$

In this context, the standard DPA adversary essentially requires a leakage model for the key byte s she targets, that can be written as:

$$\Pr[\mathbf{L} = 1|K_s = k] = \sum_t \frac{\mathsf{f}(t, s, \mathbf{l}')}{\sum_{t'} \mathsf{f}(t', s, \mathbf{l}')} \Pr[L_t = l_t|K_s = k],$$

where t is the time instant where an S-box is executed, $\mathbf{l}'$ is an optional vector containing information on the permutation p, L_t is an element of the leakage vector $\mathbf{L}$, and the function f indicates how the adversary deals with the permuted operations. In the (ideal) case where only the vector $\mathbf{L}_{\mathrm{sprf}}$ would be available, the only possibility is to perform a direct template attack assuming a uniform prior for the permutation, i.e. $\mathsf{f}(t, s, \mathbf{l}') = 1/16$. Next, and based on a leakage model $\Pr[\mathbf{L}|K_s]$, the template adversary combines the leakage vectors corresponding to q different inputs for each candidate k_s using Bayes' law as follows:

$$p_{k_s} = \prod_{j=1}^{q} \Pr[k_s|\mathbf{L}^{(j)}, p^{(j)}].$$

For each target implementation in the next section we will repeat 100 experiments and for each value q in these experiments, use the rank estimation in [19] to evaluate the time complexity needed to recover the full AES master key. Eventually, we will build security graphs, where the attack probability of success is provided in function of a time complexity and number of measurements.

Incorporating indirect leakages. The execution of 16 S-boxes is illustrated in Fig. 2 for unprotected and shuffled S-boxes. In this respect, one important observation made in [20] is the existence of *indirect leakages* on the permutation p, due to the fact that the different physical resources used to execute the S-boxes may leak according to different models. In order to capture this possibility in our simulations, we will define a family of linear leakage functions as:

$$\mathsf{L}_r(x) = \sum_{i=0}^{7} a_r^i \cdot x(i),$$

where the a_r^i are random coefficient within some interval (see next). These different leakage functions are directly reflected in the leakage vector as follows:

$$\mathbf{L}_{\mathrm{sprf}}^{\mathrm{r}} = [\mathsf{L}_{\mathsf{p}(0)}(\mathsf{S}(x \oplus k_{\mathsf{p}(0)})) + N_0, \ldots, \mathsf{L}_{\mathsf{p}(15)}(\mathsf{S}(x \oplus k_{\mathsf{p}(15)})) + N_{15}].$$

Intuitively, such resource-based indirect leakages break the assumption that all the S-boxes leak similarly, and help the adversary to know at which time instant a target S-box is executed. How strong are indirect leakages depends on the correlation between the models for different resources. In [15], FPGA experiments suggest that this correlation can rate between strong (i.e. 0.99 for S-boxes implemented in RAM) and weaker (i.e. 0.68 for combinatorial S-boxes).

Interestingly, we will show in the following that for SPRFs, the detrimental effect of leakage functions depending on the resource used is moderated by the

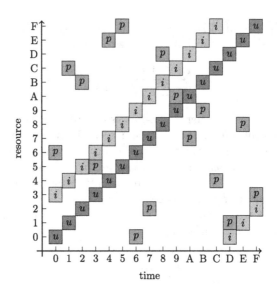

Fig. 2. S-boxes execution paths: unprotected device (u boxes, blue), shuffling with random start index (i boxes, green), shuffling with randomized permutation (p boxes, red) (Color figure online).

fact that these functions may also depend on the time instant when they are executed (e.g. because of the pipeline state of a software implementation). We incorporate this possibility in our simulations with the following definition:

$$\mathsf{L}_{r,t}(x) = \sum_{i=0}^{7} a_{r,t}^i \cdot x(i),$$

which directly leads to the leakage vectors of the form:

$$\mathbf{L}_{\mathrm{sprf}}^{r+t} = [\mathsf{L}_{\mathsf{p}(0),0}(\mathsf{S}(x \oplus k_{\mathsf{p}(0)})) + N_0, \ldots, \mathsf{L}_{\mathsf{p}(15),15}(\mathsf{S}(x \oplus k_{\mathsf{p}(15)})) + N_{15}].$$

Incorporating direct leakages. Quite naturally, indirect leakages are not the only information one can obtain about the permutation used for shuffling. If this permutation is generated on-chip, an informed adversary could also take advantage of a direct permutation leakage vector. In this context, the fact that the leakages functions depends on the resource used or time of execution has no impact on security. So we illustrate it with a Hamming weight function:

$$\mathbf{L}' = [\mathsf{HW}(\mathsf{p}(0)) + N_0, \ldots, \mathsf{HW}(\mathsf{p}(15)) + N_{15}].$$

Note however that direct permutation leakages can be avoided in certain cases, e.g. by randomizing the program memory as can be achieved (assuming a secure precomputation phase) within the recent FRAM technology [10].

4   Simulated Experiments

Simulated experiments are convenient tools to evaluate implementations in various (more or less realistic) settings and to test the impact of different parameters on their security level. In the following, the first parameter we will play with is the amount of noise in the leakage vectors defined in the previous section. It is characterized by the variance of the noise variables N_i. In order to make its reading more intuitive, we will relate this noise level with the Signal-to-Noise Ratio (SNR), defined as the quotient between the variance of the mean leakage traces (aka signal) and the noise variance [12]. For Hamming weight leakages on 8-bit values, this signal equals 2 and we considered two noise levels for illustration: a weak one corresponding to $\sigma_n^2 = 0.1$, SNR= 20 and a stronger one corresponding to $\sigma_n^2 = 10$, SNR= 0.2. Based on these parameters, we first study the ideal case with no direct permutation leakage and all S-boxes leaking identically.

4.1   Ideal setting (identical S-box leakages, no direct perm. leakage)

In this case, the adversary is only provided with the leakage vector $\mathbf{L}_{\mathrm{sprf}}$ and the only attack she can mount is a template one with uniform prior. As expected, the construction is security-bounded. That is, after a transient period, the template attack's time complexity saturates and becomes independent of the number of measurements. The impact of the noise parameter is clearly exhibited on Fig. 3, where a higher noise level (i.e. 10 vs. 0.1) ensures a higher security bound (i.e. 2^{85} vs. 2^{60}) that is also reached for larger number of measurements (i.e. 1000 vs. 100). Note that these results even improve the ones of Medwed et al. [15] for hardware implementations, since a higher noise only implied a later saturation of the bound in this case (i.e. had no impact on the value of the bound).

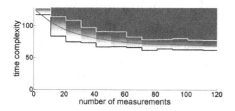 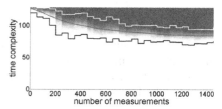

Fig. 3. Template attacks with uniform prior in the ideal scenario where all S-boxes leak identically. Left: low noise level ($\sigma^2 = 0.1$). Right: high noise level ($\sigma^2 = 10$).

4.2   Adding Indirect Resource-Based Leakages

We now move towards a more realistic scenario with indirect leakages due to the use of different resources in the implementation, helping the adversary to distinguish between the different S-boxes. That is, she can use the leakage vector $\mathbf{L}_{\mathrm{sprf}}^{\mathrm{r}}$. Note that in this case, the only possibility remains to perform a template attack with uniform prior. But the probabilities $\Pr[L_t = l_t | K_s = k]$ now depend on the byte index $s = \mathsf{p}(t)$. This indirect information is directly obtained during profiling, so the attack methodology remains identical. As a result, the main additional parameter is the "similarity" of the leakage functions $\mathsf{L}_r(.)$ for different r's. For illustration, we will consider a high (average) correlation (of $\rho_r = 0.99$) and a smaller one (of $\rho_r = 0.75$). We picked up the leakage functions (more precisely, their coefficients a_r^i) randomly for our experiments, under the additional constraint that the signal was constant and set to 2, in order for the noise levels to have a similar meaning as in our previous Hamming weight based simulations. The results in Fig. 4 clearly exhibit the weaknesses of the simulated SPRF implementations when the noise level is low and S-box leakages differ too significantly (e.g. for $\rho_r = 0.75$ in the left part of the figure) – they are not security-bounded anymore. Additional simulations performed at the higher noise level ($\sigma_n^2 = 10$) are provided in Appendix A, Fig. 12, and suggest that increasing the noise level is a simple way to preserve a security bound.

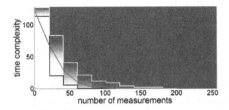 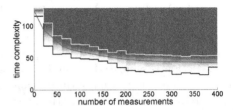

Fig. 4. Template attacks with uniform prior and indirect resource-based leakages, in the low noise scenario (i.e. $\sigma_n^2 = 0.1$). Left: $\rho_r = 0.75$. Right: $\rho_r = 0.99$.

4.3 Mitigating Resource-Based Leakages with Time-Based Ones

We now consider the possibility to reduce the previous indirect information by making the leakage functions not only dependent on the resource used, but also on the time instant when they are executed. Intuitively, such dependencies are expected to make the exploitation of resource-based indirect leakages more difficult, by introducing some additional confusion between them due to the (useless for the adversary) time dependencies. In order to illustrate their impact, we stick with the most challenging scenario in the previous subsection, with low noise ($\sigma_n^2 = 0.1$) and low similarity between the resources $\rho_r = 0.75$. We additionally consider weak and strong time-dependencies (with $\rho_t = 0.99$ and $\rho_t = 0.75$ for the leakage functions $\mathsf{L}_{r,t}(.)$, respectively). As illustrated in Fig. 5, these time-dependencies indeed provide an efficient alternative way to reach security-bounded SPRF implementations, with lower noise levels (the same figure is provided for the high noise level in Appendix A, Fig. 13).

Note that in this setting, the adversary has to estimate 16×16 templates, each of them corresponding to 256 intermediate values, which is a quite time-consuming task. Simplifying this profiling can result in a loss of informations.

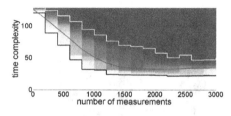
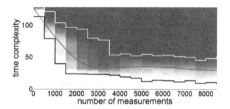

Fig. 5. Template attacks with uniform prior and indirect time + resource-based leakages ($\rho_r = 0.75$), in the low noise scenario (i.e. $\sigma_n^2 = 0.1$). Left: $\rho_t = 0.99$. Right: $\rho_t = 0.75$.

4.4 Direct Permutation Leakage

Eventually and for completeness, we add the direct permutation leakage vector and consider an adversary who can exploit $\mathbf{L}_{\mathrm{sprf}}^{\mathrm{r+t}}$ and $\mathbf{L}'$. This context has been investigated in [20]: it requires an adversary performing a template attack with non-uniform prior and considers $f(t, s, l') = \Pr[L_t' = l_t' | K_t = K_t]$, where K_t is the part of the master key that is manipulated at time instant t. As in this previous work, we see that its impact on security is limited when the shuffling is based on random permutations – yet, they allow to converge faster towards the bound.

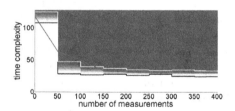
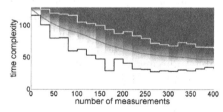

Fig. 6. Template attacks with direct and indirect (time + resource-based) leakages ($\rho_r = 0.75$), in the low noise scenario (i.e. $\sigma_n^2 = 0.1$). Left: $\rho_t = 0.99$. Right: $\rho_t = 0.75$.

5 Practical Experiments

The previous section suggests that SPRF implementations are promising candidates for designing security-bounded implementations in low-cost devices. It further puts forward that designers have two main parameters to increase their security level: the noise (as usual) and the time- vs. resource-based indirect leakages. In the latter case, we have strong incentive to design shuffled operations that only slightly depend on the resource used, and more significantly on their execution time. It naturally raises the question whether such designs exist in practice. In this respect, an interesting reference is the work on collision attacks in [7]: it shows that different implementations of the AES (e.g. always re-using

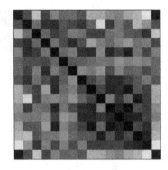 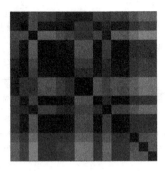

Fig. 7. Correlation between resources. Left: rand. exec. path. Right: double indexing.

the same registers or not) make the leakage models corresponding to different operations more or less similar (hence, collision attacks more or less realistic). We now provide an experimental case study based on an implementation of the SPRF construction in an Atmel AVR microcontroller. We first investigate the time- and resource-based dependencies in a shuffled AES implemented with double indexing and randomized execution path, then exhibit security evaluations based on these concrete values, and finally discuss scopes for further research.

In order to characterize the time- and resource-dependencies of the leakage models in our target AVR implementation, we build accurate templates for each S-box and time instant. As previously mentioned, this implies computing 16×16 sets of 256 templates – for each of them, we used 50,000 traces. Unfortunately, we rapidly found out that, both for the randomized execution path and the double indexing implementations, the time dependencies were small (i.e. with average values of $\hat{\rho}_t \approx 0.99$). By contrast, we could observe the quite strong resource-dependencies illustrated in Fig. 7. Interestingly, we also noticed significant differences between the two approaches to shuffling. Namely, the double indexing implementation exhibits larger average values of $\hat{\rho}_r \approx 0.86$, compared to $\hat{\rho}_r \approx 0.5$ for the randomized execution path one. This intuitively matches the expectations for these two designs, since the first one is based on the repeated exploitation of a single register, while the randomized execution path inherently requires traveling through the different resources of the target device. In view of

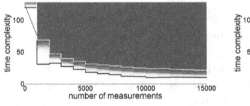 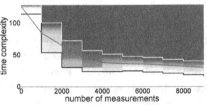

Fig. 8. Template attacks against the randomized execution path implementation ($\hat{\rho}_r = 0.5$, $\hat{\rho}_t = 0.99$, SNR = 2). Left: with direct leakages. Right: without direct leakages.

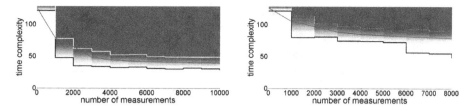

Fig. 9. Template attacks against the double indexing implementation ($\hat{\rho}_r = 0.86$, $\hat{\rho}_t = 0.84$, SNR = 2). Left: with direct leakages. Right: without direct leakages.

the performances listed in Table 1, this leads to a clear security vs. performance tradeoff.

We then launched experiments against these two implementations (with and without exploiting direct permutation leakages). In order to exhibit the impact of indirect leakages, we first analyzed an intermediate scenario, where the template mean values follow exactly the patterns of our target device, but we arranged the noise levels of all the leakage samples so that their SNR was fixed to a constant value. As expected and illustrated in Figs. 8 and 9, the implementation based on double indexing allows a better security bound in this case.

We then considered the leakage samples with their actual noise level, as measured experimentally. It turned out (see Figs. 10 and 11) that for the exploited samples, the SNR of the double indexing implementation was larger, hence canceling its advantage over the randomized execution path implementation. The exact reason of this observation is hard to state with confidence (we assume the additional memory manipulation of intermediate values in the double indexing implementation may be in cause). But this last experiment confirms the subtle dependencies between our two parameters on the concrete security level of an implementation. Since the leakage models are admittedly hard to control in cryptographic devices, this suggests that ensuring a large enough noise level may be the most reliable way to ensure large enough security levels in practice.

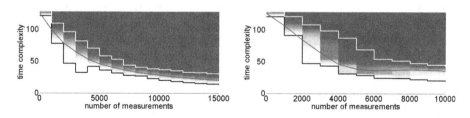

Fig. 10. Template attacks against the rand. execution path implementation ($\hat{\rho}_r = 0.5$, $\hat{\rho}_t = 0.99$, variable SNR). Left: with direct leakages. Right: without direct leakages.

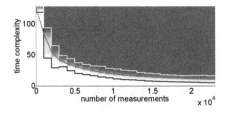 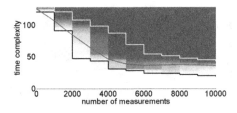

Fig. 11. Template attacks against the double indexing implementation ($\hat{\rho}_r = 0.86$, $\hat{\rho}_t = 0.84$, variable SNR). Left: with direct leakages. Right: without direct leakages.

Discussion. The previous results are worth a couple of words of interpretation as we now detail. First, from a pragmatic complexity point-of-view, the values of the security bounds obtained may not be sufficient (as the enumeration of up to 2^{50} keys is reachable by determined adversaries and improved attacks and measurement strategies can probably be deployed). Yet, the very fact of being security-bounded is already a significant improvement compared to most state-of-the-art countermeasures (e.g. the combination of masking and shuffling). Combined with the simulated results in the previous section, showing that it is possible to improve these bounds with higher noise or less informative indirect leakages, we believe this section confirms that SPRFs lead to an interesting family of protected implementations, that are certainly worth further investigation. In particular, we conjecture that combining it with a commercial security chip (including some hardware countermeasures) could already lead to much better concrete results. Furthermore, the best exploitation of time-dependent resource leakages is a nice research scope as well. In this respect, it is worth mentioning that the constructive investigation of the similarities between leakage models as we envision here is different (more demanding) than the destructive one in collisions attacks. That is, while a single sample showing good similarity is enough for these attacks to succeed, we need to guarantee that all of them are similar (for resource-based indirect leakages) or different (for time-based indirect leakages) – which also raises interesting characterization challenges. Eventually, and as for the previous (hardware) construction of CHES 2012, we recall that our current security analyses are based on first-round leakages. While we believe this is a natural first step for understanding these constructions, investigating whether (more computationally intensive) attacks against the inner block cipher rounds could be more damaging remains an important research topic.

Acknowledgements. F.-X. Standaert is a research associate of the Belgian Fund for Scientific Research (FNRS-F.R.S.). This work has been funded in parts by the European Commission through the ERC project 280141 (CRASH).

A   Additional Figures

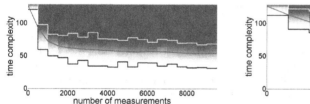
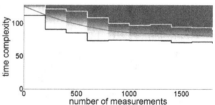

Fig. 12. Template attacks with uniform prior and indirect resource-based leakages, in the high noise scenario (i.e. $\sigma_n^2 = 10$). Left: $\rho_r = 0.75$. Right: $\rho_r = 0.99$.

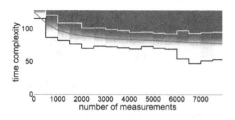
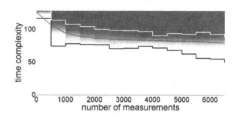

Fig. 13. Template attacks with uniform prior and indirect time+resource-based leakages ($\rho_r = 0.75$), in the high noise scenario (i.e. $\sigma_n^2 = 10$). Left: $\rho_t = 0.99$. Right: $\rho_t = 0.75$.

References

1. Abdalla, M., Belaïd, S., Fouque, P.-A.: Leakage-resilient symmetric encryption via re-keying. In: Bertoni, G., Coron, J.-S. (eds.) CHES 2013. LNCS, vol. 8086, pp. 471–488. Springer, Heidelberg (2013)
2. Chari, S., Rao, J.R., Rohatgi, P.: Template attacks. In: Kaliski Jr., B.S., Koç, Ç.K., Paar, C. (eds.) CHES 2002. LNCS, vol. 2523, pp. 13–28. Springer, Heidelberg (2003)
3. Coron, J.-S., Kizhvatov, I.: Analysis and improvement of the random delay countermeasure of CHES 2009. In: Mangard, S., Standaert, F.-X. (eds.) [14], pp. 95–109
4. Dodis, Y., Pietrzak, K.: Leakage-resilient pseudorandom functions and side-channel attacks on feistel networks. In: Rabin, T. (ed.) CRYPTO 2010. LNCS, vol. 6223, pp. 21–40. Springer, Heidelberg (2010)
5. Durvaux, F., Renauld, M., Standaert, F.-X., van Oldeneel tot Oldenzeel, L., Veyrat-Charvillon, N.: Efficient removal of random delays from embedded software implementations using hidden markov models. In: Mangard, S. (ed.) CARDIS 2012. LNCS, vol. 7771, pp. 123–140. Springer, Heidelberg (2013)

6. Dziembowski, S., Pietrzak, K.: Leakage-resilient cryptography. In: FOCS, pp. 293–302. IEEE Computer Society (2008)
7. Gérard, B., Standaert, F.-X.: Unified and optimized linear collision attacks and their application in a non-profiled setting: extended version. J. Cryptographic Eng. **3**(1), 45–58 (2013)
8. Goldreich, O., Goldwasser, S., Micali, S.: How to construct random functions (extended abstract). In: FOCS, pp. 464–479. IEEE Computer Society (1984)
9. Herbst, C., Oswald, E., Mangard, S.: An AES smart card implementation resistant to power analysis attacks. In: Zhou, J., Yung, M., Bao, F. (eds.) ACNS 2006. LNCS, vol. 3989, pp. 239–252. Springer, Heidelberg (2006)
10. Kerckhof, S., Standaert, F.-X., Peeters, E.: From new technologies to new solutions exploiting FRAM memories to enhance physical security. In: Francillon, A., Rohatgi, P. (eds.) CARDIS 2013. LNCS, vol. 8419, pp. 16–30. Springer, Heidelberg (2014)
11. Kocher, P.C.: Leak resistant cryptographic indexed key update. US Patent 6539092
12. Mangard, S.: Hardware countermeasures against DPA – a statistical analysis of their effectiveness. In: Okamoto, T. (ed.) CT-RSA 2004. LNCS, vol. 2964, pp. 222–235. Springer, Heidelberg (2004)
13. Mangard, S., Oswald, E., Standaert, F.-X.: One for all - all for one: unifying standard differential power analysis attacks. IET Inf. Secur. **5**(2), 100–110 (2011)
14. Mangard, S., Standaert, F.-X. (eds.): CHES 2010. LNCS, vol. 6225. Springer, Heidelberg (2010)
15. Medwed, M., Standaert, F.-X., Joux, A.: Towards super-exponential side-channel security with efficient leakage-resilient PRFs. In: Prouff, E., Schaumont, P. (eds.) CHES 2012. LNCS, vol. 7428, pp. 193–212. Springer, Heidelberg (2012)
16. Rivain, M., Prouff, E.: Provably secure higher-order masking of AES. In: Mangard, S., Standaert, F.-X. (eds.) [14], pp. 413–427
17. Rivain, M., Prouff, E., Doget, J.: Higher-order masking and shuffling for software implementations of block ciphers. In: Clavier, C., Gaj, K. (eds.) CHES 2009. LNCS, vol. 5747, pp. 171–188. Springer, Heidelberg (2009)
18. Standaert, F.-X., Pereira, O., Yu, Y., Quisquater, J.-J., Yung, M., Oswald, E.: Leakage resilient cryptography in practice. In: Sadeghi, A.-R., Naccache, D. (eds.) Towards Hardware-Intrinsic Security, Information Security and Cryptography, pp. 99–134. Springer, Heidelberg (2010)
19. Veyrat-Charvillon, N., Gérard, B., Standaert, F.-X.: Security evaluations beyond computing power. In: Johansson, T., Nguyen, P.Q. (eds.) EUROCRYPT 2013. LNCS, vol. 7881, pp. 126–141. Springer, Heidelberg (2013)
20. Veyrat-Charvillon, N., Medwed, M., Kerckhof, S., Standaert, F.-X.: Shuffling against side-channel attacks: a comprehensive study with cautionary note. In: Wang, X., Sako, K. (eds.) ASIACRYPT 2012. LNCS, vol. 7658, pp. 740–757. Springer, Heidelberg (2012)
21. Yu, Y., Standaert, F.-X.: Practical leakage-resilient pseudorandom objects with minimum public randomness. In: Dawson, E. (ed.) CT-RSA 2013. LNCS, vol. 7779, pp. 223–238. Springer, Heidelberg (2013)

Embedded Implementations

Double Level Montgomery Cox-Rower Architecture, New Bounds

Jean-Claude Bajard[1,2] and Nabil Merkiche[3]([✉])

[1] Sorbonnes Universités, UPMC Univ Paris 06,
UMR 7606, LIP6, 75005 Paris, France
[2] CNRS, UMR 7606, LIP6, 75005 Paris, France
jean-claude.bajard@lip6.fr
[3] DGA/MI, Rennes, France
nabil.merkiche@intradef.gouv.fr

Abstract. Recently, the Residue Number System and the Cox-Rower architecture have been used to compute efficiently Elliptic Curve Cryptography over FPGA. In this paper, we are rewriting the conditions of Kawamura's theorem for the base extension without error in order to define the maximal range of the set from which the moduli can be chosen to build a base. At the same time, we give a procedure to compute correctly the truncation function of the Cox module. We also present a modified ALU of the Rower architecture using a second level of Montgomery Representation. Such architecture allows us to select the moduli with the new upper bound defined with the condition. This modification makes the Cox-Rower architecture suitable to compute 521 bits ECC with radix downto 16 bits compared to 18 with the classical Cox-Rower architecture. We validate our results through FPGA implementation of a scalar multiplication at classical cryptography security levels (NIST curves). Our implementation uses 35 % less LUTs compared to the state of the art generic implementation of ECC using RNS for the same performance [5]. We also slightly improve the computation time (latency) and our implementation shows best ratio throughput/area for RNS computation supporting any curve independently of the chosen base.

Keywords: Residue Number System · High speed · Hardware implementation · Elliptic Curve Cryptography · FPGA

1 Introduction

The Residue Number System (RNS) has shown interest for efficient implementation and high performances in large integer computations for public key cryptography and digital signature [5,6]. Due to the ability to compute any operation quickly ($O(n)$ complexity in RNS vs $O(n^{\log_2(3)})$ in multiprecision for multiplications when using Karatsuba) without carry propagation and with natural parallelism, RNS has gained interest in the literature [1,11,12]. Recently, it has also been demonstrated to be suitable for pairing computations [3,13]. Improvement

© Springer International Publishing Switzerland 2015
M. Joye and A. Moradi (Eds.): CARDIS 2014, LNCS 8968, pp. 139–153, 2015.
DOI: 10.1007/978-3-319-16763-3_9

has been made for efficient computation of the final exponentiation in [2]. All these implementations are based on the Cox-Rower architecture proposed by Kawamura for RSA [6] and improved by Guillermin for ECC computations [5].

In this paper, we reformulate the conditions for the base extension in order to build bases for the RNS Cox-Rower. Then, we present a new ALU that takes advantages of the new conditions for the base extension.

The paper is organised as follow: in Sect. 2, we will recall briefly mathematical background about RNS, Montgomery over RNS and approximations made in the base extension. Section 3 deals with the range of the moduli set induced by the approximation made during the base extension. The truncation function of the Cox is re-evaluated under those conditions. Section 4 presents a new Rower architecture, together with its base extension algorithm, to take advantage of the maximal range of the moduli set defined in Sect. 3. Section 5 gives results with scalar multiplication as well as area and performance comparisons with the classical Rower architecture. Section 6 concludes the paper.

2   Background Review

2.1   Residue Number System

RNS represents a number using a set of smaller integers. Let $\mathfrak{B} = \{m_1, \ldots, m_n\}$ be a set of coprime natural integers. $\mathfrak{B}$ is also called a base. Let $M = \prod_{i=1}^{n} m_i$. The RNS representation of $X \in \mathbb{Z}/M\mathbb{Z}$ is the unique set of positive integers $\{X\}_\mathfrak{B} = \{x_1, \ldots, x_n\}$ with $x_i = X \mod m_i$. The conversion from RNS representation to binary representation can be computed using the Chinese Remainder Theorem (other methodology as Mixed Radix is possible):

$$X = \left(\sum_{i=1}^{n} (x_i M_i^{-1} \mod m_i) M_i \right) \mod M \text{ with } M_i = \frac{M}{m_i} \tag{1}$$

Operations in RNS are computed as follows:
$\forall X, Y \in \mathbb{Z}/M\mathbb{Z}, \exists Z \in \mathbb{Z}/M\mathbb{Z}$ s.t.:

$$Z = X \odot Y \mod M \Leftrightarrow z_i = x_i \odot y_i \mod m_i \text{ with } \odot \in \{+, -, *, \div\}$$

and $\div$ only available when Y is coprime with M and a divisor of X.

Notation: In the rest of the paper, $\{X\}_\mathfrak{B}$ will refer to the representation of X in the RNS base $\mathfrak{B}$. We use braces to denote the fact that this is a set of integers.

2.2   RNS and Montgomery

RNS arithmetic has several drawbacks over multiprecision arithmetic. One of them is that reduction over p is complex. Reduction over p is still possible when using Montgomery Reduction since it computes exactly the value using a base

---

Algorithm 1. Montgomery Reduction in RNS

   Input: $\{X\}_{\mathcal{B}}, \{X\}_{\mathcal{B}'}$
   Output: $\{S\}_{\mathcal{B}}, \{S\}_{\mathcal{B}'}$
1 **Precomputed:** $\{-p^{-1}\}_{\mathcal{B}}, \{p\}_{\mathcal{B}'}, \{M^{-1}\}_{\mathcal{B}'}$
2 $\{Q\}_{\mathcal{B}} \leftarrow \{X\}_{\mathcal{B}} * \{-p^{-1}\}_{\mathcal{B}}$
3 $\{Q\}_{\mathcal{B}'} \leftarrow BE(\{Q\}_{\mathcal{B}}, \mathcal{B}, \mathcal{B}')$
4 $\{S\}_{\mathcal{B}'} \leftarrow (\{X\}_{\mathcal{B}'} + \{Q\}_{\mathcal{B}'} * \{p\}_{\mathcal{B}'}) * \{M^{-1}\}_{\mathcal{B}'}$
5 $\{S\}_{\mathcal{B}} \leftarrow BE(\{S\}_{\mathcal{B}'}, \mathcal{B}', \mathcal{B})$

---

extension [9,10]. Thereafter, we recall the algorithm to compute the Montgomery Reduction in RNS [5,6,10].

The main part of Montgomery Reduction relies on the Base Extension function (BE in the algorithm) that is described in the next section.

2.3 Base Extension

Let n be the cardinality of the base in RNS. In [9,10], Posch and Posch introduced a floating approach to compute the base extension function. In [6], Kawamura came to a similar result, but the base extension function introduced by Kawamura supposes that the moduli m_i are pseudo-Mersenne numbers of the form $m_i = 2^r - \mu_i$ with $0 \le \mu_i \ll 2^r, \forall i \in [\![1, n]\!]$. The base extension function relies on the conversion from RNS representation to binary representation. From (1), we have:

$$x = \sum_{i=1}^{n} (x_i M_i^{-1} \mod m_i) M_i - kM,$$

for some k to be determined. Let $\xi_i(x_i) = x_i M_i^{-1} \mod m_i$ but we will use ξ_i to lighten notations. Then it follows:

$$\sum_{i=1}^{n} \xi_i/m_i = k + x/M$$

Since $0 \le x/M < 1$, we have $k \le \sum_{i=1}^{n} \xi_i/m_i < k+1$. Hence:

$$k = \left\lfloor \sum_{i=1}^{n} \xi_i/m_i \right\rfloor \tag{2}$$

Thanks to the special form of m_i and to the condition $0 \le \mu_i \ll 2^r$, Kawamura has approximated m_i by 2^r to ease the computation. Let $\hat{k}$ be:

$$\hat{k} = \sum_{i=1}^{n} \frac{trunc_q(\xi_i)}{2^r} + \alpha \text{ where } trunc_q(\xi_i) = \left\lfloor \frac{\xi_i}{2^{(r-q)}} \right\rfloor 2^{(r-q)} \text{ and } 0 \le \alpha < 1 \tag{3}$$

One can see that $0 \leq \xi_i - trunc_q(\xi_i) \leq 2^{(r-q)} - 1$. To evaluate the error due to the truncation approximation, Kawamura introduced some definitions that we recall here:

$$\epsilon_{m_i} = \frac{2^r - m_i}{2^r}, \quad \delta_{m_i} = \frac{\xi_i - trunc_q(\xi_i)}{m_i} \tag{4}$$

$$\epsilon = \max_{i \in [\![1,n]\!]} (\epsilon_{m_i}), \quad \delta = \max_{i \in [\![1,n]\!]} (\delta_{m_i}) \tag{5}$$

The denominator's approximations error is called ϵ_{m_i} whereas δ_{m_i} is due to the numerator's approximation. Then, Kawamura proved 2 theorems for the base extension function. The conditions of one of the theorems will help to find the μ_i's upper bound (called μ_{max}), which is the maximal range of the set from which we can select the moduli to build a base.

Theorem 1 (Kawamura [6]). *If $0 \leq n(\epsilon + \delta) \leq \alpha < 1$ and $0 \leq x < (1-\alpha)M$, then $\hat{k} = k$ and the base extension function extends the base without error.*

One can see from the proof of the Theorem 1 in [6] that the conditions can be relaxed in:

$$0 \leq n(\epsilon + \delta(1 - \epsilon)) \leq \alpha \text{ and } 0 \leq x < (1 - \alpha)M \text{ with } \alpha < 1 \tag{6}$$

This new condition will help us to estimate μ_{max}'s upper bound. To our knowledge, conditions on μ_{max} have not been clearly established. In order to ease the moduli selection, we define the conditions on μ_{max} in the next section.

3   New Bounds for the Cox-Rower Architecture

3.1 μ_i's Upper Bound for RNS Base

In the previous section, we have presented Kawamura's approximation of the factor k for the base extension. The only condition given by Kawamura is $0 \leq \mu_i \ll 2^r$. In this section, we will explore the different equations to evaluate the impact on μ_i's upper bound. From (4) and (5), we have:

$$\epsilon = \max \left(\frac{2^r - m_i}{2^r} \right) = \frac{2^r - \min(m_i)}{2^r} \text{ which leads to } \min(m_i) = 2^r(1 - \epsilon)$$

On the other hand, $\forall x \in \mathbb{Z}/M\mathbb{Z}$ we have:

$$0 \leq \delta = \max \left(\frac{\xi_i - trunc_q(\xi_i)}{m_i} \right) \leq \frac{2^{(r-q)} - 1}{\min(m_i)} = \frac{2^{(r-q)} - 1}{2^r(1 - \epsilon)}$$

From the new condition (6), it follows that:

$$0 \leq n \left(\epsilon + \frac{2^{(r-q)} - 1}{2^r(1 - \epsilon)}(1 - \epsilon) \right) \leq \alpha \text{ then } 0 \leq \epsilon \leq \frac{\alpha}{n} - \frac{2^{(r-q)} - 1}{2^r} \tag{7}$$

Now, we will evaluate Eq. (7) in ϵ to find the condition on m_i since $\epsilon = \frac{2^r - \min(m_i)}{2^r} = \frac{\mu_{max}}{2^r}$. Let substitute ϵ in (7):

$$0 \leq \frac{\mu_{max}}{2^r} \leq \frac{\alpha}{n} - \frac{2^{r-q} - 1}{2^r} \Leftrightarrow 0 \leq \mu_{max} \leq 2^r \frac{\alpha}{n} - 2^{r-q} + 1 \tag{8}$$

If $q = r$, then μ_{max} is maximum and is in the range of:

$$0 \leq \mu_{max} \leq 2^r \frac{\alpha}{n} \tag{9}$$

Then, we can rewrite an equivalent condition of the Theorem 1 using only the parameters α, r, n, q and μ_{max}, which is more explicit for implementations:

Theorem 2. *If* $0 \leq \mu_{max} \leq 2^r \frac{\alpha}{n} - 2^{r-q} + 1$ *and* $0 \leq x < (1 - \alpha)M$ *with* $\alpha < 1$, *then* $\hat{k} = k$ *and the base extension function extends the base without error.*

With this new formulation, we can easily build bases for the RNS Cox-Rower architecture.

3.2   Lower Bound for the Parameter Q of the Cox

In [6], Kawamura described a procedure to determine $n, \epsilon, \delta, \alpha$ and q for a given p. While n is easy to determine (same order of magnitude as $n \approx \log_2(p)/r$), q is determined using the approximations $\epsilon \ll 1$ and $2^{-(r-q)} \ll 1$ with Theorem 1's conditions. While those approximations are asymptotically correct, we want to determine q for any range of parameters. We give, here, a new procedure to determine correctly q from α, n, r and μ_{max}.

Once the bases are choosen using (9), from the Theorem 2's conditions, the following equation can be applied to find the parameter q:

$$q \geq \left\lceil -\log_2 \left(\frac{\alpha}{n} + 2^{-r} - \frac{\mu_{max}}{2^r} \right) \right\rceil \text{ with } \mu_{max} = \max_{\mu_i \in \{B, B'\}} (\mu_i) \tag{10}$$

This is a necessary and sufficient condition to get an exact computation. Unlike Kawamura's method [6], no assumption is made on ϵ (or equivalently on μ_{max}) and $2^{-(r-q)}$.

4   A New Cox-Rower Architecture

In the previous section, conditions on μ_{max} has been determined. In this section, we first present the algorithm and the classical ALU used to compute the reduction inside the Rower. To our knowledge, it is the only ALU used with the RNS Cox-Rower architecture [2,3,5,8,13].

Then, we introduce the new ALU proposed in this paper. This new ALU has been designed to fit on FPGAs, and we compare it with the classical ALU. Our comparison analysis uses 3 types of cells: DSP (Digital Signal Processing) blocks, LUTs (Look-Up Table) and registers (basic elements of FPGA) to compare the 2 ALUs. Multipliers are implemented inside DSP blocks on FPGA, with some additional features such as pre/post-adder/substracter. LUTs are the cell bases to implement any combinatorial logic.

Algorithm 2. Efficient Reduction Algorithm

Input: $a \leq 2^r, b \leq 2^r$ and $m_i = 2^r - \mu_i$ with $0 \leq \mu_i < \sqrt{2^r}$
Output: $z = (ab) \mod m_i$
1 $c \leftarrow ab = c_1 2^r + c_0$
2 $d \leftarrow c_1 \mu_i = d_1 2^r + d_0$
3 $e \leftarrow d_1 \mu_i$
4 $z \leftarrow (e + d_0 + c_0) \mod m_i$

4.1   Classical Rower Unit

The Cox-Rower architecture defined in [3,5,6,8,13] computes the reduction inside the Rower using Algorithm 2 when $0 \leq \mu_i < \sqrt{2^r}$.

The last addition (line 4 of Algorithm 2) gives a number up to $3 \cdot 2^r < 4m_i$. It is also possible to reduce the last addition during the computation of the multiplications, if the adder/reducer block are not the critical path of the design compared to the multipliers. Such implementation gives good results for efficient implementation and computation for $\mathbb{F}_p$/RSA and ECC [2,3,5,6,8,13]. Figure 1 presents the ALU of the Rower unit introduced by Guillermin [5].

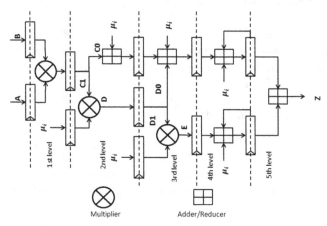

Fig. 1. Classical ALU's Rower

The first reduction stage (second level in Fig. 1) is not necessary because its output is reduced within the second stage (third level in Fig. 1) (in the design, we have $2^r + m_i < 3m_i$ but $2^r + 2^r < 3m_i$). The last part of the design is two accumulators before adding and reducing the 2 branches.

4.2   New Rower Unit

A drawback of the previous ALU is the condition $0 \leq \mu_i \leq \sqrt{2^r}$. This restriction on moduli is taken to allow efficient reduction. Notice that, on the contrary, the condition we derived in (9) has to be met to ensure a base extension without error.

Then the two following cases can be met:

(i) $0 \leq \mu_{max} \leq 2^r \frac{\alpha}{n} < \sqrt{2^r}$. In that case, choosing moduli in the range $[2^r \frac{\alpha}{n}; \sqrt{2^r}]$ may lead to erroneous computations.

(ii) $0 \leq \mu_{max} \leq \sqrt{2^r} < 2^r \frac{\alpha}{n}$. In this second case we observe that, using the classical ALU, we are restricted for the choice of moduli while our conditions (9) shows that taking more moduli without inducing errors is possible.

As an example, when $r \geq 14$ and $\log_2(p) = 521$, we are restricted by the condition $0 \leq \mu_{max} \leq \sqrt{2^r}$ to select the moduli. The condition given for efficient reduction, when r is large, is sufficient to be in (ii), which is the case in [2, 3, 5, 6, 8, 13].

We propose here a new ALU for the Rower unit to exploit the upper bound $\mu_{max} \leq 2^r \frac{\alpha}{n}$ given by our condition (9). Using this upper bound, we will be able to use smaller radix than the classical ALU for computing equivalent size of p ($r = 16$ for computing $\log_2(p) = 521$ whereas we need $r = 18$ with the classical ALU). Our ALU is based on the Montgomery reduction[1] inside the Rower unit (called inner level of Montgomery). Our ALU computes the reduction using Algorithm 3 without any assumption on m_i excepted the one that m_i is coprime with 2^r to ease the computation in hardware[2].

Algorithm 3. Inner Montgomery Reduction algorithm

Input: $a \leq 2^r, b \leq m_i, m_i = 2^r - \mu_i$ with $\gcd(m_i, 2^r) = 1, m_i < 2^r$
Output: $z = (ab2^{-r}) \mod m_i$
1   $c \leftarrow ab = c_1 2^r + c_0$
2   $q \leftarrow (c_0(-m_i^{-1})) \mod 2^r = q_0$
3   $s \leftarrow (q_0 m_i) + c = s_1 2^r + s_0$
4   $z \leftarrow s_1 \mod m_i$

The most significant bits of the last addition (line 3 of Algorithm 3) gives a number up to $2m_i$ (compared to $4m_i$ with the classical ALU). Figure 2 presents the ALU of the Rower unit proposed in this paper.

Levels of multiplication and reduction are also well separated, which makes our design fully pipelinable inside DSP blocks of the FPGA. Our ALU has also one accumulator. Moreover, we can take advantage of the adder integrated in the DSP blocks to compute the last addition of the Montgomery reduction algorithm (Algorithm 3).

4.3 Computation Algorithm

The computation of the Montgomery reduction over RNS (called outer level of Montgomery), when using the classical ALU, is given in [5]. We recall this

---

[1] Barrett reduction is also possible, but we would need larger multipliers for the same results.

[2] For $m_i = 2^r$ (only one even number can be selected), we use a classical multiplier and gather the r least significant bits of the multiplier.

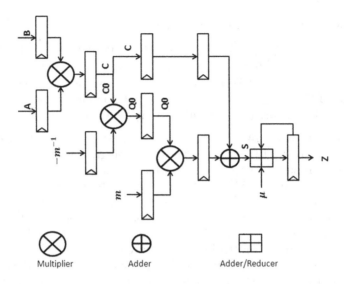

Fig. 2. New ALU's Rower

algorithm in the Appendix. It is based on precomputation of values depending on the parameters of the elliptic curve $(a4, a6, p$ with $y^2 = x^3 + a_4 x + a_6)$ and on the values of the bases $(m_i, M_i, M_i^{-1}, M, M^{-1}, m'_i, M'_i, M'^{-1}_i, M')$.

Our ALU uses the same algorithm as the one given in [5]. Differences reside in the precomputed values. Indeed, values that have to be computed are $\{X2^r\}_{\mathfrak{B}} = \{\tilde{x}_i = x_i 2^r \mod m_i\}^3$. Mainly, we precompute the values using Montgomery representation inside the ALU (which is $\times 2^r \mod m_i$ in the inner level of Montgomery). When we use the base extension function, we need to compute the real value (inner level of Montgomery representation to normal representation $\mod m_i$) to extend it to the second base. The new ALU needs the same number of cycles in order to compute the outer Montgomery compared to the classical ALU (Algorithms for outer Montgomery computation, as well as precomputed values, for the classical ALU and our ALU are given in Appendix A).

4.4 Comparison Analysis

Despite the fact that our ALU was designed specifically to fit on FPGA, we give some comparisons for ASIC implementations.

Area analysis. Size of the multipliers are not the same between the classical ALU and our ALU. When using the classical ALU, we need 3 multipliers of size $r \times r \to 2r, r \times r/2 \to 3r/2$ and $r/2 \times r/2 \to r$ (lines 1, 2 and 3 of Algorithm 2). Our ALU costs the same number of multipliers, but the size will be $r \times r \to$

---

^{3} It is well known that the Montgomery representation is stable for addition and product using Algorithm 3.

$2r, r \times r \to r$ and $r \times r \to 2r$. With our ALU, we fully used the full size of the DSP blocks on FPGA whereas quarter and half of the DSP blocks are lost with the classical ALU. When looking at LUTs used on FPGA, our ALU is less complex (in term of additions and reductions) than the classical ALU. This reduces the number of LUTs used within our ALU. The final adder in Montgomery reduction algorithm (Algorithm 3) can also be included inside the DSP blocks of the FPGA to help reducing the number of LUTs used, which is not the case with the classical ALU. Looking at Fig. 2, we can estimate that we would use 5 times less LUTs with our ALU than with the classical one. For ASIC, those considerations are no more true since the cost of the reduction level is far more important on FPGA than in ASIC (where multipliers are far more area consuming than adders).

Timing analysis. Timing path of a classical multiplier is an affine function on the size of its inputs. In the classical ALU, for each multiplications, we need the most significant bits of the previous multiplication (lines 2 and 3 of Algorithm 2). In ASIC or FPGA, this is usually the critical path of the design if it is not well pipelined. On the other hand, our ALU only needs the least significant bits from one multiplier to the next (lines 2 and 3 of Algorithm 3), which reduces the length of the critical timing path.

Others considerations. Stages of multiplications and reductions are well separated, which reduces the fanouts, placement and routing issues. Stages of multiplication are also fully pipelinable without any impact on the final reduction in our ALU.

Remarks. With the classical ALU, Kawamura's approximation on $\epsilon \ll 1$ and $2^{-(r-q)} \ll 1$ to determine q is correct when r is large enough to have $\sqrt{2^r} \ll 2^r \frac{\alpha}{n}$. With the new ALU, the procedure to determine q, defined in the previous section, is available.

5   Experiments and Comparison

5.1   Validation on FPGA

Target technology. We have implemented our ALU (and also the classical ALU [5] for the purpose of comparison) on a Xilinx Kintex-7 FPGA using the KC705 evaluation board available from Xilinx. This board includes the device xc7k325t which is a mid range FPGA on the 28 nm process node.

Parameters design. We have implemented the classical cryptography security level from NIST but no restriction is given on the parameters of the elliptic curve but to be a valid curve. DSP blocks of the Xilinx 7 series family are signed multipliers of size $25 \times 18 \to 43$. Since we need only the unsigned part of the multiplier, and we want to be base-independent, we choose to take radix $r = 17$. The base has been chosen such that we can take $\alpha = 0.5$.

Table 1. P&R performances and comparisons

Design	Curve	n	Cycles	Slices	Fmax	Latency	q	$\log_2(\mu_{max})$	Ratio
Classical ALU (C)	160	10	78892	1614	233,8	0,337 ms	5	7	293,7
Our ALU (O)				1011	285,7	0,276 ms	5	7	573,1
C	192	12	106205	1880	231,3	0,459 ms	5	7	222,4
O				1190	283,0	0,375 ms	5	7	429,8
C	224	14	137360	2249	232,5	0,590 ms	5	8	168,6
O				1358	285,0	0,481 ms	5	8	342,2
C	256	16	172520	2540	224,2	0,769 ms	5	8	130,9
O				1630	281,5	0,612 ms	5	8	256,2
O	384	23	339463	2163	281,0	1,208 ms	6	9	146,9
O	521	31	585926	2565	265,9	2,203 ms	7	10	92,2

Implementation. For both design (classical ALU and our ALU) and each curve, Table 1 gives the area in terms of slices[4], maximum frequency after Place and Route, number of cycles for a whole computation (binary to RNS or INT2RNS, scalar multiplication or MULT, final inversion or INV, and RNS to binary transformation or RNS2INT), the computation time, q (size of the adder in the Cox module), $\log_2(\mu_{max})$ and the ratio bits.s^{-1}/slices. The slice count is independent on DSP slices or BRAM (Block RAM). Table 2, in Appendix A, gives the details account on LUTs, registers, DSP and BRAM, as well as the cycles for each command. Area implementation results take the datapath, the sequencer and the interface into accounts. Only the ALU has been modified as well as the precomputations.

Comparison of the 2 ALUs. Because of the condition given for an efficient reduction ($0 \leq \mu_i \leq \sqrt{2^r} = 362$) with the classical ALU, we were not able to build 2 bases with $r = 17$ for $\log_2(p) > 256$ which is a critical size for the DSP block for the Xilinx FPGA. On the other hand, using our ALU and the condition (9) ($0 \leq \mu_{max} \leq 2^r \frac{\alpha}{n} = 2114$), we were able to build 2 bases up to $\log_2(p) = 521$. To reach similar size of p, Guillermin took $r = 18$ with the classical ALU to overcome this issue [5], which it's not acceptable if we want to use 1 DSP block per multiplication and don't want to penalize the maximal frequency and latency.

As expected in the previous section, we use 35 % less area, globally, with the Montgomery ALU than with the classical ALU. The area reduction given here takes into account the logic for the whole datapath, the sequencer and the interface. The area reduction inside the ALU is around 75 %. The area of the 256 bits with the classical ALU is almost the same as with the 521 bits for our ALU.

The gap on the maximal frequency between the 2 ALUs is due to the placement and routing issues. Indeed, critical timing paths of the classical ALU are from multipliers to adder/reducers blocks (Fig. 1). The multiple interconnections

---

[4] The slices is the cells counting system on Xilinx FPGA. A slice on a Kintex-7 includes 4 LUTs with 6 inputs and 8 registers.

make those paths really difficult to place and route efficiently (essentially due to the fanouts). On the other hand, critical timing paths of our ALU is from one multiplier to the next multiplier. Thus, if we want to increase the frequency, we will have to increase the pipeline. For scalar multiplication in ECC, a pipeline of 5 registers is enough to have 95 % of the pipeline used during the whole computation (Guillermin came to similar results [5]). For application to pairing computations, we can increased the pipeline to 10 registers thus expecting better frequency than for scalar multiplication [3,13].

5.2   Comparison

We compare our design with 3 others design RNS and non RNS. Our architecture supports any elliptic curve over $\mathbb{F}_p$ and implements the Montgomery Ladder algorithm to be SPA resistant. We used projective coordinates for computations. We considered the general elliptic curve in the Weierstrass form $y^2 = x^3 + a_4 x + a_6$ with no assumption on the parameters. Our architecture does not make assumption on the form of the moduli except that they respect Theorem 2's conditions.

(i)   First design is the one given in [5] and is based on RNS. The ALU used is the classical one. A larger size of radix has also been used in his implementation. This design shows really fast computation with any elliptic curve over $\mathbb{F}_p$. To our knowledge, it is the fastest implementation of elliptic curve scalar multiplication with generic curves independently of the choosen base on FPGA using RNS Cox-Rower architecture. For ratio comparison, a slice in recent Xilinx devices (virtex-5 and beyond) is equivalent to 3 ALMs[5] in Altera. To achieve high running frequency, all the precomputed values and the GPR are implemented into registers inside ALMs.

(ii)   Second design is an implementation of a specific curve where p is a pseudo-Mersenne number [4]. Using the property of the pseudo-Mersenne value, this implementation can be specialized to run at high frequency and quickly computing the multiplication scalar.

(iii)   Third design is based on fast quotient pipelining Montgomery multiplication algorithm in [7]. The scalar multiplication algorithm is based on window method algorithm. Jacobian coordinates is used and a_4 parameter is set to -3 (which is not a real restriction with Weierstrass form through an isogeny). To our knowledge, it is the fastest implementation of scalar multiplication over ECC and smallest design for such performance with generic curves.

Design (i) is the one we compare during the paper. Our implementation is smaller and a slightly faster than the implementation in [5].

Design (ii) used the specific form of the parameter p to improve the overall performance. This design is faster than ours, but it is dependent on the pseudo-Mersenne form of the parameter p of the elliptic curve.

---

[5] An ALM, in the Stratix-2 family, contains 2 LUTs with 5 inputs and 2 registers, and equivalent to the Xilinx Virtex-4 slice.

Design	Curve	Device	Size (DSP)	Frequency	Latency	Ratio
Our work	256 any	Kintex-7	1630 slices (46)	281,5	0,612 ms	256,2
	521 any		2565 slices (91)	265,9	2,203 ms	92,2
[5]	256 any	Stratix-2	9177 ALM (96)	157,2	0,68 ms	123,1
	512 any		17017 ALM (244)	144,97	2,23 ms	40,47
[4]	256 NIST	Virtex-4	1715 slices (32)	490	0,49 ms	304,6
[7]	256 any	Virtex-4	4655 slices (37)	250	0,44 ms	250,0
		Virtex-5	1725 slices (37)	291	0,38 ms	390,5

Design (iii) shows really fast computation of ECC scalar multiplication. Compared to our design, the gain in computation time comes from the use of Jacobian coordinates and the window method algorithm whereas we use Montgomery Ladder and projective coordinates. But when comparing the numbers of cycles to complete a multiplication and an addition/substraction, 35 cycles is needed to compute a multiplication whereas we need $2n + 3$ cycles (35 cycles for 256 bits), and 7 cycles is needed to compute an addition/substraction, whereas we need 1 cycle for an addition/substraction. Eventually, the gain in performance is not scalable to any size of elliptic curve as our work.

6 Conclusion and Perspectives

In this paper, we established the link between moduli's properties and base extension for the Cox-Rower architecture. To our knowledge, that was not clearly defined yet. Now, the given bounds are more appropriate for designers. We also give a new procedure to determine q parameter which is used for truncation in the Cox module. We propose a new ALU design, based on an inner Montgomery reduction. This ALU is designed to fully use the bounds of the Cox-Rower architecture and to reduce the combinatorial area of the architecture on FPGA without penalizing performance. Moreover, using the same pipeline depth, we manage to increase the frequency of our ALU compare to the classical one.

In future works, we will increase the pipeline depth in DSP blocks for applications to pairing computations in order to improve computation time. Furthermore, we will take advantage of the pre-substracter of the DSP block to easily compute $(-AB) \bmod p$ and reduce computation time. In the perspective of improving the algorithmic, we will study the use of different coordinates and implementations, such as Jacobian coordinates and window method. Although our ALU is designed for FPGA, we will also study the potential application of our ALU to ASIC.

A   Algorithm to Compute the Montgomery Reduction over RNS and Implementation Details

Let $\mathfrak{B}$ and $\mathfrak{B}'$ be 2 RNS bases such that $\mathfrak{B} = \{m_i\}$ and $\mathfrak{B}' = \{m'_i\}$ with $M = \prod_{i=1}^{n} m_i$, $M' = \prod_{i=1}^{n} m'_i$, $\gcd(p, M) = 1$ and $\gcd(M, M') = 1$. Algorithm 4 recalls the Montgomery reduction over RNS, when using the classical ALU. Precomputed values are in bold.

Algorithm 5 is the algorithm for the Montgomery reduction over RNS, when using our ALU. Operation $\otimes$ will denote the inner Montgomery multiplication and reduction (Algorithm 3) such that $a \otimes b \mod m = ab2^{-r} \mod m$.

Algorithm 4. Montgomery Reduction over RNS with classical ALU

Input: $\{X\}_{\mathfrak{B}} = \{x_i\}$ and $\{X\}_{\mathfrak{B}'} = \{x'_i\}$
Output: $\{S = (XM^{-1} \mod p) \mod M\}_{\mathfrak{B}} = \{s_i\}$ and $\{S = (XM^{-1} \mod p) \mod M'\}_{\mathfrak{B}'} = \{s'_i\}$

1 **for** $i = 1$ **to** n **do**
2      $q_i \leftarrow x_i(-\mathbf{p}^{-1})\mathbf{M}_{\mathbf{i}}^{-1} \mod m_i$
3      $q'_i \leftarrow 0$
4      $s_i \leftarrow 0$
5 **end**
6 $k \leftarrow 0$ // Initialization of the cox with $\alpha = 0$
7 **for** $i = 1$ **to** n **do**
8      $k \leftarrow k + trunc_q(q_i)$ // Evaluating the factor k
9   **for** $j = 1$ **to** n **do**
10          $q'_j \leftarrow (q'_j + q_i\mathbf{M_i}\mathbf{p}\mathbf{M}^{-1}\mathbf{M'}_{\mathbf{j}}^{-1}) \mod m'_j$
11   **end**
12 **end**
13 **for** $i = 1$ **to** n **do**
14      $q'_i \leftarrow (q'_i + \lfloor \frac{k}{2^r} \rfloor(-\mathbf{M})\mathbf{p}\mathbf{M}^{-1}\mathbf{M'}_{\mathbf{i}}^{-1}) \mod m'_i$
15 **end**
16 **for** $i = 1$ **to** n **do**
17      $s'_i \leftarrow (q'_i + x'_i\mathbf{M}^{-1}\mathbf{M'}_{\mathbf{i}}^{-1}) \mod m'_i$
18 **end**
19 $k \leftarrow errinit$ // Initialization of the cox with $\alpha = errinit$
20 **for** $i = 1$ **to** n **do**
21      $k \leftarrow k + trunc_q(s'_i)$ // Evaluating the factor k
22   **for** $j = 1$ **to** n **do**
23          $s_j \leftarrow (s_j + s'_i\mathbf{M'_i}) \mod m_j$
24   **end**
25 **end**
26 **for** $i = 1$ **to** n **do**
27      $s_i \leftarrow (s_i + \lfloor \frac{k}{2^r} \rfloor(-\mathbf{M'})) \mod m_i$
28      $s'_i \leftarrow (s'_i\mathbf{M'_i}) \mod m'_i$
29 **end**

Algorithm 5. Montgomery Reduction over RNS with Montgomery ALU

Input: $\{\tilde{X}\}_{\mathfrak{B}} = \{\tilde{x}_i = x_i 2^r \mod m_i\}$ and $\{\tilde{X}\}_{\mathfrak{B}'} = \{\tilde{x'}_i = x'_i 2^r \mod m'_i\}$

Output: $\{\tilde{S} = (XM^{-1} \mod p)2^r \mod M\}_{\mathfrak{B}} = \{\tilde{s}_i = s_i 2^r \mod m_i\}$ and
$\quad \{\tilde{S} = (XM^{-1} \mod p)2^r \mod M'\}_{\mathfrak{B}'} = \{\tilde{s'}_i = s'_i 2^r \mod m'_i\}$

```
1  for i = 1 to n do
2      q_i ← x̃_i ⊗ (−p⁻¹)M_i⁻¹  mod m_i
3      q'_i ← 0
4      s_i ← 0
5  end
6  k ← 0 // Initialization of the cox with α = 0
7  for i = 1 to n do
8      k ← k + trunc_q(q_i) // Evaluating the factor k
9      for j = 1 to n do
10         q'_j ← (q'_j + q_i ⊗ M_i p M⁻¹ M'_j⁻¹ 2^r)  mod m'_j
11     end
12 end
13 for i = 1 to n do
14     q'_i ← (q'_i + ⌊k/2^r⌋ ⊗ (−M)p M⁻¹ M'_i⁻¹ 2^r)  mod m'_i
15 end
16 for i = 1 to n do
17     s'_i ← (q'_i + x̃'_i ⊗ M⁻¹ M'_i⁻¹)  mod m'_i
18 end
19 k ← errinit // Initialization of the cox with α = errinit
20 for i = 1 to n do
21     k ← k + trunc_q(s'_i) // Evaluating the factor k
22     for j = 1 to n do
23         s_j ← (s_j + s'_i ⊗ M'_i 2^{2r})  mod m_j
24     end
25 end
26 for i = 1 to n do
27     s_i ← (s_i + ⌊k/2^r⌋ ⊗ (−M')2^{2r})  mod m_i
28     s'_i ← (s'_i ⊗ M'_i 2^{2r})  mod m'_i
29 end
```

Table 2. Performances details

Design	Curve	LUTs	Regs	DSP	BRAM	INT2RNS	MULT	INV	RNS2INT
Classical	160	4864	2959	28	10	228	66406	11598	682
	192	5691	3497	34	12	262	89659	15446	862
	224	6688	4028	40	14	300	116227	19805	1058
	256	7482	4605	46	16	336	146144	24804	1270
Ours	160	2988	2023	28	10	228	66406	11598	682
	192	3446	2346	34	12	262	89659	15446	862
	224	3847	2696	40	14	300	116227	19805	1058
	256	4250	3532	46	16	336	146144	24804	1270
	384	5517	4962	67	23	462	289101	47810	2090
	521	7067	5882	91	31	606	500577	81437	3306

References

1. Antão, S., Bajard, J.-C., Sousa, L.: RNS-based elliptic curve point multiplication for massive parallel architectures. Comput. J. **55**(5), 629–647 (2012)
2. Bigou, K., Tisserand, A.: Improving modular inversion in RNS using the plus-minus method. In: Bertoni, G., Coron, J.-S. (eds.) CHES 2013. LNCS, vol. 8086, pp. 233–249. Springer, Heidelberg (2013)
3. Cheung, R.C.C., Duquesne, S., Fan, J., Guillermin, N., Verbauwhede, I., Yao, G.X.: FPGA implementation of pairings using residue number system and lazy reduction. In: Preneel, B., Takagi, T. (eds.) CHES 2011. LNCS, vol. 6917, pp. 421–441. Springer, Heidelberg (2011)
4. Güneysu, T., Paar, C.: Ultra high performance ECC over NIST primes on commercial FPGAs. In: Oswald, E., Rohatgi, P. (eds.) CHES 2008. LNCS, vol. 5154, pp. 62–78. Springer, Heidelberg (2008)
5. Guillermin, N.: A high speed coprocessor for elliptic curve scalar multiplications over $\mathbb{F}_p$. In: Mangard, S., Standaert, F.-X. (eds.) CHES 2010. LNCS, vol. 6225, pp. 48–64. Springer, Heidelberg (2010)
6. Kawamura, S., Koike, M., Sano, F., Shimbo, A.: Cox-rower architecture for fast parallel montgomery multiplication. In: Preneel, B. (ed.) EUROCRYPT 2000. LNCS, vol. 1807, pp. 523–538. Springer, Heidelberg (2000)
7. Ma, Y., Liu, Z., Pan, W., Jing, J.: A high-speed elliptic curve cryptographic processor for generic curves over GF(p). In: Lange, T., Lauter, K., Lisoněk, P. (eds.) SAC 2013. LNCS, vol. 8282, pp. 421–437. Springer, Heidelberg (2014)
8. Nozaki, H., Motoyama, M., Shimbo, A., Kawamura, S.: Implementation of RSA algorithm based on RNS montgomery multiplication. In: Koç, Ç.K., Naccache, D., Paar, C. (eds.) CHES 2001. LNCS, vol. 2162, pp. 364–376. Springer, Heidelberg (2001)
9. Posch, K.C., Posch, R.: Base extension using a convolution sum in residue number systems. Computing **50**(2), 93–104 (1993)
10. Posch, K.C., Posch, R.: Modulo reduction in residue number systems. IEEE Trans. Parallel Distrib. Syst. **6**(5), 449–454 (1995)
11. Schinianakis, D.M., Fournaris, A.P., Michail, H.E., Kakarountas, A.P., Stouraitis, T.: An RNS implementation of an f_p elliptic curve point multiplier. IEEE Trans. Circuits Syst. I: Regul. Pap. **56**(6), 1202–1213 (2009)
12. Szerwinski, R., Güneysu, T.: Exploiting the power of GPUs for asymmetric cryptography. In: Oswald, E., Rohatgi, P. (eds.) CHES 2008. LNCS, vol. 5154, pp. 79–99. Springer, Heidelberg (2008)
13. Yao, G.X., Fan, J., Cheung, R.C.C., Verbauwhede, I.: Faster pairing coprocessor architecture. In: Abdalla, M., Lange, T. (eds.) Pairing 2012. LNCS, vol. 7708, pp. 160–176. Springer, Heidelberg (2013)

How to Use Koblitz Curves on Small Devices?

Kimmo Järvinen[1,2(✉)] and Ingrid Verbauwhede[1]

[1] KU Leuven ESAT/COSIC and iMinds, Kasteelpark Arenberg 10, Bus 2452,
3001 Leuven-Heverlee, Belgium
{Kimmo.Jarvinen,Ingrid.Verbauwhede}@esat.kuleuven.be
[2] Department of Information and Computer Science, Aalto University,
Konemiehentie 2, 02150 Espoo, Finland

Abstract. Koblitz curves allow very efficient scalar multiplications because point doublings can be traded for cheap Frobenius endomorphisms by representing the scalar as a τ-adic expansion. Typically elliptic curve cryptosystems, such as ECDSA, also require the scalar as an integer. This results in a need for conversions between integers and the τ-adic domain, which are costly and prevent from using Koblitz curves on very constrained devices, such as RFID tags or wireless sensors. In this paper, we provide a solution to this problem by showing how complete cryptographic processes, such as ECDSA signing, can be completed in the τ-adic domain with very few resources, consequently outsourcing the expensive conversions to a more powerful party. We also provide small circuitries that require about 76 gate equivalents on 0.13 μm CMOS and that are applicable for all Koblitz curves.

1 Introduction

Because elliptic curve cryptography (ECC) [12,18] offers high security levels with short key lengths and relatively low amounts of computation, it is one of the most feasible alternatives for implementing public-key cryptography on constrained devices where resources (e.g., circuit area, power, and energy) are extremely limited. Constrained devices that require lightweight implementations of public-key cryptography are, e.g., wireless sensor network nodes, RFID tags, and smart cards. Several researchers have proposed lightweight implementations which aim to minimize area, power, and/or energy of computing elliptic curve scalar multiplications [2,3,8,14,16], which are the fundamental operations required by every elliptic curve cryptosystem.

Koblitz curves [13] are a special class of elliptic curves offering very efficient elliptic curve operations when scalars used in scalar multiplications are given as τ-adic expansions. It is commonly known that Koblitz curves allow extremely fast scalar multiplications in both software [25] and hardware [9]. A recent paper [2] showed that they can be implemented also with very few resources (especially, in terms of energy) if the scalar is already in the τ-adic domain. Many cryptosystems require both the integer and τ-adic representations of the scalar which results in a need for conversions between the domains. All known methods for computing

© Springer International Publishing Switzerland 2015
M. Joye and A. Moradi (Eds.): CARDIS 2014, LNCS 8968, pp. 154–170, 2015.
DOI: 10.1007/978-3-319-16763-3_10

these conversions in hardware [1,5,6,10,23] require a lot of resources making them unfeasible for constrained devices. In most cases, this prevents from using Koblitz curves although they would otherwise result in very efficient lightweight implementations. A workaround to this problem is to design a protocol that operates directly in the τ-adic domain [4]. However, this approach has several drawbacks because it prevents from using standardized algorithms and protocols, which, consequently, makes the design work more laborious and may even lead to cryptographic weaknesses in the worst case.

In this paper, we show how the computationally weaker party of a cryptosystem can delegate the conversions to the more powerful party by computing all operations directly in the τ-adic domain with an extremely small circuitry. Our approach can be straightforwardly used for many existing Koblitz curve cryptosystems that require scalar multiplications on Koblitz curves and modular arithmetic with the scalar (e.g., ECDSA) without affecting the cryptographic strength of the cryptosystem. We also provide small circuitries that enable efficient lightweight implementations of the approach. Consequently, we show how Koblitz curves can be used also in lightweight implementations.

This paper is structured as follows. Section 2 surveys the preliminaries of ECC and Koblitz curves. Section 3 discusses the existing solutions for using Koblitz curves by reviewing the related work on conversions between integers and the τ-adic domain and presents the outline of the new idea. An algorithm for computing additions in the τ-adic domain is presented and analyzed in Sect. 4. Section 5 presents algorithms for computing other arithmetic operations using the algorithm from Sect. 4. Section 6 introduces an architecture for a circuitry implementing the algorithms from Sects. 4 and 5. Section 7 presents implementation results on $0.13\,\mu\text{m}$ CMOS and compares them to converters from the literature. Section 8 presents a case study of how the findings of this paper could be used in computing ECDSA signatures in lightweight implementations. The paper ends with conclusions in Sect. 9.

2 Elliptic Curve Cryptography and Koblitz Curves

In the mid-1980s, Miller [18] and Koblitz [12] showed how public-key cryptography can be based on the difficulty of computing the discrete logarithm in an additive Abelian group $\mathcal{E}$ formed by points on an elliptic curve. Let $k \in \mathbb{Z}_+$ and $\mathbf{P} \in \mathcal{E}$. The fundamental operation in ECC is the scalar multiplication which is given by:

$$k\mathbf{P} = \underbrace{\mathbf{P} + \mathbf{P} + \ldots + \mathbf{P}}_{k \text{ times}} \ . \tag{1}$$

The operation $\mathbf{Q} + \mathbf{R}$, where $\mathbf{Q}, \mathbf{R} \in \mathcal{E}$, is called point addition if $\mathbf{Q} \neq \pm\mathbf{R}$ and point doubling if $\mathbf{Q} = \mathbf{R}$. Scalar multiplication can be computed with a series of point doublings and point additions, e.g., by using the well-known double-and-add algorithm. Elliptic curves over finite fields of characteristic two $GF(2^m)$ are often preferred in implementing ECC because they allow efficient implementations, especially, in hardware. These curves are commonly called binary curves.

Koblitz curves [13] are a subclass of binary curves defined by the equation:

$$y^2 + xy = x^3 + ax^2 + 1 \tag{2}$$

where $a \in \{0, 1\}$ and $x, y \in GF(2^m)$. Let $\mathcal{K}$ denote the Abelian group of points (x, y) that satisfy (2) together with $\mathcal{O}$ which is a special point that acts as the zero element of the group. Koblitz curves have the property that if a point $\mathbf{P} = (x, y) \in \mathcal{K}$, then also its Frobenius endomorphism $F(\mathbf{P}) = (x^2, y^2) \in \mathcal{K}$. This allows devising efficient scalar multiplication algorithms where Frobenius endomorphisms are computed instead of point doublings. It can be shown that $F(F(\mathbf{P})) - \mu F(\mathbf{P}) + 2\mathbf{P} = 0$, where $\mu = (-1)^{1-a}$, holds for all $\mathbf{P} \in \mathcal{K}$ [13]. Consequently, $F(\mathbf{P})$ can be seen as a multiplication by the complex number τ that satisfies $\tau^2 - \mu\tau + 2 = 0$, which gives $\tau = (\mu + \sqrt{-7})/2$.

If the scalar k is given using the base τ as a τ-adic expansion $K = \sum K_i \tau^i$, the scalar multiplication $K\mathbf{P}$ can be computed with a Frobenius-and-add algorithm, where Frobenius endomorphisms are computed for each K_i and point additions (or subtractions) are computed for $K_i \neq 0$. This is similar to the double-and-add algorithm except that computationally expensive point doublings are replaced with cheap Frobenius endomorphisms. Hence, if a τ-adic expansion can be efficiently found, then Koblitz curves offer considerably more efficient scalar multiplications than general binary curves.

We use the following notation. Lower-case letters $a, b, c, \ldots$ denote integer values and upper-case letters $A, B, C, \ldots$ denote τ-adic expansions. If both lower-case and upper-case version of the same letter are used in the same context, then the values are related; to state this explicitly, we denote $A \overset{\circ}{=} a$. Bold-faced upper case letters $\mathbf{P}, \mathbf{Q}, \ldots$ denote points on elliptic curves.

3   Related Work and Outline of the Idea

Lightweight applications are typically asymmetric in the sense that one of the communicating parties is strictly limited in resources, whereas the other is not. As an example, we consider an application where a wireless tag communicates with a server over a radio channel. The tag is limited in computational resources, power, and energy but the server has plenty of resources for computations. The tag implements an elliptic curve cryptosystem which requires both elliptic curve operations and modular arithmetic with integers (e.g., it signs messages with ECDSA [21]). The tag uses Koblitz curves for efficient scalar multiplication resulting in a need for obtaining both τ-adic expansions and their integer equivalents. In the following, we survey two existing options for implementing the above scheme as well as a new idea which allows delegating the expensive conversions from the tag to the powerful server.

3.1   Survey of the Existing Options

The first option, which is depicted in Fig. 1(a), is to generate k as a random integer and convert it into a τ-adic expansion K for scalar multiplication.

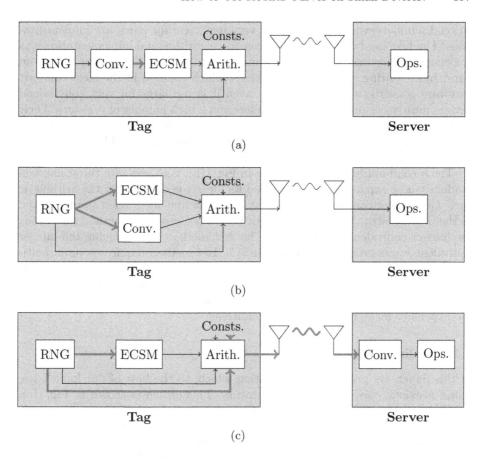

Fig. 1. Three options for using Koblitz curves on a wireless tag. Thin black arrows and thick gray arrows represent integer and τ-adic values, respectively. (a) the random number generator (RNG) generates scalar k as an integer which is converted to a τ-adic expansion K in order to use it in the elliptic curve scalar multiplication (ECSM) but k can be used as it is in the arithmetic part; (b) the RNG generates a random τ-adic expansion K which is used as it is in the ECSM but it is converted into an integer k in order to use it in the arithmetic part; and (c) the RNG generates a random τ-adic expansion K but the arithmetic part is also performed (at least partly) in the τ-adic domain. The computationally expensive conversion is delegated to the server.

The arithmetic part can be computed using the original integer k. The first method for conversion was given by Koblitz [13]. It has the drawback that the length of the τ-adic expansion is twice the length of the original scalar, consequently, reducing the efficiency of the scalar multiplication. Later, Meier and Staffelbach [17] and Solinas [24] showed that expansions of approximately the same length as the original scalar can be found. Solinas [24] also showed how to find τ-adic nonadjacent form (τNAF) and windowed NAF (w-τNAF) representations for the scalar k. These algorithms require, e.g., operations with large rational numbers, which render them very inefficient for hardware implementations. The first hardware oriented conversion algorithm and implementation was presented by Järvinen et al. [10]. Brumley and Järvinen [6] later presented an algorithm requiring only integer additions, which resulted in the most compact hardware converter to date; however, even it is too large for very constrained devices mostly because it uses long adders and a high number of registers. Their work was extended by Adikari et al. [1] and Sinha Roy et al. [23] who focused on improving speed at the expense of resource requirements, which makes them even less suitable for constrained devices.

The second option, which is shown in Fig. 1(b), is to generate the scalar as a random τ-adic expansion K and to find its integer equivalent for the arithmetic part. Generating random τ-adic expansions was first mentioned (and credited to Hendrik Lenstra) by Koblitz [13] but he did not provide a method for finding the integer equivalent of the scalar. The first method for retrieving the integer equivalent k was proposed by Lange in [15]. Her method requires several multiplications with long operands. More efficient methods were later introduced by Brumley and Järvinen in [5,6]. The resource requirements of their methods are smaller than computing conversions to the other direction [6] but even they are too expensive for lightweight implementations.

3.2   Outline of the New Idea

In this paper, we propose a third option which, to the best of our knowledge, is not previously available in the literature. This option is shown in Fig. 1(c). Similarly to the second option, the tag generates a random τ-adic expansion K and uses it for scalar multiplication. However, the tag does not compute the integer equivalent k but, instead, it uses K directly and all operations which depend on it are computed in the τ-adic domain. The results of these operations (τ-adic expansions) are transmitted over the radio channel to the server, which first converts the results to integers and then proceeds with normal server-side operations. Only the operations which depend on the scalar need to be computed in the τ-adic domain and, hence, it may be possible to compute other operations (and transmit their results) using integers. Clearly, this option improves efficiency of the tag only if operations in the τ-adic domain are cheap. In the following, we show that they can, indeed, be implemented with very few resources. From security perspective, the third option is equivalent with the second option discussed in Sect. 3.1 (c.f. [15]) because transmitting τ-adic expansions instead of their integer equivalents does not reveal any additional information about the secret scalars.

The new idea has similarities with [4], which presented a modified version of the Girault-Poupard-Stern identification scheme that handles only τ-adic expansions. Both [4] and the new idea use arithmetic in the τ-adic domain. We adapt and further develop the addition algorithm from [4]. The new idea allows delegating conversions to the more powerful party for arbitrary cryptosystems that require scalar multiplications on Koblitz curves and modular integer arithmetic with the scalar, whereas [4] presented a single identification scheme built around

τ-adic expansions only. For instance, it is unclear how to build a digital signature scheme that uses only τ-adic expansions because the ideas of [4] cannot be directly generalized to other schemes. We also provide the first hardware realizations of algorithms required to implement the new idea. These implementations may have importance also for implementing the scheme from [4].

4   Addition in the τ-adic Domain

The cornerstone of the idea discussed in Sect. 3.2 is to devise an efficient algorithm for adding two τ-adic expansions. In this section, we show how to construct such an algorithm. Our addition algorithm is close to the algorithm from [4] but we improve its efficiency and provide an analysis of the algorithm. Other arithmetic operations can be built upon the addition algorithm and they are discussed later in Sect. 5.

Let A and B be the τ-adic expansions of two positive integers a and b such that

$$A = \sum_{i=0}^{n-1} A_i \tau^i \quad \text{and} \quad B = \sum_{i=0}^{n-1} B_i \tau^i \tag{3}$$

where $A_i \in \{0, 1\}$ and $B_i \in \{-1, 0, 1\}$ so that $A_{n-1} = 1$ and/or $B_{n-1} = \pm 1$. Signed bits are allowed for B for two reasons: (a) Koblitz curve cryptosystems are typically implemented by using the τNAF) representation [24] or some other representation with signed bits (e.g., [22,27]) and (b) this allows computing subtractions with the same algorithm.

Adding the two expansions gives the following expansion:

$$C = A + B = \sum_{i=0}^{n-1} C_i \tau^i \tag{4}$$

where $C_i = A_i + B_i \in \{-1, 0, 1, 2\}$. This expansion is correct in the sense that $C \overset{\circ}{=} a + b$ but it has several drawbacks because the set of digits has grown. Hence, the expansion must be processed in order to obtain a binary-valued τ-adic expansion. Instead of allowing C to have signed binary values as in [4], we limit the set of digits to unsigned binary values (i.e., $C_i \in \{0, 1\}$) in order to decrease the storage requirements for C. This does not imply restrictions for the use of the addition algorithm in our case as long as B_i are allowed to have signed binary values because we do not use the results of additions for computing scalar multiplications.

The binary-valued expansion C can be found analogously to normal addition of binary numbers by using a carry [4]. The main difference is that the carry is a τ-adic number t. The unsigned binary valued C_i is obtained by adding the coefficients A_i and B_i with the carry from the previous iteration and by reducing this value modulo 2; i.e., by taking the least significant bit (lsb). Every τ-adic number can be represented as $t_0 + t_1\tau$ where $t_0, t_1 \in \mathbb{Z}$ [24] and, hence, also the carry t can be represented with two integer coefficients as $t = t_0 + t_1\tau$.

Input: τ-adic expansions $A = \sum_{i=0}^{n-1} A_i \tau^i \stackrel{\circ}{=} a$ and $B = \sum_{i=0}^{n-1} B_i \tau^i \stackrel{\circ}{=} b$
Output: $C = \sum_{i=0}^{n'-1} C_i \tau^i$, where $C_i \in \{0, 1\}$, such that $C \stackrel{\circ}{=} a + b$
1 $(t_0, t_1) \leftarrow (0, 0); i \leftarrow 0$;
2 **while** $i < n$ **or** $(t_0, t_1) \neq (0, 0)$ **do**
3     $r \leftarrow A_i + B_i + t_0$;
4     $C_i \leftarrow r \bmod 2$;
5     $(t_0, t_1) \leftarrow (t_1 + \mu \lfloor r/2 \rfloor, -\lfloor r/2 \rfloor)$;
6     $i \leftarrow i + 1$;
7 **return** C

Algorithm 1. Addition in the τ-adic domain

Updating the carry for the next iteration requires a division by τ. As shown by Solinas [24], $t_0 + t_1\tau$ is divisible by τ if and only if t_0 is even. Subtracting C_i (rounding towards the nearest smaller integer) ensures this and, hence, we get:

$$((t_0 - C_i) + t_1\tau)/\tau = t_1 + \mu \left\lfloor \frac{t_0}{2} \right\rfloor - \left\lfloor \frac{t_0}{2} \right\rfloor \tau . \tag{5}$$

We continue the above process for all n bits of the operands and as long as $(t_0, t_1) \neq (0, 0)$. The resulting algorithm is shown in Algorithm 1.

Remark 1. Computing subtractions with Algorithm 1 is straightforward: $A - B = A + (-B) = A + \sum_{i=0}^{n-1}(-B_i)\tau^i$. I.e., we flip the signs of B_i and compute an addition with Algorithm 1. Alternatively, we revise Algorithm 1 so that Line 3 is replaced with $r \leftarrow A_i - B_i + t_0$.

4.1 Analysis of Algorithm 1

There are certain aspects that must be analyzed before Algorithm 1 is ready for efficient hardware implementation. The most crucial one is the sizes of the carry values t_0 and t_1 because efficient hardware implementation is impossible without knowing the number of flip-flops required for the carry. The ending condition of Algorithm 1 also implies that the latency of an addition depends on the values of the operands. This might open vulnerabilities against timing attacks. The following analysis sheds light on these aspects and provides efficient solutions for them.

In order to analyze Algorithm 1, we model it as a finite state machine (FSM) so that the carry (t_0, t_1) represents the state. Algorithm 1 can find unsigned binary τ-adic expansions with any $A_i, B_i \in \mathbb{Z}$ but, in this analysis and in the following propositions, we limit them so that $A_i \in \{0, 1\}$ and $B_i \in \{-1, 0, 1\}$, as described above. The FSM is constructed starting from the state $(t_0, t_1) = (0, 0)$ by analyzing all transitions with all possible inputs $A_i + B_i \in \{-1, 0, 1, 2\}$. E.g., when $\mu = 1$, we find out that the possible next states from the initial state $(0, 0)$ are $(0, 0)$ with inputs 0 and 1 (the corresponding outputs are then 0 and 1), $(-1, 1)$ with input -1 (output 1), and $(1, -1)$ with input 2 (output 0). Next, we

Fig. 2. The FSM for Algorithm 1, when $\mu = 1$, with inputs $A_i \in \{0,1\}$ and $B_i \in \{-1,0,1\}$. The FSM is plotted on the complex plane so that each state is positioned based on its complex value $t = t_0 + t_1\tau$. The states are labeled with (t_0, t_1). State transitions are marked with *in / out* where *in* are the input values for which the transition is taken and *out* are the corresponding outputs.

analyze $(-1,1)$ or $(1,-1)$, and so on. The process is continued as long as there are states that have not been analyzed. The resulting FSM for $\mu = 1$ is depicted in Fig. 2 and it contains 21 states. We draw two major conclusions from this FSM (and the corresponding one for $\mu = -1$).

Proposition 1. *For both $\mu = \pm 1$, the carry (t_0, t_1) of Algorithm 1 can be represented with 6 bits so that both t_0 and t_1 require 3 bits.*

Proof. The FSM of Fig. 2 directly shows that $-3 \le t_0 \le 3$ and $-2 \le t_1 \le 2$. There are 7 distinct values for t_0 and 5 for t_1 and, hence, they can be represented with 3 bits, e.g., by using two's complement representation. The FSM for $\mu = -1$ can be constructed similarly and it also contains 21 states so that $-3 \le t_0 \le 3$ and $-2 \le t_1 \le 2$. Hence, t_0 and t_1 both require 3 bits for $\mu = \pm 1$. Consequently, the carry requires 6 bits. ∎

Remark 2. The FSM of Fig. 2 includes 21 states. Hence, the states could be represented with only 5 bits. Unfortunately, if the algorithm is implemented directly as an FSM, the growth in the size of the combinational part outweighs the benefits gained from the lower number of flip-flops.

Proposition 2. *Let n be the larger of the lengths of A and B; i.e., $A_{n-1} = 1$ and/or $B_{n-1} = \pm 1$. Then, Algorithm 1 returns C with a length n' that satisfies*

$$n' \le n + \lambda \tag{6}$$

where $\lambda = 7$ for both $\mu = \pm 1$.

Proof. After all n bits of A and B have been processed, the FSM can be in any of the 21 states. Hence, the constant λ is given by the longest path from any state to the state $(0,0)$ when the input is fixed to zero; i.e., $A_i = B_i = 0$. The FSM of Fig. 2 shows that the longest path starts from the state $(0,2)$ and goes through the following states $(2,0)$, $(1,-1)$, $(0,-1)$, $(-1,0)$, $(-1,1)$, and $(0,1)$ to $(0,0)$ and outputs $(0,0,1,1,1,0,1)$. Thus, $\lambda = 7$ for $\mu = 1$. It can be shown similarly that $\lambda = 7$ also for $\mu = -1$. ∎

5   Other Operations in the τ-adic Domain

In this section, we describe algorithms for other arithmetic operations in the τ-adic domain, which are required in order to implement the idea of Sect. 3.2. The algorithms are based on using the addition algorithm given in Algorithm 1.

5.1   Folding

The length of an arbitrarily long τ-adic expansion can be reduced to about m bits without changing its integer equivalent modulo q, where q is the order of the base point of the scalar multiplication. The integer equivalent of a τ-adic expansion $A = \sum_{i=0}^{n-1} A_i \tau^i$ can be retrieved by computing the sum $a = \sum_{i=0}^{n-1} A_i s^i \pmod{q}$ where s, the integer equivalent of τ, is a per-curve constant integer [15]. Because $s^m \equiv 1 \pmod{q}$,

$$a = \sum_{i=0}^{n-1} A_i s^i \equiv \sum_{j=0}^{\lfloor n/m \rfloor} \sum_{i=0}^{m-1} A_{jm+i} s^i \pmod{q}, \tag{7}$$

Input: τ-adic expansion $A = \sum_{i=0}^{n-1} A_i \tau^i \overset{\circ}{=} a$, m, and $\ell \geq m$
Output: $B = \sum_{i=0}^{n'-1} B_i \tau^i \overset{\circ}{=} b = a$ and $n' \leq \ell$
1 $B \leftarrow A^{(0)}$;
2 **for** $j = 1$ **to** $\lfloor n/m \rfloor$ **do**
3 $\quad \lfloor \ B \leftarrow B + A^{(j)}$;   /* Algorithm 1 */
4 **while** $n' > \ell$ **do**
5 $\quad \lfloor \ B \leftarrow B^{(0)} + B^{(1)} + \ldots + B^{(\lfloor n'/m \rfloor)}$;   /* Optional, Algorithm 1 */
6 **return** B

Algorithm 2. Folding

where $A_i = 0$ for $i \geq n$. As a result of (7), an expansion can be compressed to approximately m bits by "folding" the expansion; i.e., folding is analogous to modular reduction. Let $A^{(j)} = \sum_{i=0}^{m-1} A_{jm+i} \tau^i$, the j-th m-bit block of A. Then, an approximately m-bit τ-adic expansion B having the same integer equivalent with A can be obtained by computing $B = A^{(0)} + A^{(1)} + \ldots + A^{(\lfloor n/m \rfloor)}$ with $\lfloor n/m \rfloor$ applications of Algorithm 1. Because of the carry structure of Algorithm 1, the length of the expansion may still exceed m bits. Additional foldings can be computed in the end in order to trim the length of B below a predefined bound $\ell \geq m$. An algorithm for folding (including the optional trimming in the end) is given in Algorithm 2. In most practical cases, the optional trimming requires at most one addition: $B^{(0)} + B^{(1)}$.

5.2 Multiplication

Multiplication of two τ-adic expansions A and B is given as follows:

$$C = A \times B = \sum_{i=0}^{n-1} A_i \tau^i B \ . \tag{8}$$

An algorithm for multiplication in the τ-adic domain can be devised by using a variation of the binary method. An addition is computed with Algorithm 1 if $A_i = 1$ and a multiplication by τ is performed for all A_i by shifting the bit vector. Hence, multiplication requires $n - 1$ shifts and $\rho(A) - 1$ additions, where $\rho(A)$ is the Hamming weight of A. A bit-serial most significant bit (msb) first multiplication algorithm is presented in Algorithm 3. A similar multiplication algorithm was used also in [4].

It is also possible to use the binary method for computing multiplications where the other operand, say a, is an integer. Algorithm 4 presents a bit-serial msb first algorithm for computing $C = a \times B$ such that $C \overset{\circ}{=} a \times b$. It requires $n + \rho(A) - 2$ additions with Algorithm 1.

Remark 3. Algorithm 4 also serves as an algorithm for converting integers to the τ-adic domain. An integer a can be converted by computing $a \times 1$ with Algorithm 4. The algorithm returns $C = A$, the unsigned binary τ-adic expansion

---

Input: τ-adic expansions $A = \tau^{n-1} + \sum_{i=0}^{n-2} A_i \tau^i \stackrel{\circ}{=} a$, where $A_i \in \{0, 1\}$, and
$B \stackrel{\circ}{=} b$, where $B_i \in \{-1, 0, 1\}$
Output: $C = A \times B$ such that $C \stackrel{\circ}{=} a \times b$
1 $C \leftarrow B$;
2 **for** $i = n - 2$ **to** 0 **do**
3 | $C \leftarrow \tau C$;   /* Shift */
4 | **if** $A_i = 1$ **then**
5 | └ $C \leftarrow C + B$;   /* Algorithm 1 */
6 **return** C

Algorithm 3. Multiplication in the τ-adic domain

Input: Integer $a = 2^{\lfloor \log_2 a \rfloor} + \sum_{i=0}^{\lfloor \log_2 a \rfloor - 1} a_i 2^i$, where $a_i \in \{0, 1\}$, and a τ-adic
expansion $B \stackrel{\circ}{=} b$, where $B_i \in \{-1, 0, 1\}$
Output: C such that $C \stackrel{\circ}{=} a \times b$
1 $C \leftarrow B$;
2 **for** $i = \lfloor \log_2 a \rfloor - 1$ **to** 0 **do**
3 | $C \leftarrow C + C$;   /* Algorithm 1 */
4 | **if** $a_i = 1$ **then**
5 | └ $C \leftarrow C + B$;   /* Algorithm 1 */
6 **return** C

Algorithm 4. Multiplication by an integer in the τ-adic domain

---

of a. This could also be used for converting k but, in that case, K would have $\rho(K) \approx n/2$, whereas representing K in τNAF gives $\rho(K) \approx n/3$ and results in more efficient scalar multiplications.

Remark 4. Different versions of the binary method can be straightforwardly used for devising an algorithm for multiplications of τ-adic expansions (also when the other operand is an integer). Especially, using Montgomery's ladder [19] would give an algorithm with a constant sequence of operations (shifts and additions), which would provide resistance against side-channel analysis. The scalar k is typically a nonce and the adversary is limited to a single side-channel trace. Thus, constant pattern of operations offers sufficient protection against most attacks.

5.3 Multiplicative Inverse

The multiplicative inverse modulo q, a^{-1}, for an integer a can be found via Fermat's Little Theorem by computing the following exponentiation:

$$a^{-1} = a^{q-2} \pmod{q} . \tag{9}$$

Input: τ-adic expansion A of integer a and $q' = q - 2$
Output: B such that $b \equiv a^{-1} \pmod{q}$
1 $B \leftarrow A$;
2 **for** $i = \lfloor \log_2 q' \rfloor - 1$ **to** 0 **do**
3 | $B \leftarrow B \times B$;   /* Algorithm 3 */
4 | **if** $q'_i = 1$ **then**
5 | └ $B \leftarrow B \times A$;   /* Algorithm 3 */
6 **return** B

Algorithm 5. Inversion modulo q in the τ-adic domain

This exponentiation gives a straightforward way to compute inversions also with τ-adic expansions. Let $q' = q - 2$. Given a τ-adic expansion A, a τ-adic expansion A^{-1} such that $A \times A^{-1} \stackrel{\circ}{=} a \times a^{-1} \equiv 1 \pmod{q}$ can be found by computing:

$$A^{-1} = A^{q'} = \prod_{i=0}^{\lfloor \log_2 q' \rfloor} A^{q'_i 2^i} . \tag{10}$$

Algorithm 5 shows an algorithm for computing (10) by using Algorithm 3.

6   Architecture

The objective of this work was to provide an efficient circuitry with small resource requirements that could be used for computing τ-adic arithmetic in lightweight implementations. Figure 3 presents an architecture that implements Algorithm 1 for $\mu = 1$. Because $B_i \in \{-1, 0, 1\}$, it can be used for K given using signed-bit representations (e.g., [22, 24, 27]). Because $t_0 \in [-3, 3]$ and $A_i + B_i \in [-1, 2]$, $r \in [-4, 5]$ and we need 4 bits to represent it. The division $\lfloor r/2 \rfloor$ can be trivially performed by dropping off the lsb of r, which is used directly as C_i. The carry values t_0 and t_1 are represented as 3-bit two's complement numbers (see Proposition 1). Hence, $-\lfloor r/2 \rfloor$ is obtained by flipping the bits and adding one, which results in the circuitry shown on the right in Fig. 3. The while loop can be implemented as a for loop from 0 to $n + \lambda - 1$ (see Proposition 2). The rest of Algorithm 1 and the other algorithms (e.g., Algorithm 3) can be implemented with a simple control logic and shift registers for the operands. Algorithm 1 and the architecture of Fig. 3 are independent of the field size m and, hence, the same architecture can be used for all Koblitz curves with $\mu = 1$.

A circuitry for $\mu = -1$ can be devised similarly but we omit the description because of space restrictions. We merely state that it is almost similar: the only difference is that the adders updating t_0 (on the left in Fig. 3) use the outputs of the negation part that computes $-\lfloor r/2 \rfloor$ (on the right in Fig. 3) instead of taking $\lfloor r/2 \rfloor$ directly. Hence, the area requirements should, in theory, remain the same but the critical path becomes longer by one NOT and two XORs (in the half adders).

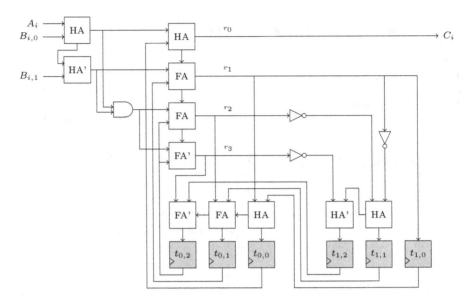

Fig. 3. Architecture for $\mu = 1$. The circuit consists of 4 half adders (HA), 3 full adders (FA), 2 half adders without carry logic (HA'), 2 full adders without carry logic (FA'), 3 NOTs, and 6 flip-flops. All wires are single bit wires

The circuitry of Fig. 3 computes additions in the τ-adic domain with a constant latency of $n+\lambda$ clock cycles. Assuming that $n \approx m$, we get that an addition requires $m + 7$ clock cycles; this gives 170 clock cycles for the NIST curve K-163 from [21]. If multiplication by τ (shift) takes one clock cycle, Algorithm 3 requires approximately $m(m + \lambda + 2)/2$ clock cycles and Algorithm 4 requires approximately $3m(m+\lambda)/2$ clock cycles; this gives roughly 14000 or 41600 clock cycles, respectively, for NIST K-163. These latencies are small compared to the latency of scalar multiplication [2,3,8,14,16]. It is also typical for lightweight implementations that area, power, and energy consumption are more important than latency.

7   Results and Comparison

We described the circuitry of Fig. 3 and the corresponding one for $\mu = -1$ in VHDL and simulated them with ModelSim SE 6.6d. We used Synopsys Design Compiler D-2010.03-SP4 with Faraday FSC0L standard cell libraries for synthesizing them for UMC $0.13\,\mu\mathrm{m}$ CMOS with voltage of 1.2 V. When synthesized using the 'compile ultra' process without additional constraints, the areas of the circuitries were 75.25 and 76.25 gate equivalents (GE) for $\mu = 1$ and $\mu = -1$, respectively.

The converter architectures available in the literature have been implemented on field-programmable gate arrays (FPGA) and, consequently, their area and performance characteristics are available only for FPGAs. Hence, comparing the

Table 1. Comparison to the state-of-the-art converters for NIST K-163 ($\mu = 1$)

Work	Technology	Area / Notes	GE
[6], integer-to-τNAF	FPGA, Stratix II S60C4	948 ALUTs, 683 FFs	> 7200
[6], τ-adic-to-integer	FPGA, Stratix II S60C4	850 ALUTs, 491 FFs	> 3600
This work, $\mu = 1$	ASIC, $0.13\,\mu$m CMOS	Fig. 3	75.25
This work, $\mu = 1$	ASIC, $0.13\,\mu$m CMOS	Fig. 3, 340 FFs	~ 2000

circuitries presented above to the state-of-the-art converters is not straightforward. In order to perform a fair comparison, we estimate the GE counts of the converters from [6], which are the most compact converters available in the literature. These estimates in the case of NIST K-163 are collected in Table 1.

The integer to τNAF converter [6] includes two m-bit and four $m/2$-bit adders and registers as well as several multiplexers and comparators. A full adder and a flip-flop both require 5.5 GE on $0.13\,\mu$m CMOS and, hence, we can estimate that only the adders and registers occupy an area of about 7200 GE if $m = 163$. The area of the τ-adic expansion to integer converter [6] that requires two m-bit adders, two m-bit registers, multiplexers, and comparators can be estimated similarly. The adders and registers alone give an area estimate of about 3600 GE if $m = 163$.

Algorithms 3–4 require two $(m + \lambda)$-bit registers. We anticipate that in most implementations these registers can be shared with the circuitry computing scalar multiplications. In that case, the overhead of the circuitries is only about one hundred GEs (including the control logic), which is negligible compared to the converters. If none of these registers can be shared with the scalar multiplier, then the circuitry for NIST K-163 including registers has an area of approximately 2000 GE. This area is still only about half of the area of the smallest converter available today.

8   Case Study: ECDSA

In this section, we present a case study of how the new scheme could be used for ECDSA. The tag computes an ECDSA signature for a message $\mathcal{M}$ and sends it to a more powerful server for verification. The signature (r, s) is computed as follows [21]:

$$k \in_R [1, q - 1] \tag{11}$$

$$r = [k\mathbf{P}]_x \tag{12}$$

$$e = H(\mathcal{M}) \tag{13}$$

$$s = k^{-1}(e + dr) \mod q \tag{14}$$

where d is the signer's private key, $[k\mathbf{P}]_x$ denotes the x-coordinate of the result point of the scalar multiplication $k\mathbf{P}$, and $H(\mathcal{M})$ is the hash value of $\mathcal{M}$ (e.g., SHA-256).

Equation (12) can be efficiently computed using Koblitz curves if k is given as a τ-adic expansion; i.e., we compute $r = [K\mathbf{P}]_x$. We can use the τNAF representation for K in order to speedup computations. If the compact encoding proposed by Joye and Tymen [11] is used, then K can be obtained by generating m random bits. In order to avoid computing the expensive inversion of (14), we can transmit the nominator and denominator separately after blinding them with $b \in_R [1, q-1]$ as proposed in [20]: $s_n = b(e + dr) \mod q$ and $s_d = bk \mod q$. Because K affects only s_d, we compute s_n using cheaper integer arithmetic. The denominator can be computed with a single multiplication in the τ-adic domain: $S_d = b \times K$ by using Algorithm 4. The result of the multiplication should be compressed by folding it with Algorithm 2 after (and at any time during) the execution of Algorithm 4. Instead of transmitting a $2m$-bit (r, s), we now transmit approximately $3m$-bit (r, s_n, S_d). The server computes s_d from S_d and performs the modular division $s = s_n/s_d \pmod{q}$, after which it proceeds normally with the signature verification procedure from [21].

If transmission is expensive, the transmittable amount can be reduced to $2m$ bits by computing the inversion in the tag and transmitting (r, S). In this case, it is preferable to compute $e + dr$ using integers, invert K using Algorithm 5, and compute $S = (e + dr) \times K^{-1}$ with Algorithm 4. Both S and intermediate values should be folded with Algorithm 2 in order to limit the amount of storage and transmission. In this case, the server simply converts S to s before proceeding normally.

9   Conclusions and Future Work

In this paper, we showed that, contrary to previous beliefs, Koblitz curves can be efficiently used in lightweight implementations even if integer arithmetic is required with the scalar k. Because Koblitz curves offer more efficient scalar multiplications compared to general binary curves, utilizing the findings of this paper will probably enable more efficient lightweight implementations of ECC than what has been possible in the past. We conclude with the following suggestions for future research:

Future work 1. For Koblitz curve cryptosystems, resistance against side-channel attacks can be achieved by using dummy point additions [7], randomized representations for the scalar [7], or more efficiently with a zerofree representation for the scalar [22,27]. The approach presented in this paper can be straightforwardly applied also in these cases. As mentioned in Remark 4, the side-channel resistivity of the algorithms proposed in this paper can be improved, e.g., by using Montgomery's ladder [19] in Algorithms 3 and 4. The circuitries of Sect. 6 can be implemented with secure logic styles (e.g., [26]) in order to limit side-channel leakage. Although the more significant side-channel leakages are typically in scalar multiplication parts, resistance against side-channel attacks deserves further research in the future.

Future work 2. The registers for t occupy almost half of the areas of the addition circuits. Hence, significant speedups and area-speed ratio improvements could be achieved by processing several A_i and B_i in one iteration because this would affect only the amount of logic, not the number of flip-flops.

Future work 3. As discussed in Sect. 7, the circuitries have negligible area overheads if the shift registers for the operands can be shared with the circuitry computing scalar multiplications. It will be studied in the future how registers could be shared, e.g., with the compact architecture presented in [2].

Acknowledgments. We would like to thank the anonymous reviewers for their valuable comments and improvement suggestions. The work was partly funded by KU Leuven under GOA TENSE (GOA/11/007) and the F+ fellowship (F+/13/039) and by the Hercules Foundation (AKUL/11/19).

References

1. Adikari, J., Dimitrov, V., Järvinen, K.: A fast hardware architecture for integer to τNAF conversion for Koblitz curves. IEEE Trans. Comput. **61**(5), 732–737 (2012)
2. Azarderakhsh, R., Järvinen, K.U., Mozaffari-Kermani, M.: Efficient algorithm and architecture for elliptic curve cryptography for extremely constrained secure applications. IEEE Trans. Circ. Syst. I-Regul. Pap. **61**(4), 1144–1155 (2014)
3. Batina, L., Mentens, N., Sakiyama, K., Preneel, B., Verbauwhede, I.: Low-cost elliptic curve cryptography for wireless sensor networks. In: Buttyán, L., Gligor, V.D., Westhoff, D. (eds.) ESAS 2006. LNCS, vol. 4357, pp. 6–17. Springer, Heidelberg (2006)
4. Benits Jr, W.D., Galbraith, S.D.: The GPS identification scheme using frobenius expansions. In: Lucks, S., Sadeghi, A.-R., Wolf, C. (eds.) WEWoRC 2007. LNCS, vol. 4945, pp. 13–27. Springer, Heidelberg (2008)
5. Brumley, B.B., Järvinen, K.U.: Koblitz curves and integer equivalents of frobenius expansions. In: Adams, C., Miri, A., Wiener, M. (eds.) SAC 2007. LNCS, vol. 4876, pp. 126–137. Springer, Heidelberg (2007)
6. Brumley, B.B., Järvinen, K.U.: Conversion algorithms and implementations for Koblitz curve cryptography. IEEE Trans. Comput. **59**(1), 81–92 (2010)
7. Hasan, M.A.: Power analysis attacks and algorithmic approaches to their countermeasures for Koblitz curve cryptosystems. IEEE Trans. Comput. **50**(10), 1071–1083 (2001)
8. Hein, D., Wolkerstorfer, J., Felber, N.: ECC is ready for RFID – a proof in silicon. In: Avanzi, R.M., Keliher, L., Sica, F. (eds.) SAC 2008. LNCS, vol. 5381, pp. 401–413. Springer, Heidelberg (2009)
9. Järvinen, K.: Optimized FPGA-based elliptic curve cryptography processor for high-speed applications. Integr. VLSI J. **44**(4), 270–279 (2011)
10. Järvinen, K., Forsten, J., Skyttä, J.: Efficient circuitry for computing τ-adic non-adjacent form. In: Proceedings of the 13th IEEE International Conference on Electronics, Circuits and Systems – ICECS 2006, pp. 232–235. IEEE (2006)
11. Joye, M., Tymen, C.: Compact encoding of non-adjacent forms with applications to elliptic curve cryptography. In: Kim, K. (ed.) PKC 2001. LNCS, vol. 1992, pp. 353–364. Springer, Heidelberg (2001)

12. Koblitz, N.: Elliptic curve cryptosystems. Math. Comput. **48**(177), 203–209 (1987)
13. Koblitz, N.: CM-curves with good cryptographic properties. In: Feigenbaum, J. (ed.) CRYPTO 1991. LNCS, vol. 576, pp. 279–287. Springer, Heidelberg (1992)
14. Koçabas, Ü., Fan, J., Verbauwhede, I.: Implementation of binary edwards curves for very-constrained devices. In: Proceedings of the 21st IEEE International Conference on Application-specific Systems Architectures and Processors – ASAP 2010, pp. 185–191. IEEE (2010)
15. Lange, T.: Koblitz curve cryptosystems. Finite Fields Appl. **11**, 200–229 (2005)
16. Lee, Y.K., Sakiyama, K., Batina, L., Verbauwhede, I.: Elliptic-curve-based security processor for RFID. IEEE Trans. Comput. **57**(11), 1514–1527 (2008)
17. Meier, W., Staffelbach, O.: Efficient multiplication on certain nonsupersingular elliptic curves. In: Brickell, E.F. (ed.) CRYPTO 1992. LNCS, vol. 740, pp. 333–344. Springer, Heidelberg (1993)
18. Miller, V.S.: Use of elliptic curves in cryptography. In: Williams, H.C. (ed.) CRYPTO 1985. LNCS, vol. 218, pp. 417–426. Springer, Heidelberg (1986)
19. Montgomery, P.L.: Speeding the Pollard and elliptic curve methods of factorization. Math. Comput. **48**, 243–264 (1987)
20. Naccache, D., M'Raïhi, D., Vaudenay, S., Raphaeli, D.: Can D.S.A. be improved? In: De Santis, A. (ed.) EUROCRYPT 1994. LNCS, vol. 950, pp. 77–85. Springer, Heidelberg (1995)
21. National Institute of Standards and Technology (NIST): Digital signature standard (DSS). Federal Information Processing Standard, FIPS PUB 186-4 (July 2013)
22. Okeya, K., Takagi, T., Vuillaume, C.: Efficient representations on Koblitz curves with resistance to side channel attacks. In: Boyd, C., González Nieto, J.M. (eds.) ACISP 2005. LNCS, vol. 3574, pp. 218–229. Springer, Heidelberg (2005)
23. Sinha Roy, S., Fan, J., Verbauwhede, I.: Accelerating scalar conversion for Koblitz curve cryptoprocessors on hardware platforms. In: IEEE Transactions on Very Large Scale Integration (VLSI) Systems (to appear)
24. Solinas, J.A.: Efficient arithmetic on Koblitz curves. Des. Codes Crypt. **19**(2–3), 195–249 (2000)
25. Taverne, J., Faz-Hernández, A., Aranha, D.F., Rodríguez-Henríquez, F., Hankerson, D., López, J.: Speeding scalar multiplication over binary elliptic curves using the new carry-less multiplication instruction. J. Crypt. Eng. **1**(3), 187–199 (2011)
26. Tiri, K., Verbauwhede, I.: A logic level design methodology for a secure DPA resistant ASIC or FPGA implementation. In: Proceedings of Design, Automation and Test in Europe Conference and Exhibition – DATE 2004, vol. 1, pp. 246–251. IEEE (2004)
27. Vuillaume, C., Okeya, K., Takagi, T.: Defeating simple power analysis on Koblitz curves. In: IEICE Transactions on Fundamentals of Electronics, Communications and Computer Sciences E89-A(5), pp. 1362–1369 (May 2006)

Public-Key Cryptography

Caml Crush: A PKCS#11 Filtering Proxy

Ryad Benadjila, Thomas Calderon, and Marion Daubignard$^{(\boxtimes)}$

ANSSI, Paris, France
{ryad.benadjila,thomas.calderon,marion.daubignard}@ssi.gouv.fr

Abstract. PKCS#11 is a very popular cryptographic API: it is the standard used by many Hardware Security Modules, smartcards and software cryptographic tokens. Several attacks have been uncovered against PKCS#11 at different levels: intrinsic logical flaws, cryptographic vulnerabilities or severe compliance issues. Since affected hardware remains widespread in computer infrastructures, we propose a user-centric and pragmatic approach for secure usage of vulnerable devices. We introduce *Caml Crush*, a PKCS#11 filtering proxy. Our solution allows to dynamically protect PKCS#11 cryptographic tokens from state of the art attacks. This is the first approach that is immediately applicable to commercially available products. We provide a fully functional open source implementation with an extensible filter engine effectively shielding critical resources. This yields additional advantages to using *Caml Crush* that go beyond classical PKCS#11 weakness mitigations.

Keywords: PKCS#11 · Filter · Proxy · OCaml · Software

Introduction

The ever increasing needs for confidentiality and privacy of information advocates for a pervasive use of cryptography. However, the security provided by cryptography itself completely relies on the confidentiality and integrity of some (quite small) pieces of data, e.g., secret keys. Therefore, sound management of this sensitive data proves to be as critical in ensuring any amount of security as the use of cryptography itself. In practise, cryptographic material is accessed and operated on through an Application Programming Interface (API). Protection and handling of sensitive objects thus fall back on *security APIs*, which enable external applications to perform cryptographic operations.

Normalization efforts have yielded the RSA PKCS#11 standard, which nowadays appears as the *de facto* standard adopted by the industry [18]. Therefore, much effort should be devoted to the provision of solutions allowing for safe and sound implementations of the PKCS#11 security API. In this article we present *Caml Crush*, a secure architecture meant to protect vulnerable PKCS#11 *middlewares*. As an additional software layer sitting between applications and the original PKCS#11 middleware, *Caml Crush* acts as a mandatory checkpoint controlling the flow of operations. The result is a PKCS#11 filtering proxy which

© Springer International Publishing Switzerland 2015
M. Joye and A. Moradi (Eds.): CARDIS 2014, LNCS 8968, pp. 173–192, 2015.
DOI: 10.1007/978-3-319-16763-3_11

can enforce dynamic protection of cryptographic resources through the use of an extensible filtering engine.

Though software tokens do exist, it is rather classical to depend on hardware assisted solutions, such as smartcards and Hardware Security Modules (HSMs). Having put to test numerous platforms exposing the PKCS#11 interface, it has come to our attention that the available implementations, be it open-source or commercial solutions, often do not meet average requirements in terms of standard compliance, robustness, let alone security properties. As many end-users of HSMs are not granted the ability to modify (or even access) the source code of their interface, tending to these diverse weaknesses whilst preserving standard compliance commends for a global approach. Additionally, we aim to provide users with means to dynamically customize such APIs according to self-imposed restrictions or needs for vulnerability patches.

Possible improvements of the exposed API. The first and rather obvious step to take is to *enforce more acute conformity* to the PKCS#11 standard. Elementary as it seems, it really forms an inescapable axis of improvement, as there exist deployed tokens dutifully answering direct requests to output sensitive values, oblivious to the fact that the standard does explicitly prohibit it (see, e.g., [11]). That being said, security requirements stated in the PKCS#11 specification cannot be reached by solely implementing the standard to the letter. Indeed, the quite generic API described in the document bears inherent flaws which enable logical key-revealing attacks, such as the notorious wrap-and-decrypt attack. References depicting such attacks include [11,13,15][1]. It is worth mentioning that Bortolozzo et al. introduce in [11] a tool, Tookan, allowing for automatic API analysis and attack search. A second relevant amelioration of tokens consists in *patching PKCS#11 logical defects* while remaining as close as possible to the standard. In the meantime, it seems welcome to *address possible cryptographic attacks* such as padding oracle existence.

Fixing the PKCS#11 standard. Two main alternatives can be chosen to get a secure API: either try and fix the ubiquitous standard, or start over from scratch. This latter possibility has been explored by Cortier and Steel in [14], and by Cachin and Chandran in [12], who propose a server-centric approach. As mentioned earlier, the need we address is to allow for a secure use of already available – and even possibly deployed – tokens. This calls for the choice of the first and more pragmatic alternative.

In [11], the authors exhibit a successfully fixed PKCS#11 middleware: the software token named CryptokiX [2], whose security has been verified using the Tookan tool. CryptokiX is the work that bears the more similarities to our approach, in the sense that it successfully patches a number of the PKCS#11 standard flaws. There is no way to ensure that vendors provide customers with a patched version of their software. Hence, we believe that CryptokiX might not be a viable alternative for customers using HSMs as they operate the cryptographic resource with a proprietary and binary-only middleware. This objection put

---

[1] We refer the reader to the extended version of this paper [17] for more details.

aside, this work proves their patches realistic, and we reuse them in our work. Though it is clear that no piece of software can replace a secure API embedded in the hardware itself, we advocate a best-of-both-worlds approach in which users can suit to their needs and constraints the trade-off between security, performance and confidence in the token native implementation.

Our contributions. In this paper, we propose an additional middleware and a software stack running a filtering proxy service between client applications using cryptography and PKCS#11 compatible security devices. The idea is to exclusively expose to regular users - or potential adversaries - the API as made available by the proxy, rather than letting them interact with the commercially available middleware. We show that *Caml Crush* provides the means to effectively augment the security properties of the resulting solution. Obviously, these security guarantees rely on the assumption that adversaries cannot bypass the proxy - which we find to be relevant, according to several examples of deployment scenarios presented in the paper.

We emphasize that *Caml Crush* allows to adequately patch problems in PKCS#11 implementations, but not to search for them. Indeed, our architecture includes a filtering engine able to hook API function calls to either simply block them or filter them based on a run-time policy. Our proxy can feature any tailored filtering functionality throughout the client connection's lifetime. In particular, it can be configured to enforce some or all of the aforementioned hardening measures on top of any PKCS#11 interface.

Below is a non-exhaustive list of noticeable functionalities:

- every feature offered by CryptokiX is implemented in the filter module included in *Caml Crush*: patches to all known logical attacks are readily available.
- the PKCS#11 standard allows to tag cryptographic objects using labels or identifiers. *Caml Crush* twists this feature to filter objects and thus restrict their visibility. It finds an immediate application in virtualized environments or resource sharing scenarios.
- our implementation and design choices ensure great portability and interoperability even on platforms with different operating systems and endianness.
- we provide solutions to other attacks (coding flaws, buffer overflows vulnerabilities, etc.) by blocking, altering, or detecting and disabling repeated calls to a function.

We have validated our solution using both known attack implementations of our own and the more exhaustive trials performed by the Tookan tool. Finally, we underline the practical relevance of our work on several accounts. The filter engine possible configurations allow for flexible filtering policies. The complete source code of our implementation is made publicly available [1]. Moreover, the project was architectured with modularity in mind: it features user-defined extensions through plug-ins. Lastly, the performance cost measured in concrete deployment scenarios turns out to be reasonable.

Outline. Section 1 introduces PKCS#11 key concepts, briefly describes shortcomings of the API and details our motivations. Section 2 depicts the proxy architecture while justifying our design choices. Section 3 focuses on the filtering engine. Section 4 discusses deployment scenarios to secure various classes of devices, while Sect. 5 is both a security and performance evaluation.

1 Motivations of the Work

1.1 An Introduction to PKCS#11

PKCS are a set of standards developed to allow interoperability and compatibility between vendor devices and implementations. The PKCS#11 standard specifies a cryptographic API. This allows the cryptographic resource vendors to expose common interfaces so that application developers can implement portable code, while hiding low-level implementation details. A common way of exposing the API is through OS shared libraries.

To abstract away from the cryptographic resource, PKCS#11 defines a logical view of the devices: the **tokens**. To interact with the token, an application opens a **session** in which **objects** are manipulated. Objects can be keys, data or certificates and are used as input of cryptographic **mechanisms** defined by the standard. The objects can differ in their lifetime and visibility. Non-volatile objects are called **token objects**. They are accessible from all client applications. They differ from **session objects** are not meant to be shared between applications, and are destroyed once the session ends. Visibility of objects is also conditioned on whether a user is authenticated. When no authentication has been carried out, an application is only allowed to handle **public objects**, whereas authenticated users can use **private objects**. Once a session is opened with a resource, users traditionally achieve authentication by providing a PIN.

On top of implementing cryptography, tokens are meant to enforce security measures w.r.t. the objects they store. Namely, the main feature expected from tamper-resistant devices is that even legitimate users logging in on the token cannot **clone** it using the API. Thus, one of the key concepts behind PKCS#11 is to enable the use of cryptographic mechanisms without passing sensitive values in plaintext as arguments. The API uses **handles** to refer to objects, they are local to an application and bound to a session.

PKCS#11 objects can be exported from or injected into a token. This allows to save and restore keys (useful in case of broken or obsolete devices), but also to share keys over public channels between tokens. PKCS#11 objects are defined by a set of **attributes** which may vary depending on the object nature: symmetric secret keys have their value as an attribute, while asymmetric private keys have their modulus and exponents as attributes. Some attributes are common to all the storage objects though: examples are the `private` attribute and the `token` attribute characterizing the nature of the object (session vs. token objects as introduced previously).

Since the confidentiality of secret objects must be preserved, only their encrypted values are to be given to the user. PKCS#11 offers specific functions to export and import objects: `C_WrapKey` for **wrapping** and `C_UnwrapKey` for **unwrapping**. The result of a wrapping operation is an encrypted key value with a key that is inside the token, so that only the ciphertext is exported. In turn, keys used to protect other objects must be carefully managed. The PKCS#11 standard defines a few specific attributes to capture properties of keys allowing to monitor their use. Briefly, the `sensitive` attribute, when set to `TRUE`, is meant to prevent the user from fetching the value of the object, while an `extractable` attribute with value `FALSE` should prevent the user from exporting the object through a wrapping operation. Keys with attributes amongst `encrypt`, `decrypt`, `sign`, `verify`, `wrap` and `unwrap` can be used for the corresponding operation.

1.2 Attacker Model and Usual Shortcomings Exhibited by PKCS#11 Middlewares

Cryptographic resources implementing the standard are formed by some combination of software and hardware, and need a piece of software to export the PKCS#11 API. This latter is usually referred to as a PKCS#11 middleware. In the case of a Hardware Security Module, this middleware might be partly hosted inside the token, whereas for smartcards, it is a library to be loaded by the operating system.

The issues addressed by *Caml Crush* mainly fall into two categories. Firstly, *Caml Crush* allows to **fix defects** in the way middlewares implement the PKCS#11 API, leading to unexpected behaviors that can break applications expecting standardized answers. Secondly, *Caml Crush* enables the **prevention of purposeful attacks** that consist in any interaction with the PKCS#11 middleware resulting in the leak of sensitive information (such as the values of sensitive keys), or in tampering with the middleware itself (through classical buffer overflow attacks for instance).

In a nutshell, our attacker model encompasses applications or users (be it legitimate or not) forging **any sequence of API calls leading to a successful leak of sensitive information or API defect**. Compared to usual definitions of a successful attack – typically resulting in sensitive information disclosure – our success criterion takes into account less obvious threats. Let us also emphasize that the attackers that we consider remain at the PKCS#11 API level: this implies that they only interact with the resource through the PKCS#11 middleware and never gain a direct lower level access to the token. We discuss this attacker model in Sect. 1.3 and give valid use cases in Sect. 4. In this model, PKCS#11 issues can be classified in three categories.

Compliance Defects. The PKCS#11 standard comprehends a broad set of features without providing a reference implementation, compliance is therefore hard to achieve. Most tokens only implement part of the specification. Even then, quite trivial inconsistencies have been found. Serious mishandling of the attributes of keys probably feature amongst the most critical disagreements with the standard requirements. Indeed, they very concretely lead to the output in plaintext of the value of secret keys. Such **behaviors** are explicitly **not compliant with the specification**.

PKCS#11 API-level Attacks. Even strict compliance with the standard is not enough. **Logical attacks** that only exploit flaws in the API design itself confirm it. The most famous example is perhaps the so-called wrap-and-decrypt attack. It exploits the possibility to use keys for more than one type of operation, in order to extract sensitive keys from the token. Other attacks exploit use of **obsolete cryptographic schemes** (e.g., DES) and of combinations of mechanisms yielding **padding oracle attacks**. Details about flaws and possible patches can be found in the extended version of this paper [17], and in the seminal references [11,13,15].

Classic Vulnerabilities. Middlewares are also prone to the **generic** pitfalls yielding **vulnerabilities** that an adversary can exploit in any piece of code. These oversights include absence of checking for errors, presence of buffer overflows or null-pointer dereferences. Consequences range from the pure and simple crash of the middleware to the redirection of the control flow of the programs or execution of arbitrary code. The large size and relatively low-level at which the PKCS#11 standard is specified make the resulting token implementations rather subject to exhibit such weaknesses.

1.3   Our Motivations for Providing a Filtering Proxy

Limitations of State of the Art Solutions. In [11], Bortolozzo et al. introduce Tookan, a tool to automatically search for attacks on PKCS#11 tokens, along with CryptokiX, a reference implementation of a fixed software token. A fork of openCryptoki [5], a famous PKCS#11 software implementation of the standard, CryptokiX implements patches that turn out sufficient to fix the API against logical and cryptographic attacks.

However, these works suffer from two practical limitations. Firstly, they only take into consideration a subset of the attacks described in Sect. 1.2 (namely PKCS#11 API-level attacks). Thus, compliance defects as well as classic vulnerabilities are not covered. Secondly, they can be of interest to token vendors, but are of limited interest to token users in the field. Users are able to check with Tookan whether their token is vulnerable to certain classes of attacks. Unfortunately, without the vendor support nothing can be done, and the user still ends up using his token despite its possible vulnerabilities.

As a consequence, the matter of fixing commercially available tokens is not addressed by the related work. We envision two possible scenarios regarding this issue. One can hope that vendors successfully repair existing vulnerable tokens and integrate the countermeasures in their future designs. In our experience, it takes a long time to achieve such a goal. We rather believe that vulnerable tokens are not to completely disappear anytime soon. Many PKCS#11 devices, e.g., smartcards, cannot be updated easily, if they are updatable at all. Furthermore, vendors will probably not maintain obsolete PKCS#11 devices, even if some are still being used. Finally, when some vendors provide a patch for their tokens, it is very likely that only the most recent platforms benefit from them. Deprecated operating systems interfacing with the token will not be able to get updates.

Using *Caml Crush* to Dynamically Protect Vulnerable Tokens. Previous limitations call for the design of a suitable solution for users who want to protect potentially vulnerable tokens, but are deprived of patches. With *Caml Crush*, we aim at dynamically detecting and applying mitigations against attacks on PKCS#11 requests **before they reach the token.** To do so, our solution consists in a PKCS#11 proxy that sits between the original middleware and the PKCS#11 applications. Alternatives include developing a replacement middleware, but low-level interfaces with devices are often proprietary. Therefore, we opted for a lightweight and more portable solution. This induces some limitations, though, discussed in 5.3.

Not only does our design implement the state of the art patches inherited from [11], but it also comes with supplementary features. *Caml Crush* adds to tokens a detection and protection layer against adversaries who can forge PKCS#11 requests that exploit vulnerabilities on tokens that are known to be vulnerable (e.g., to a buffer overflow on a PKCS#11 function argument). We stress out that the hardware device remains in charge of secure key storage and cryptographic operations.

We recall that we make one working hypothesis about the attacker capabilities though: no adversary can bypass the PKCS#11 proxy and directly communicate with the resource (see the attacker model discussed in Sect. 1.2). This is obviously not a limitation in cases where the cryptographic resource is a – part of – a dedicated machine on a managed network. This approach is easily applied to network HSMs and more thoroughly discussed in Sect. 4.

2   Architecture

Using a proxy is an efficient approach in order to protect cryptographic resources and vulnerable PKCS#11 middlewares. Though there exist some projects implementing PKCS#11 proxies – among which GNOME Keyring [3] and pkcs11-proxy [6] – they rather focus on performance, usability or ergonomic concern, which are orthogonal to our motives. Thus, we have chosen to propose a completely new architecture. In this section, we motivate our design choices and present the components of *Caml Crush*.

2.1   Design Choices

Critical pieces of the software use the OCaml language: it offers a static type system, a type-inferring compiler and relieves the programmer from memory management issues. The functional programming paradigm is well-suited to express filtering rules.

The communication layer plays an essential role in a proxy architecture. *Caml Crush* uses standard *Sun RPC* [8] Remote Procedure Call and its XDR [10] data serialization format. This ensures greater portability as most operating systems have a native implementation of this standard. *Caml Crush* can operate over

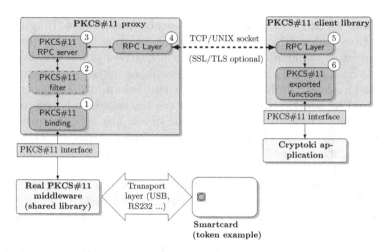

Fig. 1. *Caml Crush* architecture overview

Unix domain or TCP sockets and the link can be secured using TLS mutual authentication. Acceptable TLS cipher suites are tunable on the server side.

To end up with code of higher quality, we generalize the use of automatic code generation. We thus rely on the code of the tool, which is generally smaller and well tested-out. It is very likely that it also reduces the introduction of vulnerabilities in the resulting code (bad memory management, human errors...).

The PKCS#11 API matches each application with a context, mainly a list of handles and session states (read-only, user logged, etc.). The standard outlines that "an application consists of a single address space and all the threads of control running in it", meaning that an application is mapped to a single process. Therefore the logical separation of processes is supposed to isolate multiple PKCS#11 contexts. This is handled by all operating systems supporting virtual memory. In our opinion, using a *multi-threaded* architecture for the proxy is in contradiction with the standard and bound to create unforeseen issues. This partially explains why thread-based projects such as GNOME-Keyring or pkcs11-proxy [3,6] were not reused. *Caml Crush* is a *multi-process* architecture handling client connections through *fork-exec*. Each process is tied to a client and runs its own instance of the filter engine, with its own object and session handles stored in its memory space.

2.2   Components

One of the design goals of *Caml Crush* is modularity. Having the possibility to replace portions of code while minimizing the impact is essential. This is why *Caml Crush* is split in several sub-components. Figure 1 illustrates this architecture.

OCaml PKCS#11 Binding ①. PKCS#11 middlewares are shared libraries. Before performing calls to PKCS#11 functions, client applications must load the middleware. While OCaml does not natively support loading a C shared library, calling C foreign functions is allowed.

The binding is the low-level part of *Caml Crush*. It is used to load the middleware and forward calls to the cryptographic resource. The code of this component is mostly generated with the help of CamlIDL [9]. This tool can generate the necessary stubbing code to interface OCaml with C. CamlIDL works with an IDL file whose syntax is derived from C and enhanced to add type information. This greatly simplified our work as the conversion code and memory allocation are handled automatically. The resulting stubbing functions point to corresponding symbols that call the PKCS#11 functions of the real middleware. These were manually written and mainly act as a pass-through.

PKCS#11 Filter ②. Thoroughly detailed in Sect. 3, the filtering engine relies on the OCaml PKCS#11 binding ① to communicate with the real middleware.

PKCS#11 Proxy ③ ④. The proxy server is a critical component of this architecture. Because it is facing potentially hostile clients it has to be robust and secure. As motivated earlier, we choose to use one process per client to avoid abusive sharing of handles, be it with honest or hostile clients.

We based our proxy service on the **Ocamlnet** library, and more specifically the **Netplex** subclass, used to implement our PKCS#11 RPC listening service ③. We benefit from the support for the *Sun RPC* standard in **OCamlnet**. As for the binding described earlier, we use a description file to produce the code in charge of data serialization on the transport layer ④. A file with the XDR syntax describes the available RPC functions and the various structures. Both the client and server take advantage of this.

Best security practices recommend dropping all unnecessary privileges for system daemons. Since OCaml does not provide the necessary APIs to accomplish this task to harden the server process we provide a custom primitive. After its initialization, we instruct **Netplex** to call a function that performs capabilities dropping and privilege reduction from our C bindings. Further hardening can be achieved depending on the sandboxing features available on the operating system running the *Caml Crush* daemon.

PKCS#11 Client Library ⑤ ⑥. The final component is the PKCS#11 shared library that substitutes to the original middleware. Client applications load it to perform cryptographic operations. The main task of the client library is to set up a communication channel with the server, export PKCS#11 symbols ⑥ to the calling application and relay function calls to the proxy server with serialized arguments. As for the proxy, the transport layer code ⑤ is generated from the XDR file. Some sanity checks are performed within the library to prevent invalid requests from reaching the proxy server. However, we want to stress that the client library **plays no role** in the security of this architecture (i.e. an attacker controlling the library does not reduce the overall security).

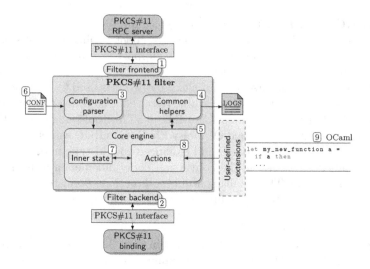

Fig. 2. *Caml Crush* filtering engine overview

3   PKCS#11 Filtering Engine

3.1   Architecture of the Filter

Overview. The engine is divided into several components detailed in Fig. 2. Firstly, it is isolated from the PKCS#11 proxy by a frontend ① and from the OCaml PKCS#11 binding by a backend ②. Secondly, it includes a configuration parser ③, to process set-up data provided by the administrator. Helpers ④ are also used for common tasks such as logging. Eventually, the filter core engine ⑤ performs the filtering actions within PKCS#11 calls, helped by requests to the backend.

Core Engine ⑤. The configuration parser takes as input a configuration ⑥ (defined by the administrator) and uses it to build a static filtering policy. This policy is expressed as a mapping from PKCS#11 function names to a sequence of operations performed each time the given function is called ⑧. The most basic example of operation consists in simply forwarding the call to the backend, getting the matching output and forwarding it back to the frontend. A filter instance is loaded when an application opens a connection with the server, a new process is forked on the proxy side. It is unloaded when the connection is closed. The *multi-process* model grants *Caml Crush* the ability to load and isolate multiple PKCS#11 middlewares. The filter configuration allows to apply fine-grained filtering policies depending on the target middleware.

Actions ⑧ and User Extensions ⑨. The engine is architectured to allow precise tuning of the filtering policy and user-specific extensions. To achieve such modularity, we introduce an intermediate abstraction layer, built on the notion of *filtering actions* ⑧.

Two alternatives are available to users to adapt the filter to their needs. Firstly, predefined configurations ⑥ are proposed, based on concrete use-cases. They comprise all of PKCS#11 patches as well as function blocking and *label/id* filtering (see Sect. 3.2). Secondly, users can write plug-ins in OCaml to suit their needs. Since each PKCS#11 function is hooked inside the filter, it can be configured to call any other user-defined function implemented in the plug-ins.

3.2   Filtering Features Involving Standard PKCS#11 Mitigations

Mitigations Against Logical Attacks. Logical attacks detailed in Sect. 1.2 are mainly due to exposing wrap and unwrap functions. **Completely removing them** partially fixes the API, and proves relevant as most use cases do not use them. To address the generic case, Fröschle *et al.* have proposed patches in [16], then extended in [11]. They put forward two sets of patches, that each presents their own advantages and drawbacks. Details about the patches can be found in the extended version of this paper [17]. In our proxy design, these fixes are naturally implemented as **filtering actions**. The checks are **dynamically enforced** at runtime each time a PKCS#11 request is sent to the middleware. *Caml Crush* provides the same security level as CryptokiX against logical attacks.

Mitigations Against Cryptographic Attacks. Efficiently preventing the usage of **obsolete ciphers and mechanisms** implies prohibiting their usage in the token. Our filter engine allows to mimic the absence from a token of weak mechanisms – e.g., substandard cipher suites or poor key derivation schemes. Indeed, all the cryptographic functions called with these mechanisms can be blocked, as well as the creation of keys supporting them. To avoid impacting client applications, we also amend the behavior of functions listing mechanisms supported by the token. **Padding oracle attacks** can also be prevented this way: mechanisms as PKCS#1 v1.5 and CBC_PAD can be deemed "weak mechanisms". As padding oracles exploit the unwrapping functionality, these latter can be suppressed when useless. When removal is unrealistic, a better alternative is provided by the *wrapping format* patch (see details in [17]). This patch precludes the decryption of malformed ciphertexts, thus preventing the information leakage useful to these attacks.

3.3   Object and Structure Filtering

Resource Sharing and Label/Id Filtering. Though client applications can have different criticality levels, they most likely share the same cryptographic resource. This can lead to involuntary information leaks: as PKCS#11 defines a single user mode of operation, an application authenticated to the token can use any private token object.

PKCS#11 allows applications to search for objects matching certain attributes. One can fetch a handle to a specific object using its `label` or `identifier` attribute. We propose to use both attributes in the filter engine to restrict the set of token objects with which an application can operate. It can be done in a completely transparent way. For instance, by prefixing or suffixing labels used by applications with criticality levels. Then, calls to PKCS#11 functions with which objects can be accessed, read or modified are adapted by the filter to simulate a token containing only the objects of a given criticality level. A concrete use case of this feature is given in Sect. 4.2.

Key Usage Segregation. As mentioned earlier, many PKCS#11 flaws result from some keys being allowed multiple usages or roles. Even subtle ways of disrespecting the key separation principle yield confusions at the API level and enable attacks. The fixes presented in [11,16] mainly focus on `wrap/unwrap` and `encrypt/decrypt` segregation. One might also want to push this logic further with the `sign/verify` attributes. For example, a PKI (Public Key Infrastructure) application only needs to sign and verify data with the asymmetric keys. Disabling other uses of these keys seems relevant. All these patches have been easily integrated to the filtering rules we provide.

Token Information Filtering. PKCS#11 describes a set of structures that characterize a token. For instance, the `CK_TOKEN_INFO` structure contains information such as a serial number, a manufacturer ID and so on. The filtering proxy can be used to transparently modify such information: for instance, a PIN length policy can be set up by changing the `ulMinPinLen` and `ulMaxPinLen` fields. A policy on the characters set as well as protection against dictionary attacks can also be enforced when setting PINs. It is readily enabled by the hooking of PKCS#11 functions `C_InitToken` and `C_SetPIN` performed in the filter engine, to allow returning an error if the PIN disrespects the policy.

3.4   Blocking PKCS#11 Functions and Mechanisms

Function blocking offers a simple way to deactivate unused or dangerous features of PKCS#11. Though rather elementary, disabling functions can prove effective to prevent security breaches often left unaddressed by usual PKCS#11 patches. For example, one can express a filtering policy to block administration functions, thus only allowing regular use of the token to clients connecting to this instance.

Furthermore, we recall that provided that the user is authenticated, he can freely create and modify objects on the token. This in turn potentially enables him to tamper with the device to force known values as keys. Blocking object creation and modification offers a way to impede such attacks, thus addressing the issue of hostile users, while object management can still be performed on a dedicated trusted filter instance.

Finally, as pointed out before, mechanisms filtering can also be of interest, be it to completely block unwanted mechanisms, or to filter out some combination of operations.

3.5   Security Breaches Beyond PKCS#11 Flaws

Fixing Generic Coding Errors. Since the filter sits between the client application and the PKCS#11 middleware, one can detect, filter and alter any known bad request or behaviour of malicious applications. Thus, **prevention of vulnerability exploitation,** or more generally mending design flaws in middlewares, puts the proxy to good use. Let us illustrate these words with a realistic example of an error that we found in an existing middleware, in the PKCS#11 C_SetPIN function call, as presented on Listing 1.1.

```
CK_RV C_SetPIN(CK_SESSION_HANDLE hSession, CK_UTF8CHAR_PTR pOldPin, CK_ULONG
    ulOldLen, CK_UTF8CHAR_PTR pNewPin, CK_ULONG ulNewLen){
  ...
  /* Compare stored PIN with old PIN */
  if(memcmp(StoredPin, pOldPin, ulOldLen) == 0){
    /* If test is ok, store the new PIN */
    *StoredPinLen = ulNewLen;
    memcpy(StoredPin, pNewPin, ulOldLen);
    return CKR_OK;
  }
  /* Provided old PIN is incorrect */
  return CKR_PIN_INCORRECT;
}
```

Listing 1.1. C_SetPIN coding error example

As we can see, the newly stored PIN is either truncated or extended to the old PIN length; either way it is rendered erroneous by a call to C_SetPIN. The inherent risk is to block the underlying token, the user having no clue which PIN is actually set. Even though it is not possible to truly patch this error without modifying the code or the binary of the middleware, the filtering proxy can help avoiding such a pitfall. The filtering actions associated to the C_SetPIN function can consist in checking that the old and new PIN share the same length before forwarding the call to the middleware. In case lengths do not coincide, the proxy returns the error CKR_PIN_LEN_RANGE and the PIN is not modified. The client application can later fetch the correct length it needs using another PKCS#11 function and call C_SetPIN again. Although a constant PIN length is forced, the entered PIN and the stored one are consistent.

Preventing Denial of Service. PKCS#11 defines a calling convention described in [18, p. 101] for functions returning variable-length output data. In some cases, the affected functions are supposed to handle either null or valid pointers. During our development we observed that some middlewares end up dereferencing null pointers. These vulnerabilities are easily prevented by implementing a filter action that performs input sanitizing.

Another example we encountered is that using a cryptographic function with a malformed input (a non-standard mechanism) we could freeze a token, leading to the unavailability of the cryptographic resource. Again, this behavior was corrected using a custom filter action, the malformed input is not sent to the device and a PKCS#11 compliant error is returned to the client application.

We advocate that a large set of such coding errors and vulnerabilities can similarly be corrected by stopping or modifying malformed requests before they reach the middleware.

4   Deployment Scenarios

Security guarantees provided by *Caml Crush* rest upon the assumption that going through the proxy is mandatory. Yet it is potentially still possible to connect to the cryptographic resource directly. For instance, an attacker could try to load the vendor middleware or use the transport layer to directly communicate with the device. Though such attacks are realistic, we advocate that for any type of token, complementary security measures can mitigate this issue. This section discusses secure deployment strategies for *Caml Crush*.

4.1   HSMs in Corporate Networks

Network HSMs provide a convenient way to perform cryptographic operations and securely store keys in a corporate environment. They are frequently used as backends for PKI solutions, timestamping servers and document or code signing applications. Traditionally, these devices can be considered as black boxes, accessed using the interfaces provided by the vendor (usually PKCS#11). In this context of use, *Caml Crush* is to be installed on a dedicated server with at least two network cards. The first card shall be directly connected to the network HSM, thus shielding the device from any other hosts, while the second network card shall be connected to the corporate network. Since the HSM is only linked to the proxy, client applications are forced to access the cryptographic resource through our filtering proxy using the *Caml Crush* client library. Clearly, meticulous users can apply complementary hardening measures to further reduce the attack surface of the server hosting *Caml Crush*.

In rare cases, HSM vendors allow non-proprietary code to run on their platform. These particular devices offer a way to tightly couple *Caml Crush* with the cryptographic device without needing additional hardware. We also point out that OEM vendors who integrate standalone HSMs (such as PCI devices) can benefit from *Caml Crush* when it is accessed using PKCS#11. As they may face the same issues as customers when provided with binary-only middlewares, they shall integrate *Caml Crush* within their designs.

4.2   Virtualized Environment

Caml Crush can be used within virtualized operating systems in order to securely use a cryptographic resource. Figure 3 illustrates such a deployment scenario. In this example, the PKCS#11 device is only exposed to the trusted hypervisor, virtual machines wishing to use the resource can only do so using the *Caml Crush* client library. This architecture also leverages *Caml Crush* resource sharing capabilities using a filtering policy dedicated to each virtual machine.

Here, the policy for Virtual Machine 1 restricts PKCS#11 applications to use objects with a label in the set A (resp. B for VM 2). Therefore, the filtering engine transparently compels virtualized environments to use objects matching their respective policy.

While this scenario uses the hypervisor isolation features, more lightweight isolation alternatives exist for standalone desktops using USB smartcards. The Linux operating system can be enhanced with Mandatory Access Control (MAC) support such as SELinux [7] or Grsecurity role-based access control [4]. Building on discretionary access control and MAC enforces a security policy restricting PKCS#11 and low-level smartcard access to *Caml Crush* instances.

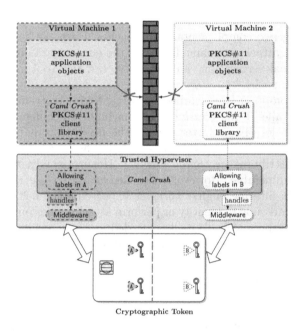

Fig. 3. *Caml Crush* used for resource sharing in a virtualized environment

4.3 Mobile and Embedded Platforms

Given the fact that vendors provide binary-only PKCS#11 middlewares, compatibility is generally limited to mainstream operating systems and microarchitectures. In our opinion, running an unconventional CPU platform (such as MIPS or ARM to a lesser extent) should not stand in the way of the use of hardware-assisted cryptography. Having chosen standardised communication protocols ensures great portability of our code. Our initial implementation was Linux specific but it is worth mentioning that porting to Mac OS X and FreeBSD required little efforts. Windows support is limited to the client library, running the server code through Cygwin is a work in progress. A native Windows port for the server is not excluded but requires significant development. We stress that

Caml Crush is fully capable of handling clients with a foreign endianness. We have successfully validated interoperability scenarios using our PKCS#11 client library on ARM, MIPS and PowerPC architectures. Corporate environments can benefit from the variety of systems supported, from embedded to mobile devices or legacy systems, in order to access remote PKCS#11 resources through the use of *Caml Crush*.

5   Evaluation

5.1   Security Evaluation

We ensure that the filtering engine performs as expected, i.e. protects vulnerable devices, using two complementary approaches. First, we have implemented classic PKCS#11 attacks to manually verify the efficiency of our filtering rules. Then, since manual verification can only go so far, the Tookan tool is used to try finding attack paths.

On a Linux computer, we installed openCryptoki, a software HSM. We also compiled and installed *Caml Crush* on this machine and configured it to use the default filtering rules. These latter enforce the needed properties described in the extended version of this paper [17] to secure the PKCS#11 API (*conflicting* and *sticky* attributes, *wrapping format*). Unsurprisingly, the unprotected device remains vulnerable. However, once instructed to use the *Caml Crush* client library, our filtering engine works as expected since neither Tookan nor our manual tools are able to identify or perform attacks. The completeness result obtained by the authors of Tookan allows to deduce that the filter efficiently prevents all attacks that can be carried out in the model underlying their tool.

5.2   Performance Evaluation

In this section we present the various test cases that we used to quantify the performance impact of our solution. The experiments were conducted on three different platforms, a PCI HSM, a network HSM and a USB smartcard. For each cryptographic device, our benchmark is run three times. First, the raw performance is computed using various cryptographic operations. Second, we run the same benchmarks using *Caml Crush* with the filtering engine disabled to measure the architectural cost. Finally, we enable all of our filtering rules to add up the remaining cost of *Caml Crush*. Figure 4 summarizes the types of operations we used during our performance testing, as well as the number of such operations performed on each type of device. We point out that the card is a USB smartcard using an open source middleware and has fewer capabilities compared to HSMs. We iterated the type of operation depending on the device performance. HSMs and network HSMs are fast devices capable of handling multiple requests at the same time. Therefore, we also ran benchmarks simulating multiple client applications performing the described operations (about ten clients running various operations).

PCI HSM. Figure 4 illustrates the performance impact of *Caml Crush* using a sequential client application. The most significant performance drop affects the aes operations. These are fast operations and adding *Caml Crush* on top of such local devices reduces throughput. The key-gen and rand-dgst operations respectively have a 25 % and 50 % performance penalty. On the other hand, rsa tests are time-consuming operations and the impact is negligible. The right side of the figure clearly demonstrates that when the resource is accessed using multiple applications at the same time, the impact of *Caml Crush* is low.

Network HSM. We now focus on the evaluation on a network HSM, the results are shown in Fig. 4. The observation is similar to the PCI-HSM, using a single sequential client, *Caml Crush* has roughly the same performance impact. We recall that the filter engine fetches attributes from the device when processing PKCS#11 calls (using C_GetAttributeValue). Those supplementary calls account for a large portion of the throughput drop. Again, *Caml Crush* cost is reduced when the cryptographic resource is under heavier load from multiple clients.

Smartcard. The performance impact of *Caml Crush* related to the smartcard at our disposal is illustrated in Fig. 4. Smartcards are rather slow devices and perform through the USB bus. Given this, we observe a 20 % drop on rsa tests and less than 10 % on the rand-dgst operations.

We used various benchmarks to quantify the performance cost of our solution. Assembling a software layer on top of another one obviously consumes some resources. In our case, the RPC layer accounts for a substantial part of the performance penalty. Furthermore, the supplementary calls needed by the filtering logic add an overhead that is device-specific. Nevertheless, we state that the performance trade-off remains acceptable.

5.3   Filter Limitations and Future Work

Currently, the filtering engine lacks the ability to adapt filtering actions based on the state between different client connections. We described in Sect. 2.1 that each client's connection is isolated in separate processes. *Caml Crush* would need to use Inter-Process Communication (IPC) mechanisms in order to exchange state-related messages. It could prove useful in some filtering scenarios but would require development of synchronization primitives and significantly increase the code complexity. Such feature would probably have further impact on the overall performance.

Another limitation is that the current filter plug-ins use the OCaml marshalling module that lacks type safety: this means that extra care must be taken by users when writing code as filter extensions. Errors in the plug-in code could indeed evade the compile-time checks, and might allow an attacker to tamper with the memory of the server instance (process) dealing with the client. The implications of such memory tampering of OCaml native structures is not clear, but it would at least provide the attacker with a denial of service capability

	Token types			
	PCI HSM and NetHSM		USB Smartcards	
	Operation type	Number[†]	Operation type	Number[†]
key-gen	AES-128 Generate keys	10^4	✗	✗
rand-dgst	random/SHA-1 Generate random then hash it	10^4	random/SHA-1 Generate random then hash it	10^3
rsa	RSA-2048 encrypt/decrypt sign/verify	10^4	RSA-2048 sign/verify	10^3
aes	AES-128 encrypt/decrypt	10^5	✗	✗

✗ The token does not support the operation types.
[†]Number of operations performed on the token to measure performance.

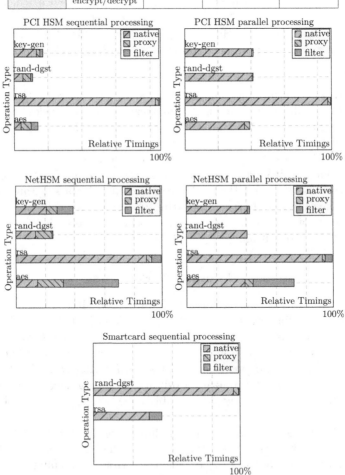

Fig. 4. Performance of Net/PCI-HSM and smartcards. Relative timings are used, the operation taking maximum time is at 100 %

on the instance. Albeit, the attacker would not be able to attack other clients instances thanks to the fork-exec model (provided that appropriate operating system level protections and sandboxing features are used).

Furthermore, writing plug-ins requires expertise in OCaml. We are currently working toward the removal of marshalling functions. We profit from this step in the filter development to rethink the way filter actions are encoded. We plan on introducing an intermediate domain-specific language using more generic and fine-grained atomic actions. This would allow advanced users to use this intermediate language to specify filter actions. Such an abstraction is meant to relieve users from dealing with the complexity of OCaml and adherence to our design choices in the filter backend.

Conclusion

We are able to dynamically address security issues of the PKCS#11 API. Related work has paved the way to resolve these issues with a reference PKCS#11 software implementation. However, applying such countermeasures is left to the vendors of cryptographic devices. This is insufficient as commercially available and already deployed devices remain vulnerable. *Caml Crush* offers an alternative to protect cryptographic resources from state of the art attacks. Substituting the original middleware with our proxy and filtering PKCS#11 function calls is a pragmatic and effective approach. Moreover, the filter engine is conceived to be modular: it is possible to customize and extend the filter with plug-ins written in OCaml.

The filtering engine of *Caml Crush* is versatile enough to enable complementary features such as function blocking, improved PKCS#11 compliance and secure resource sharing We are confident that these functionalities find immediate application for users of compliant cryptographic devices.

References

1. **Caml Crush**. https://github.com/ANSSI-FR/caml-crush/
2. CryptokiX. http://secgroup.dais.unive.it/projects/security-apis/cryptokix/
3. GNOME Keyring. http://live.gnome.org/GnomeKeyring
4. **grsecurity**. http://grsecurity.net/
5. openCryptoki. http://sourceforge.net/projects/opencryptoki/
6. pkcs11-proxy. http://floss.commonit.com/pkcs11-proxy.html
7. **SELinux**. http://selinuxproject.org/
8. Sun RPC RFC 1057 (1988). http://www.ietf.org/rfc/rfc1057.txt
9. CamlIDL project page (2004). http://caml.inria.fr/pub/old_caml_site/camlidl/
10. Xdr, RFC 4506 (2006). http://tools.ietf.org/html/rfc4506
11. Bortolozzo, M., Centenaro, M., Focardi, R., Steel, G.: Attacking and fixing PKCS#11 security tokens. In: ACM Conference on Computer and Communications Security, pp. 260–269. ACM Press, October 2010
12. Cachin, C., Chandran, N.: A secure cryptographic token interface. In: CSF 2009, pp. 141–153. IEEE Computer Society (2009)

13. Clulow, J.: On the security of PKCS #11. In: Walter, C.D., Koç, Ç.K., Paar, C. (eds.) CHES 2003. LNCS, vol. 2779, pp. 411–425. Springer, Heidelberg (2003)
14. Cortier, V., Steel, G.: A generic security API for symmetric key management on cryptographic devices. In: Backes, M., Ning, P. (eds.) ESORICS 2009. LNCS, vol. 5789, pp. 605–620. Springer, Heidelberg (2009)
15. Delaune, S., Kremer, S., Steel, G.: Formal security analysis of PKCS#11 and proprietary extensions. J. Comput. Secur. **18**(6), 1211–1245 (2010)
16. Fröschle, S., Steel, G.: Analysing PKCS#11 key management APIs with unbounded fresh data. In: Degano, P., Viganò, L. (eds.) ARSPA-WITS 2009. LNCS, vol. 5511, pp. 92–106. Springer, Heidelberg (2009)
17. Benadjila, R., Calderon, T., Daubignard, M.: CamlCrush: a PKCS#11 Filtering Proxy (2014). http://eprint.iacr.org/2015/063
18. RSA Security Inc.: PKCS#11 v2.20: Cryptographic Token Interface Standard (2004)

Algorithms for Outsourcing Pairing Computation

Aurore Guillevic[2,3]([⊠]) and Damien Vergnaud[1]

[1] Département d'Informatique, École normale supérieure, Paris, France
[2] Inria, Paris, France
aurore.guillevic@ens.fr
[3] École Polytechnique/LIX, Palaiseau, France

Abstract. We address the question of how a computationally limited device may outsource pairing computation in cryptography to another, potentially malicious, but much more computationally powerful device. We introduce two new efficient protocols for securely outsourcing pairing computations to an untrusted helper. The first generic scheme is proven computationally secure (and can be proven statistically secure at the expense of worse performance). It allows various communication-efficiency trade-offs. The second specific scheme – for optimal Ate pairing on a Barreto-Naehrig curve – is unconditionally secure, and do not rely on any hardness assumptions. Both protocols are more efficient than the actual computation of the pairing by the restricted device and in particular they are more efficient than all previous proposals.

1 Introduction

Pairings (or bilinear maps) were introduced in cryptography in 2000 by Joux [14] and Boneh-Franklin [4]. A pairing is a bilinear, non-degenerate and computable map $e : \mathbb{G}_1 \times \mathbb{G}_2 \to \mathbb{G}_T$. In practice, the first two groups $\mathbb{G}_1$ and $\mathbb{G}_2$ are prime-order r subgroups of the group of points $E(\mathbb{F}_q)$ of an elliptic curve E defined over a finite field $\mathbb{F}_q$. The so-called *target* group $\mathbb{G}_T$ is the order r subgroup of a finite field extension $\mathbb{F}_{q^k}$. Bilinear pairings proved to be an amazingly flexible and useful tool for the construction of cryptosystems with unique features (*e.g.* efficient identity based cryptography or short signatures). However, the pairing computation is more resource consuming compared to a scalar multiplication on the elliptic curve $E(\mathbb{F}_q)$.

In the last decade, several papers [7,9,12] studied the question of how a computationally limited device may outsource pairing computation to another, potentially malicious, but much more computationally powerful device. In this setting, one wants to efficiently delegate the computation of a pairing $e(\mathcal{SK}_1, \mathcal{SK}_2)$ of two secret keys, or a pairing $e(\mathcal{SK}, \mathcal{PP})$ of a secret key and some public parameter. Obviously, one needs to ensure that this malicious device does not learn anything about what it is actually computing (*secrecy*) and sometimes one also needs to, when possible, detect any failures (*verifiability*, also called correctness).

© Springer International Publishing Switzerland 2015
M. Joye and A. Moradi (Eds.): CARDIS 2014, LNCS 8968, pp. 193–211, 2015.
DOI: 10.1007/978-3-319-16763-3_12

As mentioned in [7,9], a delegation protocol that does not ensure verifiability may cause severe security problems (in particular if the pairing computation occurs in the verification algorithm of some authentication protocol). Unfortunately, the different proposals for verifiable pairing delegation are very inefficient and it is actually better in practice to directly embed the pairing computation inside the restricted device than using these solutions. The main interest is then to save of area that is required to implement a pairing in the restricted device such as smart card.

However, if verifiability is mandatory in authentication protocols, this is not necessarily the case in scenarios where the delegated pairing value is used in an encryption scheme as a session key. In this case, one can indeed use additional cryptographic techniques to ensure that the values returned by the powerful device are correct (e.g. by adding a MAC or other redundancy to the ciphertext). One can even consider settings where the powerful device actually learns the pairing value. For instance, in a pay-TV scenario, the set-up box (provided by the pay-TV company) needs to know the (one-time) session key $\mathcal{K}$ used to decipher the content (e.g. movie, football match) but it does not know the secret key $\mathcal{SK}$ securely stored in the smartcard. If the smartcard delegates the pairing computation to the set-up box there is no harm to let it know the session key $\mathcal{K}$ since it will learn it anyway.

In 2005, Girault and Lefranc [12] introduced the first secure pairing delegation protocol through the *Server-Aided Verification* notion which consists in speeding up the verification step of an authentication/signature scheme. Their pairing delegation protocol only achieves secrecy with unconditional security (and the verifiability is achieved *via* a different mean). Chevallier-Mames, Coron, McCullagh, Naccache and Scott introduced in 2005 the security notions for pairing delegation [8,9] and they provided a verifiable delegation protocol for pairing computation. Their protocols are much more resource consuming for the restricted device than directly computing the pairing.

Recently, Canard, Devigne and Sanders proposed a more efficient protocol for verifiable pairing delegation. The authors showed that their proposal is more efficient than the computation of the pairing for optimal ate pairing on a so-called KSS-18 curve [15]. Unfortunately, we will show in this paper that this is not the case for state-of-the-art optimal Ate pairing on a Barreto-Naehrig curve [3].

Contributions of the paper. We propose two new efficient protocols for secret pairing delegation. Our protocols are not verifiable but as explained above, this is not really an issue for encryption primitives where verifiability can be achieved by other means. In particular, our typical usecases are Pay-TV where a smartcard delegates a pairing computation to the set-up box and encrypted GSM communication where the sim-card delegates a pairing computation to the smartphone processor (e.g. an ARM or Intel processor with high competitive performances). In these scenarios, one can even assume that the set-up box or the smartphone actually learns the pairing value (but of course not the secret information stored by the smartcard or the sim-card). Both methods enable to delegate the computation of a pairing $e(\mathcal{SK}, \mathcal{PP})$ of a secret key $\mathcal{SK}$ and some public parameter $\mathcal{PP}$. They achieve better efficiency than actual computation of the pairing by the restricted device and in particular they are more efficient than all previous proposals.

We first present a (generalized) knapsack-based approach which uses different endomorphisms on the groups $\mathbb{G}_1, \mathbb{G}_2, \mathbb{G}_T$ to speed-up the method. Instead of masking the secret point $\mathcal{SK}$ by a scalar multiplication with a random secret exponent, it is masked by adding to it a sum of (small) multiple of random points that are also sent to the powerful device. It computes several pairings of these points with the public parameter $\mathcal{PP}$ and the restricted device combines them to get the actual value. The method is generic and can be applied to any pairing instantiation. The method increases the communication complexity between the two devices but one can propose different communication-efficiency trade-off.

In our second approach, we present a way to delegate only the non-critical steps in the pairing algorithm, looking carefully at each instruction in Miller algorithm. The powerful device does not learn any information on the secret point $\mathcal{SK}$ except the actual value of the pairing $e(\mathcal{SK}, \mathcal{PP})$ (which is perfectly suitable in our usecases). The technique can be applied to any instantiation of pairings but we concentrate on the state-of-the-art optimal Ate pairing on a Barreto-Naehrig curve [3]. We obtain a 65 % improvement (for a 128-bit security level) for the restricted device compared to the computation of the pairing.

2   Preliminaries

Timing Estimates Using the Relic Library. To illustrate the algorithms presented in this paper, we estimate the various costs of scalar multiplication, exponentiations and pairings. We choose as a practical example a Barreto–Naehrig (BN) curve [3] at the 128-bit security level with the implementation provided in Relic library of Aranha [1].

This library is at the state of the art for pairing computation [2] and is freely available for research purpose. We assume that scalar multiplications $[a]P$ and exponentiations z^a are performed with a binary signed representation of a. So it requires roughly $\log a$ doublings (resp. squarings) and $\log a/3$ additions (resp. multiplications). A doubling on a BN curve (with $a_4 = 0$) costs $2M_p + 5S_p$ (multiplications and squarings in a finite field $\mathbb{F}_p$) and a mixed addition costs $7M_p + 4S_p$ [1]. We assume that $M_p = S_p$ first because it is the case for Relic library and secondly to simplify (but the estimation $S_p = 0.9M_p$ would also be accurate for another implementation). We obtain a total cost of $\approx 256 \, \mathrm{Dbl}_{E(\mathbb{F}_p)} + 86 \, \mathrm{Add}_{E(\mathbb{F}_p)} \approx 2738M_p$ for a scalar multiplication on $\mathbb{G}_1$, 2.4 times this cost: $\approx 6590M_p$ for a scalar multiplication in $\mathbb{G}_2$ and $\approx 256S_{p^{12}} + 86M_{p^{12}} \approx 9252M_p$ for an exponentiation in $\mathbb{G}_T$. We note that checking that an element is in $\mathbb{G}_T$ is much more expensive than performing an exponentiation in $\mathbb{G}_T$. Indeed $\mathbb{G}_T$ is an order-r subgroup in a large finite field $\mathbb{F}_{p^k}$. $\mathbb{G}_T$ has particular properties permitting very fast squaring that $\mathbb{F}_{p^k}$ does not. We summarize these estimates in Table 1 (which may be of independent interest).

Table 1. Estimations for common operations in algorithms, for a BN curve with $\log p = 256$ bits and Relic [1] implementation (Running Relic toolkit on a Intel Xeon E5-1603 at 2.80 GHz).

Operation	Cost	Total over $\mathbb{F}_p$	Relic
$\mathbb{F}_{p^k}$ arithmetic			
		M_p	$0.149\,\mu s$
M_{p^2}	$3M_p$	$3M_p$	$0.427\,\mu s$
S_{p^2}	$2M_p$	$2M_p$	$0.360\,\mu s$
M_{p^6}	$6M_{p^2}$	$18M_p$	$3.362\,\mu s$
S_{p^6}	$2M_{p^2} + 3S_{p^2}$	$12M_p$	$2.523\,\mu s$
$M_{p^{12}}$	$3M_{p^6}$	$54M_p$	$10.856\,\mu s$
$S_{p^{12}}$	$2M_{p^6}$	$36M_p$	$7.598\,\mu s$
$S_{\phi_{12}(p)}$	z^2, $z \in \mathbb{F}_{p^{12}}$, $\mathrm{Norm}(z) = 1$	$18M_p$	$4.731\,\mu s$
z^a, for any z, a	$\log a\ S_{p^{12}} + \log a\ /3\ M_{p^{12}}$	$54 \log a\ M_p$	$3.864\,ms$
z^a, $\mathrm{Norm}_{\mathbb{F}_{p^{12}}/\mathbb{F}_p}(z) = 1$	$\log a\ S_{\phi_{12}(p)} + \log a\ /3\ M_{p^{12}}$	$36 \log a\ M_p$	$2.818\,ms$
$\mathrm{Norm}_{\mathbb{F}_{p^{12}}/\mathbb{F}_p}(z)$, for any z	$\mathrm{Norm}_{\mathbb{F}_{p^{12}}/\mathbb{F}_{p^6}/\mathbb{F}_{p^2}/\mathbb{F}_p}(z)$	$59\ M_p$	–
z^r, $\mathrm{Norm}_{\mathbb{F}_{p^{12}}/\mathbb{F}_p}(z) = 1$	$z^p z^{1-t} = z^p (z^{p^6})^{t-1}$	$4616\ M_p$	–
check order$(z) = r$ in $\mathbb{F}_{p^k}$	$\mathrm{Norm}_{\mathbb{F}_{p^{12}}/\mathbb{F}_p}(z) = 1$; $z^r = 1$	$4675\ M_p$	–
$E(\mathbb{F}_p)$ arithmetic			
Doubling (Dbl$_p$)	$2M_p + 5S_p$	$7M_p$	$1.043\,\mu s$
Addition (Add$_p$)	$7M_p + 4S_p$	$11M_p$	$1.639\,\mu s$
Scalar mult. $[a]P$	$\log a\ \mathrm{Dbl} + \log a\ /3\ \mathrm{Add}$	$10.7 \log a\ M_p$	–
$[a_1]P_1 + [a_2]P_2$	$\max(\log a_1, \log a_2)$ (Dbl $+2/3$ Add)	$\max(\log a_1, \log a_2)$ $14.33 M_p$	–
$E(\mathbb{F}_{p^2})$ arithmetic			
Doubling (Dbl$_{p^2}$)	$2M_{p^2} + 5S_{p^2}$	$16M_p$	$3.137\,\mu s$
Addition (Add$_{p^2}$)	$7M_{p^2} + 4S_{p^2}$	$29M_p$	$4.866\,\mu s$
Scalar mult. $[b]Q$	$\log b\ \mathrm{Dbl}_{p^2} + \log b\ /3\ \mathrm{Add}_{p^2}$	$25.7 \log b\ M_p$	$2.017\,ms$
$[b_1]Q_1 + [b_2]Q_2$	$\max(\log b_1, \log b_2)$ (Dbl$_{p^2}$ $+2/3$ Add$_{p^2}$)	$\max(\log b_1, \log b_2)$ $35.33 M_p$	–
Pairing on a BN curve with $\log_2 p = 256$			
Dbl step $+ \ell_{T,T}(P)$	$3M_{p^2} + 7S_{p^2} + 4M_p$	$27\ M_p$	$6.036\,\mu s$
Add step $+ \ell_{T,Q}(P)$	$11M_{p^2} + 2S_{p^2} + 4M_p$	$41\ M_p$	$7.593\,\mu s$
Miller loop	see Algorithm 1	$8425 M_p$	$1.776\,ms$
Final powering	see Algorithm 1	$7911 M_p$	$1.465\,ms$
Pairing	see Algorithm 1	$16336 M_p$	$3.241\,ms$

Algorithm 1. Optimal Ate Pairing $e_{\text{OptAte}}(P, Q)$ on a BN curve

Input: $E(\mathbb{F}_p) : y^2 = x^3 + b$, $P(x_P, y_P) \in E(\mathbb{F}_p)[r]$, $Q(x_Q, y_Q) \in E'(\mathbb{F}_{p^2})[r]$, t trace, x curve parameter

Output: $e_{\text{OptAte}}(P, Q) \in \mathbb{G}_T \subset \mathbb{F}_{p^{12}}^*$

1	$R(X_R : Y_R : Z_R) \leftarrow (x_Q : y_Q : 1)$	
2	$f \leftarrow 1$	
3	$s \leftarrow 6x + 2$	
4	**for** $m \leftarrow \lfloor \log_2(s) \rfloor - 1, \ldots, 0$ **do**	
5	$\quad R \leftarrow [2]R; \ell \leftarrow \ell_{R,R}(P)$	$3M_{p^2} + 7S_{p^2} + 4M_p = 27M_p$
6	$\quad f \leftarrow f^2 \cdot \ell$	$S_{p^{12}} + 13M_{p^2} = 36 + 39 = 75M_p$
7	$\quad$ **if** $s_m = 1$ *or* $s_m = -1$ **then**	
8	$\quad\quad R \leftarrow R \pm Q; \ell \leftarrow \ell_{R,\pm Q}(P)$	$11M_{p^2} + 2S_{p^2} + 4M_p = 41M_p$
9	$\quad\quad f \leftarrow f \cdot \ell$	$13M_{p^2} = 39M_p$

total Miller function:$\log s \cdot 102M_p + \log s/3 \cdot 80M_p$
Miller function (e.g. $\log_2 s = 64$): $6528 + 1760 = 8288M_p$

10	$Q_1 \leftarrow \pi_p(Q)$	$M_{p^2} = 3M_p$
11	$R \leftarrow R + Q_1; \ell \leftarrow \ell_{R,Q_1}(P)$	$3M_{p^2} + 7S_{p^2} + 4M_p = 27M_p$
12	$f \leftarrow f \cdot \ell$	$13M_{p^2} = 39M_p$
13	$Q_2 \leftarrow \pi_{p^2}(Q)$	$2M_p$
14	$R \leftarrow R - Q_2; \ell \leftarrow \ell_{R,-Q_2}(P)$	$3M_{p^2} + 7S_{p^2} + 4M_p = 27M_p$
15	$f \leftarrow f \cdot \ell$	$13M_{p^2} = 39M_p$

total: $137M_p$
total Miller Loop: $137 + 8288 = 8425M_p$

16	$f \leftarrow f^{p^6-1}$ $3M_{p^6} + 2S_{p^6} + 10M_{p^2} + 3S_{p^2} + 2M_p + 2S_p + I_p = 118M_p + I_p$	
17	$f \leftarrow f^{p^2+1}$ $10M_p + M_{p^{12}} = 64M_p$	
18	**if** $x < 0$ **then**	
19	$\quad a \leftarrow f^{6|x|-5}$	
20	**else** $(f^{p^6} = f^{-1})$	
21	$\quad a \leftarrow (f^{p^6})^{6x+5}$	

$\frac{\log p}{4}S_{\Phi_6(p^2)} + \frac{\log p}{12}M_{p^{12}} = 64 \cdot 18 + 22 \cdot 54M_p = (1152 + 1188)M_p = 2340M_p$

22	$b \leftarrow a^p$	$5M_{p^2} = 15M_p$
23	$b \leftarrow ab$	$M_{p^{12}} = 54M_p$
24	Compute f^p, f^{p^2} and f^{p^3}	$5M_{p^2} + 10M_p + 5M_{p^2} = 40M_p$
25	$c \leftarrow b \cdot (f^p)^2 \cdot f^{p^2}$	$S_{\Phi_6(p^2)} + 2M_{p^{12}} = 126M_p$
26	$c \leftarrow c^{6x^2+1}$	

$\frac{\log p}{2}S_{\Phi_6(p^2)} + \frac{\log p}{6}M_{p^{12}} = 128 \cdot 18 + 43 \cdot 54M_p = 2304 + 2322 = 4626M_p$

27	$f \leftarrow f^{p^3} \cdot c \cdot b \cdot (f^p \cdot f)^9 \cdot a \cdot f^4$	$7M_{p^{12}} + 5S_{\Phi_6(p^2)} = 468M_p$

Exponentiation $f \leftarrow f^{(p^6-1)(p^2+1)(p^4-p^2+1)/r}$: $7851M_p + I_p \approx \mathbf{7911M_p}$

28	**return** f	**Pairing: $16336M_p$**

Optimal Ate Pairing on a Barreto–Naehrig Curve. A pairing is computed in two steps (see Algorithm 1): a Miller function $f \leftarrow f_{r,Q}(P)$ (Algorithm 1, lines 1–15) followed by a final powering $f^{\frac{p^k-1}{r}}$ (Algorithm 1, lines 16–27) to obtain a unique value in $\mathbb{G}_T$, the subgroup of order r of $\mathbb{F}_{p^k}^*$.

There are several papers on pairing computation on BN curves. We present in Algorithm 1 all the steps for an optimal ate pairing computation on a BN curve. Our global estimate is 16 336 M_p (multiplications in $\mathbb{F}_p$) for one pairing. The Miller loop takes 8425 M_p (52 %) and the exponentiation 7911 M_p (48 %). From Relic benchmarks on an Intel Xeon CPU E5-1603 0 at 2.8 GHz, we obtain one pairing in 3.241 ms, the Miller loop in 1.776 ms (55 %) and the exponentiation in 1.465 ms (45 %).

Security Model for Pairing Delegation. In this subsection, we provide an informal description of the security model for pairing delegation protocol and refer the reader to the papers [7,9] for more details. We consider only protocols for delegation of a pairing $e(\mathcal{SK}, \mathcal{PP})$ of a secret key $\mathcal{SK}$ and some public parameter $\mathcal{PP}$. The security notions defined in [7,9] are the following:

Secrecy requires that the powerful device cannot learn any information on $\mathcal{SK}$.

Verifiability requires that the restricted device, even interacting with a dishonest powerful device, will not output a wrong value for $e(\mathcal{SK}, \mathcal{PP})$.

The formal security game for secrecy is similar to the indistinguishability security notion for encryption schemes. The adversary chooses two secret points $\mathcal{SK}_0$ and $\mathcal{SK}_1$ and runs the delegation protocol with the restricted device for the secret point $\mathcal{SK}_b$ for some bit b. The scheme achieves secrecy if the probability that a (polynomial-time) adversary guesses the bit b is negligibly close to $1/2$. The formal security game for verifiability ensures that at the end of the delegation protocol, the restricted device obtains the actual value $e(\mathcal{SK}, \mathcal{PP})$ or knows that the powerful device cheated in the protocol.

As mentioned above, in some cases, the secrecy property is too strong if the powerful device is allowed to learn the value $e(\mathcal{SK}, \mathcal{PP})$ afterwards. Indeed this value reveals some information on $\mathcal{SK}$ and the complete protocol does not achieve the secrecy property. Therefore, we propose the following notion which is weaker than the secrecy notion but well-suited for our usecases of Pay-TV and encrypted GSM communication:

Weak Secrecy requires that the powerful device cannot learn any information about $\mathcal{SK}$ except what can be deduced from the value $e(\mathcal{SK}, \mathcal{PP})$.

Let us assume that we use a pairing delegation protocol for the decryption in a pairing-based scheme (such as the well-known Boneh-Franklin identity-based encryption [4]). If the delegation protocol achieves only Weak Secrecy, a malicious powerful device can mount a lunch-time attack (or CCA1) against the encryption scheme (using the restricted device in the delegation protocol as a decryption oracle). However, since it does not learn any information about $\mathcal{SK}$ (except from the one-time session keys $e(\mathcal{SK}, \mathcal{PP}_i)$ for several public parameters $\mathcal{PP}_i$'s), it is not able to decrypt any ciphertext if the restricted device is no longer active (e.g. after revocation of the decryption rights in the Pay-TV scenario).

3   Review of Previous Proposals

3.1   Girault-Lefranc Pairing Delegation Protocol

In this subsection, we present Girault-Lefranc protocol for server-aided signature verification [12, Sect. 4.1] in Algorithm 2 with a performance estimation on a BN curve at a 128-bit security level ($\log r = \log p = 256$) using the Relic library described above.

Our cost estimation concludes that the delegation of $e(\mathcal{SK}, \mathcal{SP})$ with secret $\mathcal{SK}, \mathcal{SP}$ costs $\approx 18640 M_p$ which is more than a pairing computation at the state of the art (we estimate this for $16336 M_p$ in Relic library).

Note that if pre-computation is possible, then the computation of $[a]\mathcal{SK}$ in the first step of Algorithm 2 can actually be done *off-line*. If moreover, the point $\mathcal{SP}$ is public, then the complexity of the delegation protocol falls down to $9252\ M_p$ (i.e. 0.6 pairing). This basic scheme (with pre-computation) is the most efficient pairing delegation protocol (without verifiability) of a pairing $e(\mathcal{SK}, \mathcal{PP})$ of a secret key $\mathcal{SK}$ and some public parameter $\mathcal{PP}$.

In Girault-Lefranc delegation, as f is a pairing output, we can use the optimized squaring formula of Granger and Scott [13] when computing $f^{(ab)^{-1}}$, hence $S_{p^{12}} = 18 M_p$ instead of $36 M_p$. The computations over the group $\mathbb{G}_1$ might be available on the restricted device such as a smartcard. More precisely, we need multiplication (M_p), addition - subtraction (A_p) and inversion I_p in $\mathbb{F}_p$. Finite field operations are implemented on a smartcard e.g. for ECDSA but the arithmetic operations are not available for the user. We can use the RSA primitives to simulate $\mathbb{F}_p$ arithmetic. We set no padding, the exponent to 2 and the "RSA modulus" to p to get squares mod p, then simulate multiplications through $2xy = (x + y)^2 - x^2 - y^2$. Computations in the group $\mathbb{G}_T$ are not available and must be implemented. If a BN curve [3] is used, $\mathbb{G}_T \subset \mathbb{F}^*_{p^{12}}$ hence a complicated arithmetic must be implemented.

Remark 1 (Lightening the Girault-Lefranc scheme). If the session key $\mathcal{K}$ can be known by the untrusted helper (*i.e.* if one only needs weak secrecy), we

---

Algorithm 2. Girault-Lefranc Secure pairing delegation [12].

Input: secret points $\mathcal{SK} \in \mathbb{G}_1$ and $\mathcal{SP} \in \mathbb{G}_2$ of prime order r, elliptic curve parameters
Output: corresponding session key $\mathcal{K} = e(\mathcal{SK}, \mathcal{SP})$

1 Sample random $a, b \in \mathbb{Z}_r$ and compute $I = [a]\mathcal{SK}, J = [b]\mathcal{SP}$.
  $[a]\mathcal{SK}$ on $E(\mathbb{F}_p)$: $\approx 256\ \mathrm{Dbl}_{E(\mathbb{F}_p)} + 86\ \mathrm{Add}_{E(\mathbb{F}_p)} \approx 256 \cdot (2M_p + 5S_p) + 86 \cdot (7M_p + 4S_p)$
  $\approx 2738 M_p$

  $[b]\mathcal{SP}$ on $E'(\mathbb{F}_{p^2})$: $\approx 256\mathrm{Dbl}_{E'(\mathbb{F}_{p^2})} + 86\ \mathrm{Add}_{E'(\mathbb{F}_{p^2})}$ $\approx 6590 M_p$

  If $\mathcal{SP}$ is public we can set $b = 1$
2 Send I, J to the server.
3 Compute $(ab)^{-1} \mod r$. $\approx 60 M_p$
4 Receive $f = e(I, J)$.   delegated: $\approx 16336 M_p$
5 Compute $f^{(ab)^{-1}}$ to retrieve $\mathcal{K} = e(\mathcal{SK}, \mathcal{SP})$. $\approx 9252 M_p$
6 **return** $\mathcal{K}$.   Total cost ($b = 1$): $\approx 9252 + 60 + 2738 \approx 12050 M_p = 0.74$ pairing
      Total cost $a, b \neq 1$: $\approx 12050 + 6590 \approx 18640 M_p = 1.14$ pairing

---

note that a variant of the protocol may be used in some cases. We propose to ask the external resource to compute $e([\alpha]\mathcal{SK}, [\alpha^{-1}]\mathcal{SP}) = e(\mathcal{SK}, \mathcal{SP}) = \mathcal{K}$ with α taken at random. The output will be exactly $\mathcal{K}$. This solution is not very efficient as it costs $9388/16336 = 0.6$ pairing. To improve it slightly in practice, we can swap $\mathcal{SK}$ and $\mathcal{PP}$, i.e. put $\mathcal{SK}$ in $E'(\mathbb{F}_{p^2})$ and $\mathcal{PP} \in E(\mathbb{F}_p)$. In this way, $[\alpha]\mathcal{SK}$ is the costly part and can be computed offline. Note that this delegation procedure reveals some information on the secret key $\mathcal{SK}$ and it is necessary to reprove the security of the underlying scheme if it is used to improve its efficiency.

3.2 Chevallier-Mames *et al.* Pairing Delegation Protocol

Another pairing delegation protocol was introduced by Chevallier-Mames, Coron, McCullagh, Naccache and Scott in 2005 [8,9]. Contrary to Girault-Lefranc's protocol, the protocol proposed by Chevallier-Mames *et al.* achieves secrecy (unconditionnally) and verifiability. Unfortunately, the protocol is very inefficient since the overall cost for the restricted device is 3.5 times the cost for computing the pairing (3.3 if pre-computation is possible). The main advantage

---

Algorithm 3. Pairing delegation with public right-side point [7, Sect. 4.1].

Input: secret point $\mathcal{SK} \in \mathbb{G}_1$ and public point $\mathcal{PP} \in \mathbb{G}_2$ of prime order r, G_1 generator of $\mathbb{G}_1$, G_2 of $\mathbb{G}_2$, elliptic curve parameters

Output: Pairing value $e(\mathcal{SK}, \mathcal{PP})$

1 Sample a random $a \in \mathbb{Z}_r$ and compute $I_1 = [a]G_1$. $[a]G_1$ on $E(\mathbb{F}_p)$: $\approx 2738M_p$
2 Sample a random $b \in \mathbb{Z}_r$ and compute $I_2 = [b]G_2$. $[b]G_1$ on $E(\mathbb{F}_p)$: $\approx 2738M_p$
3 Compute $\chi = e(G_1, G_2)^{ab}$ 1 exp. in $\mathbb{G}_T$ $\approx 9216M_p$
4 Compute $(a)^{-1}$ mod r and $(b)^{-1}$ mod r $I_p + 3M_p \approx 63M_p$
5 Sample c random $c \in \mathbb{Z}_r$ and compute $J_0 = [c]\mathcal{SK}$. $[c]\mathcal{SK}$ on $E(\mathbb{F}_p)$: $\approx 2738M_p$
6 Compute $J_1 = [b^{-1}]J_0 + I_1$. $[b^{-1}]J_0$ on $E(\mathbb{F}_p)$: $\approx 2738M_p$
7 Compute $J_2 = [a^{-1}]\mathcal{PP} + I_2$. $[a^{-1}]\mathcal{PP}$ on $E(\mathbb{F}_p)$: $\approx 2738M_p$
8 Send $J_1, J_2, \mathcal{PP}$ to the server.
9 Ask for $\alpha_1 = e(J_1, J_2)(e(G_1, \mathcal{PP})e(J_0, G_2))^{-1}, \alpha_2 = e(J_0, \mathcal{PP})$ **delegated:**
   $\approx 4 \cdot 16336M_p = 65344M_p$
10 Receive α_1, α_2
11 Check that $\alpha_2 \in \mathbb{G}_T$: compute α_2^r $4675M_p$
12 **if** $\alpha_2^r \neq 1$ **then**
13 $\quad$ outputs $\perp$ and halt.

14 Compute $\chi' = \chi \cdot \alpha_2^{(ab)^{-1}}$ 1 exp. in $\mathbb{G}_T$ $\approx 9216M_p$
15 **if** $\chi' = \alpha_1$ **then**
16 $\quad$ compute $(c)^{-1}$ mod r $I_p \approx 60M_p$
17 $\quad$ outputs $\alpha_2^{(c)^{-1}}$ and halt.   1 exp. in $\mathbb{G}_T$ $\approx 9216M_p$
18 **else**
19 $\quad$ outputs $\perp$ and halt.

Total cost: $46136M_p = 2.8$ **pairings**
Cost w/o pre-computation: $25905M_p = 1.6$ **pairings**

---

of the scheme is to save of area that is required to implement a pairing in the restricted device such a smart card. However, as mentioned above, even if we can use tricks, computations in the group $\mathbb{G}_T$ are usually not available and must be implemented (i.e. complex arithmetic in $\mathbb{G}_T \subset \mathbb{F}_{p^{12}}^*$ for a BN curve).

3.3 Canard-Devigne-Sanders Pairing Delegation Protocol

We present in Algorithm 3 the pairing delegation protocol proposed recently by Canard, Devigne and Sanders [7]. The protocol is more efficient than the previous one. It also achieves secrecy (unconditionnally) and verifiability. Canard *et al.* actually showed that their proposal is in fact more efficient than the computation of the pairing for optimal ate pairing on a so-called KSS-18 curve [15]. Unfortunately, as shown by the precise complexity of Algorithm 3, this is not the case for state-of-the-art optimal Ate pairing on a BN curve [3]. More precisely, we show that the overall cost for the restricted device is 2.8 times the cost for computing the pairing (1.6 if pre-computation is possible).

4   Pairing Delegation with Knapsack

We present in this section a new approach to perform pairing delegation (without verifiability) of a pairing $e(\mathcal{SK}, \mathcal{PP})$ of a secret key $\mathcal{SK}$ and some public parameter $\mathcal{PP}$. The restricted device (e.g. a smartcard) generates random points and sends them to the powerful device to compute several pairings. The smartcard receives the pairings and combines some of them to get the actual value $e(\mathcal{SK}, \mathcal{PP})$. The basic idea is to mask the secret value $\mathcal{SK}$ by a linear combination of those random points with "small" coefficients to improve efficiency. A similar approach has been used successfully in the setting of server-aided exponentiation [6, 16].

4.1   Security Analysis

Let $\mathbb{G}$ be a cyclic group of order p denoted additively. We consider the two following distributions:

$$\mathcal{U}_n = \{(P_1, P_2, \dots, P_n, Q) \xleftarrow{R} \mathbb{G}^{n+1}\}$$

and

$$\mathcal{K}_{n,A} = \left\{ (P_1, P_2, \dots, P_n, Q), \text{ s.t. } \begin{array}{c} (P_1, P_2, \dots, P_n) \xleftarrow{R} \mathbb{G}^n \\ Q \leftarrow [a_1]P_1 + \dots + [a_n]P_n \\ \text{where } (a_1, \dots, a_n) \xleftarrow{R} [\![0, A-1]\!]^n \end{array} \right\}.$$

$\mathcal{U}_n$ is the uniform distribution on $\mathbb{G}^{n+1}$ and $\mathcal{K}_{n,A}$ outputs $(n+1)$-tuples where the first n components are picked uniformly at random in $\mathbb{G}$ while the last component is a linear combination of those elements with exponents picked uniformly at random in the interval $[\![0, A-1]\!]$. In a basic version of our delegation protocol, the restricted device sends the elements $(P_1, \ldots, P_n)$ and $P_{n+1} = (\mathcal{SK} - Q)$ to the powerful device. It replies by sending back the pairings $e(P_i, \mathcal{PP})$ for $i \in \{1, \ldots, n+1\}$. The restricted device finally gets $e(\mathcal{SK}, \mathcal{PP})$ as $e(P_{n+1}, \mathcal{PP}) \cdot \prod_{i=1}^{n} e(g_i, \mathcal{PP})^{a_i}$. If the two distributions $\mathcal{U}_n$ and $\mathcal{K}_{n,A}$ are indistinguishable, the protocol will readily achieve the secrecy property.

- *Perfect indistinguishability.* It is straightforward to see that if $A = p$, then the two distributions are identical (even if $n = 1$) and the delegation scheme as outlined above achieves unconditional secrecy. Unfortunately, as we will see in the next paragraph, the efficiency of our schemes depends crucially on the size of A and one wants to use smaller A in practice.
- *Statistical indistinguishability.* By using classical results on the distribution of modular sums [16], one can prove that if $A^n = \Omega(p^2)$, then the two distributions $\mathcal{U}_n$ and $\mathcal{K}_{n,A}$ are statistically indistinguishable (see [10,16] for details). For these parameters, the delegation protocol achieves statistical (and therefore computational) secrecy. For cryptographic purposes, the order p of $\mathbb{G}$ needs to be of $2k$-bit size to achieve a k-bit security level. Therefore, to achieve statistical indistinguishability, we need to have $A^n = \Omega(2^{4k})$ and the resulting delegation protocol is not really efficient.
- *Computational indistinguishability.* For smaller parameters (i.e. $A^n = o(p^2)$), we cannot prove that the $\mathcal{U}_n$ and $\mathcal{K}_{n,A}$ are statistically indistinguishable. However, it may be possible to prove that they are computationally indistinguishable. Using a variant of Shanks "baby-step giant-step" algorithm, one can see easily that it is possible to find the scalars $(a_1, \ldots, a_n)$ (if they exist) such that $Q = [a_1]P_1 + \cdots + [a_n]P_n$ in $O(A^{n/2})$ group operations in $\mathbb{G}$ (i.e. to solve the *generalized knapsack problem* in $\mathbb{G}$). Therefore, to achieve computational indistinguishability for a k-bit security parameter, one needs to have at least $A^n = \Omega(2^{2k}) = \Omega(p)$.

To conclude this paragraph, we will prove that the two distributions $\mathcal{U}_n$ and $\mathcal{K}_{n,A}$ are computationally indistinguishable in the generic group model when $A^n = \Omega(2^{2k}) = \Omega(p)$. Our delegation protocol therefore achieves secrecy in the generic group model when $A^n = \Omega(2^{2k}) = \Omega(p)$. This model was introduced by Shoup [17] for measuring the exact difficulty of solving discrete logarithm problems. Algorithms in generic groups do not exploit any properties of the encodings of group elements. They can access group elements only via a random encoding algorithm that encodes group elements as random bit-strings.

Let $\mathcal{A}$ be a generic group adversary. As usual, the generic group model is implemented by choosing a random encoding $\sigma : \mathbb{G} \longrightarrow \{0, 1\}^m$. Instead of working directly with group elements, $\mathcal{A}$ takes as input their image under σ. This way, all $\mathcal{A}$ can test is string equality. $\mathcal{A}$ is also given access to an oracle computing group addition and subtraction: taking $\sigma(R_1)$ and $\sigma(R_2)$ and returning $\sigma(R_1 + R_2)$, similarly for subtraction. Finally, we can assume that $\mathcal{A}$ submits to the oracle only encodings of elements it had previously received. This is because we can choose m large enough so that the probability of choosing a string that is also in the image of σ is negligible.

Theorem 1. *Let $\mathcal{A}$ be a generic algorithm that distinguishes the two distribu-tions $\mathcal{U}_n$ and $\mathcal{K}_{n,A}$ that makes at most τ group oracle queries, then $\mathcal{A}$'s advantage in distinguishing the two distributions is upper-bounded by $O(\tau^2/A^n)$.*

To prove this theorem, we consider the following distributions in a product group $\mathbb{G}_1 \times \cdots \times \mathbb{G}_n$ where each $\mathbb{G}_i$ is cyclic group of prime order p (for $i \in \{1, \ldots, n\}$).

$$\mathcal{U'}_n = \{(P_1, P_2, \ldots, P_n, Q) \xleftarrow{R} \mathbb{G}_1 \times \mathbb{G}_2 \times \cdots \times \mathbb{G}_n \times (\mathbb{G}_1 \times \mathbb{G}_2 \times \cdots \times \mathbb{G}_n)\}$$

and

$$\mathcal{K'}_{n,A} = \left\{ (P_1, P_2, \ldots, P_n, Q), \text{ s.t. } \begin{array}{c} (P_1, P_2, \ldots, P_n) \xleftarrow{R} \mathbb{G}_1 \times \mathbb{G}_2 \times \cdots \times \mathbb{G}_n \\ Q \leftarrow [a_1]P_1 + \cdots + [a_n]P_n \\ \text{where } (a_1, \ldots, a_n) \xleftarrow{R} [\![0, A-1]\!]^n \end{array} \right\}$$

It is worth mentioning that the use of these product groups in cryptography is not interesting since even if their order is p^n, the complexity of discrete loga-rithm computation in them is not much harder than in cyclic groups of order p. We will only use them as a tool in order to prove our Theorem 1.

Following Shoup's technique [17], it is easy to prove that a generic algorithm in the product group $\mathbb{G}_1 \times \cdots \times \mathbb{G}_n$ (or equivalently in $\mathbb{Z}_p^n$) has a negligible advantage in distinguishing the two distributions $\mathcal{U'}_n$ and $\mathcal{K'}_{n,A}$ if it makes a polynomial number of group oracle queries. More precisely, we can prove the following proposition:

Proposition 1. *Let $\mathcal{A}$ be a generic algorithm that distinguishes the two dis-tributions $\mathcal{U'}_n$ and $\mathcal{K'}_{n,A}$ and makes at most τ group oracle queries, then $\mathcal{A}$'s advantage in distinguishing the two distributions is upper-bounded by $O(\tau^2/A^n)$.*

Proof. We consider an algorithm $\mathcal{B}$ playing the following game with $\mathcal{A}$. Algo-rithm $\mathcal{B}$ chooses $n+1$ bit strings $\sigma_1, \ldots, \sigma_n, \sigma_{n+1}$ uniformly in $\{0,1\}^m$. Internally, $\mathcal{B}$ keeps track of the encoded elements using elements in the ring $\mathbb{Z}_p[X_1] \times \cdots \times \mathbb{Z}_p[X_n]$. To maintain consistency with the bit strings given to $\mathcal{A}$, $\mathcal{B}$ creates a lists $\mathcal{L}$ of pairs (F, σ) where F is a polynomial vector in the ring $\mathbb{Z}_p[X_1] \times \cdots \times \mathbb{Z}_p[X_n]$ and $\sigma \in \{0,1\}^m$ is the encoding of a group element. The polynomial vector F represents the exponent of the encoded element in the group $\mathbb{G}_1 \times \cdots \times \mathbb{G}_n$. Initially, $\mathcal{L}$ is set to

$$\{((1,0,\ldots,0),\sigma_1),((0,1,\ldots,0),\sigma_2),\ldots,((0,0,\ldots,1),\sigma_n),((X_1,\ldots,X_n),\sigma_{n+1})\}$$

Algorithm $\mathcal{B}$ starts the game providing $\mathcal{A}$ with $\sigma_1, \ldots, \sigma_n, \sigma_{n+1}$. The simulation of the group operations oracle goes as follows:

Group Operation: Given two encodings σ_i and σ_j in $\mathcal{L}$, $\mathcal{B}$ recovers the cor-responding vectors F_i and F_j and computes $F_i + F_j$ (or $F_i - F_j$) termwise. If $F_i + F_j$ (or $F_i - F_j$) is already in $\mathcal{L}$, $\mathcal{B}$ returns to $\mathcal{A}$ the corresponding bit string; otherwise it returns a uniform element $\sigma \xleftarrow{R} \{0,1\}^m$ and stores $(F_i + F_j, \sigma)$ (or $(F_i - F_j, \sigma)$) in $\mathcal{L}$.

After $\mathcal{A}$ queried the oracles, it outputs a bit b. At this point, $\mathcal{B}$ chooses a random bit $b^* \in \{0,1\}$ and uniform values $x_1, \ldots, x_n \in \mathbb{Z}_p$ if $b^* = 0$ or uniform values $x_1, \ldots, x_n \in [\![0, A - 1]\!]$ if $b^* = 1$. The algorithm $\mathcal{B}$ sets $X_i = x_i$ for $i \in \{1, \ldots, n\}$.

If the simulation provided by $\mathcal{B}$ is consistent, it reveals nothing about b. This means that the probability of $\mathcal{A}$ guessing the correct value for b^* is $1/2$. The only way in which the simulation could be inconsistent is if, after we choose value for $x_1, \ldots, x_n$, two different polynomial vectors in $\mathcal{L}$ happen to produce the same value. First, note that $\mathcal{A}$ is unable to cause such a collision on its own. Indeed, notice that $\mathcal{L}$ is initially populated with polynomials of degree at most one in each coordinate and that both the group addition and subtraction oracle do not increase the degree of the polynomial. Thus, all polynomials contained in $\mathcal{L}$ have degree at most one. This is enough to conclude that $\mathcal{A}$ cannot purposely produce a collision.

It remains to prove that the probability of a collision happening due to a unlucky choice of values is negligible. In other words, we have to bound the probability that two distinct F_i, F_j in $\mathcal{L}$ evaluate to the same value after the substitution, namely $F_i(x_1, \ldots, x_n) - F_j(x_1, \ldots, x_n) = 0$. This reduces to bound the probability of hitting a zero of $F_i - F_j$. By the simulation, this happens only if $F_i - F_j$ is a non-constant polynomial vector and in this case, each coordinate is a degree one polynomial in one X_i's.

Recall that the Schwartz-Zippel lemma says that, if F is a degree d polynomial in $\mathbb{Z}_p[X_1, \ldots, X_n]$ and $S \subseteq \mathbb{Z}_p$ then

$$\Pr[F(x_1, \ldots, x_n) = 0] \leq \frac{d}{|S|}$$

where $x_1, \ldots, x_n$ are chosen uniformly from S. Going back to our case, we obtain by applying the Schwartz-Zippel lemma to each coordinate:

$$\Pr[(F_i - F_j)(x_1, \ldots, x_n) = \mathbf{0} \in \mathbb{Z}_p^n] \leq \begin{cases} 1/p^n & \text{if } b^* = 0 \\ 1/A^n & \text{if } b^* = 1 \end{cases}$$

Therefore, the probability that the simulation provided by $\mathcal{B}$ is inconsistent is upper-bounded by $\tau(\tau - 1)/A^n$. □

We will now prove that, provided m is large enough, a generic algorithm is not able to decide whether it is given as inputs n generators $(P_1, \ldots, P_n)$ in a cyclic group $\mathbb{G}$ of prime order p or n order-p elements

$$(P_1, 1_{\mathbb{G}_2}, \ldots, 1_{\mathbb{G}_n}), (1_{\mathbb{G}_1}, P_2, \ldots, 1_{\mathbb{G}_n}), \ldots, (1_{\mathbb{G}_1}, 1_{\mathbb{G}_2}, \ldots, P_n)$$

in a product group $\mathbb{G}_1 \times \cdots \times \mathbb{G}_n$ where each $\mathbb{G}_i$ is cyclic group of prime order p. Note that the groups $\mathbb{G}$ and $\mathbb{G}_1 \times \cdots \times \mathbb{G}_n$ are not of the same order and in practice, it will probably be easy to distinguish them. We only claim that this is difficult for a generic algorithm.

Proposition 2. *Let $\mathcal{A}$ be a generic algorithm that distinguishes these two settings and makes at most τ group oracle queries, then $\mathcal{A}$'s advantage in distinguishing the two distributions is upper-bounded by $O(\tau^2/p)$.*

Proof. We consider an algorithm $\mathcal{B}$ playing the following game with $\mathcal{A}$. Algorithm $\mathcal{B}$ chooses a random bit b^* and runs one of the following simulation depending on the bit b^*

- If $b^* = 0$, $\mathcal{B}$ chooses n bit strings $\sigma_1, \ldots, \sigma_n$ uniformly in $\{0,1\}^m$. Internally, $\mathcal{B}$ keeps track of the encoded elements using elements in the ring $\mathbb{Z}_p[X_1, \ldots, X_n]$. To maintain consistency with the bit strings given to $\mathcal{A}$, $\mathcal{B}$ creates a list $\mathcal{L}$ of pairs (F, σ) where F is a polynomial in the ring $\mathbb{Z}_p[X_1, \ldots, X_n]$ and $\sigma \in \{0,1\}^m$ is the encoding of a group element. The polynomial F represents the exponent of the encoded element in the group $\mathbb{G}$. Initially, $\mathcal{L}$ is set to

$$\{(X_1, \sigma_1), (X_2, \sigma_2), \ldots, (X_n, \sigma_n)\}$$

- If $b^* = 1$, $\mathcal{B}$ chooses also n bit strings $\sigma_1, \ldots, \sigma_n$ uniformly in $\{0,1\}^m$. Internally, $\mathcal{B}$ keeps track of the encoded elements using elements in the ring $\mathbb{Z}_p[X_1] \times \cdots \times \mathbb{Z}_p[X_n]$. To maintain consistency with the bit strings given to $\mathcal{A}$, $\mathcal{B}$ creates a list $\mathcal{L}$ of pairs (F, σ) where F is a polynomial vector in the ring $\mathbb{Z}_p[X_1] \times \cdots \times \mathbb{Z}_p[X_n]$ and $\sigma \in \{0,1\}^m$ is the encoding of a group element. The polynomial vector F represents the exponent of the encoded element in the group $\mathbb{G}_1 \times \cdots \times \mathbb{G}_n$. Initially, $\mathcal{L}$ is set to

$$\{((X_1, 0, 0, \ldots, 0), \sigma_1), ((0, X_2, 0, \ldots, 0), \sigma_2), \ldots, ((0, 0, \ldots, 0, X_n), \sigma_n)\}$$

In each cases, algorithm $\mathcal{B}$ starts the game providing $\mathcal{A}$ with $\sigma_1, \ldots, \sigma_n$. The simulation of the group operations oracle goes as follows:

Group operation: Given two encodings σ_i and σ_j in $\mathcal{L}$, $\mathcal{B}$ recovers the corresponding polynomials (or polynomial vectors, depending on b^*) F_i and F_j and computes $F_i + F_j$ (or $F_i - F_j$) termwise. If $F_i + F_j$ (or $F_i - F_j$) is already in $\mathcal{L}$, $\mathcal{B}$ returns to $\mathcal{A}$ the corresponding bit string; otherwise it returns a uniform element $\sigma \xleftarrow{R} \{0,1\}^m$ and stores $(F_i + F_j, \sigma)$ (or $(F_i - F_j, \sigma)$) in $\mathcal{L}$.

After $\mathcal{A}$ queried the oracles, it outputs a bit b. At this point, $\mathcal{B}$ chooses uniform values $x_1, \ldots, x_n \in \mathbb{Z}_p$. The algorithm $\mathcal{B}$ sets $X_i = x_i$ for $i \in \{1, \ldots, n\}$.

If the simulation provided by $\mathcal{B}$ is consistent, it reveals nothing about b. This means that the probability of $\mathcal{A}$ guessing the correct value for b^* is $1/2$. The only way in which the simulation could be inconsistent is if, after we choose value for $x_1, \ldots, x_n$, two different polynomial vectors in $\mathcal{L}$ happen to produce the same value. First, note that $\mathcal{A}$ is unable to cause such a collision on its own. Indeed, notice that $\mathcal{L}$ is initially populated with polynomials of degree at most one in each coordinate and that both the group addition and subtraction oracle do not increase the degree of the polynomial. Thus, all polynomials contained in $\mathcal{L}$ have degree at most one. This is enough to conclude that $\mathcal{A}$ cannot purposely produce a collision.

It remains to prove that the probability of a collision happening due to a unlucky choice of values is negligible. If $b^* = 1$, the probability of a collision happening is equal to 0. If $b^* = 0$, we have to bound the probability that two distinct F_i, F_j in $\mathcal{L}$ evaluate to the same value after the substitution, namely $F_i(x_1, \ldots, x_n) - F_j(x_1, \ldots, x_n) = 0$. This reduces to bound the probability of hitting a zero of $F_i - F_j$.

Applying the Schwartz-Zippel lemma, we obtain

$$\Pr[(F_i - F_j)(x_1, \ldots, x_n) = 0 \in \mathbb{Z}_p] \leq 1/p$$

Therefore, the probability that the simulation provided by $\mathcal{B}$ is inconsistent is upper-bounded by $\tau(\tau - 1)/p$. □

To prove Theorem 1, it is then enough to prove that if there exists a generic algorithm that distinguishes the two distributions $\mathcal{U}_n$ and $\mathcal{K}_{n,A}$ that makes at most τ group oracle queries with an advantage larger than $\Omega(\tau^2/A^n)$, it gives an adversary able to distinguish the cyclic group setting from the product group setting making at most τ group oracle queries and with advantage $\Omega(\tau^2/A^n)$ (due to Proposition 1) and this result contradicts Proposition 2.

4.2   Description of Our Protocol

In the previous subsection, we provided a description of a basic version of our protocol. In this subsection, we consider an improved version of it on elliptic curves equipped with efficient endomorphisms. In this improved scheme, instead of masking $\mathcal{SK}$ with $[a_1]P_1 + \cdots + [a_{n-1}]P_{n-1}$ with $(a_1, \ldots, a_{n-1}) \xleftarrow{R} [0, A - 1]^{n-1}$, we will mask it with $[a_1]Q_1 + \cdots + [a_{n-1}]Q_{n-1}$ with $(a_1, \ldots, a_{n-1}) \xleftarrow{R} [0, A - 1]^{n-1}$ where the Q_i's are images of the P_i under one of the efficient endomorphisms defined on the curve. If we denote $\mathcal{S}$ the set of efficient endomorphisms on the curve (that can also be efficiently evaluated in the group $\mathbb{G}_T$), we obtained a scheme with generic security $\Omega(\#\mathcal{S}^{n-1} \cdot A^{n-1/2})$.

Setup (could be offline). In the following, the smartcard has to generate several random points on an elliptic curve $E(\mathbb{F}_p)$. Fouque and Tibouchi [11] proposed an efficient method to do it on a BN curve.

1. Let $\mathcal{I}$ a set of small integers, $\mathcal{I} = \{0, 1, 2, 3, 4, 5, \ldots, 2^\ell - 1\}$ with $\#\mathcal{I} = 2^\ell = A$.
2. The smartcard generates $n - 1$ random points $P_1, P_2, \ldots, P_{n-1}$ on the elliptic curve $E(\mathbb{F}_p)$.
3. The smartcard chooses an endomorphism $\sigma_i \in \mathcal{S}$ to apply to P_i and sets $Q_i = \sigma_i(P_i)$.
4. For each point Q_i, the smartcard takes at random $\alpha_i \in \mathcal{I}$ and sets

$$P_n = \mathcal{SK} - ([\alpha_1]Q_1 + [\alpha_2]Q_2 + \ldots + [\alpha_{n-1}]Q_{n-1} = \mathcal{SK} - \sum_{i=1}^{n-1}[\alpha_i]Q_i .$$

Delegation

5. The smartcard sends $P_1, P_2, \ldots, P_n$ to the server.
6. The server computes the n pairings $f_i = e(Q_i, \mathcal{PP})$ and sends them back to the smartcard.

Session key computation

7. The smartcard computes $(f_1^{\sigma_1})^{\alpha_1} \cdot (f_2^{\sigma_2})^{\alpha_2} \cdots (f_{n-1}^{\sigma_{n-1}})^{\alpha_{n-1}} \cdot f_n = \mathcal{K}$. The σ_i are also almost free. Thanks to the bilinearity property,

$$
\begin{aligned}
e(\mathcal{SK}, \mathcal{PP}) &= e(\alpha_1 Q_1 + \alpha_2 Q_2 \ldots + \alpha_{n-1} Q_{n-1} + P_n, \mathcal{PP}) \\
&= e(\alpha_1 Q_1, \mathcal{PP}) e(\alpha_2 Q_2, \mathcal{PP}) \cdots e(\alpha_{n-1} Q_{n-1}, \mathcal{PP}) e(P_n, \mathcal{PP}) \\
&= (e(P_1, \mathcal{PP})^{\sigma_1})^{\alpha_1} \cdots (e(P_{n-1}, \mathcal{PP})^{\sigma_{n-1}})^{\alpha_{n-1}} (e(P_n, \mathcal{PP}))
\end{aligned}
$$

with σ_i a cheap endomorphism in $\mathbb{F}_{p^k}^*$ such that $e(\sigma_i(P_i), \mathcal{PP}) = e(P_i, \mathcal{PP})^{\sigma_i}$.

Example on a Barreto–Naehrig curve. For optimal Ate pairing on a BN curve with 128-bit security level (i.e. 256-bit prime number p), the endomorphism set $\mathcal{S}$ can be defined as $\{\mathrm{Id}, -\mathrm{Id}, \phi, \phi^2, -\phi, -\phi^2\}$ where ϕ is computed from the complex multiplication endomorphism available on the curve. These endomorphisms are almost free on $E(\mathbb{F}_p)$ if $D = 1$ or $D = 3$. They cost at most one multiplication and one subtraction in $\mathbb{F}_p$ and the resulting point Q_i is still in affine coordinates [5].

In the Setup procedure, the smartcard has to obtain P_n in affine coordinates, this costs one inversion in $\mathbb{F}_p$ plus four multiplications, resulting in an additional cost of (say) $64M_p$. The cost of computing P_n is $(n-1) \cdot (\ell \cdot 7 + \ell/2 \cdot 11 + 16) + 64M_p$. Indeed, in Jacobian coordinates, one addition on $E(\mathbb{F}_p)$ with one of the two points in affine coordinates costs $11M_p$, if none of the points are in affine coordinates, this costs $16M_p$, and one doubling costs $8M_p$. If moreover we use a BN curve ($a_4 = 0$), a doubling costs $7M_p$.

The computation cost for the powerful device is $16336(0.84(n-1)+1) \, M_p$. Indeed, the first pairing costs $\approx 16336M_p$ and the $(n-1)$ other ones cost 0.84 of one pairing (since the second argument is the fixed point $\mathcal{PP}$, the tangents and lines can be computed from $\mathcal{PP}$ one single time for all the pairings).

Finally, the smartcard computes[1] $n-1$ exponentiations and multiplies n elements in $\mathbb{G}_T$ to obtain the session key $\mathcal{K} = e(\mathcal{SK}, \mathcal{PP})$. An exponentiation costs in average ℓ squaring plus $\ell/2$ multiplications in $\mathbb{F}_{p^{12}}$. The $n-1$ exponentiations cost $(n-1)(18\ell + 54\ell/3)M_p$. It remains to compute $n-1$ multiplications.

Overall, we obtain the global cost for the restricted device is: $(n-1)(73M_p + 46, 7\ell M_p)$ (and $(n-1)(73M_p + 36\ell M_p)$ is pre-computation is possible). We summarize our proposition in Algorithm 4. By choosing appropriate values for n and ℓ, one can achieve various communication-efficiency trade-off as shown in Table 2. To achieve statistical security (instead of generic computational security), one basically needs to double the value of ℓ. One can find parameters for which the delegation procedure is more efficient than the pairing computation (0.5 pairing for practical parameters).

---

[1] It is worth mentioning that this computational cost can be further decreased by using classical multi-exponentiation techniques (in particular for small values of n (e.g. $n = 5$).

Algorithm 4. Pairing delegation with knapsack.

Input: secret key $\mathcal{SK}$, public value $\mathcal{PP}$, set I of small integers with $\#I = 2^\ell$
Output: Session key $\mathcal{K} = e(\mathcal{SK}, \mathcal{PP})$

1 Offline:
2 Generate $n-1$ random points $P_1, P_2, \ldots, P_n \in E(\mathbb{F}_p)$.
3 **foreach** P_i **do**
4 $\quad$ Choose at random an endomorphism $\sigma_i \in \{\mathrm{Id}, -\mathrm{Id}, \phi, -\phi, \phi^2, -\phi^2\}$ $\quad$ σ_i **on**
   $\quad$ $E(\mathbb{F}_p)$: **at most** $1M_p$
5 $\quad$ Choose at random an integer $\alpha_i \in \mathcal{I}$
6 $\quad$ Compute $Q_i = [\alpha_i]\sigma(P_i)$ $\quad$ $[\alpha_i]$: $\log_2 \alpha_i(\mathrm{Dbl}_{E(\mathbb{F}_p)} + \frac{1}{3}\mathrm{Add}_{E(\mathbb{F}_p)}) \leqslant 10.7\ell M_p$

7 Online:
8 Compute $P_n = \mathcal{SK} - ([\alpha_1]\sigma_i(P_1) + [\alpha_2]\sigma_2(P_2) + \ldots + [\alpha_{n-1}]\sigma_{n-1}(P_{n-1}) = \mathcal{SK} - \sum_{i=1}^{n-1}[\alpha_i]\sigma_i(P_i)$

$$n - 1 \;\; \mathrm{Add}_{E(\mathbb{F}_p)} = (n-1)11M_p$$

9 Send $\mathcal{PP}$ and all the $P_1, \ldots, P_n$ to the server. **communication:** $\log(p) \cdot (n+1)$
   bits
10 Ask for all the $f_i = e(P_i, \mathcal{PP}), 1 \leqslant i \leqslant n$ $\quad\quad$ **Delegated:** $\approx 16336n \;\; M_p$
11 Compute $\mathcal{K} = (f_1^{\sigma_1})^{\alpha_1} \cdot (f_2^{\sigma_2})^{\alpha_2} \cdots (f_{n-1}^{\sigma_{n-1}})^{\alpha_{n-1}} \cdot f_n$ $\quad$ $(n-1)(\sigma_i + \alpha_i + \mathrm{Mult.}) = (n-1)(8M_p + \ell(S_{\Phi_{12}(p)} + \frac{1}{3}M_{p^{12}}) + M_{p^{12}}) = (n-1)(62M_p + 36\ell M_p)$
12 **return** $\mathcal{K}$. $\quad\quad\quad\quad\quad\quad\quad\quad$ **Total cost:** $(n-1)(73M_p + 46, 7\ell M_p)$
$\quad\quad\quad\quad\quad\quad$ Cost w/o pre-computation: $(n-1)(73M_p + 36\ell M_p)$
$\quad\quad\quad\quad\quad\quad\quad\quad$ **for** $n = 20$ **and** $\ell = 8$: $6859M_p = 0.4$ **pairing**

---

5 Partial Pairing Computation Delegation

In this final section, we propose a completely different approach based on the arithmetic of the pairing computation (without verifiability) of a pairing $e(\mathcal{SK}, \mathcal{PP})$ of a secret key $\mathcal{SK}$ and some public parameter $\mathcal{PP}$. More precisely, we delegate only the non-critical steps in the pairing algorithm, looking carefully at each instruction in Miller algorithm. The protocol only achieves *weak secrecy*: the helper will learn the session key $\mathcal{K}$ (but still not the secret key $\mathcal{SK}$).

Final Powering Delegation. We can blind the output $f' \leftarrow u \cdot f$ of the Miller function by an element $u \in \mathbb{F}_{p^k}^*$ which is an r-th power (there exists a $u' \in \mathbb{F}_{p^k}^*$ such that $u'^r = u$), see Algorithm 5. Hence u will disappear after the final powering $f^{\frac{p^k-1}{r}}$ (Algorithm 1, lines 16–27) since $u^{\frac{p^k-1}{r}} = u'^{p^k-1} = 1$. So we can delegate the final powering thanks to the equality $f'^{(p^k-1)/r} = (uf)^{(p^k-1)/r} = \mathcal{K}$ the session key. The helper learns the session key $\mathcal{K}$ but has no additional information on f (in particular pairing inversion is not possible).

Tangent and line Delegation. The two points P, Q play two different roles in a Tate-like pairing computation. In an ate pairing, the point P is used to evaluate the intermediate line functions $\ell(P)$. The line functions ℓ are computed through a scalar multiplication $[s]Q$ (with s a public parameter of the curve). The coefficients arising in the lines and tangent computation are re-used to update the

Table 2. Communication/Efficiency Trade-off of our knapsack delegation protocol

ℓ	n	Generic security	Computational cost	Communication
59	5	128	$8788M_p = 0.53$ pairing	15360 bits
23	10	126	$8109M_p = 0.49$ pairing	30720 bits
13	15	127	$7574M_p = 0.46$ pairing	46080 bits
8	20	125	$6859M_p = 0.41$ pairing	61440 bits
8	20	125	$6859M_p = 0.41$ pairing	61440 bits
5	25	122	$6072M_p = 0.37$ pairing	76800 bits
3	30	118	$5249M_p = 0.32$ pairing	92160 bits
0	51	128	$3650M_p = 0.22$ pairing	156672 bits

Algorithm 5. Partial reduced Tate pairing delegation

Input: Elliptic curve $E(\mathbb{F}_p)$ of embedding degree k and prime order r subgroup, with degree d twist available, points $P \in E(\mathbb{F}_p)$,
$Q \in E(\mathbb{F}_{p^k}) \cap \mathrm{Ker}(\pi_{p^{k/d}} - [p^{k/d}])$

Output: Reduced Tate pairing $e_r(P, Q)^{\frac{p^k-1}{r}}$

1 $f = f_{r,P}(Q)$ Miller function
2 Compute a random r-th power $u \in \mathbb{F}_{p^k}^*$ i.e. such that $\exists v \in \mathbb{F}_{p^k}^*, u = v^r$
3 $f' = f \cdot u$
4 Send f' to the external resource
5 Receive $h = (f')^{\frac{p^k-1}{r}} = u^{p^k-1} f^{\frac{p^k-1}{r}} = f^{\frac{p^k-1}{r}} = K$
6 Return K

Miller function $f_{s,\mathcal{PP}}(\mathcal{SK})$. If Q is actually a public parameter $\mathcal{PP}$, then the line computation $\ell_{\mathcal{PP}}$ can be delegated. The restricted device (such as a smartcard) will ask for the successive intermediate values ℓ then evaluate them at the secret point $P = \mathcal{SK}$.

For an ate pairing on a BN curve, the line is of the form $\ell = \ell_0 + \ell_1\omega + \ell_3\omega^3$, with $\mathbb{F}_{p^{12}} = \mathbb{F}_{p^2}[\omega] = \mathbb{F}_{p^2}[\omega]/(\omega^6 - \xi)$. The smartcard can delegate the computation of the three coefficients then compute the line equation evaluated at $\mathcal{SK}$.

Tangent and line computation. One can found Relic [1] formulas for tangent and line computation in `src/pp/relic_pp_dbl.c` (function `pp_dbl_k12_projc_basic`) and `src/pp/relic_pp_add.c` (function `pp_add_k12_projc_basic`).

We recall the formula from [2, Eq. (10)]:

$$\ell_{2T}(P) = -2YZ\, y_P + 3X^2\, x_P\, \omega + (3b'Z^2 - Y^2)\omega^3 \tag{1}$$

with ω such that $\mathbb{F}_{p^{12}} = \mathbb{F}_{p^2}[\omega]/(\omega^6 - \xi)$, $X, Y, Z \in \mathbb{F}_{p^2}$ and $x_P, y_P \in \mathbb{F}_p$.

The second formula is the following [2, Eq. (13)], with $L = X - x_Q Z$ and $M = Y - y_Q Z$:

$$\ell_{T+Q}(P) = -L y_P - M x_P \omega + (MX - LY)\omega^3 \tag{2}$$

In both cases the coefficients of ℓ are computed from a public parameter $Q = \mathcal{P}P$ hence can be delegated. The smart card saves $2S_{p^2} + 7M_{p^2} = 25M_p$. It remains for the smart card to evaluate the line ℓ at $\mathcal{SK} = P = (x_P, y_P)$. This costs $4M_p$ in both cases.

Efficiency improvement. To sum up, the smartcard sends the point $\mathcal{P}P$ to the external computer and computes the intermediate values of the Miller function on the fly, when receiving the coefficients of the intermediate values. No information on $\mathcal{SK}$ is provided to the external helper (except f' which does not reveal more information than the session key $\mathcal{K}$). For an optimal Ate pairing on a Barreto-Naehrig curve, this saves 31% of the Miller loop, then we delegate 100% of the final powering, saving at the end 65% of the pairing cost. Note that the idea can be adapted to achieve (strong) secrecy by further masking the final powering but the efficiency improvement is smaller if pre-computation is not possible. Note also that the same idea can be applied to any instantiation of pairings (but requires a specific analysis).

Acknowledgements. The authors thank Olivier Blazy, Renaud Dubois and Fabien Laguillaumie for their fruitful comments. This work was supported in part by the French ANR-12-INSE-0014 SIMPATIC Project.

References

1. Aranha, D.F., Gouvêa, C.P.L.: RELIC is an Efficient LIbrary for Cryptography, September 2013. http://code.google.com/p/relic-toolkit/
2. Aranha, D.F., Barreto, P.S.L.M., Longa, P., Ricardini, J.E.: The realm of the pairings. In: Lange, T., Lauter, K., Lisoněk, P. (eds.) SAC 2013. LNCS, vol. 8282, pp. 3–25. Springer, Heidelberg (2014)
3. Barreto, P.S.L.M., Naehrig, M.: Pairing-friendly elliptic curves of prime order. In: Preneel, B., Tavares, S. (eds.) SAC 2005. LNCS, vol. 3897, pp. 319–331. Springer, Heidelberg (2006)
4. Boneh, D., Franklin, M.: Identity-based encryption from the Weil pairing. In: Kilian, J. (ed.) CRYPTO 2001. LNCS, vol. 2139, pp. 213–229. Springer, Heidelberg (2001)
5. Bos, J.W., Costello, C., Naehrig, M.: Exponentiating in pairing groups. Cryptology ePrint Archive, Report 2013/458 (2013)
6. Boyko, V., Peinado, M., Venkatesan, R.: Speeding up discrete log and factoring based schemes via precomputations. In: Nyberg, K. (ed.) EUROCRYPT 1998. LNCS, vol. 1403, pp. 221–235. Springer, Heidelberg (1998)
7. Canard, S., Devigne, J., Sanders, O.: Delegating a pairing can be both secure and efficient. In: Boureanu, I., Owesarski, P., Vaudenay, S. (eds.) ACNS 2014. LNCS, vol. 8479, pp. 549–565. Springer, Heidelberg (2014)

8. Chevallier-Mames, B., Coron, J.-S., McCullagh, N., Naccache, D., Scott, M.: Secure delegation of elliptic-curve pairing. Cryptology ePrint Archive, Report 2005/150 (2005)

9. Chevallier-Mames, B., Coron, J.-S., McCullagh, N., Naccache, D., Scott, M.: Secure delegation of elliptic-curve pairing. In: Gollmann, D., Lanet, J.-L., Iguchi-Cartigny, J. (eds.) CARDIS 2010. LNCS, vol. 6035, pp. 24–35. Springer, Heidelberg (2010)

10. Coron, J.-S., M'Raïhi, D., Tymen, C.: Fast generation of pairs $(k, [k]P)$ for Koblitz elliptic curves. In: Vaudenay, S., Youssef, A.M. (eds.) SAC 2001. LNCS, vol. 2259, pp. 151–164. Springer, Heidelberg (2001)

11. Fouque, P.-A., Tibouchi, M.: Indifferentiable hashing to Barreto–Naehrig curves. In: Hevia, A., Neven, G. (eds.) LatinCrypt 2012. LNCS, vol. 7533, pp. 1–17. Springer, Heidelberg (2012)

12. Girault, M., Lefranc, D.: Server-aided verification: theory and practice. In: Roy, B. (ed.) ASIACRYPT 2005. LNCS, vol. 3788, pp. 605–623. Springer, Heidelberg (2005)

13. Granger, R., Scott, M.: Faster squaring in the cyclotomic subgroup of sixth degree extensions. In: Nguyen, P.Q., Pointcheval, D. (eds.) PKC 2010. LNCS, vol. 6056, pp. 209–223. Springer, Heidelberg (2010)

14. Joux, A.: A one round protocol for tripartite Diffie-Hellman. In: Bosma, W. (ed.) ANTS 2000. LNCS, vol. 1838, pp. 385–394. Springer, Heidelberg (2000)

15. Kachisa, E.J., Schaefer, E.F., Scott, M.: Constructing Brezing-Weng pairing-friendly elliptic curves using elements in the cyclotomic field. In: Galbraith, S.D., Paterson, K.G. (eds.) Pairing 2008. LNCS, vol. 5209, pp. 126–135. Springer, Heidelberg (2008)

16. Nguyen, P.Q., Shparlinski, I.E., Stern, J.: Distribution of modular sums and the security of the server aided exponentiation. In: Lam, K.-Y., Shparlinski, I., Wang, H., Xing, C. (eds.) Cryptography and Computational Number Theory. Progress in Computer Science and Applied Logic, vol. 20, pp. 331–342. Birkhäuser, Basel (2001)

17. Shoup, V.: Lower bounds for discrete logarithms and related problems. In: Fumy, W. (ed.) EUROCRYPT 1997. LNCS, vol. 1233, pp. 256–266. Springer, Heidelberg (1997)

Leakage and Fault Attacks

Bounded, yet Sufficient? How to Determine Whether Limited Side Channel Information Enables Key Recovery

Xin Ye[✉], Thomas Eisenbarth, and William Martin

Worcester Polytechnic Institute, Worcester, MA 01609, USA
{xye,teisenbarth,martin}@wpi.edu

Abstract. This work presents a novel algorithm to quantify the relation between three factors that characterize a side channel adversary: the amount of observed side channel leakage, the workload of full key recovery, and its achievable success rate. The proposed algorithm can be used by security evaluators to derive a realistic bound on the capabilities of a side channel adversary. Furthermore, it provides an optimal strategy for combining subkey guesses to achieve any predefined success rate. Hence, it can be used by a side channel adversary to determine whether observed leakage suffices for key recovery before expending computation time. The algorithm is applied to a series of side channel measurements of a microcontroller AES implementation and simulations. A comparison to related work shows that the new algorithm improves on existing algorithms in several respects.

Keywords: Side channel analysis · Security evaluation · Guesswork · Full key recovery · Weak maximum likelihood

1 Motivation

Side channel analysis (SCA) of embedded cryptographic implementations has been studied for more than 15 years [6,8]. Recently, there has been a growing interest in studying and quantifying the amount of information that can be extracted from a *limited* number of side channel observations. Knowing how much leakage actually suffices for a *full* key recovery is of high practical relevance. This question is closely tied to the computational capabilities of the side channel adversary, since SCA often include an extensive key search component. A good comparison of algorithms using tradeoffs between side channel information and computation are the submissions to the DPA contest [1], where the success metric was solely based on the number of needed observations, without a clear limitation of computation. Another emerging trend in SCA are new attacks that are made feasible only by tapping into the massive parallel computing power as provided by GPUs, such as [12]. This indicates that computational power of the adversary needs to be considered as part of side channel security metrics. Finally, *leakage resilient cryptography* usually assumes limited leakage of a given key or secret

© Springer International Publishing Switzerland 2015
M. Joye and A. Moradi (Eds.): CARDIS 2014, LNCS 8968, pp. 215–232, 2015.
DOI: 10.1007/978-3-319-16763-3_13

state (c.f. [4,7,11,19]) before it is updated. The schemes provide security if an adversary cannot successfully exploit more than the bounded leakage. In all of these cases, it is of high interest to know how much leakage the adversary can get from the observed measurements. Closely related is the question of the remaining attack complexity—given the limited side channel information—and the resulting search strategy.

So far only little effort has been put into the quantification of the remaining computational complexity when limited leakage is available but insufficient to narrow the key space down to a simply searchable size. While systematic metrics to quantify side channel leakage exist [10,17,18,21], many of them perform relative comparisons of implementations or attacks [5,9,16]. The most promising approach has been presented in [22,23]. The authors present a full key enumeration algorithm [22] as well as a key ranking algorithm [23] in the case where only limited side channel leakage can be extracted. These algorithms enables estimating the remaining full key recovery complexity even if the experimental verification is infeasible. However their algorithms assume the correct key to be known. In other words, their results can be used by evaluation labs, but not by the key recovering adversary.

Our Contribution. This work proposes an alternative approach to evaluate side channel security for full key recovery attacks. The security level is expressed as the relation between the amount of observed leakage, the success probability and the necessary attack complexity. Following this approach, a constructive Key Space Finding (KSF) algorithm is presented. It not only provides an estimation on the remaining guessing complexity, but also allows the adversary, for the first time, to derive a probabilistic winning strategy for each specific side channel observation. Further, by statistical bootstrapping the size of returned key spaces, the algorithm can also be used by evaluation labs to approximate a *realistic* security level for various extents of information leakage.

2   Background

This section formalizes common assumptions for SCA and revisits useful metrics and algorithms that quantifies side channel leakages.

2.1   Adversarial Model and Notations

Most SCA follow the divide-and-conquer strategy. The full secret key sk is divided into b parts, i.e. $sk = k_1\|...\|k_b$ where each subkey k_i is a n bit string. In the general setting of SCA, an adversary runs the crypto algorithm $E_{sk}()$ and records side channel observations. This is followed by a leakage exploitation phase where the adversary independently recovers information about each subkey k_i from the measured observations. We assume the adversary to be q-limited, i.e. she can run the algorithm up to q times and get the respective leakages. We denote the inputs as $\boldsymbol{X}^q = [X_{i,j}]_{b \times q} \in (\mathbb{F}_2^n)^{bq}$ where each row $[X_{i,j}]$ with

$1 \leq j \leq q$ corresponds to the inputs at the i-th part for the q queries. Similarly, the leakages are denoted as $\boldsymbol{L}^q = [L_{i,j}]_{b \times q} \in \mathbb{R}^{bq}$. Each row $[L_{i,j}]$ with $1 \leq j \leq q$ represents the q leakage observations related to the i-th subkey part k_i. With the knowntexts (either plaintexts or ciphertexts) $\boldsymbol{X}^q$ and leakages $\boldsymbol{L}^q$, the adversary chooses a side channel distinguisher such as DPA, CPA, MIA, template attack, etc. and outputs an *ordered* list of subkey candidates $g_{i,[1]}, g_{i,[2]}, ...$ for guessing the correct subkey k_i. Here, $[\cdot]$ indicates a reordering of subkey candidates in the order of decreasing likelihood, i.e. $g_{i,[j]}$ refers the j-th most likely candidate. For example, for CPA it is the descending order of the absolute value of Pearson correlation coefficients; for template attacks it is the descending order of the posterior probabilities.

2.2 Existing Metrics and Maximum Likelihood Principle

For evaluating side channel security on *subkey* recovery, the framework in [18] proposes the (t-th order) Success Rate (SR) and the Guessing Entropy (GE). The t-th order SR is defined as $\mathsf{SR}^{k_i}(t) = \Pr[k_i \in \{g_{i,[1]}, ..., g_{i,[t]}\}]$. It describes the probability that the correct subkey k_i is compromised in the first t prioritized guesses. The GE is defined as the expected rank of the correct subkey, i.e., $\mathrm{GE} := \sum_{t=1}^{2^n} t \cdot \Pr[k_i = g_{i,[t]}]$. Clearly, GE can be expressed as a function from the t-th order SR.

In addition, Pliam introduces *marginal guesswork* in [14] (also referred to as *work-factor* in [13]) as a metric to benchmark password recovery attacks, or more generically, *smart* exhaustive key searches. 'Smart' refers to adversaries that have and utilize prior information about the key distribution. Thus, marginal guesswork is well suited to describe adversaries that can assign probabilities to subkey candidates. In fact, it relates the success probability to its minimum computational complexity. More specifically, let $\sigma \in [0,1]$ be the probability of success the adversary expects to achieve, the σ-*marginal guesswork* is defined to be the minimum number t of guesses to ensure finding the correct subkey k_i with at least σ success rate, i.e. $w_\sigma(k_i) = \min\{t : \sum_{j=1}^{t} p_{i,[j]} \geq \sigma\}$. Here subkey guesses $g_{i,[j]}$ are sorted decreasingly in terms of probabilities such that $p_{i,[j]} \geq p_{i,[j+1]} \geq \ldots$ where $p_{i,[j]} = \Pr[k_i = g_{i,[j]}]$.

This approach is also known as *Maximum Likelihood* (ML) attack. Based on side channel information, namely the inputs $\boldsymbol{x}^q$ and leakages $\boldsymbol{l}^q$, it first assigns posterior probability $p_{i,j} = \Pr[g_{i,j} \mid \boldsymbol{x}^q, \boldsymbol{l}^q]$ to subkey candidates $g_{i,j}$. Next, it enumerates them in a descending order $g_{i,[j]}$ according to the posterior likelihood $p_{i,[j]}$. Since $p_{i,j}$ is interpreted by definition as the likelihood of the true subkey k_i being the candidate $g_{i,j}$, the guess $g_{i,j}$ ensures subkey success rate $p_{i,j}$. Therefore the t-th order success rate using ML approach is

$$\mathsf{SR}^{k_i}(t) = \sum_{j=1}^{t} p_{i,[j]} \tag{1}$$

It also establishes a connection between the t-th order SR and the σ-marginal guess work as : $w_\sigma(k_i) = \min\{t : \mathsf{SR}^{k_i}(t) \geq \sigma\}$. To sum up, the adversary using *maximum likelihood* approach is expected to have the minimum complexity to find the correct subkey.

2.3   Full Key Ranking Algorithm

The aforementioned metrics have mostly been applied for *subkey* recovery experiments. This changed with the algorithms by Veyrat-Charvillon et al. in [22,23]. The authors present algorithms to enumerate full keys [22] and to estimate the rank of the correct full key among all full key candidates [23]. With the latter algorithm they manage, for the first time, to approximate the computational complexity of successful side channel adversaries for cases where experimental verification is no longer possible or just too expensive. This means, the work pioneers in actually getting meaningful metrics for the *expected guesswork* of an adversary achieving *full key recovery*. Furthermore, they apply statistical bootstrapping to achieve cost evaluation and approximate a ML approach adversary for full key recovery.

The rank estimation algorithm [23], referred to as VGS algorithm, works as follows: As input it receives probabilities for all subkeys from a single side channel experiment, as well as the knowledge of the correct key (and consequently its probability). After sorting each of these subkey probabilities decreasingly, the different dimensions are combined to create the key space. Next, volumes where keys have higher (or lower) probabilities than the correct key are removed from the space and their size is added to the lower (or upper) bound for the rank of the correct key. The VGS algorithm stops either after a set time or once the bounds are close enough, i.e. once the key rank has been narrowed down sufficiently. Finally, it outputs (upper and lower bounds for) the key rank of the correct key.

By itself, the key rank only provides the placement of the probability of the correct key. It cannot specify, in each *individual* side channel experiment, how much probability of success one can achieve by guessing full key candidates up to the correct key. Instead, the probability of success is derived by statistical bootstrapping: the side channel experiment is repeated e.g. $n = 100$ times, and the success probability is derived as the percentiles of the key ranks in *different* experiments are turned into success probabilities. The VGS algorithm is used for comparison and as a benchmark for our algorithm that we introduce next.

3   Evaluating Full Key Security

Side channel leakage enables assigning scores or posterior probabilities to subkey candidates. However, to verify the correctness of a guess, different subkey parts must be combined and checked. That is to say, as long as the leakage is not strong enough to reveal each subkey part with a negligible error probability, the remaining full key security is not trivially evaluated and is worthy of investigation. Conceptually, the ML approach can be extended to cover full key recovery attacks so that all the metrics described in Sect. 2.2 can also be applied to evaluate *full* key security. However, the size of the key space is 2^{bn}, e.g. in AES-128 it is 2^{128}, and it makes it infeasible to calculate the posterior probabilities to all full key candidates and then to enumerate them strictly following the ML principle. In this section, we introduce a weaker but computationally efficient approach to evaluate full key security. We call this approach the weak Maximum Likelihood (wML) approach. We describe its basic idea, followed by a Key Space Finding (KSF) algorithm as its realization and explain how it differs from a true ML approach.

3.1 Weak Maximum Likelihood Approach

Since computing and enumerating probabilities for all full key candidates is infeasible, the adversary can, nevertheless, adopt the following straightforward strategy. For each subkey part k_i, the adversary only considers the top e_i subkey candidates. When making full key guesses, she checks the Cartesian product of such selected candidates from all subkey parts. More specifically, the adversary considers the prioritized guesses $\{g_{i,[1]}, ..., g_{i,[e_i]}\}$ for the true subkey part k_i and verifies all possible combinations $\{g_{1,[j_1]}\|...\|g_{b,[j_b]}$ where $1 \le j_i \le e_i, 1 \le i \le b\}$ as full key candidates. It is clear that this approach ensures a subkey success rate of $\mathsf{SR}^{k_i}(e_i)$ with e_i guesses for the subkey part k_i. Therefore, a full key success rate of $\prod_{i=1}^{b} \mathsf{SR}^{k_i}(e_i)$ is achieved, implying a full key verification cost of $\prod_{i=1}^{b} e_i$. The vector $\boldsymbol{e} = (e_1, ..., e_b)$ is called an *effort distributor* or simply a node. The node defines how the adversary distributes her verification complexity (or guesswork) over different subkey parts. It is easy to see from the definition above that an effort distributor not only determines the full key success rate $\mathsf{Prob}(\boldsymbol{e})$ that is achieved through guessing all candidates in the Cartesian product, but also determines the full key verification cost $\mathsf{Cost}(\boldsymbol{e})$, or *guesswork*. They are expressed as

$$\mathsf{Prob}(\boldsymbol{e}) = \prod_{i=1}^{b} \mathsf{SR}^{k_i}(e_i) = \prod_{i=1}^{b} \sum_{j=1}^{e_i} p_{i,[j]} \qquad \mathsf{Cost}(\boldsymbol{e}) = \prod_{i=1}^{b} e_i \quad (2)$$

In general, the adversary is interested in finding the minimal necessary guesswork to achieve a σ success rate for a full key recovery attack. The procedure of finding minimal full key recovery guesswork through finding optimal effort distributors is referred to as the *weak Maximum Likelihood* (wML) approach. Intuitively and informally, the observed leakage l^q reveals different amounts of secret information for different subkey parts. The more information is leaked of a certain key part, the more confidence the adversary gets for prioritized subkey guesses. Therefore, she can include more subkey candidates for the subkey positions where she has less confidence in the correctness of the output hypothesis (cf. e.g. [20]).

Formally, the wML approach can be stated as an optimization problem with the objective function and restriction condition defined as below.

$$\text{Objective: } \textbf{Minimize } \mathsf{Cost}(\boldsymbol{e}) \qquad (3)$$

$$\text{Restriction Condition: } \mathsf{Prob}(\boldsymbol{e}) \ge \sigma \qquad (4)$$

We will show how to solve this optimization problem in Sect. 3.3.

There are differences between the wML and the true ML approaches. In ML, all full key candidates are ordered according to their posterior probability. In wML, this is not necessarily the case. In fact, full key candidates that are inside the Cartesian product of selected subkey guesses are prior to combinations that are not defined by the effort distributor. For example, given an effort distributor $e = (e_1, ..., e_b)$, the full key candidate $g_x = g_{1,[e_1]} \| g_{2,[e_2]} \| g_{3,[e_3]} \| \cdots \| g_{b,[e_b]}$ is inside the Cartesian product, while the candidate $g_y = g_{1,[e_1-1]} \| g_{2,[e_2+1]} \| g_{3,[e_3]} \| \cdots \| g_{b,[e_b]}$ is not. The former is to be considered by the wML approach while the latter is not. Therefore wML sets priority of the former over the latter. However, it is not always the case that g_x is more probable than g_y. This means using wML will unavoidably cause some ordering violation. The impact of such violation is discussed in Sect. 4.4 and it turns out that the penalty is rather low, which confirms the usability of wML approach.

3.2   The Search Domain and Its Calculus Model

An optimization problem in the continuous domain can usually be turned into a searching problem. Tools from differential calculus such as the gradient vector can help providing efficient search directions. Here we adjust it to our search space which is a discretized domain and build the model for the problem of searching optimal effort distributors. All concepts introduced here will be used in the KSF algorithm in Sect. 3.3. For a clear illustration we use AES-128 as an example. It can be easily applied in other block cipher scenarios.

Structure of the Search Domain. We first define the search space. Each effort distributor e is treated as a node in the b-dimensional discrete space. For AES-128, the key has 16 subkey parts (bytes) and each effort entry—the number of guesses for each subkey part—can be any integer between 1 and 256 inclusively. Therefore, the entire search space is 16 dimensional with each dimension taking integers in $[1 : 256]$, namely $\mathcal{E} = [1 : 256]^{16}$. The optimization problem is now equivalent to finding the optimum node $e^* \in \mathcal{E}$ that minimizes the full cost or guesswork while achieving the required full key success probability. To better understand the structure of the search space and enable an efficient search, we introduce the following concepts.

Definition 1: a node $e' = (e'_1, ..., e'_b)$ is called the j-th *decremental neighbor* of the node $e = (e_1, ..., e_b)$ if $e'_j = e_j - 1$ and $e'_i = e_i$ for all $i \neq j$. It is also denoted as $e^-_j = (e_1, ..., e_j - 1, ..., e_b))$. Similarly, the j-th *incremental neighbor* of node e is denoted as $e^+_j = (e_1, ..., e_j + 1, ..., e_b)$.

Definition 2: a node $e \in \mathcal{E}$ is said to be σ-*feasible* if it satisfies the restriction condition (4). The set of all σ-feasible nodes is denoted as $\mathcal{E}_\sigma := \{e \mid \text{Prob}(e) \geq \sigma\}$.

Definition 3: a σ-feasible node $e \in \mathcal{E}_\sigma$ is said to be on the boundary if none of its decremental neighbors is σ-feasible, i.e. $e^-_j \notin \mathcal{E}_\sigma, \forall j$. The set of all nodes on the boundary is called the σ-*feasible boundary* and denoted as

$$\partial\left(\mathcal{E}_\sigma\right) := \left\{e \in \mathcal{E}_\sigma \mid e_j^- \notin \mathcal{E}_\sigma, \forall j\right\}$$

Definition 4: a node e^* is called σ-*optimal* if it is a σ-feasible node and has minimal complexity among all σ-feasible nodes, i.e. $\mathtt{Cost}(e^*) \le \mathtt{Cost}(e), \forall e \in \mathcal{E}_\sigma$

An immediate but important result can now be summarized as follows.

Boundary Property: the σ-optimal nodes are inside the σ-feasible boundary, i.e. $e^* \in \partial\left(\mathcal{E}_\sigma\right) \subset \mathcal{E}_\sigma$.

The proof is straightforward. If $e_j^{*-} \in \mathcal{E}_\sigma$, then

$$\mathtt{Cost}\left(e_j^{*-}\right) = \mathtt{Cost}\left(e^*\right) \cdot \frac{e_j^* - 1}{e_j^*} < \mathtt{Cost}\left(e^*\right)$$

contradicting the definition of node e^* being σ-optimal.

This property explains the fact that if making one less subkey guess at any subkey part from an optimal effort distributor, the achieved success rate does not reach the desired level σ. It indicates that the wML approach is to find an σ-optimal effort distributor from the σ-feasible boundary.

A Calculus Model for the Search Problem. Now we define some calculus tools for enabling an efficient search algorithm for finding the optimum node in the discrete search domain. For a function in continuous space, the partial derivative $\frac{\partial f}{\partial x_j}$ indicates the instantaneous change of the output of the function f caused by the change at the j-th coordinate x_j of the input. We define similar concepts for the objective function $\mathtt{Cost}(e)$ and restriction condition $\mathtt{Prob}(e)$.

The discrete nature of our search domain $[1:256]^{16}$ gives two situations: the change caused by unit *incrementing* or *decrementing* on each effort coordinate e_j. More specifically, we define the incremental partial derivative of $\mathtt{Prob}(e)$ with respect to e_j as

$$\nabla P_j^+ = \mathtt{Prob}(e_j^+) - \mathtt{Prob}(e) = [\frac{\mathsf{SR}^{k_j}(e_j + 1) - \mathsf{SR}^{k_j}(e_j)}{\mathsf{SR}^{k_j}(e_j)}]\mathtt{Prob}(e) \qquad (5)$$

Each ∇P_j^+ is a non-negative value[1] and it indicates the amount of additional success rate that could be achieved by incrementing effort by 1 at the j-th coordinate. Similarly, the decremental partial derivative of $Prob(e)$ is defined as

$$\nabla P_j^- = \mathtt{Prob}(e) - \mathtt{Prob}(e_j^-) = [\frac{\mathsf{SR}^{k_j}(e_j) - \mathsf{SR}^{k_j}(e_j - 1)}{\mathsf{SR}^{k_j}(e_j - 1)}]\mathtt{Prob}(e) \qquad (6)$$

---

[1] The cases are considered separately if incrementing or decrementing is impossible, i.e. $e_j = 1$ or $e_j = 256$ for Eqs. (5), (6) and (7).

This is also a non-negative value and it tells the loss of full key success rate caused by decreasing effort by 1 at the j-th coordinate.

With the above defined partial derivatives, we can now obtain the *incremental gradient* $\nabla P^+ = (\nabla P_1^+, ... \nabla P_{16}^+)$ and the *decremental gradient* $\nabla P^- = (\nabla P_1^-, ... \nabla P_{16}^-)$ of the restriction condition $\texttt{Prob}(e)$. It is important to see that the coordinates for the largest partial derivatives in the incremental (or decremental respectively) gradient vector tells the full key success rate is increased (or decreased resp.) mostly due to a unit effort increment (or decrement resp.).

The same concept is defined for the objective function $\texttt{Cost}(e)$. The gradient vectors in both incrementing and decrementing cases result in the same expression because

$$\nabla C_j^+ = \texttt{Cost}(e_j^+) - \texttt{Cost}(e) = \prod_{i \neq j} e_i = \texttt{Cost}(e) - \texttt{Cost}(e_j^-) = \nabla C_j^- \quad (7)$$

For notational convenience, both ∇C_j^+ and ∇C_j^- are replaced by ∇C_j and the gradient of the full key complexity $\texttt{Cost}(e)$ becomes $\nabla C = (\nabla C_1, ... \nabla C_{16})$. Again, each coordinate is a non-negative value and it indicates the change in full key recovery complexity which is caused by incrementing/decrementing effort by 1 at the j-th entry of effort node e.

Lastly, we consider the *direction vector* u which is the negation of the gradient $-\nabla C$ projected onto the hyper-surface that is perpendicular to the gradient ∇P.

$$u = -\nabla C \text{ projected onto } (\nabla P)^{\perp} = \frac{\nabla P \cdot \nabla C}{\|\nabla P\|^2} \nabla P - \nabla C \quad (8)$$

where $\nabla P = (\nabla P_1, ..., \nabla P_{16})$ is the averaged gradient, i.e. $\nabla P_j = (\nabla P_j^+ + \nabla P_j^-)/2$. This direction vector u satisfies the intuition to keep the restriction condition $\texttt{Prob}(e)$ unchanged (seen from the vanishing of the inner product $u \cdot \nabla P = 0$) while decreasing the objective function $\texttt{Cost}(e)$ as much as possible. A visualization can be seen in Fig. 2.

3.3   An Optimized Key Space Finding Algorithm

We now show how to realize the weak maximum likelihood approach to find the optimum effort distributor by using the KSF algorithm.

The **inputs** of the algorithm include the desired full key success probability σ and the sorted posterior probabilities $p_{i,[j]}$ (and hence the subkey success rates $\mathsf{SR}^{k_i}(t)$ according to Eq. (1)) for all subkey candidates $g_{i,[j]}$. Note that this algorithm, unlike the VGS algorithm, does not require knowledge of the correct key, i.e. can also be used by a key recovering adversary. The applicability of this algorithm is not restricted to the profiling adversary. In [22] it is suggested that a non-profiling adversary can also assign likelihoods to subkey candidates to achieve a justified full key ranking, which could also be applied in our case.

The algorithm returns two **outputs**: the minimum verification complexity $\min \{\texttt{Cost}(e) \mid e \in \mathcal{E}_\sigma\}$ that ensures the desired full key success rate σ together

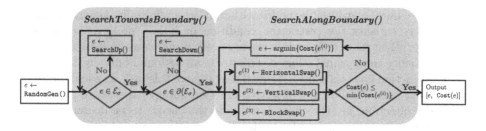

Fig. 1. Flow Chart of the KSF algorithm.

with an optimal effort distributor $e^* = \text{argmin}\{\text{Cost}(e) \mid e \in \mathcal{E}_\sigma\}$ that achieves this complexity lower bound.

The flow chart of the KSF algorithm is shown in Fig. 1. It uses several subroutines. The algorithm begins by generating a random node $e \leftarrow [1 : 256]^{16}$ using `RandomGen()`. This node serves as the starting point in the searching space. The initial node is then passed sequentially into two subroutines: `SearchTowardsBoundary()` and `SearchAlongBoundary()`. The former moves a node onto the feasible boundary $\partial(\mathcal{E}_\sigma)$ by calling `SearchUp()` and `SearchDown()`. The latter searches for nodes within the boundary that feature an even lower value of the objective `Cost(e)`. It uses the `Swap()` family of subfunctions. Note that the algorithm is a probabilistic algorithm to finding the point on the surface that has minimal cost. It finds local minima. In practice, it is executed several times to ensure that the local optimization also yields the global minimum.

The `SearchTowardsBoundary()` Function. The task of this function is to move a node onto the feasible boundary $\partial(\mathcal{E}_\sigma)$. If the input node e does not satisfy the restriction condition, i.e. $\text{Prob}(e) < \sigma$, it calls the function `SearchUp()` (as shown in Alg. 1) to search for a node that is σ-feasible. More specifically, `SearchUp()` iteratively increases the number of subkey guesses for some part of the subkey and updates the node. In each iteration, the search direction, i.e. the coordinate of the subkey part that needs to be incremented, is determined by the incremental gradient ∇P^+ as defined in Sect. 3.2. The effort coordinate that maximizes the gain in success rate through a unit effort increase is chosen, i.e. $i = \text{argmax}_j\{\nabla P_j^+\}$. The node is updated by a unit increment on the chosen effort coordinate. The process continues until a σ-feasible node is reached, namely, the restriction condition is satisfied as $\text{Prob}(e) \geq \sigma$.

Algorithm 1. SearchUp()	**Algorithm 2.** SearchDown()
1: **while** $\text{Prob}(e) < \sigma$ **do**	1: **while** $e \notin \partial(\mathcal{E}_\sigma)$ **do**
2: $i \leftarrow \text{argmax}_j\{\nabla P_j^+\}$	2: $i \leftarrow \text{argmax}_j\{\nabla C_j \text{ s.t. } \text{Prob}(e) - \nabla P_j^- \geq \sigma\}$
3: $e_i \leftarrow e_i + 1$	3: $e_i \leftarrow e_i - 1$
4: **end while**	4: **end while**
5: **return** e	5: **return** e

Now we have a σ-feasible node—either it is an initially generated node that already satisfies the restriction condition or it is a node returned from SearchUp(). The remaining task is to search for a node on the feasible boundary $\partial(\mathcal{E}_\sigma)$ since the optimal effort distributors can be found only on the boundary. The function SearchDown() is called to complete this task. In each iteration, the gradient vector ∇C of the objective function Cost(e) is used to determine the search direction, i.e. the effort coordinate that needs to be decremented as shown in line 2 of Alg. 2. It reflects the direction where the objective function Cost(e) has the biggest complexity drop through a unit effort decrementing while not violating the restriction condition. This means that the updated node is still σ-feasible. The process continues until the Boundary Property (as defined in Sect. 3.2) is satisfied. In other words, it returns a node $e \in \partial(\mathcal{E}_\sigma)$.

The SearchAlongBoundary() Function. So far the search algorithm has found a node on the σ-feasible boundary. The next step is to search for nodes within the boundary, which achieve σ-feasibility at a lower cost Cost(e). The subroutine SearchAlongBoundary() is called to accomplish this task. We have seen from the Boundary Property in Sect. 3.2 that any decremental neighbor of a node on the boundary is not σ-feasible. It implies that the only way to find a node with lower full key cost is through trading-off (or swapping) efforts between different coordinates, which is realized in the Swap() family of subroutines.

More specifically, the coordinates for swapping are determined from the direction vector u defined in Eq. (8) as it follows the intuition that the search should decrease the overall guesswork while not compromising the full key success probability. The direction vector u suggests to increase effort on coordinate j if u_j is positive, and decrease if negative. The order of the effort coordinates being incremented or decremented is determined by the order of the absolute values of the entries u_j. The higher the absolute value, the higher the priority that is assigned to the coordinates for incrementing and decrementing.

Similar to search problems defined in continuous domain, the algorithm also handles the problem of local minima that prevent effective searching. In particular, we implement three different swapping modes –HorizontalSwap(), VerticalSwap() and BlockSwap() – to "escape" from many local minima and therefore mitigate the risk of being terminated in advance. The HorizontalSwap() allows trading-off multiple efforts between the positive most and negative most coordinates, i.e. u_i^+ and u_j^-. The VerticalSwap() in each iteration enables trading-off one effort between multiple coordinates where u_js are of different signs. Finally, the BlockSwap() mode enables trading-off multiple efforts on multiple coordinates. All three modes ensure that the swap does not compromise the required full key success probability, i.e. $e \in \mathcal{E}_\sigma$ always hold. The updated node (after efforts being swapped) is again passed through SearchDown() to ensure that the search is still performed on the boundary. The three modes prevent infinite loops because the swap action occurs only if the cost of the updated node is lower than the cost for the session node.

Algorithm 3. SearchAlongBoundary()

1: $e' \leftarrow$ Swap()
2: **while** Cost$(e) >$ Cost(e') **do**
3:     $e \leftarrow e'$
4: **end while**
5: **return** $[e,$ Cost$(e)]$

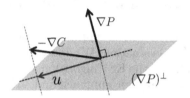

Fig. 2. Direction vector u is the projection of cost gradient $-\nabla C$ onto $(\nabla P)^\perp$

As shown in Alg. 3, a temporary node e' is returned from the Swap() family of functions in each iteration. If the cost for the temporary node is lower than the current session node, then the session node e is replaced by before being passed into the next iteration. Otherwise the search is terminated and the algorithm outputs the current node e and its full key verification cost Cost(e).

3.4 Usage of the KSF algorithm

Full key security evaluation used to stay as an analysis that is beyond computing power. The KSF algorithm provides practical meaning to the security evaluation. Firstly, the adversary can use it to determine if the leakage is strong enough to enable full key recovery at her accessible computing power. More specifically, upon a particular set of observations (x^q, l^q), the returned global minimum of Cost(e) serves as an *individual* lower bound of the optimum guesswork w_σ. If the guesswork is acceptable, the associated optimal effort distributor e provides a winning strategy: checking all the full key candidates defined by the Cartesian product of this optimal node. This strategy ensures he adversary with success rate being at least σ. Even if in one session the observed leakages are not strong enough, namely requires high w_σ, she can just wait for the next session until a "good" observation appeared. This can be the case if the guesswork is impacted a lot from different observations, which is in fact verified in our experiments in the next section.

Secondly, it can be used by a security evaluation lab. By feeding the algorithm with independently generated observations (x^q, l^q), an evaluator can bootstrap the individual lower bounds and obtain the distribution of the guesswork w_σ at any fixed σ. This informs the evaluator the resistance of some DUT against a probabilistic SCA. In other words, if the adversary intends σ success rate, how much chance does she have by waiting until a strong enough leakage occurs. A simple example would be computing the *expected* lower bound of guesswork— the average of all individual lower bounds—and using it as a metric. The metric indicates the averaged level of security of the full key as the expectation is with respect to various experiments, i.e. not only different choices of input x^q, but also leakages observations l^q.

4   Experiment Results and Comparison

In this section we apply the proposed wML approach to practical side channel leakage evaluation. We first explain the experimental setup. Next, we verify the validity of the KSF algorithm and discuss its possible influencing factors. Finally, we compare our approach and VGS algorithm.

4.1   Experiment Setup

We conduct the leakage evaluation experiments in two settings: real measurements and simulations. For the former, we target on an unprotected AES software implementation, the RjindaelFurious [15] running on an 8-bit AVR ATXMega A3B processor. A total of 200,000 measurements were taken using a Tektronix DPO 5104 oscilloscope at a sampling rate of 200 MS/s. Among all the collected traces, 20,000 are used for building Gaussian templates. The remaining traces are used as needed for the evaluation step. In the other setting, we simulate side channel leakage using the widely accepted Hamming weight leakage model with additive Gaussian noise. In both cases the targeted leakage is that of the s-box output of the first round for each of the 16 state bytes.

4.2   Posterior Probabilities Derivation

As a preparation step of leakage evaluation, posterior probabilities for all subkey candidates need to be estimated from side channel observations. The probably most popular method is through Templates [2,10] where the adversary creates a precise model of the leakage in the profiling phase and derives posterior probabilities in the attack phase. An in-depth discussion of modeling errors for Gaussian templates can be found in [3]. For our experiments, we build Gaussian templates $\mathcal{N}(L; \boldsymbol{\mu}_v, \Sigma_v^2)$ regarding the internal state $Y = S(X \oplus K)$ over all the 16 bytes. In the attack phase, the adversary obtains the observations $(\boldsymbol{x}^q, \boldsymbol{l}^q)$. Since the predicted internal state for the j-th query is $y_{i,j,g} = f(x_{i,j}, g)$ under the subkey hypothesis g at the i-th subkey part, the observed leakage $l_{i,j}$ has conditional probability density $\mathrm{P}[l_{i,j} \mid g] = \mathcal{N}(l_{i,j}; \boldsymbol{\mu}_v, \Sigma_v^2)$, where $v = y_{i,j,g}$. Since side channel leakages in different queries are independent, the conditional probability density $\mathrm{P}[\boldsymbol{l}_i^q \mid g]$ of observing the q leakages $\boldsymbol{l}_i^q = (l_{i,1}, ..., l_{i,q})$ on the i-th subkey part is the product of each $\mathrm{P}[l_{i,j} \mid g]$. Namely,

$$\mathrm{P}[l_{i,1}, ..., l_{i,q} \mid g] = \prod_{j=1}^{q} \mathrm{P}[l_{i,j} \mid g] = \prod_{j=1}^{q} \mathcal{N}(l_{i,j}; \boldsymbol{\mu}_v, \Sigma_v^2). \tag{9}$$

Further, the Bayesian formula returns posterior probabilities $p_{i,g} := \Pr[g \mid \boldsymbol{l}_i^q]$ of subkey hypothesis g given the q observations $\boldsymbol{l}_i^q$ as

$$p_{i,g} := \Pr[g \mid \boldsymbol{l}_i^q] = \frac{\mathrm{P}[\boldsymbol{l}_i^q \mid g] \cdot \Pr[g]}{\sum_{g^*} \mathrm{P}[\boldsymbol{l}_i^q \mid g^*] \cdot \Pr[g^*]} = \frac{\mathrm{P}[\boldsymbol{l}_i^q \mid g]}{\sum_{g^*} \mathrm{P}[\boldsymbol{l}_i^q \mid g^*]} \tag{10}$$

Finally the posterior probabilities $p_{i,g}$ are sorted into a descending sequence $p_{i,[g]}$ as detailed in Sect. 2.2. They determine the subkey success rates in Eq. (1) which are the inputs for the KSF algorithm and the VGS algorithm.

4.3   Correctness and Influencing Factors of the KSF Algorithm

Verifying the correctness of the KSF algorithm is rather simple: if the returned optimal effort distributor e^* covers the ranks of the posterior probability of every subkey k_i, then the search space defined by the Cartesian product includes the correct full key as explained in Sect. 3.1. In the following, we check if the algorithm in fact achieves the promised success rate for various experiments. We provide a set of observations for a range of q from 1 to 40: higher value for q indicates more leaked information. We furthermore set 19 different levels of desired success rate from 0.05 to 0.95 incrementing at 0.05. For each possible (q, σ), 200 experiments are performed for the scenario using real measurements, and 100 experiments for the scenario using simulated leakage.

Figure 3(a) compares the promised full key success rate of the KSF algorithm with the actually achieved success rate for real measurements. One can see that when the leakage is strong (high value of q), the achieved success rate is far beyond what is promised. However, when the leakage is weak, the two rates only differ slightly. A probable reason for the achieved success rate being *lower* than the desired success rate for small values of q is due to the assumption that the Gaussian templates fully capture the underlying leakage distribution. In fact, the empirically obtained Gaussian templates only serve as approximation to the true leakage distribution, and hence the derived posterior probabilities are unavoidably biased. This claim is also supported by the results for simulated leakage, as given in Fig. 3(b), where the underachieving never happens. Nevertheless, for almost all cases, especially when $q \geq 8$, the KSF algorithm fulfills the promised full key success rate.

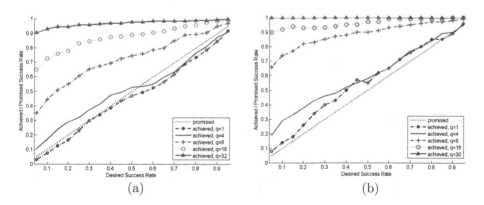

Fig. 3. Correctness verification for real measurements (a) and simulation (b); The success rate that KSF achieves (y-axis) is more than what it promised (x-axis).

Other influencing factors of the KSF algorithm are the leakage observations and the number of independent initial nodes used for finding local minima, as discussed in Sect. 3. To investigate their impact, we run 50 experiments associated with independent sets of observations (x^q, l^q). In each experiment, we compare the performance of KSF algorithm at fixed $\sigma = 50\%$ using 100 and 10000 initial nodes. The global minimum guessworks in each experiments are returned and compared in Fig. 4(a). The x-axis is the index of experiments indicating a different set of observation (x^q, l^q) and the y-axis is the guesswork in bits. As we can see, different leakage observations causes more than 40 bits guesswork differences while the influence from the number of initial nodes (the distance between the two curves) are rather small. In fact, the biggest difference between the two curves is less than 2.5 bits and most of the times the difference is smaller than one bit.

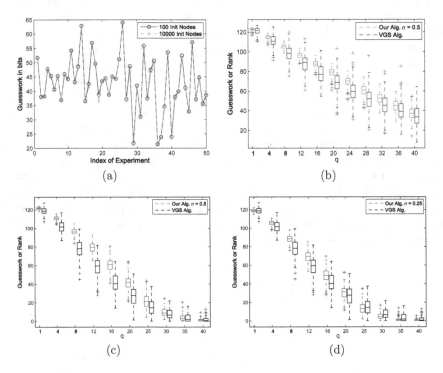

Fig. 4. Figure (a) shows the impact on guesswork (y-axis) from the number of starting nodes for KSF algorithm is far less than the impact from the set of observations (x^q, l^q) in each experiment (X-axis); Figure (b,c,d) compares the size of the key space from the KSF algorithm to the key rank from the VGS algorithmÉxperiments are performed over real measurement with success rate $\sigma = 50\%$ (b); over simulation with $\sigma = 50\%$ (c); and over simulation with $\sigma = 25\%$ (d)

4.4 Comparing the KSF algorithm with the VGS algorithm

As mentioned in Sect. 2.3, the VGS algorithm estimates the rank of the correct key among all full key candidates. By bootstrapping this rank statistic, or namely, by repeating the rank estimation from different side channel observations, one can get a security evaluation based on the success percentiles to see the rank distributions given random side channel inputs.

We first provide several comparisons between the bootstrapping of the rank statistic from repeating VGS algorithm and the bootstrapping of guesswork w_σ KSF algorithm. Figure 4(b) compares the two over the real measurement. We fix the full key success rate in KSF algorithm to $\sigma = 50\%$. For each q (x-axis), we perform 200 experiments using the algorithms on the same sets of observations. The box plot indicates quartiles and outliers of the guesswork and rank statistics. We see that the results from the two algorithms are relatively close to each other. Further, the impact of different leakages on the rank statistic using VGS algorithm is heavier than that on the guesswork returned from our algorithm. This can be seen from the difference of the height of boxes for the two algorithms. More importantly, we see that the medians of the two analyzed cases do not align exactly. In fact, ours are always slightly higher than the VGS algorithm. The reason is two folds. On one side, the KSF algorithm is following wML approach, which introduces ordering violation comparing to the true ML approach, as explained in Sect. 3. On another, since in each individual experiment the VGS algorithm does not return a fixed success probability $\sum_{t=1}^{\text{rank}} p_{[t]}$ (the ML adversary should guesses all the top rank full key candidates), the 50th percentile of the rank does not necessarily ensure the adversary achieves 50% success rate in an averaged experiment either. This is even more clearly seen from the simulated leakage scenario as shown in Fig. 4(c) (rank compared to $w_{0.5}$) and 4(d) (rank compared to $w_{0.25}$). In the simulated case, the ML approach is closer to the $w_{0.25}$ bootstrapping with the weak ML approach. It indicates that the guessing the top rank most likely full key candidates in the ML approach roughly returns winning probability of 25%. In general, it might suggest the evaluator to find the appropriate σ level such that the bootstrapping of the guesswork w_σ matches the bootstrapping of the key rank. By doing so, the evaluator can estimate the success rate $\sum_{t=1}^{\text{rank}} p_{[t]}$ in an average experiment that the top rank full key candidates contain.

The next comparison of the two leakage evaluation algorithms is between the *expected* guesswork lower bound (Fig. 5(a)) and the bootstrapping of the rank (Fig. 5(b)). Experiments use the data from the microcontroller measurements. The x-axis for both represents the number q of accessible leakages in each experiment. In Fig. 5(a), the y-axis is the desired full key success probability σ. The color or gray-scale for the pixel at coordinate $(x, y) = (q, \sigma)$ represents the *expected* lower bound (as explained in Sect. 3.4) of the guesswork in log scale. The darker a pixel is, the more guesswork is needed to achieve the specified success rate σ. In particular, the expected lower bound at each (q, σ) is derived from 200 independent experiments. Each experiment uses an independent set of observations $(\boldsymbol{x}^q, \boldsymbol{l}^q)$ which yields different posterior probabilities $p_{i,[g]}$

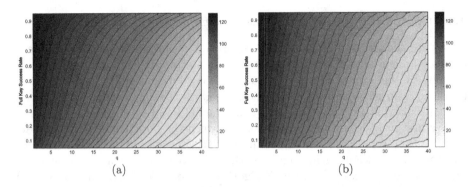

Fig. 5. Security evaluation using KSF algorithm showing the remaining guesswork (color in (a)) and using VGS algorithm showing the key rank (color in (b)) over the number of observations q (x-axis) and success rate/percentile (y-axis) (Color figure online).

computed as described in Sect. 4.2. The number of initial node is set to 100 (Fig. 4(a) already shows this number is sufficient). The global minimum guesswork from the 100 searches is returned as the *individual* lower bound of the guesswork for this single experiment. Upon the completion of the 200 experiments, the average of the 200 individual lower bounds yields the *expected* lower bound as reflected in the color of pixel in Fig. 5(a). In short, the color at pixel (q, σ) indicates the expected minimum guesswork that a q-limited adversary should spend in order to achieve full key recovery with probability σ. In Fig. 5(b), VGS algorithm is executed with the same sets of observations (x^q, l^q). The returned 200 **ranks** (represented in the color of each pixel) derive the statistical bootstrapping of the success percentile (the same as in bootstrapping) which is represented on the y-axis. Two contour plots are fairly close to each other.

5   Conclusion

The presented algorithm finds the optimal key search space that allows the adversary to achieve a predefined probability of success. Unlike prior work, the algorithm provides a connection between remaining full key security and success probability even for a single set of side channel observations. It furthermore is a constructive algorithm, since it not only bounds the remaining key search space, but also provides an optimized yet simple strategy to search that space. As a consequence, the algorithm can be used by embedded security evaluators to quantify the resistance of a device to SCA. It can also be used by an adversary to determine whether the leakage suffices for a successful key recovery attack.

Acknowledgments. This material is based upon work supported by the National Science Foundation under Grant No. #1261399 and Grant No. #1314770. We would like to thank François-Xavier Standaert for the helpful discussion. We would also like to thank the anonymous reviewers for their helpful comments.

References

1. Dpa contest (versions 1 and 2). http://www.dpacontest.org/home/
2. Chari, S., Rao, J., Rohatgi, P.: Template attacks. In: Kaliski, B.S., Koç, Ç.K., Paar, C. (eds.) Cryptographic Hardware and Embedded Systems - CHES 2002. Lecture Notes in Computer Science, vol. 2523, pp. 13–28. Springer, Heidelberg (2003)
3. Durvaux, F., Standaert, F.-X., Veyrat-Charvillon, N.: How to certify the leakage of a chip? In: Nguyen, P.Q., Oswald, E. (eds.) EUROCRYPT 2014. LNCS, vol. 8441, pp. 459–476. Springer, Heidelberg (2014)
4. Faust, S., Pietrzak, K., Schipper, J.: Practical leakage-resilient symmetric cryptography. In: Prouff, E., Schaumont, P. (eds.) CHES 2012. LNCS, vol. 7428, pp. 213–232. Springer, Heidelberg (2012)
5. Gierlichs, B., Lemke-Rust, K., Paar, C.: Templates vs. stochastic methods. In: Goubin, L., Matsui, M. (eds.) CHES 2006. LNCS, vol. 4249, pp. 15–29. Springer, Heidelberg (2006)
6. Kocher, P.C.: Timing attacks on implementations of diffie-hellman, rsa, dss, and other systems. In: Koblitz, N. (ed.) CRYPTO 1996. LNCS, vol. 1109, pp. 104–113. Springer, Heidelberg (1996)
7. Kocher, P.C.: Leak-resistant cryptographic indexed key update (US patent 6539092) (2003)
8. Kocher, P.C., Jaffe, J., Jun, B.: Differential power analysis. In: Wiener, M. (ed.) CRYPTO 1999. LNCS, vol. 1666, pp. 388–397. Springer, Heidelberg (1999)
9. Macé, F., Standaert, F.-X., Quisquater, J.-J.: Information theoretic evaluation of side-channel resistant logic styles. In: Paillier, P., Verbauwhede, I. (eds.) CHES 2007. LNCS, vol. 4727, pp. 427–442. Springer, Heidelberg (2007)
10. Mangard, S., Oswald, E., Popp, T.: Power Analysis Attacks: Revealing the Secrets of Smartcards. Springer-Verlag, New York (2007)
11. Medwed, M., Standaert, F.-X., Joux, A.: Towards super-exponential side-channel security with efficient leakage-resilient PRFs. In: Prouff, E., Schaumont, P. (eds.) CHES 2012. LNCS, vol. 7428, pp. 193–212. Springer, Heidelberg (2012)
12. Moradi, A., Kasper, M., Paar, C.: Black-box side-channel attacks highlight the importance of countermeasures. In: Dunkelman, O. (ed.) CT-RSA 2012. LNCS, vol. 7178, pp. 1–18. Springer, Heidelberg (2012)
13. Pliam, J.: The disparity between work and entropy in cryptology. Cryptology ePrint Archive, report 1998/024 (1998). http://eprint.iacr.org/
14. Pliam, J.O.: On the incomparability of entropy and marginal guesswork in brute-force attacks. In: Roy, B., Okamoto, E. (eds.) INDOCRYPT 2000. LNCS, vol. 1977, pp. 67–79. Springer, Heidelberg (2000)
15. Poettering, B.: Rijndael Furious. Implementation. http://point-at-infinity.org/avraes/
16. Regazzoni, F., Badel, S., Eisenbarth, T., Großschädl, J., Poschmann, A., Deniz, Z.T., Macchetti, M., Pozzi, L., Paar, C., Leblebici, Y., Ienne, P.: A simulation-based methodology for evaluating the DPA-resistance of cryptographic functional units with application to CMOS and MCML technologies. In: International Symposium on Systems, Architectures, Modeling and Simulation (SAMOS VII) (2007)
17. Rivain, M.: On the exact success rate of side channel analysis in the Gaussian model. In: Avanzi, R.M., Keliher, L., Sica, F. (eds.) SAC 2008. LNCS, vol. 5381, pp. 165–183. Springer, Heidelberg (2009)

18. Standaert, F.-X., Malkin, T.G., Yung, M.: A unified framework for the analysis of side-channel key recovery attacks. In: Joux, A. (ed.) EUROCRYPT 2009. LNCS, vol. 5479, pp. 443–461. Springer, Heidelberg (2009)

19. Standaert, F.-X., Pereira, O., Yu, Y., Quisquater, J.-J., Yung, M., Oswald, E.: Leakage resilient cryptography in practice. In: Sadeghi, A.-R., Naccache, D. (eds.) Towards Hardware-Intrinsic Security. Information Security and Cryptography, pp. 99–134. Springer, Berlin Heidelberg (2010)

20. Thillard, A., Prouff, E., Roche, T.: Success through confidence: evaluating the effectiveness of a side-channel attack. In: Bertoni, G., Coron, J.-S. (eds.) CHES 2013. LNCS, vol. 8086, pp. 21–36. Springer, Heidelberg (2013)

21. Tiri, K., Akmal, M., Verbauwhede, I.: A dynamic and differential CMOS logic with signal independent power consumption to withstand differential power analysis on smart cards. In: Proceedings of the 28th European Solid-State Circuits Conference, 2002. ESSCIRC 2002, pp. 403–406 (September 2002)

22. Veyrat-Charvillon, N., Gérard, B., Renauld, M., Standaert, F.-X.: An optimal key enumeration algorithm and its application to side-channel attacks. In: Knudsen, L.R., Wu, H. (eds.) SAC 2012. LNCS, vol. 7707, pp. 390–406. Springer, Heidelberg (2013)

23. Veyrat-Charvillon, N., Gérard, B., Standaert, F.-X.: Security evaluations beyond computing power. In: Johansson, T., Nguyen, P.Q. (eds.) EUROCRYPT 2013. LNCS, vol. 7881, pp. 126–141. Springer, Heidelberg (2013)

On the Security of Fresh Re-keying
to Counteract Side-Channel and Fault Attacks

Christoph Dobraunig$^{(\boxtimes)}$, Maria Eichlseder, Stefan Mangard,
and Florian Mendel

IAIK, Graz University of Technology, Graz, Austria
christoph.dobraunig@iaik.tugraz.at

Abstract. At AFRICACRYPT 2010 and CARDIS 2011, fresh re-keying schemes to counter side-channel and fault attacks were introduced. The idea behind those schemes is to shift the main burden of side-channel protection to a re-keying function g that is easier to protect than the main block cipher. This function produces new session keys based on the secret master key and random nonces for every block of message that is encrypted. In this paper, we present a generic chosen-plaintext key-recovery attack on both fresh re-keying schemes. The attack is based on two observations: Since session key collisions for the same message are easy to detect, it is possible to recover one session key with a simple time-memory trade-off strategy; and if the re-keying function is easy to invert (such as the suggested multiplication constructions), the attacker can use the session key to recover the master key. The attack has a complexity of about $2 \cdot 2^{n/2}$ (instead of the expected 2^n) for an n-bit key. For the typically employed block cipher AES-128, this would result in a key-recovery attack complexity of only 2^{65}. If weaker primitives like 80-bit PRESENT are used, even lower attack complexities are possible.

Keywords: Side-channel attacks · Fresh re-keying · Key-recovery attack

1 Introduction

The design of efficient and effective countermeasures against side-channel and fault attacks is a very challenging task. In fact, more than 15 years ago a kind of an arms race between attackers and designers of countermeasures started and still has not come to an end. In the early years, the main goal of designers of embedded systems was to engineer systems in such a way that they do not leak side-channel information at all [18], or to randomize the power consumption by masking techniques [2]. However, over the years it has become more and more clear that such countermeasures are very expensive to implement for settings with high security requirements. An overview of costs for countermeasures can for example be found in [11].

The main driver for these costs is the fact that in typical settings an attacker can observe the execution of a cryptographic algorithm multiple times with the same key. A good example for such a setting is the mutual authentication of

© Springer International Publishing Switzerland 2015
M. Joye and A. Moradi (Eds.): CARDIS 2014, LNCS 8968, pp. 233–244, 2015.
DOI: 10.1007/978-3-319-16763-3_14

two communicating parties via a challenge-response protocol. In such a setting, the attacker can send an arbitrary number of challenges to a device in order to obtain an arbitrary number of side-channel measurements or to induce faults to generate pairs of faulty and correct ciphertexts. During each execution of the algorithm, the attacker learns information about the secret key and accumulates this information. This is the basic idea of differential power analysis (DPA) [9] as well as differential fault attacks (DFA) [3].

In [12,13], Medwed et al. propose a re-keying scheme that prevents DPA and DFA attacks by preventing multiple executions of an algorithm with the same key. The basic idea of this re-keying scheme is to never use a long-term key k directly in a cryptographic algorithm, but to derive a fresh session key k^* from k upon each invocation of the algorithm. In fact, for each invocation a random nonce is generated and used in a key derivation function g to generate a session key k^* that is then used by the cryptographic algorithm. This construction prevents an attacker from performing differential attacks on the cryptographic algorithm and this reduces the effort for countermeasures significantly. However, while the cryptographic algorithm needs less protection in this construction, it is clear that it is possible to mount differential attacks on the key derivation function g. Hence, this re-keying approach obviously only pays off in practice if it is significantly easier to protect g against differential attacks than it is to protect the original algorithm.

Medwed et al. provide several arguments for this in [12,13]. In fact, they argue that it is not necessary to have a cryptographic algorithm for the key derivation and propose to use a modular multiplication for the key derivation. A modular multiplication can be protected against differential attacks in a straightforward and efficient way by using blinding techniques [11].

The proposal of Medwed et al. triggered several follow-up works. In fact, several articles [1,4,7] treat the question of how to construct a key derivation function that can be implemented efficiently and that at the same time provides a high level of protection against differential attacks. Finding such a function is a central research question in the field of side-channel attacks and countermeasures. This research question is in particular relevant for low-cost systems, such as RFIDs, that typically rely on communication protocols based on symmetric key cryptography. A key derivation function that can be protected efficiently allows to do authentication and session-key derivation based on a symmetric cipher without the need to protect it against differential side-channel and fault attacks. Such a construction can also be used to negotiate a session key that is then used in a leakage-resilient mode of operation [16] for communication.

Our Contribution. In this paper, we show that the requirements for the key derivation function that have been formulated in [12,13] are not sufficient. In fact, we present a simple key-recovery attack on the fresh re-keying schemes proposed in [12,13]. The basic idea of the attack is that since the scheme changes the block cipher key for every encrypted message block, a time-memory trade-off strategy is possible. An adversary can recover a session key by requesting multiple encryptions of the same message (under different unknown session keys) and searching for collisions with a table of pre-computed encryptions under known session keys. We also demonstrate how knowledge of one or a few session keys allows to recover the master key for the proposed re-keying functions.

This chosen-plaintext key recovery attack has a complexity as low as $2 \cdot 2^{n/2}$ with similar memory requirements, while the complexity should ideally be 2^n. Due to the properties of the function g (that derives the session key from the master key and random nonces) proposed for these schemes, the master key can be recovered out of one or more recovered session keys. Our attack allows a free trade-off between memory (precomputation) and time/number of queries (online phase), and as such can be tailored to different attack scenarios. In all variants, it is significantly more efficient than Hellman's generic time-memory trade-off.

Outline. The remainder of the paper is organized as follows. We describe the generic construction of the fresh re-keying scheme by Medwed et al. in Sect. 2. We present our generic key-recovery attack in Sect. 3 and discuss how the scheme might be fixed in Sect. 5. Moreover, we give a brief outline to the application of the presented attacks to other re-keying schemes in Sect. 6. Finally, we conclude in Sect. 7.

2 Fresh Re-keying Schemes of Medwed et al.

The basic idea of the re-keying schemes described in this section is to perform every encryption under a new session key k^* to limit the available side-channel information during the encryption for one key. By doing so, the requirements to limit the leakage of side-channel information for the cipher in use can be relaxed. In this section, we describe the two re-keying schemes presented in [12,13].

2.1 Basic Re-keying Scheme (AFRICACRYPT 2010)

The scheme from AFRICACRYPT 2010 [13] targets scenarios where one of the two communication parties only allows limited support for side-channel protection mechanisms. Such a scenario is the communication between an RFID tag and a reader. RFID tags are low cost and low performance devices. Therefore, no overly expensive countermeasures can be included in the RFID tag's block cipher implementation, whereas the protection mechanisms on the more expensive reader can be more complex.

Figure 1 shows the working principle of the re-keying scheme. This scheme uses two functions: the re-keying function $g(k, r)$ to derive new session keys, and the block cipher $E(k^*, m)$ to encrypt message blocks. For every message block m, a new public nonce r has to be randomly generated on the tag. From this nonce r and the secret master key k, a new session key k^* is then generated via $k^* = g(k, r)$. The session key k^* is then used to encrypt one message block $c = E(k^*, m)$. With the help of the publicly known r and the master key k, the reader is able to decrypt c to $m = E^{-1}(k^*, c)$.

Since the reader cannot contribute to the nonce, an attacker that impersonates the tag can hold the nonce r constant for several different decryptions

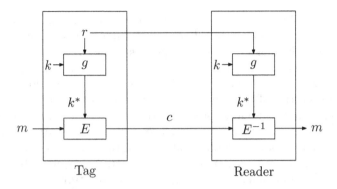

Fig. 1. Structure of the basic re-keying scheme from AFRICACRYPT 2010 [13].

and increase the available side-channel information for the reader's implementation. This means that we need different levels of protection for the block cipher implementation E on the reader and on the tag. Medwed et al. argue [13] that both g and E have to be protected against side-channel attacks in the reader's implementation. However, for the tag, only g needs full protection, whereas E does not need to be protected against differential power analysis.

An open question for this re-keying scheme is how to find a suitable function g. In [13], Medwed et al. list six required properties for g:

1. Good diffusion of k.
2. No need for synchronization between parties, i.e., g should be stateless.
3. No additional key material, i.e., k and k^* should be the same size.
4. Little hardware overhead.
5. Easy to protect against side channel attacks.
6. Regularity.

As we show in Sect. 3, adding another property to the list is necessary:

7. Hard to invert, i.e., it should be hard to recover k from k^*, r.

Medwed et al. [13] propose the following modular multiplication as a specific instance of g:

$$g\colon (\mathbb{F}_{2^8}[y]/p(y))^2 \to \mathbb{F}_{2^8}[y]/p(y), \quad (k, r) \mapsto k \cdot r,$$

where $\cdot$ denotes polynomial multiplication in $\mathbb{F}_{2^8}[y]$ modulo $p(y)$. The polynomial $p(y)$ is defined as $p(y) = y^d + 1$ with $d \in \{4, 8, 16\}$ for 128-bit master keys k (typically $d = 16$).

Since $\mathbb{F}_{2^8}[y]/p(y)$ is not a field, but only a ring, and zero divisors exist, $g(k, \cdot)$ it not necessarily bijective for any $k \neq 0$. Master keys k that are zero divisors (not co-prime to $p(y)$) can be considered weak keys since they generate a smaller key space for k^*. Medwed et al. state in [13] that only a fraction of all possible keys k are such weak keys, and that the reduction of the key-space if weak keys are excluded can be neglected. The same holds true for the nonce r, and randomly generated values for r are unlikely to be 'weak nonces'.

Note that if r is co-prime to $p(y)$, r^{-1} can be calculated easily. Now we can define g', the inverse function to g, easily via $k = g'(k^*, r) = k^* \cdot r^{-1}$. Thus, the master key k can be calculated from a known session key k^* and the corresponding nonce r. We will make use of the function g' in the attack of Sect. 3.

2.2 Advanced Re-keying Scheme for Multiple Parties (CARDIS 2011)

The basic scheme Medwed et al. proposed at AFRICACRYPT 2010 [13] (Sect. 2.1) only allows low cost side-channel countermeasures for one of the two communication parties. To overcome this drawback, Medwed et al. proposed a second scheme at CARDIS 2011 [12]. This scheme is suitable for multi-party communication (with a common, shared secret key) and allows cheaper side-channel countermeasures for all parties. For clarity, we focus on two-party communication, but the attack can easily be generalized for n parties.

Figure 2 illustrates the scheme for two-party communication. In contrast to the scheme of Sect. 2.1, both communication parties are involved in the generation of the session key k^* by contributing a randomly generated nonce.

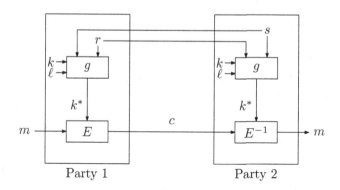

Fig. 2. Structure of the multi-party re-keying scheme from CARDIS 2011 [12] for two parties.

In [12], Medwed et al. propose two different re-keying schemes. The first one uses n different (common, secret) keys for an n-party communication. Each party contributes a random nonce, which is combined with one of the n keys. In the case of a two-party communication, the session key is $k^* = k \cdot r + \ell \cdot s$ (see Fig. 2), where k and ℓ are the secret master keys. r is the public nonce randomly generated by party 1, and s is the public nonce randomly generated by party 2. The ring operations $+$ and $\cdot$ are defined over $\mathbb{F}_{2^8}[y]/p(y)$, as in the AFRICACRYPT paper.

The second proposed scheme [12] uses only one master key k, and expands this to n keys by using powers of k. For the two-party case, the session key is computed as $k^* = r \cdot k + s \cdot k^2$. In general, the n nonces are used as coefficients of a polynomial that is evaluated in k to derive the session key k. In both schemes, the used master keys are restricted to the invertible elements in $\mathbb{F}_{2^8}[y]/p(y)$.

3   Generic Key-Recovery Attack

In this section, we describe simple key-recovery attacks on the encryption scheme of [12,13]. In both schemes, the session key k^* is new for every single new encrypted block. In Sect. 3.1, we show that we are able to recover one of the used session keys k^* with a complexity as low as $2 \cdot 2^{n/2}$ for an n-bit key. Since the function g to derive the session key is easy to invert for both re-keying schemes, we are able to compute the secret master key k out of recovered session keys and the corresponding nonces. We present attacks on the basic re-keying scheme presented at AFRICACRYPT 2010 [13] in Sect. 3.3 and on the multi-party re-keying scheme from CARDIS 2011 [12] in Sect. 3.4. Note that similar attacks have been recently published on several authenticated encryption schemes [5,14].

Throughout this section, k is the n-bit master key, k^* an n-bit session key, and r an n-bit nonce.

3.1   Recovery of the Session Key

As a first step of the attack, we want to recover one of several used session keys. This step consist of two phases: an offline (precomputation) phase and an online (query) phase. The attack is a chosen-plaintext attack with a time complexity of about $2 \cdot 2^{n/2}$. The complexity in memory and number of queries is $2^{n/2}$. Different trade-offs between the memory complexity and the number of queries are possible, at the cost of a higher overall complexity. Chosen-plaintext attacks are not unlikely to be practically applicable if, for instance, protocols based on challenge-response techniques are used.

The basic idea of our attack is to recover the session key k^* from collisions with pre-computed keys. The encryption scheme changes the session key k^* for every block of plaintext that is encrypted. By keeping the plaintext message input to the block cipher fixed, the adversary can apply a basic time-memory trade-off strategy to recover one of the session keys. We will demonstrate in Sect. 3.3 that this is already enough to also recover the master key k if no additional precautions are taken.

Let $E(k^*, m)$ denote the raw block cipher encryption operation with key k^* and plaintext m. Then the attack strategy is given in Algorithm 1, where m is a fixed message throughout.

A match between an entry in list L and a received ciphertext c gives a candidate session key k^* and the according nonce r. Since there is on average only one possible session key k^* that maps m to c, the possibility of false positives

---

Algorithm 1. Recover a session key k^*

Fix a message block m.

I. **Offline Phase** (Precomputation)
   Repeat t times:
   1. Guess a new value for k^*.
   2. Compute $c = E(k^*, m)$ and save the pair (c, k^*) in a list L.
II. **Online Phase** (Queries)
   Repeat $t' = 2^n/t$ times:
   1. Request ciphertext c and random nonce r for an encryption of m.
   2. If list L contains an entry (c, k^*) for some k^*, return r and k^*.

---

is negligible. (If in doubt, the candidate k^* and the derived master key k can be verified with a few additional queries.)

The number of iterations is such that the success probability of finding at least one collision is $\geq 1 - \frac{1}{e} \approx 63.21\,\%$, where e is Euler's number. We assume that no key candidate k^* in the offline phase is selected twice (drawing without replacement), but duplicates may occur in the online phase. Then, the probability of failure is $\left(1 - \frac{t}{2^n}\right)^{t'} = (1 - t')^{t'}$, which increases monotonically from 0 up to $\frac{1}{e}$ as the number t' of online queries grows (while t decreases accordingly). Since the expected number of false alarms is small, we can state that the algorithm finds a correct used session key k^* with high probability with a total complexity of t offline encryptions plus $2^n/t$ online chosen-plaintext queries. The best overall complexity of $2 \cdot 2^{n/2}$ is achieved for $t = 2^{n/2}$.

Sometimes, an attacker wants to recover more than only a single master key. In this case, only the second phase of the attack has to be repeated, while the precomputation phase has to be done only once. In such settings, in particular if the number of attacked keys is large, other values of t might result in a better overall complexity. In Table 1, we give the complexities and memory requirements for different choices of t.

Table 1. Complexities and memory requirements for both phases of the attack with different choices of t.

$\log_2(t)$	Offline phase	Online phase	Memory	Total
$n/4$	$2^{n/4}$	$2^{3n/4}$	$2^{n/4}$	$2^{3n/4}$
$n/3$	$2^{n/3}$	$2^{2n/3}$	$2^{n/3}$	$2^{2n/3}$
$n/2$	$2^{n/2}$	$2^{n/2}$	$2^{n/2}$	$2 \cdot 2^{n/2}$
$2n/3$	$2^{2n/3}$	$2^{n/3}$	$2^{2n/3}$	$2^{2n/3}$
$3n/4$	$2^{3n/4}$	$2^{n/4}$	$2^{3n/4}$	$2^{3n/4}$

3.2   Memoryless Session Key Recovery

In practice, the memory requirements are typically the most significant restriction for this attack. Unfortunately, since the values of the online phase are not under the attacker's control, standard memoryless collision search techniques are not directly applicable. If the attacker could additionally choose the nonce r for online queries, memoryless cycle finding algorithms would reduce the memory requirements to constant or logarithmic while only marginally (by a small constant factor) increasing the necessary number of online queries.

There are two possible modifications to the attack that allow this. Both attack the reader instead of the tag in the basic scheme of Sect. 2.1. The first assumes that the reader can also send messages to the tag by requesting a new nonce from the tag and then encrypting under this nonce. This would require the tag to remember the nonce until it receives the corresponding encrypted message. Then, the attacker can send chosen nonces r together with the fixed message m for encryption, and apply the memoryless algorithm described below.

The other variant does not make any such assumptions, but simply attacks decryption instead of encryption in a chosen-ciphertext setting. Instead of a fixed plaintext m, a fixed ciphertext c is sent to the reader together with a chosen nonce r. The collision target, then, is the received plaintext m.

Either of these two versions can be used for memoryless session key recovery as follows. We construct a helper function $f : \{0,1\}^n \to \{0,1\}^n$:

$$f(x) = \begin{cases} D(x,c) & \text{if the last bit of } x \text{ is } 0 \quad \text{(offline, session key guess } x), \\ D(g(k,x),c) & \text{if the last bit of } x \text{ is } 1 \quad \text{(query with nonce } x), \end{cases}$$

where $D(k^*,c)$ denotes decryption of a fixed ciphertext c. A collision $f(x_1) = f(x_2)$ for f will give us a session key $k^* = x_1$ and corresponding nonce $r = x_2$ with a probability of $\frac{1}{2}$ (otherwise, we have to repeat the procedure).

Now, we can consider the sequence generated by $x_i = f(x_{i-1})$ and apply a standard cycle finding algorithm to determine the periodicity of this sequence and derive a collision. For example, using Brent's algorithm [6], the expected number of evaluations of f to find a collision (for a random mapping) is

$$\sqrt{\frac{\pi}{8}} \cdot \left(\frac{3}{\log 4} + 2\right) \cdot 2^{n/2} \approx 2.6094 \cdot 2^{n/2}.$$

Since the expected necessary number of collisions to recover a session key is 2, the overall complexity of this approach is slightly higher than before, but the memory requirements are negligible.

For minimizing the overall complexity for a fixed given memory size, better trade-offs are achieved by distinguished-point searches and similar methods. Examples include Quisquater and Delescaille's [17] or van Oorschot and Wiener's [15] algorithms. In particular, the latter is useful if multiple collisions are required.

3.3 Master Key Recovery for the Basic AFRICACRYPT 2010 Scheme

For the attack on the basic re-keying scheme of AFRICACRYPT 2010 [13], we can directly apply the standard or memoryless collision searches from Sect. 3.1. Assume we successfully recovered one session key k^* and the corresponding nonce r. The re-keying function used in this scheme is $k^* = g(k, r) = k \cdot r$.

As already discussed in Sect. 2.1, the majority of the nonces r is coprime to $y^d + 1$ and the inverse r^{-1} exists. Therefore, we can define the inverse function $k = g'(k^*, r) = k^* \cdot r^{-1}$ and simply derive the master key k in use. The overall complexity of this attack is dominated by the session-key recovery complexity of $2 \cdot 2^{n/2}$.

3.4 Master Key Recovery for the CARDIS 2011 Multi-party Scheme

Two different functions g for re-keying are proposed in [12]. We first consider the version with $k^* = r \cdot k + s \cdot \ell$ in the two-party case. Recall that k and ℓ are the two master keys, and r and s are nonces chosen freshly by the two communicating parties. We attack the device during the online phase, where the attacker has control over the nonce s. For simplicity, the nonce s is kept constant during the whole online phase, although the attack works just as well for random nonces. Now, we need to recover two session keys k_1^* and k_2^* with two corresponding nonces r_1 and r_2 to determine the master key. We can then set up the following equations:

$$k_1^* = r_1 \cdot k + s \cdot \ell,$$
$$k_2^* = r_2 \cdot k + s \cdot \ell.$$

By combining them, we get

$$k_1^* - k_2^* = (r_1 - r_2) \cdot k.$$

If the inverse of $(r_1 - r_2)$ exists (which holds with overwhelming probability), we can calculate the first master key k as

$$k = (r_1 - r_2)^{-1} \cdot (k_1^* - k_2^*)$$

As s is also invertible (trivially if we control s, with high probability otherwise), we also get ℓ:

$$\ell = s^{-1} \cdot (k_1^* - r_1 \cdot k).$$

As nearly every difference of $(r_1 - r_2)$ is coprime to $y^{16} + 1$, the complexity of this attack is determined by finding the two necessary session keys. By increasing the precomputed table size and the number of online queries to $t = t' = \sqrt{2} \cdot 2^{n/2}$, we can achieve this with an overall complexity of $2\sqrt{2} \cdot 2^{n/2} \approx 2.8284 \cdot 2^{n/2}$ encryptions and a success probability of about $1 - \frac{3}{e^2} \approx 59.40\,\%$. Note that the memoryless version cannot realistically be used in this scenario, since we are unlikely to be able to control both parties' nonces.

Clearly, the same attack applies if k^2 is used instead of ℓ. For m parties, we need m session keys to recover the m unknown master keys. The necessary table size and number of queries grow accordingly.

4   Comparison to Hellman's Time-Memory Trade-Off Attack

Hellman [8] described a generic cryptanalytic time-memory trade-off attack on block ciphers. For a block cipher with a key size of n bits, after a precomputation with time complexity of about 2^n, Hellman's method has an (online) time complexity of $T = 2^{2n/3}$ and memory requirements of $M = 2^{2n/3}$ to recover the key. In more detail, it allows a time/memory trade-off curve of $M \cdot \sqrt{T} = 2^n$. Since we are only interested in attacks with $T \leq 2^n$ (faster than brute force), M has to be at least $2^{n/2}$. We want to note that the attack described in this paper is on a much better time/memory trade-off curve, $M \cdot T = 2^n$, and in particular does not require a 2^n precomputation.

5   Fixing the Scheme

The main problem of the construction is that the function g is easy to invert. This allows to extend the time-memory trade-off attacks for session key recovery to full master key recovery as demonstrated in Sect. 3. A simple, but unsatisfactory solution to prevent this kind of attack is to increase the master key, session key, and nonce sizes to twice the security level each. For example, if the desired security level is 128 bits, AES-256 is a natural choice for the block cipher E, with a performance overhead of about 40 % compared to AES-128. Additionally, the nonce transmission overhead becomes twice as large. This is clearly not compatible with resource-constrained application scenarios.

The alternative is to fix the construction by using a function g that is hard to invert, as for instance the one suggested in [4]. It should be hard to recover the master key k from the knowledge of one or a few session keys k^* and corresponding nonces r. However, this raises the question how such a cryptographically strong function can be constructed without in turn being very costly to protect against side-channel attacks. It is not sufficient to simply postprocess k^* with some preimage-resistant function that does not additionally depend on any secret information (i.e., parts of the key). Clearly, additional research is necessary to identify suitable constructions and desirable properties for g.

6   Application to Other Re-keying Schemes

The attacked schemes [12,13] are nonce-based and stateless. In short, this means that the communicating parties share a secret key and derive the session key by using the exchanged nonces. Besides this type of schemes, other schemes have been proposed, such as the re-keying scheme by Kocher [10]. This scheme works without nonces. To generate the session keys, the communicating parties traverse a tree-like structure. We call schemes like Kocher's [10] stateful schemes.

It is easy to see that similar time-memory trade-off attacks are also possible on stateful schemes. To mount such attacks and recover the master key, the used functions to generate the session keys have to be publicly known and must be easy to invert.

7   Conclusions

In this paper, we have analyzed fresh re-keying schemes from a generic point of view. We demonstrated how to recover one (of many) used session keys with a complexity of about $2 \cdot 2^{n/2}$ chosen-plaintext queries. Depending on the function g used for deriving the session key, knowledge of one or a few session keys may allow to even recover the master key. In case of the simple and multi-party re-keying schemes suggested by Medwed et al. [12,13], recovering the master key is easily possible since their function g is easy to invert. The effect of our attacks is that the complexity to recover the master key is reduced from the ideal 2^n to about $2 \cdot 2^{n/2}$.

A simple, but unsatisfactory solution to prevent this kind of attacks is to increase the master key, session key and nonce sizes to twice the security level each. More promising approaches focus on the properties of g, in particular the hardness to invert $g(\cdot, r)$ to deduce the key k, as in the scheme by Belaid et al. [4]. Our results show that designing secure, efficient re-keying functions remains a challenging task, and that frequent re-keying opens up problems of its own that are not yet fully understood.

Acknowledgments. This work has been supported in part by the Austrian Science Fund (project P26494-N15) and by the Austrian Government through the research program ICT of the Future under the project number 4593209 (project SCALAS).

References

1. Abdalla, M., Belaïd, S., Fouque, P.-A.: Leakage-resilient symmetric encryption via re-keying. In: Bertoni, G., Coron, J.-S. (eds.) CHES 2013. LNCS, vol. 8086, pp. 471–488. Springer, Heidelberg (2013)
2. Akkar, M.-L., Giraud, C.: An implementation of DES and AES, secure against some attacks. In: Koç, Ç.K., Naccache, D., Paar, C. (eds.) CHES 2001. LNCS, vol. 2162, pp. 309–318. Springer, Heidelberg (2001)
3. Ali, S., Mukhopadhyay, D., Tunstall, M.: Differential fault analysis of AES: towards reaching its limits. J. Cryptographic Eng. **3**(2), 73–97 (2013)
4. Belaïd, S., Santis, F.D., Heyszl, J., Mangard, S., Medwed, M., Schmidt, J., Standaert, F., Tillich, S.: Towards fresh re-keying with leakage-resilient PRFs: cipher design principles and analysis. J. Cryptographic Eng. **4**(3), 157–171 (2014)
5. Bogdanov, A., Dobraunig, C., Eichlseder, M., Lauridsen, M., Mendel, F., Schläffer, M., Tischhauser, E.: Key Recovery Attacks on Recent Authenticated Ciphers. In: Aranha, D., Menezes, A. (eds.) LATINCRYPT. LNCS, Springer (2014) (to appear)
6. Brent, R.P.: An improved Monte Carlo factorization algorithm. BIT, Nord. Tidskr. Inf.-behandl. **20**, 176–184 (1980)
7. Grosso, V., Poussier, R., Standaert, F.X., Gaspar, L.: Combining leakage-resilient PRFs and shuffling (Towards Bounded Security for Small Embedded Devices). IACR Cryptology ePrint Archive 2014, p. 411 (2014)
8. Hellman, M.E.: A cryptanalytic time-memory trade-off. IEEE Trans. Inf. Theory **26**(4), 401–406 (1980)

9. Kocher, P.C., Jaffe, J., Jun, B.: Differential power analysis. In: Wiener, M. (ed.) CRYPTO 1999. LNCS, vol. 1666, pp. 388–397. Springer, Heidelberg (1999)

10. Kocher, P.: Leak-resistant cryptographic indexed key update (Mar 25 2003). http://www.google.com/patents/US6539092. US Patent 6,539,092

11. Mangard, S., Oswald, E., Popp, T.: Power Analysis Attacks - Revealing the Secrets of Smart Cards. Springer, New York (2007)

12. Medwed, M., Petit, C., Regazzoni, F., Renauld, M., Standaert, F.-X.: Fresh re-keying II: Securing multiple parties against side-channel and fault attacks. In: Prouff, E. (ed.) CARDIS 2011. LNCS, vol. 7079, pp. 115–132. Springer, Heidelberg (2011)

13. Medwed, M., Standaert, F.-X., Großschädl, J., Regazzoni, F.: Fresh re-keying: Security against side-channel and fault attacks for low-cost devices. In: Bernstein, D.J., Lange, T. (eds.) AFRICACRYPT 2010. LNCS, vol. 6055, pp. 279–296. Springer, Heidelberg (2010)

14. Mendel, F., Mennink, B., Rijmen, V., Tischhauser, E.: A simple key-recovery attack on McOE-X. In: Pieprzyk, J., Sadeghi, A.-R., Manulis, M. (eds.) CANS 2012. LNCS, vol. 7712, pp. 23–31. Springer, Heidelberg (2012)

15. van Oorschot, P.C., Wiener, M.J.: Parallel collision search with application to hash functions and discrete logarithms. In: ACM Conference on Computer and Communications Security, pp. 210–218 (1994)

16. Pietrzak, K.: A leakage-resilient mode of operation. In: Joux, A. (ed.) EURO-CRYPT 2009. LNCS, vol. 5479, pp. 462–482. Springer, Heidelberg (2009)

17. Quisquater, J.-J., Delescaille, J.-P.: How easy is collision search. New results and applications to DES. In: Brassard, G. (ed.) CRYPTO 1989. LNCS, vol. 435, pp. 408–413. Springer, Heidelberg (1990)

18. Tiri, K., Verbauwhede, I.: Securing encryption algorithms against DPA at the logic level: Next generation smart card technology. In: Walter, C.D., Koç, Ç.K., Paar, C. (eds.) CHES 2003. LNCS, vol. 2779, pp. 125–136. Springer, Heidelberg (2003)

Evidence of a Larger EM-Induced Fault Model

S. Ordas[2]([⊠]), L. Guillaume-Sage[2], K. Tobich[2], J.-M. Dutertre[1],
and P. Maurine[1,2]

[1] CEA-TECH and ENSMSE, Centre Microélectronique de Provence G. Charpak,
80 Avenue de Mimet, 13120 Gardanne, France
dutertre@emse.fr, philippe.maurine@cea.fr
[2] LIRMM-University of Montpellier, 161 Rue Ada, 34392 Montpellier, France
{ordas,guillaume-sage,tobich}@lirmm.fr

Abstract. Electromagnetic waves have been recently pointed out as a medium for fault injection within circuits featuring cryptographic modules. Indeed, it has been experimentally demonstrated by A. Dehbaoui et al. [3] that an electromagnetic pulse, produced with a high voltage pulse generator and a probe similar to that used to perform EM analyses, was susceptible to create faults exploitable from a cryptanalysis viewpoint. An analysis of the induced faults [4] revealed that they originated from timing constraint violations.

This paper experimentally demonstrates that EM injection, performed with enhanced probes is very local and can produce not only timing faults but also bit-set and bit-reset faults. This result clearly extends the range of the threats associated with EM fault injection.

1 Introduction

Besides power and EM analyses [5,6], fault injection constitutes [2] a serious threat against secure circuits. Among the means used to inject faults within cryptographic circuits, the laser [11] is undoubtedly the most popular because of its high spatial and temporal resolutions. However, fault injection with laser is facing difficulties. Among them one can identify the increasing number of metal layers (up to 12 levels) used to rout signals in a chip, this may forbids the use of laser to inject fault through the frontside. The second difficulty one may point out is the long practice of laser injection and the related and progressive development of more and more efficient countermeasures like embedded laser shot detectors. It is therefore not surprising that adversaries looks for new mediums for injecting faults. Two fault injection means appeared recently. One of them is the injection of a voltage spike directly into the substrate of the targeted integrated circuit to produce ground bounces or voltage drops according to the polarity of the spike [12]. The other is EM injection which, despite the early warning of Quisquater et al. in 2002 [1], did only find recently a larger echo in the scientific bibliography thanks to its inherent advantages: its ability to inject faults through the package and the frontside being the most important as highlighted in [10] in which a high frequency spark gap is used to produce faults in a CRT-RSA.

© Springer International Publishing Switzerland 2015
M. Joye and A. Moradi (Eds.): CARDIS 2014, LNCS 8968, pp. 245–259, 2015.
DOI: 10.1007/978-3-319-16763-3_15

Two types of EM injection platforms can be mounted to induce faults into circuits. Harmonic EM injection platform refers to the first type. It produces sine EM waves, that can be modulated in amplitude or not, to produce faults. Such type of platform has been reported efficient in [9] to disturb the behavior of an internal clock generator and in [1] to bias a true random number generator.

EM Pulse (EMP) platform refers to the second type of platform which is detailed in Sect. 2. It produces a single but powerful electromagnetic pulse that creates a sudden current flow in the power/ground networks of an integrated circuit (IC) and therefore voltage drops and/or ground bounces. Such type of platform was first reported efficient in [3] to inject faults into a quite old microcontroller (designed with a 350 nm technology). The analysis of the fault obtained using such a platform was conducted in [4]. This paper concludes that EM injection produces timing faults and more precisely setup time constraint violations as described in Sect. 3. As a result of this observation, a delay-based glitch detector was evaluated against EM injection in [13] and demonstrated partially efficient.

If the results reported in [3] are convincing, they limit de facto the interest of EM Pulses (EMP) for injecting faults into smartcards. Indeed, nowadays smartcards are typically designed with the 90 nm process and operate at a reduced clock frequencies (<40 MHz). They are therefore characterized by large timing slacks i.e. the time margin between a circuit critical time and the clock period). They are thus quite robust to EM injection (considering the ranges and the slew rates of modern high speed voltage generators) if the latter does only produce timing faults. Indeed, producing timing faults in such circuits requires the use of extremely powerful pulse generator to produce sufficiently intense EMP. Additionally producing such EMP reduces the spatial resolution of the EM injection.

This paper addresses this limitation. It experimentally shows that EM injection can also produce other types of faults, like bit-set and bit-reset faults, provided enhanced injectors, that allow to concentrate the magnetic flux on a small part of the IC surface, are used. The rest of the paper is organized as follows. First, the EM injection platform, including the enhanced injectors, used to demonstrate that EM injection can produced bit-set and bit-reset fault is described in Sect. 2. In Sect. 3, the ability of EM injection in producing timing fault is verified and the conditions at which timing faults appear in an AES embedded into an FPGA (90 nm) are characterized. Then Sect. 4 gives evidences that EM injection is able to produce bit-set and bit-reset faults into the same FPGA. Conditions at which the bit-set and bit-reset faults appear are also characterized. Finally, Sect. 5 proposes a discussion related to the EM fault model before concluding in Sect. 6.

2   Experimental Setup

EM injection platforms, both harmonic and pulsed, are briefly described in [7]. In this section, a more detail description of the EM pulsed injection platform used to obtain the experimental results reported in this paper is given. Both the setup and EM injectors are discussed.

2.1   EM Pulse Platform (EMP Platform)

The goal of an EMP platform is to generate, in the close vicinity of the targeted device, an intense and sudden variation of the magnetic field. This variation of the magnetic flow is then captured by some of the metallic loops formed by the power/ground networks. A sudden and intense current variation thus appears in the IC and results in voltage drops and ground bounces. Because, the IC does not operate under its normal voltage conditions, faults are expected to appear.

The EMP platform considered in the rest of the paper is shown in Fig. 1. It features a laptop that controls the whole platform through serial ports, a 3-axis positioning system to place the EM injector with an accuracy of $\pm 5\,\mu$m at the surface of the Device Under Analysis (DUA), a 3-axes vision system made of USB microscopes connected to the laptop. An oscilloscope is also used in order to monitor the synchronization between the EMP and the target's operations. The pulse generator is a main element of the platform. It delivers, to the EM injector, a voltage pulse of amplitude V_{pulse} as high as 200 V (current 8 A), with a width that ranges between 5 ns and 100 ns. Its settling times are lower than 2 ns. Because an adversary aims at injecting faults in some specific part of the target's computations while letting the other parts' computations fault free, the EMP should be localized in the smallest possible area. For that, the adversary can design some specific and miniaturized EM injectors.

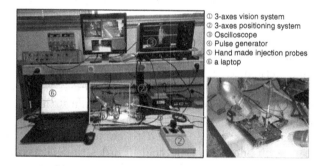

Fig. 1. EMP platform used for all experiments reported in this paper.

2.2   EM-Injectors

Various EM-injectors can be used according to the context of the analysis. Figure 2 shows three types of injectors we typically use. All are hand made and designed around a ferrite core to guide the magnetic field lines toward the target. All are also designed in different sizes. 'Flat' injectors (see Fig. 2-a) were designed with ferrite diameter ranging between 750 μm and 300 μm. 'Sharp' injectors were designed with tip end as small as 50 μm (see Fig. 2-b). Finally, 'Crescent' injectors were designed with an air gap separation 's' (see Fig. 2-c) of the ends as small as 450 μm.

The 'Flat' and 'Sharp' Injectors have been typically designed to localize the magnetic flow below the ferrite tip end. In that case, sharpening the tip-end of the ferrite (see Fig. 2-b), as proposed in [8], allows to further concentrate the flow into a smaller area and thus to expect a higher spatial resolution. Note however that contrarily to what has been obtained by simulation in [8], practice showed that 4–7 turns around the ferrite provide better results than 1 or 2. However, practice also shows that increasing further the number of turns does not help in producing faults and can be counterproductive. Some magnetic field lines can couple with interconnects quite far from the tip end indeed.

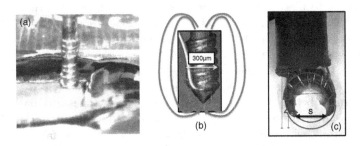

EM-Injectors: (a) 'Flat' Injector (b) 'Sharp' Injector and (c) 'Crescent' Injector

Fig. 2. EM-Injectors: (a) 'Flat' Injector (b) 'Sharp' Injector and (c) 'Crescent' Injector (Color figure online).

If both the 'Flat' and 'Sharp' injectors are efficient, they suffer from a same drawback. The magnetic field lines form close loops from one tip end to the other in an ellipsoid shape as this is roughly represented in Fig. 2-b by the red arrows. This implies that the resolution can be not so high even if the magnetic field is extremely strong below the tip end of the 'Sharp' Injectors.

'Crescent' EM injectors were designed to circumvent this limitation. The idea was to create a circular magnetic field in order to concentrate it between the two ends of the crescent-shaped ferrite. This is expected to avoid (or limit) any magnetic pollution all around the space separating the two ends because the magnetic lines should get out from one end, then surround the top layer of the power/ground network before coming back into the ferrite by the other end. Additionally, because of their geometry, 'crescent' EM injectors have an interesting property: they are directional. If rotated around the z-axis, the field lines direction will also rotate of the same angle. This may modify the properties of the coupling between the injector and the target. This is not the case for the 'Flat' and 'Sharp' injectors because of their cylindrical geometry.

3   Occurrence of Timing Faults

Almost all digital ICs are synchronous. Their internal operations are synchronized with a common clock signal. Figure 3 depicts the principle of their internal architecture: blocks of computational logic, to process the data, surrounded by 'launch' and 'capture' registers (or DFF, D flip-flop). The data stored in a 'launch' DFF are released at the logic's input on a clock rising edge, processed through the logic, then latched into a 'capture' DFF at the next clock rising edge. The use of synchrony leads to timing constraint requirements (as partially exposed hereafter) which violation may induce computation faults. Thus the authors of [3] showed on experimental grounds that EM injection, performed with raw EM injectors, produces timing faults (induced by setup time constraint violations). This observation should explain why a glitch detector was tested and find partially efficient in detecting EM injection in [13]. The setup time constraint is related to the amount of time spent by the circuit to process a data. This time, roughly speaking, should be lower than the clock period of the target as written more precisely in Eq. 1:

$$T_{Clk} > D_{Clk2Q} + D_{pMax} + T_{setup} + T_{skew} + T_{jitter} \qquad (1)$$

where T_{Clk} is the clock period, D_{Clk2q} the delay spent by the 'capturing' DFF to launch a new data on its outputs after the clock rising edge (see Fig. 3), T_{setup} the setup time of the DFF capturing one bit of the resulting computation, T_{skew} and T_{jitter} the skew that may exist between the clock signals of 'launch' and 'capture' DFFs and its jitter. Finally, D_{pMax} is the biggest propagation delay of the signal in the computational logic of the device. The time margin that exists between the two hand-sides of Eq. 1 is commonly called the timing slack.

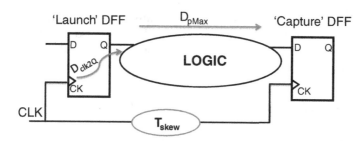

Fig. 3. Setup timing constraint in a synchronous IC.

D_{pMax} depends on many factors. Among them, the most interesting, when dealing with EM fault injection, are the supply voltage Vdd and the processed data. Indeed, EM injection is expected to alter Vdd locally and thus to modify the value of D_{pMax} so that a fault appears by violation of Eq. 1 (i.e. a setup time constraint violation). In this instance, EM injection leads to an increase of D_{pMax} that makes the right hand-side part of Eq. 1 bigger than its left hand-side part (the timing slack became negative). Similarly, when changing the data processed by the circuit, all terms in Eq. 1 remain unchanged except D_{pMax} that can change significantly. This change in the D_{pMax} value from one dataset to the other thus alters the value V_{pulse} that must be chosen to produce a fault.

The data dependence of D_{pMax} is illustrated in Fig. 4. We performed EM fault injection on an FPGA that embeds an AES hardware module (AES, or advanced encryption standard, is a symmetric encryption algorithm) processing random texts. EMPs targeted the 9th round of the AES. For any given dataset, the magnitude V_{pulse} of the voltage pulse inducing the EM perturbation was progressively increased from 60 V to 200 V. A first set of experiments was carried out with the FPGA running at a clock frequency of 100 MHz. The obtained fault occurrence rate is drawn as a function of V_{pulse} in Fig. 4. Below ~120 V no fault was injected. As V_{pulse} increased further to ~175 V, the fault occurrence rate grew progressively from 0 % to 100 %. This range corresponds to the appearance of timing violations. However, depending on D_{pMax}, which changes with the currently handled data, the fault probability increases progressively. Beyond a ~175 V V_{pulse}, EM fault injection became systematic.

A second set of experiments was performed with the FPGA running at 50 MHz and also processing the same dataset. We were expecting that this increase of the clock period, which is obviously related to an increase of the timing slack, would shift the fault occurrence rate towards higher V_{pulse} magnitudes. The obtained fault probability curve at 50 MHz is depicted in Fig. 4, it exhibits a 15 V shift. Moreover, the induced faults were the same at both 50 MHz and 100 MHz for any given dataset. These results are consistent with an EM fault injection mechanism related to timing violations, it is a further experimental reassurance. At that stage, it should be noticed that lowering further the clock frequency (below 20 MHz) leads to a probability of obtaining a fault stuck at 0 % for $V_{pulse} \in [-200\,V, 200\,V]$ for this positioning of the EM injector. This is a direct illustration of the limitation associated to EM injection if the latter produces only timing faults. Nevertheless, faults were also observed when the AES was forced to operate at a low clock frequency. This observation suggested us that EM injection does not only produce timing faults.

4   Evidence of a Bit-Set/Bit-Reset Fault Model

In Sect. 3, the occurrence of timing faults was confirmed. This section intends to experimentally demonstrate that EMPs are also able to induce both bit-set

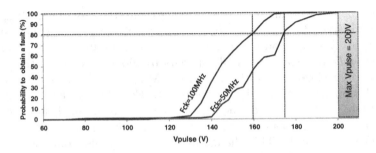

Fig. 4. Probability to obtain a faulty response from the same AES when operated at a clock frequency equal to 50 MHz and 100 MHz respectively.

and bit-reset faults into the DFFs of an IC. We define a bit-set (resp. bit-reset) fault as forcing to high (resp. low) level the state of a DFF initially at low (resp. high) level as a result of a disturbance (an EMP injection in our case). To avoid injecting timing faults while performing the experiments reported in this section, the target's clock was stopped during EMP injection.

4.1   Detecting Bit-Set and Bit-Reset Faults: Test Chip and Experimental Procedure

Aiming at demonstrating the occurrence of bit-set and bit-reset faults, a specific test chip was designed. Our intend was to be able to easily write and read the content of DFFs to detect, by simple comparison, the occurrence of bit-set or bit-reset faults. A large FIFO featuring (640×8) DFFs (64 bytes) was mapped into a Xilinx spartan 3E-1000 (technology node 90 nm). Figure 5 shows the floorplan of this design. At that point, it should be noticed for the remainder of the paper that all DFFs were mapped with their reset signal active low and their set signal active high.

This test chip was exposed to EMPs for the purpose of drawing a fault sensitivity map. The following and automated procedure was adopted in order to detect (i.e. experimentally demonstrate) the occurrence of bit-set and bit-reset faults:

- 1st step: the EM injector is placed at a given $\{X, Y\}$ (initial value $\{0, 0\}$) coordinate above the test chip, in its close vicinity (i.e. close to contact) in order to maximize the spatial resolution of the EM injection,
- 2nd step: the content of each byte of the FIFO is set to the hexadecimal value 'AA' ('10101010' in binary),
- 3rd step: the clock signal is stopped in order to avoid the occurrence of a timing fault,
- 4th step: an EM pulse, with an amplitude V_{pulse} ranging between -200 V and 200 V is delivered to the EM injector,
- 5th step: the clock signal is re-activated after a while (several μs) and the content of the FIFO recovered,
- 6th step: the initial and final contents are compared (a xor operation) in order to detect the occurrence of bit-set and bit-reset faults, and the result of the comparison is stored in a log file.
- 7th step: steps #2 to #6 are repeated 9 times in order to estimate the probabilities to obtain bit-set and bit-reset faults at the current position $\{X, Y\}$,
- 8th step: restart the procedure at step #1 at a new $\{X, Y\}$ coordinate in order to obtain a fault sensitivity map of the target.

4.2   Occurrence of Bit-Set and Bit-Reset Faults

Many fault sensitivity maps of the target were drawn according to the procedure described in Subsect. 4.1 for different values of V_{pulse} ranging from -200 V to 200 V. Different probes were used. However, we report herein only the results

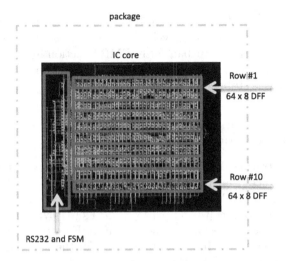

Fig. 5. Large chain of registers (FIFO) designed to demonstrate the occurrence of bit-set and bit-reset faults.

obtained with a 'crescent' injector characterized by '$s = 450\,\mu m$' because these results are the best from a spatial resolution point of view.

During all these experiments, four types of circuit's behavior were observed:

– injection of bit-set faults into a given number of DFFs,
– injection of bit-reset faults into a given number of DFFs,
– 'Mute' or loss of communication with the circuit,
– fault free.

Figure 6 shows three fault sensitivity maps obtained with a displacement step of the EM injector equal to $300\,\mu m$ ($<$ to the air gap of the crescent probe). The whole die surface ($5500\,\mu m \times 5000\,\mu m$) was scanned resulting in $4500\,\mu m \times 2400\,\mu m$ fault sensitivity maps because of the shape of the EM injector and a of guard-banding to avoid any collision of the injector with bondings. These maps were obtained with the following settings: $V_{pulse} = +170\,V$ and a pulse width $PW = 8\,ns$. Figure 6-a shows the probability to have faults regardless of the type of the obtained faults (either bit-set, bit-reset or Mute). Figure 6-b reports the probability to have bit-set faults while Fig. 6-c gives the probability to have 'Mutes'. Finally, Fig. 6-d shows the orientation of the injector above the IC surface, a parameter that will be discussed later because of the directionality of the injector. Two kind of 'Mutes' were observed. The first category is characterized by a no response of the IC that does not imply to reprogram the FPGA in order to relaunch the cartography. This suggests the occurrence of a fault in one of the DFF of the finite state machine. The second category was more severe. Indeed relaunching the cartography requires in that case to reprogram the FPGA. This suggests that the bitstream was corrupted by the EM injection.

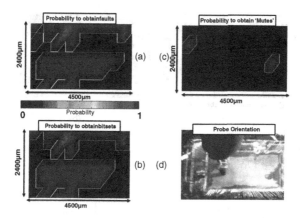

Fig. 6. Probabilities to produce (a) faults regardless of the fault type (b) bit-set faults (c) 'mutes' and (d) injector orientation (air gap along the y-axis) – (170 V, 8 ns) EMP.

Obtaining these sensitivity maps, especially the one of Fig. 6-b, constitutes an experimental demonstration that EM injection, conducted with enhanced injectors, is able to produce bit-set faults. This was our first objective. Additionally, one may observe once again that EM injection is local and reproducible. Indeed, we did verify that the bit-set faults obtained, at a given coordinate from one injection to another, were exactly the same.

4.3   Correlation Between the EMP Polarity and the Occurrence of Bit-Set and Bit-Reset Faults

Despite being a proof that EMP injection may inject faults into registers which are not related to timing violations, the experiments reported in Subsect. 4.2 never leaded to a bit-reset fault. Considering that the set signal of the DFFs was active high and that their reset signal active low, a similar set of experiments was relaunched for both achievable polarities of the EMPs: with $V_{pulse} = -140$ V and $+140$ V instead of $+170$ V only. The idea that motivated this experiment was the assumption that a pulse of a given polarity may affect more the ground network than the power network (or vice-versa). Therefore, it may be easier to induce bit-set than bit-reset faults (or the contrary) depending on the EMP polarity. Note however that the polarity is here an arbitrary notion that depends in our case of both the injector orientation and the sign of the voltage spike. For the sake of simplicity, we choose here to define the polarity as positive when the pulse affects more the 'set' signal which is active high than the 'reset' signal which is active low.

Figure 7-a gives the probability to obtain bit-set faults when applying a positive pulse of amplitude $+140$ V instead of $+170$ V for Fig. 6-b. Comparing these two figures (Figs. 6-b and 7-a) allows observing that reducing V_{pulse} reduces the size of the fault sensitive areas. Note however, that the two maps remain

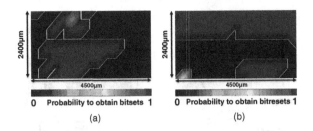

Fig. 7. Probabilities to obtain (a) bit-set faults with $V_{pulse} = +140\,\text{V}$ and (b) bit-reset faults with $V_{pulse} = -140\,\text{V}$

similar in shape. This indicates that the magnitude V_{pulse} is an efficient control parameter for EM injection, as it was expected.

Figure 7-b gives the probability to obtain bit-reset faults when applying a negative pulse of amplitude $-140\,\text{V}$; during this set of experiments not any bit-set fault was induced. One may observed that the two cartographies are completely different indicating that the susceptibility of an IC to a positive or a negative pulse may be radically different.

Nevertheless, the main conclusion that can be drawn from these experiments is that the pulse polarity (and therefore the injector orientation) is a key factor in controlling the type of EMP-induced faults. It seems to allow targeting more the ground network than the power network according to the topology of the IC. These results also suggest that according to their occurrence, bit-set and bit-reset faults are related to the way DFF are designed (set/reset signals active low or high). However, further investigations are mandatory to sustain this assumption.

4.4   Threshold Voltage for the Occurrence of Bit-Set Faults

The evolution with V_{pulse} of the probability to obtain timing faults has been experimentally estimated in Sect. 3. According to [4], this evolution should be smooth when random plaintexts are passed to the AES because the electrical paths and therefore the minimum timing slack changes with the processed plaintexts. This has been verified in Sect. 3. Indeed, this evolution has been found, for the AES mapped into the FPGA and the considered positioning of the injector, varying from 10 % to 90 % for V_{pulse} ranging from 130 V to 180 V when the AES operates at 100 MHz.

The evolution with V_{pulse} of the probability to obtain bit-set faults has also been measured at several $\{X, Y\}$ coordinates for different values of the supply voltage, Vdd, of the FPGA. Figure 8 shows the result obtained for one positioning of the injector but for different Vdd values. As depicted, for this positioning, as well as for many other that have been tested, the evolution is really sharp. The probabilities vary from 10 % to 90 % when the the magnitude of V_{pulse} varies from less than 1 V, which is the voltage resolution of our pulse generator. This confirms the crossing of a threshold, V_{pulse}^{th}, above which the probability to obtain a bit-set (or a bit-reset) is equal to 1. Additionally, this threshold voltage slowly

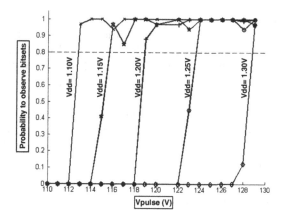

Fig. 8. Evolutions of the probabilities to obtain bit-set faults when the FPGA is supplied with different Vdd values.

varies with the supply voltage of the FPGA. It should also be noticed that from one positioning of the EM injector to another one, $V_{pulse}^{th,bit-set}$ can vary for several tens or even move out of the voltage range of our pulse generator (-200 V to $+200$ V).

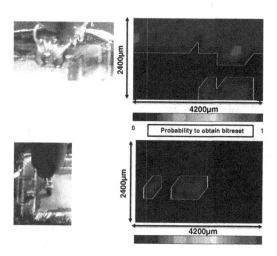

Fig. 9. Evolutions of the probabilities to obtain bit-set faults with V_{pulse} when the EM injector is parallel or orthogonal to the X-axis.

4.5   EM Injector Orientation

In Sect. 2, it is mentioned that 'crescent' injectors, because of their geometry, produce a polarized magnetic field, i.e. are directional. This characteristic of these enhanced EM injectors was experimentally verified. Two fault sensitivity maps were drawn ($V_{pulse} = -140$ V) with the EM-injector positioned parallel and perpendicular to the X-axis as illustrated in Fig. 9 which also discloses the obtained maps. It is obvious that the susceptibility of the IC to magnetic fields parallel and perpendicular to the X-axis is different. This could may be be explained by the way the top metal layers of the power (Vdd) and ground (Gnd) networks are routed. It is common practice to route perpendicular to each other the Vdd and Gnd metal lines. However, we didn't have this information for the FPGA under consideration. Nevertheless, this result confirms that 'crescent' injector are, as expected, directional.

4.6   Fault Types and Spatial Resolution

Considering the legacy from laser injection techniques, one may wonder what is the spatial resolution of EM fault injection, but also the types of faults it produces. The experimental faults maps were further analyzed: Fig. 10 reports some results illustrating what was observed. More precisely each sub-figure gives the number of faulted bits per byte for all bytes, for given position and orientation of the injector (shown by the large dot and the dotted rectangles) and given polarity and amplitude of the pulse (given in the caption). It is therefore possible to observe, for several settings of the EM injection, the spatial resolution of the EM injection and the type of induced faults. Figure 10-a and -b (resp. -e and -f) show the effect of the positioning of the injector; all others settings being constant. These sub-figures highlight that EM injection can be very local. Figure 10-a and -c allow to observe the effect of V_{pulse}. Figure 10-a, -b and -c should be compared to Fig. 10-d, -e and -f to observe the impact of the injector

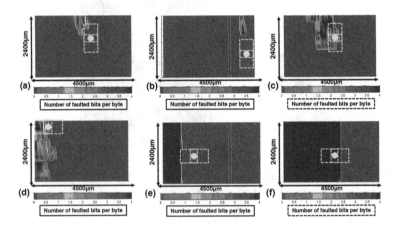

Fig. 10. Fault types and illustration of EM injection effects for four different settings of injection parameters: (a) $V_{pulse} = -100$ V, perpendicular; (b) $V_{pulse} = -100$ V, perpendicular; (c) $V_{pulse} = -140$ V, perpendicular; (d) 110 V, parallel; (e) -110 V, parallel; (f) $V_{pulse} = -110$ V, parallel.

orientation. Figure 10-d should be compared to -e or -f to observe the effect of polarity.

These six maps allow to observe that both the area affected (let's denote it by spatial resolution even if it is not the most appropriated term) by the EM injection and the types of induced faults (from single bit to multi-bits and from single byte to multi bytes that were all observed during our experiments) strongly depend on several parameters: the pulse amplitude and its polarity, the injector position and its orientation. It was also observed (not illustrated herein) that the distance d (d = 0 to d = 1.5 mm in our experiments) separating the injector from the IC surface changes significantly the obtained results. Nevertheless, even if the size of the area affected by the EM injection significantly varies with the aforementioned parameters, one may observe the effect is not global but more or less local according to the settings of the injection.

These observations could be explained by the mechanism exploited by EM injection: a local EM coupling between an emitting antenna and one or several receiving antennas. This implies that the spatial resolution and the effects produced by EM injection depend of course on the characteristics the EM injector (emitting antenna) but also on the characteristics of the receiving antennas, i.e. on the way the supply network of the IC is designed. It is therefore extremely difficult to define the spatial resolution of an EM injection, or to give any figure. It depends on both the Device Under Test and the settings of the injection. One may only characterize the spatial resolution of its injector in free space; but this is of reduced interest for the practice of EM injection.

As a result, let us conclude that there are several parameters (additional parameters with respect to laser injection) allowing to select the area affected by the EM injection and the faults that are produced. The EM injection can thus be perceived as more complex than laser injection in this regard. However, EM injection offers more degrees of freedom (more tuning parameters), to obtain the desired faults. However, their induction remain conditioned by the presence of the appropriated receiving antenna(s) in the IC. Experiments revealed there are plenty. One has just to target the right ones with an efficient EM injector, i.e. with the EM injector having the best spatial resolution in the empty space. At the moment, no general recipe emerges to quickly and directly find the rights settings for a given desired effect. Experimentation still prevails.

5 Discussion

At that stage, it has been experimentally observed that EM injection can produce timing faults. This result was expected from [4]. It has also been verified that the minimum pulse amplitude, $V_{pulse}^{th,timing}$, to produce, with a high probability (>0.8), a timing fault depends on the plaintext processed by the AES: it could vary for one or four tens of volts from one plaintext to the other.

Additionally to these results, we experimentally demonstrated that EM injection, conducted with enhanced EM injectors, can produce bit-set and bit-reset faults in more or less local manner according to the settings of the EM injection.

It was also observed that the minimum pulse amplitudes related to the injection of bit-sets or bit-resets with a probability higher than 0.8 can vary for several tens of volts from one positioning of the EM injector to another one.

All these considerations suggest that it is particularly difficult to decide if a fault induced by an EMP is a timing fault, a bit-set or a bit-reset. It is even possible that all type of faults coexist during a same EM injection. Nevertheless, the experimental demonstration that EM injection can produce bit-set or bit-reset faults significantly enlarges the scope of what can be done with EM injection.

6 Conclusion

In this paper, we have experimentally demonstrated that EM injection, conducted with enhanced EM injectors, is able to produce bit-set and bit-reset faults in addition to timing faults. This experimental demonstration significantly enlarges the scope of what can be done with EM injection, i.e. the EM fault model. Indeed, if this was not the case, EM injection would have been of reduced interest for the evaluation of IC designed with modern technologies but operating at reduced clock frequency, such as smartcards.

Such a result was obtained thanks to the design of EM injectors according to a simple idea: concentrating the magnetic field on the smallest possible area at constant power rather than increasing the power delivered to the EM injector. It should be noticed that there is still room to enhance EM injectors.

References

1. Bayon, P., Bossuet, L., Aubert, A., Fischer, V., Poucheret, F., Robisson, B., Maurine, P.: Contactless electromagnetic active attack on ring oscillator based true random number generator. In: Schindler, W., Huss, S.A. (eds.) COSADE 2012. LNCS, vol. 7275, pp. 151–166. Springer, Heidelberg (2012)
2. Boneh, D., DeMillo, R.A., Lipton, R.J.: On the importance of checking cryptographic protocols for faults (extended abstract). In: Fumy, W. (ed.) EUROCRYPT 1997. LNCS, vol. 1233, pp. 37–51. Springer, Heidelberg (1997)
3. Dehbaoui, A., Dutertre, J.-M., Robisson, B., Orsatelli, P., Maurine, P., Tria, A.: Injection of transient faults using electromagnetic pulses -practical results on a cryptographic system. IACR Cryptology ePrint Archive, 2012:123 (2012)
4. Dehbaoui, A., Dutertre, J.-M., Robisson, B., Tria, A.: Electromagnetic transient faults injection on a hardware and a software implementations of AES. In: FDTC, pp. 7–15 (2012)
5. Gandolfi, K., Mourtel, C., Olivier, F.: Electromagnetic analysis: concrete results. In: Koç, Ç.K., Naccache, D., Paar, C. (eds.) CHES 2001. LNCS, vol. 2162, pp. 251–261. Springer, Heidelberg (2001)
6. Kocher, P.C.: Timing attacks on implementations of Diffie-Hellman, RSA, DSS, and other systems. In: Koblitz, N. (ed.) CRYPTO 1996. LNCS, vol. 1109, pp. 104–113. Springer, Heidelberg (1996)
7. Maurine, P.: Techniques for em fault injection: equipments and experimental results. In: FDTC, pp. 3–4 (2012)

8. Omarouayache, R., Raoult, J., Jarrix, S., Chusseau, L., Maurine, P.: Magnetic microprobe design for em fault attackmagnetic microprobe design for EM fault attack. In: EMC Europe (2013)
9. Poucheret, F., Tobich, K., Lisart, M., Chusseau, L., Robisson, B., Maurine, P.: Local and direct EM injection of power into CMOS integrated circuits. In: FDTC, pp. 100–104 (2011)
10. Schmidt, J.-M., Hutter, M.: Optical and EM fault-attacks on CRT-based RSA: concrete results. In: Posch, J.W.K.C. (ed.) Austrochip 2007, 15th Austrian Workhop on Microelectronics, Proceedings, Graz, Austria, 11 October 2007, pp. 61–67. Verlag der Technischen Universität Graz (2007)
11. Skorobogatov, S.P., Anderson, R.J.: Optical fault induction attacks. In: Kaliski, B.S., Koç, Ç.K., Paar, C. (eds.) CHES 2002. LNCS, vol. 2523, pp. 2–12. Springer, Heidelberg (2003)
12. Tobich, K., Maurine, P., Liardet, P.-Y., Lisart, M., Ordas, T.: Voltage spikes on the substrate to obtain timing faults. In: DSD, pp. 483–486 (2013)
13. Zussa, L., Dehbaoui, A., Tobich, K., Dutertre, J.-M., Maurine, P., Guillaume-Sage, L., Clédière, J., Tria, A.: Efficiency of a glitch detector against electromagnetic fault injection. In: DATE, pp. 1–6 (2014)

Author Index

Printed in the United States
By Bookmasters